Pragmatics & Language Learning

Pragmatics & Language Learning
Series Editor
Gabriele Kasper

Pragmatics & Language Learning ("PLL"), a refereed series sponsored by the National Foreign Language Resource Center at the University of Hawai'i, publishes selected papers from the biennial International Conference on Pragmatics & Language Learning under the editorship of the conference hosts and the series editor. Check the NFLRC website (nflrc.hawaii.edu) for upcoming PLL conferences and PLL volumes.

Pragmatics and language learning (Vol. 11)
Kathleen Bardovi-Harlig, César Félix-Brasdefer, & Alwiya S. Omar (Eds.), 2006
ISBN 978-0-8248313-7-0

Pragmatics and language learning (Vol. 12)
Gabriele Kasper, Hanh thi Nguyen, Dina Rudolph Yoshimi,
Jim K. Yoshioka (Eds.), 2010
ISBN 978-09800459-6-3

Pragmatics & Language Learning

volume 13, 2013

editors Tim Greer
Donna Tatsuki
Carsten Roever

NATIONAL FOREIGN LANGUAGE RESOURCE CENTER
University of Hawai'i at Mānoa

(cc) 2013 Tim Greer
This work is licensed under the Creative Commons Attribution-NonCommercial-ShareAlike 3.0 Unported License. To view a copy of this license, visit http://creativecommons.org/licenses/by-nc-sa/3.0/
Manufactured in the United States of America.

The contents of this publication were developed in part under a grant from the U.S. Department of Education (CFDA 84.229, P229A100001). However, the contents do not necessarily represent the policy of the Department of Education, and one should not assume endorsement by the Federal Government.

ISBN: 978–0–9835816–4–2
ISSN: 1943–6947

distributed by
National Foreign Language Resource Center
University of Hawai'i
1859 East-West Road #106
Honolulu HI 96822–2322
nflrc.hawaii.edu

contents

vii	Acknowledgements
1	Introduction *Tim Greer* *Donna Tatsuki* *Carsten Roever*
5	A Coming of Age of Conversation Analysis and Applied Linguistics *Jean Wong*
29	Expanding Resources for Marking Direct Reported Speech *Eric Hauser*
55	Prioritization: A Formulation Practice and Its Relevance for Interaction in Teaching and Testing Contexts *Yusuke Okada*
79	Turn-taking Practices in Conversation-For-Learning *Tomomi Otsu* *Nathan P. Krug*
103	Working Through Disagreement in English Academic Discussions Between L1 Speakers of Japanese and L1 Speakers of English *Noël Houck* *Seiko Fujii*

133	Collaborative Creation of Spoken Language Corpora *Michael Haugh* *Wei-Lin Melody Chang*
161	Acquisition of the Pragmatic Marker 'Like' by German Study Abroad Adolescents *Averil Grieve*
191	On Saying the Same Thing: Issues in the Analysis of Conventional Expressions in L2 Pragmatics *Kathleen Bardovi-Harlig*
213	The Effects of Explicit Metapragmatic Instruction on EFL Learners' Performance of Constructive Criticism in an Academic Setting *Nguyen Thi Thuy Minh* *Pham Minh Tam* *Cao Thuy Hong*
245	Pragmatic Awareness of Japanese EFL Learners in Relation to Individual Differences: A Cluster Analytic Approach *Kazuhito Yamato* *Kenji Tagashira* *Takamichi Isoda*
267	About the Contributors

acknowledgements

This volume has greatly benefited from helpful commentaries at different stages of the editorial process. The editors gratefully acknowledge the following reviewers:

Machiko Akiba, *Tokyo Woman's Christian University*
David Aline, *Kanagawa University*
Michael Bamberg, *Clark University*
Kathleen Bardovi-Harlig, *Indiana University Bloomington*
Jack Bilmes, *University of Hawai'i at Mānoa*
Don Carroll, *Shikoku Gakuin University*
Eton Churchill, *Kanagawa University*
Rebecca Clift, *University of Essex*
Andrew Cohen, *University of Minnesota*
Haruko Cook, *University of Hawai'i at Mānoa*
Pico Cutrone, *Nagasaki University*
John Davis, *University of Hawai'i at Mānoa*
Zohreh Eslami, *Texas A&M University*
Mayumi Fujioka, *Kinki University*
Rod Gardner, *Griffith University*
Andrea Golato, *University of Illinois at Urbana-Champaign*
Marta González-Lloret, *University of Hawai'i at Mānoa*
Averil Grieve, *University of Melbourne*
Michael Haugh, *Griffith University*
Eric Hauser, *University of Electro-Communications, Tokyo*
Beverley Horne, *Chiba University*
Yuri Hosoda, *Kanagawa University*
Noël Houck, *California State Polytechnic University*
Kylie Hsu, *California State University Los Angeles*

Thorsten Huth, *University of Tennessee Knoxville*
Shin'ichiro Ishikawa, *Kobe University*
Laurel Kamada, *Tohoku University*
Gabriele Kasper, *University of Hawai'i at Mānoa*
Paul Kay, *University of California, Berkeley*
Yuriko Kite, *Kansai University*
Mai Kuha, *Ball State University*
Anthony Liddicoat, *University of South Australia*
Allyssa McCabe, *University of Massachusetts Lowell*
Junko Mori, *University of Wisconsin-Madison*
Ian Nakamura, *Okayama University*
Kazumi Namiki, *University of Melbourne*
Hanh thi Nguyen, *Hawai'i Pacific University*
Mary Noguchi, *Kansai University*
Yusuke Okada, *Ritsumeikan University*
Carol Rinnert, *Hiroshima City University*
Steven Ross, *University of Maryland*
Scott Saft, *University of Hawai'i at Hilo*
Gila Schauer, *University of Erfurt*
Norbert Schmitt, *University of Nottingham*
Greg Sholdt, *Kobe University*
Naoko Taguchi, *Carnegie Mellon University*
Satomi Takahashi, *Rikkyo University*
Yumiko Tateyama, *University of Hawai'i at Mānoa*
Hansun Zhang Waring, *Teachers College, Columbia University*
Jean Wong, *College of New Jersey*
Lynda Yates, *Macquarie University*
Lori Zenuk-Nishide, *Kobe City University of Foreign Studies*

Introduction

Tim Greer
Kobe University

Donna Tatsuki
Kobe City University of Foreign Studies

Carsten Roever
University of Melbourne

With contributions from a variety of learning contexts and participant language backgrounds, the chapters in this, the 13th volume of *Pragmatics and Language Learning*, reflect the latest inquiry into second language use as social action. The collection contains a range of methodological approaches, including qualitative investigations into talk and text as well as quantitative studies on second language and the acquisition of linguistic functions. From conversation analytic and interactional approaches to experimental studies of motivation and pragmatic competence, a central concern of the collection is the pursuit of evidence for how learners can put their languages to use in order to "do things with words."

The collection begins with a reflective and somewhat autobiographical narrative by Jean Wong that traces the history of Conversation Analysis as it relates to the field of Applied Linguistics. This firsthand account goes behind the scenes to document the early connections between the sociological approach of Conversation Analysis (CA) and the fields of Applied Linguistics and Second Language Acquisition (SLA). Wong reminiscences about what it was like to be a student of CA at a time when there was very little interaction between these fields and offers a rare glimpse into the early connections that led to increased crossover between CA and SLA, which has played a large part in the social turn that Applied Linguistics has witnessed over the past ten or fifteen years. Several of the subsequent chapters then go on to reveal how such research looks today.

One of the relatively recent interests among applied linguistics researchers who use CA is the search for evidence of the development of interactional resources over time. Eric Hauser takes up this challenge by using a series of longitudinal recordings to provide empirical insight into the way one adult learner's use of direct reported speech markers changes over a seven-month period. The analysis provides corroboration from two levels of sequence; the local emergence of new resources at the turn-by-turn level and their increasing stability across episodes. Hauser argues that this approach suggests that learning within CA-for-SLA can be conducted without recourse to an exogenous theory of learning, such as situated learning theory.

Likewise dealing with the resources interactants use in formulating a turn one way over another, Yusuke Okada takes up the topic of word selection and the reflexivity between a particular formulation choice, the local sequential context, and macro-level contexts. He focuses on the notion of prioritization in language teaching and Oral Proficiency Interview (OPI) role-play testing situations to draw attention to how teachers and testers prioritize certain social actions to efficiently accomplish the institutional aims of the interaction. This work points to potential links between research into lexicon and social interaction, and pushes the boundaries of CA in areas such as reference and recipient design.

Another fundamental concern for CA research involves the practices for constructing and allocating turns. Tomomi Otsu and Nathan Krug consider how this becomes an issue for L2 speakers of English in a conversation room where there is no L1 speaker. They uncover some of the fundamental interactional practices these novice language users employ to negotiate speakership and progress the talk. Their close examination of features of both spoken and embodied interaction (such as gaze shift and bodily orientation) provides a viable account of turn allocation among L2 speakers of English.

Likewise inspired by the CA approach, Noël Houck and Seiko Fujii investigate disagreement sequences between peers in academic discussions where one speaker has English as a first language and the other is an L2 speaker. In particular, they focus on how the pairs work through the disagreement and resolve the issue, pointing to specific interactional and embodied strategies that speakers have available for encouraging discussion, or winding it down. Common to this and many of the other studies in the volume is the fact that language is first and foremost being used for communication, rather than being imparted as an object in itself. Whether learners are arguing, role-playing or simply chatting, the act of talking can provide opportunities for learning and implementing language. Doing and learning go hand in hand.

Collecting, transcribing and analyzing spoken data is a long and arduous task for researchers of naturally occurring interaction, and it is all the more difficult for novice researchers, such as undergraduate students of linguistics. With this in mind, Michael Haugh and Melody Chang report on a project they conducted for collaboratively creating a corpus of spoken interaction. They 'crowdsourced' their data collection by having students record and transcribe small sections of interaction and pooling these into a corpus that could be used by all, which allowed everyone access to more data than they would otherwise have been able to process. Haugh and Chang report on how this corpus was used by their students of Applied Linguistics to analyze pragmatic aspects of spoken interaction as part of their assessment.

Of course, a conversation analytic view is not the only possible perspective on second language pragmatic development, and the chapters in the second half of the volume showcase other approaches. The chapter by Averil Grieve, for example, looks at how a group of German teenagers naturally acquire the pragmatic marker 'like' while on a ten-month study abroad trip to Australia. Although maligned by some adults, 'like' is an important expression of, like, identity for teenagers and its proficient use can be seen as an indicator of the extent to which a learner has socially integrated into the target culture of adolescent English speakers. Comparing their development to that of German adolescents on a five-month exchange, German teenagers learning English in Germany and Australian native speakers of around the same age, Grieve finds that the students' use of 'like' increased significantly during the first five months of the exchange, while there was no change for those who stayed in Germany. Her study combines both qualitative and quantitative analysis to make a convincing case for the natural acquisition of pragmatic markers over time.

Nguyen Thi Thuy Minh and her colleagues report on a project for university students with both practical and theoretical implications. Adding to our understanding of how pragmatics can be explicitly taught, their study focuses on the notion of providing constructive criticism for giving feedback to peers on their writing. By comparing the progress of the target group with that of a group of students who were not taught how to word such advice, the authors demonstrate that making the various formulations of this speech act set available to learners through meta-pragmatic instruction increased their ability to use constructive criticisms in peer feedback. Such research has obvious practical implications for learners from cultural backgrounds where direct feedback on a peer's work is not commonly part of the pedagogical approach to teaching L2 writing.

Another feature of formulations is that certain strings of words are often used in predictable ways to accomplish certain actions. "That'd be great" is a routine way of accepting an offer while "No, that's okay" does the opposite. These patterns are not reinvented by speakers each time they use them, but instead represent formulaic expressions that serve pragmatic purposes.

Kathleen Bardovi-Harlig's chapter considers some of the issues that arise when analyzing conventional expressions in L2 pragmatics, including identifying their use by native speakers through the criteria of recurrence of sequences, context dependence, and community-wide use. In addition, it discusses how native speakers' and L2 learners' use of such expressions can differ. The issues raised in this paper will be particularly instructive to researchers who are attempting to code conventional formulations.

Finally, Kazuhito Yamato and his collaborators use a cluster analytic approach to examine the pragmatic awareness of Japanese EFL learners in relation to individual difference factors. They compile learner profiles based on motivation and language proficiency to uncover the relationship between pragmatic awareness and learner types. They find that those learners with more self-determined motivation had a greater awareness of language that was pragmatically inappropriate. In contrast, students who were extrinsically motivated were less aware of pragmatic inappropriateness, even though their English proficiency was higher. The authors hypothesize that students with lower motivation are more likely to notice only the form of the language without having a deeper understanding of its pragmatic function.

This volume simultaneously showcases the breadth of research in interlanguage pragmatics and the increasingly important role of participant-centered analytical approaches to the study of how learners become competent interactants in a second language. We hope it stimulates more research in interlanguage pragmatics and helps lead it in new directions.

A Coming of Age of Conversation Analysis and Applied Linguistics

Jean Wong
The College of New Jersey

This chapter[1] traces the history of early connections between Conversation Analysis (CA) and Applied Linguistics/SLA that developed at the University of California, Los Angeles (UCLA).Through reminiscences of what it was like to be a student of CA studying with Professor Emanuel Schegloff at UCLA in the 1980s and early 1990s, this personal narrative documents the flowering of a new direction in second language studies. It also recounts a time when CA and Applied Linguistics/Second Language Acquisition were separate academic fields with minimal, if any, cross-over or mutual interest. Much as a bottle of wine gets defined with age, connections between CA and Applied Linguistics / SLA have, over time, become more robust and full-bodied. This article is not intended as a state-of-the-art piece, but it will revisit some of the early signposts for a bridging between CA and Applied Linguistics/SLA.

Introduction

I treat my contribution to this volume as an opportunity to relate an oral history, to capture on tape, so to speak, some of the early footage that recounts the joint engagement of "allied" forces, for some may not realize that the connections between CA and Applied Linguistics/SLA were neither obvious nor wholeheartedly promoted some 30 years ago. Yet given three decades of research history, particularly the last 10 years and counting, the lines of connection are now "clear and busy" and CA and Applied Linguistics/SLA have much to gain in talking with one another. Much as a bottle of wine gets defined with age, the connections between CA and Applied Linguistics/SLA have, over time, become more robust and full-bodied. Looking back over the past three decades, give or take a few years, many changes have taken place in a blending of Applied Linguistics/SLA with CA. This article is not intended as a state-of-the-art piece, but it will revisit some of the early signposts for a bridging between CA and Applied Linguistics/SLA, doing so largely by way of personal reminiscences.[2]

When I was a master's level graduate student at the University of California at Los Angeles (UCLA) in the early 1980s and training to become an English as a Second Language (ESL) teacher, I first heard of Conversation Analysis during a class on discourse analysis that I took with Professor Peter Shaw in the Spring of 1983. Professor Shaw had said, "There's a guy named Emanuel Schegloff in the sociology department here, who does this stuff called CA, which examines the details of conversation." I thought, "Gee, if I'm going to teach English, I should know how conversation works just as I should know how grammar works" (Wong & Waring, 2010, p. 3). So, I enrolled in Professor Schegloff's CA course in the Fall of 1983. When I arrived for the first class, I was the only one sitting in the classroom waiting for the professor. I began to wonder whether I had confused the time and day. But within a few minutes, Professor Schegloff walked through the door. After going through the typical opening sequences, the significance of which I had not registered at the time, he asked me who I was, what my academic interests were, and why I wanted to take the course. After I answered all those questions, he informed me that I could not take the course. He suggested that I return in the following Fall and take the first of a two-course introductory sequence on CA. He explained that the Fall course was a prerequisite for the Spring one.[3]

I was only mildly disappointed because I had no idea how the CA courses would tie in with my interests in learning how to become an ESL teacher. In fact, in 1983 I had not heard of anyone else in the applied linguistics program at UCLA speak about Conversation Analysis except, as I said above, Professor Shaw's mention of it in a discourse analysis class – and he hadn't been particularly advocating CA. He had simply stated in passing that in addition to discourse analysis, there was something called Conversation Analysis offered in the sociology department. In order to get a preliminary sense, at that first meeting in the empty classroom I asked Schegloff what the study of CA was about so that I could decide whether or not to wait to take his course. He replied, "The best way to find out is to read some CA literature." He told me to drop by his office, which I did, and he gave me two papers to read, which turned out to be the classic papers on the organizations of turn-taking (Sacks, Schegloff, & Jefferson, 1974) and repair (Schegloff, Jefferson, & Sacks, 1977).

About a month later, I went to Schegloff's office to return the articles. This time, we talked about the turn-taking and repair systems now that I was becoming an informed consumer. I was intrigued that anyone would consider the turn-taking system or the organization of repair as worthy of analytic investment.

Those were not familiar paths in my prior regimen of courses in the TESL and applied linguistics department. Yet ironically, being denied access to Schegloff's CA course in the Spring of 1983 marked my entry into a world that I have yet to find compelling reason to exit almost three decades later. In fact, I feel as if I have only just arrived, so surely it cannot be time to leave just as the party is getting started. Some twenty-nine years later, I have finally reached an 'anchor point,' as we might call it in telephone openings (Schegloff, 1986), a point at which "reasons-for-the-calling" between CA and applied linguistics are due, now that we are well past openings. What are some of those "reasons-for-the-calling?" In observance of the 'distribution rule' in telephone talk (Schegloff, 1986), allow me to be the "answerer" who speaks first here.

Reasons-for-the-calling

During the academic year of 1983–1984, I was the only student from the TESL and applied linguistics department at UCLA who was taking a course in CA. I felt as if I had transferred to sociology because I was mingling with sociology graduate students in the CA courses more than I was mingling with applied linguists. CA and applied linguistics were separate academic departments to the extent that when I inquired about whether I could work with Professor Schegloff in doing my doctoral thesis and have him as my academic program advisor, I was told that I had to obtain special permission. I recall the late Professor Russell Campbell, then chair of TESL and applied linguistics at UCLA, saying, "Okay, we will sign a form that will allow you to be in Applied Linguistics, but go across the ways to Haines Hall and work with Manny Schegloff." Still, Schegloff could only serve as co-chair and not chair of my dissertation committee because he was regarded as an outside member, a third party to my academic discipline. Also, Schegloff had asked me why I did not consider applying to the Sociology department instead. I told him the route was shorter from applied linguistics given my master's degree.

Sometimes I wondered whether I was an applied linguist masquerading as a conversation analyst or a conversation analyst masquerading as an applied linguist. I even contemplated whether the two identities were entirely compatible or whether I had to choose one of them. The discomfort with the dual identity was sometimes made apparent when I shuffled back and forth in discussions with Schegloff and professors in Applied Linguistics. I felt as if I were in the middle, coming between two different points of view. The "linguistic" divide spoke to differences in perspectives, differences in what was considered acceptable or required; what one could use as data, how one should analyze data collected, whether hypotheses were allowed in doing research, and so on. Professor Junko Mori expressed similar sentiments when she delivered a plenary address at the 17th Pragmatics and Language Learning conference in Hawai'i (2006). Her talk was aptly entitled "Border Crossings," a version of which was published in *The*

Modern Language Journal (Mori, 2007; see also Mori, 2010). Imagine how I must have felt in the 1980s harboring those sorts of identity issues when similar ones are still being raised now.

I left UCLA and the Los Angeles area in 1988 and at some point thereafter, many transformations have led to flavorful blends between CA and Applied Linguistics. As far as I know, there is no longer the bureaucratic red tape that I had faced. For instance, students may now enter the program as applied linguists and concentrate on CA, or they may come from sociology and take applied linguistics courses. Special permission is no longer needed for those coming from applied linguistics but interested in working on CA with faculty in the sociology or anthropology department. CA, applied linguistics, sociology and anthropology at UCLA have undergone considerable cross-pollination since the 1980s and early 1990s. We should take note of this milestone, a case of academic "bad news" turned "good news" (Maynard, 2003), because up until the 1990s this kind of interdisciplinarity was far less common.

At UCLA in the 1970s and 1980s, early bridges between CA and applied linguistics were primarily at the master's level. Daden was the first one to leave a paper trail, writing the first in a line of four master's theses that were to come along at UCLA that bridged CA with applied linguistics or SLA (Daden, 1975; Gaskill, 1977; Schwartz, 1977; Wong, 1984). The topic of her thesis, evident from its title, "Conversational analysis and its relevance to teaching English as a second language," was impressively decades ahead of its time and began the CA/applied linguistics ball rolling (uphill, of course). Daden remarked:

> There are few practical fields which could benefit more from the analysis of conversation than the field of language teaching. One of the major aims of the language teacher is to enable the student to participate in natural conversation with native speakers of the target language and to engage in social interaction with them. Given this premise, it is reasonable to assume that a knowledge of the rules that govern conversation and an understanding of the implications that arise from a disregard for them would constitute invaluable tools not only for the language teacher but also for the textbook writer. (Daden, 1975, p. 1)

When I was at UCLA, among the few references that Schegloff recommended to me on the connection between CA and applied linguistics was Daden's work, along with Gaskill's and Schwartz's theses.[4] The latter two studies constituted the very beginning of research on repair in SLA from a CA perspective.[5] Larsen-Freeman had the foresight to publish revised versions of Gaskill's and Schwartz's theses in an edited volume entitled *Discourse Analysis in Second Language Research* (Larsen-Freeman, 1980). At one time, Larsen-Freeman was at UCLA in the TESL and applied linguistics program along with other now retired *emerita* scholars, Professors Marianne Celce-Murcia and Evelyn Hatch. Indeed, Celce-Murcia and Hatch advised and mentored many papers and theses at UCLA that used CA in examining naturally-occurring talk-in-interaction. Undoubtedly, their early efforts have had an influence on the current engagement between CA and Applied Linguistics, which gave birth to a long list of studies in edited volumes and in journals that argue, directly or indirectly, for the significance and relevance of CA in helping us to unpack and repackage interaction, second language acquisition, and second language pedagogy in more "naturalistic" ways.

From those early laborious days, but rest assured we are *still* in labor, the notion that conversation is the foundation of language acquisition and its attendant attraction to the input and interaction hypothesis, proposed by another UCLA scholar (Long, 1983), most likely had its inception in Hatch's observation that one learns how to "do" conversation and out of this syntactic structures develop" (Hatch, 1978). Viewing CA as a form of discourse analysis (although radically different in some respects), Hatch and Long (1980) were among the first to introduce CA to applied linguists. Also, Hatch's (1992) textbook situated CA against the larger realm of discourse and language education. She introduced CA concepts and findings about turn-taking, openings, and closings within Goffman's work on ritual and system constraints (Goffman, 1976).

Around the same time, when discourse analysis became a new avenue or intersection for applied linguistics, Celce-Murcia (1980) proposed doing contextual analysis, which was consonant with a CA perspective, since this kind of analysis necessitated examining naturally-occurring, recorded and transcribed spoken language (as well as written language). Her work using contextual analysis not only focused on grammar but also on social and pragmatic functions of language. In fact, Celce-Murcia (1991, 1995) is well-known for advocating discourse-based understandings of grammar and discourse-based approaches to language teaching (Celce-Murcia & Olshtain, 2000).[6]

So with the benefit of hindsight, we can appreciate the lines of "conception" between CA and Applied Linguistics. Those ways of thinking about language and the works that have emanated from them, a list too long to reproduce here, constitute an ultra-sound moment and movement, for they have set in motion new undulating waves, e.g., a spoken grammar in interaction or a 'syntax-for-conversation' (Hayashi, 1999, 2003; Ford, Fox & Thompson, 2002; Ochs, Schegloff & Thompson, 1996; Schegloff, 1979). In a similar vein, Professor Sandra Thompson, also formerly of UCLA,[7] encouraged students to explore grammar as an emergent, dynamic, full-bodied and not to mention *em*bodied social phenomenon (Thompson & Hopper, 1994).

In related areas in the greater applied linguistics research arena, other scholars were writing about the notion of 'communication strategies' with the ultimate goal being to influence theories of second or foreign language teaching and learning (Færch & Kasper, 1983; 1984; Tarone, 1977, 1981). Some of the communication strategies which were referred to as compensatory strategies, i.e., paraphrase, circumlocution, word search, appeal for assistance, or the like

(Færch & Kasper, 1983, 1984; Tarone, 1977) might be thought of as harbingers of the research that examined repair in SLA from a CA perspective (Hosoda, 2006; Kasper, 1985; Macbeth, 2004: Seedhouse, 2004; van Lier, 1988; Wong, 2000a). In addition, Swain (1985) was very much onto something in calling for a balancing of Krashen's (1985) notion of 'input' with that of 'output.' The notion of output found resonance with CA's preoccupation with naturally-occurring language use.

Fortunately, that preoccupation is also an occupation for many. Not only is CA strongly impacting the form and shape of scholarship in Applied Linguistics, but applied linguistics has also left its (birth) mark on CA, altering its "lines" of work as well. The current focus in CA on comparative perspectives (Bolden, 2009; Heinemann, 2009; Lindstrom, 2009; Schegloff, 2009; Sidnell, 2009; Wu, 2009) may have had its pre-beginning after the official blessing of CA and applied linguistics in the article aptly entitled "Conversation analysis and applied linguistics," which appeared in the *Annual Review of Applied Linguistics,* the official journal of the American Association for Applied Linguistics (Schegloff, Koshik, Jacoby, & Olsher, 2002).

Now it should be clear that within the confines of the space provided here that I cannot do justice to the myriad works that have indeed entered into the picture in the intellectual engagement of CA and Applied Linguistics/SLA, not to speak of one of the most penetrating debates in SLA history, which was initiated by Firth and Wagner (1997) and re-examined a decade later (Firth & Wagner, 2007). This discussion, which amounted to a call for a reconceptualization of how SLA research is executed, including what and how to analyze data, has spawned numerous debates and counter debates appearing in *The Modern Language Journal* (1997/1998, 2004, 2007) and elsewhere. Some might consider that the debates have led to two (entrenched) SLA camps, i.e., traditional/ mainstream SLA and contemporary SLA (Gass, 2004; Gass, Lee & Roots, 2007; Kasper, 1997) with the former emphasizing language acquisition and the latter emphasizing language use, although this distinction may, in actuality, become quite blurred.

Daden's work (Daden, 1975) would put us at a 35th anniversary, but the relationship between CA and Applied Linguistics/SLA did not take hold until the 1990s and early 2000 (e.g., Koshik, 1999; Firth & Wagner, 1997; Markee, 1994, 1995, 2000; Wong, 1994, 2000a, 2000b, 2000c). During the early years, among the first group to connect Applied Linguistics/SLA and CA at the doctoral level were Ford (1988), Markee (1988), Riggenbach (1989), Lazaraton (1992), and Wong (1994). Koshik's (1999, 2005) works were the first to examine second language conversations in tutorial settings.[8] Markee's (1995) article was one of the first to call for a methodological shift in the way SLA research is conducted, particularly when using naturally-occurring data. He also authored the first book that proposed 'CA-for-SLA' (Markee, 2000), which was followed by three edited volumes by other scholars that used CA as a methodological framework in examining issues and concerns in language acquisition or language pedagogy (Gardner & Wagner, 2004; Richards & Seedhouse, 2005; Bowles & Seedhouse, 2007). In my doctoral thesis (Wong, 1994), among the topics that I addressed was the notion of delayed next turn repair initiation in native/nonnative speaker English conversation. This notion had not been raised in the classic paper on the organization of repair in everyday conversation by Schegloff, Sacks and Jefferson (1977). In fact, in Schegloff (2000), we find a modification of that seminal paper, which was written as a companion article to Wong (2000a).

How was the tentative joint venture between CA and applied linguistics in the 1980s and early 1990s different from how it is now? What is now possible and what interest has accrued that was virtually unimaginable three decades ago? One way of answering these questions is to look at a number of past *definite no-no*'s regarding research that have since morphed into welcome and emphatic *yes-yes*'s.

Ordinary conversation vs. institutional talk

At UCLA in the early 1980s, the focus was on "ordinary conversation," even though the initial recordings on which Sacks and Schegloff based their earliest observations were, in fact, made in institutional settings, such as calls to the police, a suicide prevention center, and group therapy sessions. By and large, this emphasis on ordinary conversation had to do with the fact that only Schegloff was teaching CA at UCLA at that time and his primary concern was with mundane conversation as the primordial site of human sociality (Sacks, Schegloff & Jefferson, 1974). Yet, in the greater CA arena outside the confines of UCLA, there was an early interest in examining interaction in the courtroom and in workplace settings (Atkinson & Drew, 1979; Drew & Heritage, 1992). This broader perspective brought about a shift in CA's object-of-inquiry from ordinary conversation to the more inclusive description, *talk-in-interaction*.[9] Nevertheless, when I was at UCLA, the vast expanse of acceptable data types, e.g., interviews, news broadcast interviews, doctor-patient interaction, classroom discourse, tutorial sessions, still lay on the horizon – let alone the analysis of gestures and other embodied behaviors that would soon become commonplace in CA work.

In fact, when I was a doctoral student in applied linguistics at UCLA in the years immediately following the completion of my master's degree, I recall telling Schegloff about some interview data that I had, that I was going to use for a paper in a linguistics course. He advised against using the data, stating that it would not provide access to understanding how participants use talk in everyday interaction. In other words, he did not say, "yes, go ahead and work with the data and see what you can find out about institutional talk." In terms of "doing CA" at UCLA in the 1980s and early 1990s, interview data was a *no-no*, as was classroom discourse, since neither was regarded as ordinary (enough) conversation. One line of reasoning that had yet to come into sharper focus was that the practices of ordinary conversation, e.g., turn-taking and repair, may be used as a benchmark against which to scrutinize talk in specialized institutional settings, e.g., doctor-patient talk, classroom discourse, interview, workplace talk, etc. (e.g., Drew & Heritage, 1992).

No children, no pets!

In the late 1980s at UCLA, the focus of CA research was unequivocally on adult talk. This was later confirmed in an interview conducted with Schegloff (Wong & Olsher, 2000). Use of children's data (that is, recordings of child interactions) was not allowed. This prohibition was in place largely because Schegloff thought that using children's talk as data was not efficacious for learning how to do CA. Besides, children were regarded as "not-yet-competent" in the language of interaction (Schegloff, Jefferson & Sacks, 1977). Published CA research on children's data was also sparse. The only work that I recall Schegloff mentioning at that time was Ochs' study of repair between a mother and child in Samoan culture (Ochs, 1984, 1991).[10]

Since then, the research landscape has changed spectacularly, absorbing and reflecting hues and color combinations that one could not have envisioned either as background or foreground some 30 years ago. As just one example of this sea-change, Schegloff (2009) now reports on the "quickening pace of CA work on 'very young children'" (p. 361) and he cites mainline CA scholars such as Kidwell (2005), Kidwell & Zimmerman (2006, 2007), Lerner & Zimmerman (2003) and Lerner, Zimmerman & Kidwell (2011) in this regard.[11] Schegloff underscores three important foci for future research: (1) the way adults interact with children and the elderly (2) the way children interact with adults and (3) the way children interact with each other (Schegloff, 2009, p. 362). Furthermore, Schegloff (2009) now draws our attention to the absence of research using children's data (in Sidnell, 2009), and reminds us that age is an important dimension of comparative work. Clearly we have come a long way since the days of "No children, no pets!" It is quite literally a Coming of Age for this type of data. Indeed, there are two very recent volumes devoted entirely to children's talk-in-interaction, e.g., Filippi (2009) and Gardner & Forrester (2009). And there is at least one ethnomethodological study that examines interaction between humans and pets (Goode, 2007). Thus, it is a worthwhile pursuit to investigate communication between "competent" speakers and their "non-speaking" but "vocal" participants, i.e., dogs.

No children, no non-natives & English only! (mostly)

In addition to the prohibition against using children's talk as data, it was "native-only" when I was studying CA at UCLA – and those natives were overwhelmingly native speakers of English.[12] Relatedly, when I was embarking on my dissertation research at UCLA, the only work in another language and of another culture that Schegloff directed my attention to was an unpublished paper on same-turn repair in a Guatemalan language known as Quiche (Daden & McClaren, n.d.). However, it didn't take long for CA to spread beyond the borders of the English-speaking world. For example, CA research was soon being applied to talk in Dutch (Houtkoop-Steenstra, 1991), Swedish (Lindstrom, 1994), Mandarin-Chinese (Wu, 2004), and Thai (Moerman, 1988), among other languages. Thus, in looking back, we can now appreciate that there were already the pre-beginnings of research into "talking culture into being" (Daden & McClaren, n.d.; Moerman, 1988; Ochs, 1984, 1991).

In 1999, Zimmerman called for more horizontal and vertical work in language and social interaction (Zimmerman, 1999). He indicated that for journals such as *Research on Language and Social Interaction* to truly achieve international stature, they would have to publish more work on horizontal and vertical dimensions. By horizontal CA, he meant research that is cross-cultural and cross-linguistic, and by vertical CA, he meant studies using children's first language (Zimmerman, 1999). In the 21st century, comparative CA analyses are the hot topic of the day, CA's wave to the future, as exemplified in numerous articles and four recent volumes on comparative perspectives, e.g., Enfield and Stivers (2007), Sidnell (2007), Haakana, Laakso and Lindstrom (2009), Nguyen and Kasper (2009) and Sidnell (2009). What was once nebulous backgrounding has stepped forth boldly as foreground in the current landscape.

When Schegloff was asked why prior CA research had ignored the talk of non-native speakers of English, he replied that that was the agenda of those with interests in TESL and SLA. He stated that individuals coming from those academic areas were looking for succor and support in terms of CA-related research, but did not find any. However, he emphasized that it was not that anyone was specifically turning away from non-native talk, but that that kind of data had not come up yet as a relevant category or a category that was of interest to him or others working in CA at the time (Wong & Olsher, 2000). By the time I was proposing a dissertation topic in 1988, however, Schegloff was agreeable to my using native/non-native speaker interaction data. Nevertheless, as he stated in Wong and Olsher, he regarded the analysis of native/non-native speaker conversation as akin to analyzing non-English talk, i.e., as an undertaking largely out of his territory. From CA's formative years of adult mono-lingual English conversation, it is quite astonishing to register the current diversity of CA research on "talk-in-other-languages" as well as the many strides that have been taken in working with interaction involving the so-called "not-yet-competent" including children and non-native speakers of several languages (e.g., Hosoda, 2006; Kurhila, 2006). The prohibition against working with data of the "not-yet-competent" has now vanished or morphed into an active *yes-yes*.

Research is a humbling enterprise. We are wiser with age, or so we would like to think. We have aged and matured. I see so many more lines or connections between CA and applied linguistics and not wrinkles—but there are those as well. We now appreciate that those other languages, such as Quiche, Thai or Japanese, were not "exotic" languages—they were just languages which ordinary people used to live their lives. Similarly, we now recognize the great variety and richness of *first* and *second* languages and *lingua franca* speakers (Firth, 1996; 2009) and no longer fret so much about the native/non-native dichotomy. There has been extensive growth separately within both CA and Applied Linguistics, yet within these "fields" there has also been an expansion of the "plots of common territory," for example, Bowles & Seedhouse (2007), Enfield & Stivers (2007), Firth & Wagner (1997; 2007), Gardner & Wagner (2004), Houck & Tatsuki (2011), Richards & Seedhouse (2004), and Wong & Waring (2010). Undoubtedly, there are more varieties and a richness of flavors in CA research and its connections with applied linguistics and second language acquisition than there was 30 years ago.

CA, applied linguistics, and second language acquisition

One debate that has arisen over the past ten years or so is whether employing a CA framework should be referred to as "applied" CA or "pure" CA. Terminology aside, anyone who is fully adhering to a CA methodological framework is *doing* CA, and whether one calls that applying CA or not seems beside the point. However, in a strict sense of the terms, *applied CA* or, more dynamically, *applying CA* can and perhaps should be reserved for studies that consider how findings and insights from CA are used or transferred to professional practice by teachers, clinicians, doctors, therapists, and so on (Antaki, 2011). This might be one way to differentiate between "applied" and "pure" CA. In fact, perhaps it is better just to leave off the word "pure" and speak simply of "CA" and "applied CA." For example, an application of CA might involve a teacher's discussion with language learners about how to do openings in the target language and showing learners examples from naturally occurring talk and pointing out the various sequences that are involved as illuminated through CA research (Wong & Waring, 2010). Or if a physician changes the way in which s/he interacts with his/her patients because s/he has been influenced by insights and findings gleaned from CA studies of doctor-patient interaction, then that might be regarded as an application of CA in professional contexts (Heritage & Robinson, 2011).

CA-SLA (or CA-for-SLA)

Another domain of applied research is what is sometimes referred to as CA-SLA or CA-for-SLA (Kasper & Wagner, 2011) (and it is referred to as such more frequently by those coming to CA from mainstream perspectives on applied linguistics and second language research). But this work really should just be called CA – pure and simple (no pun intended). That is, unless one only partially adopts a CA methodological framework or changes it somehow to suit one's purposes, it is still CA. Now understandably, the term CA-for-SLA may have evolved with respect to informing or convincing those from a traditional SLA perspective about the benefits of using CA to examine issues and concerns in second or foreign language acquisition. Yet, those in SLA and applied linguistics who do CA and refer to their work as CA-SLA or CA-for-SLA may run the risk of separating themselves from the mainstream body of CA research.

The use of the term CA-SLA (and CA-for-SLA) positions language learning firmly in the center of the researcher's universe – and suggests it is the only suitable object of attention. Yet this point of view can potentially conflict with CA's emic perspective, where one does not begin with (preconceived) hypotheses. Not all of the so-called CA-SLA studies need be concerned with or look for evidence of language learning in the first instance (cf. Firth, 2009; Mori, 2009; Wong, 2000a, 2000b, 2000c). A better approach, and many scholars already do this since it is more compatible with the spirit of CA, would be to let language learning, if indeed it is observable, arise naturally from the data. That said, it might be useful to reflect upon the following three questions:

1. Do CA-SLA studies fall into the category of CA in comparative perspective, whether horizontal, vertical or both?
2. Are CA-SLA studies in some way(s) different from other CA studies? If so, how? If not, why not call them CA studies rather than CA-SLA?
3. Do the above questions relate to publishing venues and/or audiences, for example, CA-SLA being used when the engagement is (more) with mainstream SLA scholars rather than CA analysts?

My stance on the questions raised immediately above, and I can only be very brief here, is that we should continue to do CA, to use CA research to help us to understand the practices of talk-in-interaction regardless of whether we are dealing with ordinary conversation, *lingua franca* discourse, talk in institutional settings, and so on. At this stage in the joint venture of CA and SLA, we no longer need to persuade those in "mainstream" SLA research about the advantages or benefits of CA (since CA has joined the mainstream) – and this need for persuasion may have been a rationale behind the use of the phrase CA-for-SLA in the first place. Kasper (2006) writes about CA's current role and contribution in discursive pragmatics in the following manner:

> Of the different proposals for the analysis of speech acts in interaction, conversation analysis (CA) has accrued by far the largest and most coherent cumulative body of research, lending high credibility to its theoretical foundations and methodology. CA therefore recommends itself not only as a lens for critical scrutiny of speech act research but provides a well documented alternative. (Kasper, 2006, p. 283)

Being true to CA and its methodological stance, we can (continue to) let the data speak for themselves. Researchers, teachers and practitioners may come along as they may (or not), but the burden is no longer on us to advocate for CA as the phrase CA-for-SLA or CA-SLA implies.

Notably, CA research on children's L1 data is not referred to as CA-for-FLA. It is just CA. The only thing different is the kind of interaction data being examined (Kidwell, 2005; Kidwell & Zimmerman, 2006, 2007; Lerner & Zimmerman, 2003). Similarly, scholars doing CA in other academic areas, for example, those doing work in speech pathology, hearing-impaired and aphasia do not refer to their work as CA-for-speech pathology, CA-for-hearing-impaired discourse, or the like. These are all just branches of the same CA tree. What is crucial is to remain committed to the spirit, methods, and practices of CA, which is why my "preference" is for the term CA to describe our body of work rather than CA-SLA or CA-for-SLA. Since we are well past "openings" and "identification" issues in forging the new direction for research, perhaps it is time to throw out this particular anchor!

This branch of CA research has, to a great extent, been influenced by socio-cultural theories of learning (Lave & Wenger, 1991; Vygotsky, 1978). For example, there is work that focuses on learning opportunities (Mori, 2004; Waring, 2008, 2009; Wong & Waring, 2009), participation structures (Hellermann, 2005) and gestures and their relation to talk (Olsher, 2004). Research that has honed in on classroom talks (note the use of the plural) has reminded us that classroom discourse is not a monolithic genre (Markee & Kasper, 2004; Seedhouse, 2004). Moreover, CA-based research on task-based instruction has helped to confirm the importance of cooperative learning environments in education (Brouwer, 2003; Mori, 2002; Hellermann, 2008); Mondada & Pekarek Doehler, 2004).

Increasingly CA researchers may use longitudinal data to examine some of the same issues that traditional SLA scholars have explored (Brouwer & Wagner, 2004; Hellermann, 2005, 2008). Many of these CA studies have focused on how instructional practices are directly tied to the extent to which learners can participate in the learning process (e.g., Hellermann, 2005, 2009; Kasper & Kim, 2007; Waring, 2008, 2009). Taken together these CA studies provide another window through which to view the significance of interaction, input and output in language but within locally managed interactional sites.

Overall, this type of CA research augments what we already know about the importance of input and interaction in second language acquisition research (Gass, 2005; Gass & Selinker, 2008). CA adds another dimension, another puzzle piece to shape our notions of language, language learning and social interaction. Certainly, if we come at the research puzzle from as many angles as possible, the greater are our chances of glimpsing the total picture.

CA and second language pedagogy

CA has played a central role in advancing our understanding of communicative competence (Hymes, 1974), and, most importantly, has given us an empirically-grounded sense of the notion of interactional competence. It has helped us to fine-tune what the interactional practices of talk-in-interaction consist of, what they sound and look like, including practices as fine-grained as a micro-pause or a smiley voice. CA provides a way of systematically articulating the nature of authentic language; we can use this knowledge to think about how to teach language learners and particularly to raise their level of awareness of pragmatics, but we must begin by raising teachers' awareness of these interactional practices as well (Houck & Tatsuki, 2011; Kasper, 2006; Tatsuki & Houck, 2010; Wong & Waring, 2010). CA has helped to ground our notion of interaction and speech acts through an empirical examination of the organization of actions (Schegloff, 1997, 2006, 2007).

Not only are there differences between what second or foreign language learners of English may find in textbooks and what they may have been taught (Barraja-Rohan, 2011; Barraja-Rohan & Pritchard, 1997; Bernsten, 2002; Carroll, 2010; Olsher, 2011; Wong, 2002, 2007, 2011a, 2011b), but our learners come from a vast array of first and second languages and backgrounds, and this affects the teaching of language enormously. No longer do languages and cultures stand in monolithic isolation. Globally, there is much cross-breeding of cultures and languages as people from differing languages and places of origin come into contact and influence one another on an ongoing basis. Teachers have to understand and appreciate what the diversity of linguistic and cultural competences entails and brings to the interactional table, for example, with respect to pragmatics, interlanguage pragmatics or cross-linguistic and cross-cultural issues (Barraja-Rohan, 2011; Golato, 2002; Greer, 2010; Houck & Tatsuki, 2011; Huth, 2006; Huth & Taleghani-Nikazm, 2006; Kasper, 2006; Sidnell, 2009; Taleghani-Nikazm, 2002).

Closing remarks

Just as language is traditionally thought of as a system with components (e.g., phonology, morphology, syntax, etc.), CA provides a powerful tool for hearing and seeing the components, i.e., the "machinery" of talk-in-interaction, such as turn-taking, sequencing, and repair. The interactional system more likely escapes our notice than, say, the grammatical system and yet can have more far-reaching consequences for our social well-being. Once we come to see and to appreciate that there are other tracks in this changing landscape, e.g., a 'syntax-for-conversation' (Schegloff, 1979), which leads to an intersection between grammar and interaction (Ochs, Schegloff & Thompson, 1996), we realize that we may need to go back to the drawing board as far as figuring out what and how to teach our second or foreign language learners about language. That's enough to keep us drastically away from "closings" (Button, 1987) for a very long time!

Notes

1. This article was conceived as the first of three parts of the Opening Plenary Address that I delivered at the 18th Pragmatics and Language Learning conference held at Kobe University, Kobe, Japan in July 2010. I am deeply indebted to the conference organizers, Tim Greer, Donna Tatsuki and Yuriko Kite, who invited me to speak. They provided me with the occasion to reflect upon part of what is written here. I am most appreciative of the insightful and helpful comments offered by two anonymous reviewers as well as that of the editors of this volume. All remaining errors are mine
2. See Seedhouse (2005) for a state-of-the-art piece on CA and language pedagogy.
3. If my memory is correct, it was not that I was the only student who enrolled for Schegloff's Spring semester course in 1983, but rather, that the students who had enrolled in that course had already taken a Fall semester course with Schegloff and were previously informed of a scheduling change so did not show up on the same day and time that I did.
4. I consulted the references cited in my doctoral dissertation to see what I could include in this article. I was amazed to rediscover (I had forgotten) how few references there were to cite in terms of CA and applied linguistics research. I cited a handful of studies at most. This rechecking of references has helped me to see that we have truly made progress and headway in thirty years. It is even astonishing to think of how much progress has been made in such a short amount of time in terms of the number of publications.
5. In the 1980s and early 1990s, Gaskill's (1980) and Schwartz's (1980) works were cited quite often.
6. Professors Marianne Celce-Murcia and Evelyn Hatch served on my master's and doctoral thesis committees. Hatch was chair of my master's thesis. Celce-Murcia, along with Schegloff, were co-chairs of my doctoral thesis committee.
7. Professor Sandra Thompson is now retired emerita professor from University of California, Santa Barbara, CA, USA.
8. For more recent work on tutorial settings, see Waring (2005, 2007a, 2007b) and Waring & Hruska (2011).
9. If I am not mistaken, Schegloff introduced the term talk-in-interaction officially in a 1999 article, which was a revised version of his Opening Plenary Address delivered at the International Pragmatics Association conference in Mexico City (Schegloff, 1996).
10. Schegloff also mentioned Garvey's (1984) work on children's repair but her work did not employ a CA framework.
11. By "mainline CA scholars" my point is that these researchers are not, strictly speaking, from Applied Linguistics departments.

12 Over the years, even the terms or labels have "grown and matured." We can no longer draw a definitive line between native and non-native speaker because, for instance, a "non-native" may have full command of the language, i.e., as well as "natives" do. Also, "non-native" speakers of English now outnumber "native" speakers by a ratio of 3 to 1 (Crystal, 2003). More and more, researchers are switching to use alternative terminology such as expert speaker, fluent speaker, proficient speaker, novice speaker, second language user, *lingua franca* speaker (Firth, 1996), or the like.

References

Antaki, C. (Ed.) (2011). *Applied conversation analysis*. Basingstoke: Palgrave.

Atkinson, J. M., & Drew, P. (1979). *Order in court: The organization of verbal interaction in judicial settings*. London: Macmillan.

Barraja-Rohan, A.-M. (2011). Using conversation analysis in the second language classroom to teach interactional competence. *Language Teaching Research*. 1–29.

Barraja-Rohan, A.-M., & Pritchard, C. (1997). *Beyond talk: A course in communication and conversation for intermediate adult learners of English*. Melbourne,: Western Melbourne Institute of TAFE (now Victoria University of Technology).

Bernsten, S. (2002). *Using conversation analysis to examine pre-sequences in invitation, offer and request dialogues in ESL textbooks*. Unpublished Master's thesis, University of Illinois at Urbana-Champaign.

Bolden, G. (2009). Implementing delayed actions. In J. Sidnell (Ed.). *Conversation analysis: Comparative perspectives* (pp. 326–354). Cambridge: Cambridge University Press.

Bowles, H., & Seedhouse, P. (Eds.), (2007). *Conversation Analysis and language for specific purposes*. Bern: Peter Lang.

Brouwer, C. E. (2003). Word searches in NNS-NS interaction: opportunities for language learning? *Modern Language Journal, 87*, 534–545.

Brouwer, C. E., & Wagner, J. (2004). Developmental issues in second language conversation. *Journal of Applied Linguistics, 1*, 29–47.

Button, G. (1987). Moving out of closings. In G. Button & J. R. E. Lee (Eds.), *Talk and social organization* (pp. 101–151). Clevedon/Philadelphia: Multilingual Matters.

Carroll, D. (2010). Conversation analysis and language teaching: A call to action. In T. Greer (Ed.), *Observing talk: Conversation analytic studies of second language interaction* (pp. 7–22). Tokyo: The Japan Association for Language Teaching, Pragmatics Special Interest Group.

Celce-Murcia, M. (1980). Contextual analysis of English: Application to TESL. In D. Larsen-Freeman (Ed.), *Discourse analysis in second language research* (p. 41–55). Rowley, MA: Newbury House.

Celce-Murcia, M. (1991). Discourse analysis and grammar instruction. *Annual Review of Applied Linguistics, 11,* 135–151.

Celce-Murcia, M. (1995). On the need for discourse analysis in curriculum development. In P. Hashemipour, R. Maldonado & M. Van Naerssen (Eds.), *Studies in language learning and Spanish linguistics, a festschrift for Tracy Terrell* (pp. 200–213). San Francisco: McGraw-Hill.

Celce-Murcia, M., & Olshtain, E. (2000). *Discourse and context in language teaching: A guide for language teachers.* Cambridge: Cambridge University Press.

Crystal, D. (2003). *The Cambridge encyclopedia of the English language,* Cambridge: Cambridge University Press.

Daden, I. (1975). *Conversational analysis and its relevance to the teaching of English as a second language.* Unpublished master's thesis, University of California, Los Angeles.

Daden, I., & McClaran, M. (n.d.) *Same turn repair in Quiche (Maya) conversation: An initial report.* Unpublished paper, Department of Anthropology, University of California, Los Angeles.

Drew, P., & Heritage, J. (1992). *Talk at work.* Cambridge: Cambridge University Press.

Enfield, N., & Stivers, T. (Eds.) (2007). *Person reference in interaction: Linguistic, cultural and social perspectives.* Cambridge: Cambridge University Press.

Færch, C., & Kasper, G. (Eds.) (1983). *Strategies in interlanguage.* London: Longman.

Færch, C. & Kasper, G. (1984). Two ways of defining communication strategies. *Language Learning, 34,* 45–63.

Filippi, A. (2009), *Toddler and parent interaction: The organization of gaze, pointing and vocalisation.* Amsterdam: John Benjamins.

Firth, A. (1996). The discursive accomplishment of normality: On 'lingua franca' English and conversation analysis. *Journal of Pragmatics, 26,* 237–259.

Firth, A. (2009). Doing "not" being a foreign language learner in English as a "lingua franca" in the workplace and (some) implications for SLA. *International Review of Applied Linguistics, 47,* 127–156.

Firth, A., & Wagner, J. (1997). On discourse, communication, and (some) fundamental concepts in SLA research. *The Modern Language Journal, 81,* 285–300.

Firth, A., & Wagner, J. (2007). Second/foreign language as a social accomplishment: Elaboration on a reconceptualized SLA. *The Modern Language Journal, 91,* 798–817.

Ford, C. (1988). *Grammar in interaction: Adverbial clauses in American English conversation.* Unpublished doctoral dissertation, University of California, Los Angeles.

Ford, C., Fox, B., & Thompson, S. (Eds.) (2002). *The language of turn and sequence.* Oxford: Oxford University Press.

Gardner, H., & Forrester, M. (Eds.), (2010). *Analysing interactions in childhood: Insights from Conversation Analysis.* Oxford: Wiley/Blackwell.

Gardner, R., & Wagner, J. (Eds.), (2004). *Second language conversations,* New York: Continuum.

Garvey, C. (1984). *Children's talk.* Cambridge, MA: Harvard University Press.

Gaskill, W. (1977). *Conversation Analysis in adult native speaker-non-native speaker interaction*. Unpublished master's thesis, University of California, Los Angeles.

Gaskill, W. (1980). Correction in native speaker – nonnative speaker conversation. In D. Larsen-Freeman (Ed.), *Discourse analysis in second language research* (pp. 125–137). Rowley, MA: Newbury House.

Gass, S. (2004). Conversation analysis and input-interaction. *Modern Language Journal, 88,* 597–602.

Gass, S. (2005). Input and interaction. In C. Doughty & M. Long (Eds.), *The handbook of second language acquisition* (pp. 224 – 255), Oxford: Blackwell.

Gass, S., Lee, J., & Roots, R. (2007). New ideas or a new articulation? *Modern Language Journal, 91,* 788–799.

Gass, S., & Selinker, L. (2008). *Second language acquisition*. New York: Routledge.

Goffman, E. (1976). Replies and responses. *Language in Society, 5,* 254–313.

Golato, A. (2002). German compliment responses. *Journal of Pragmatics, 34,* 547–571.

Goode, D. (2007). *Playing with my dog Katie: An ethnomethodological study of dog-human interaction*. West Lafayette, Indiana: Purdue University Press.

Greer, T. (Ed.). (2010). *Observing talk: Conversation analytic studies of second language interaction*. Tokyo: The Japan Association for Language Teaching.

Haakana, M., Laakso, M., & Lindstrom, J. (Eds.). (2009). *Talk in interaction: Comparative dimensions*. Helsinki: Finnish Literature Society.

Hatch, E. (1978). Discourse analysis and second language acquisition. In E. Hatch (Ed.), *Second language acquisition*. Rowley, MA: Newbury House.

Hatch, E. (1992). *Discourse and language education*. Cambridge: Cambridge University Press.

Hatch, E., & Long, M. (1980). Discourse analysis: What's that? In D. Larsen-Freeman (Ed.), *Discourse analysis in second language research* (pp. 1–40). Rowley, MA: Newbury House.

Hayashi, M. (1999). Where grammar and interaction meet: A study of co-participant completion in Japanese conversation. *Human Studies* 22: 475–499.

Hayashi, M. (2003). Language and the body as resources for collaborative action: A study of word searches in Japanese conversation. *Research on Language and Social Interaction* 36, 109–141.

Heinemann, T. (2009). Two answers to inapposite inquiries. In J. Sidnell (Ed.), *Conversation analysis: Comparative perspectives* (pp. 159–186), Cambridge: Cambridge University Press.

Hellermann, J. (2005). The sequential and prosodic co-construction of a "quiz game" activity in classroom talk. *Journal of Pragmatics, 37,* 919–944.

Hellermann, J. (2008). *Social actions for classroom language learning*. Clevedon: Multilingual Matters.

Heritage, J. & Robinson, D. (2011). 'Some' versus 'Any' medical issues: Encouraging patients to reveal their unmet concerns. In C. Antaki (ed.) *Applied conversation analysis* (pp 15–31). Basingstoke:Palgrave-Macmillan.

Hosoda, Y. (2006). Repair and relevance of differential language expertise. *Applied Linguistics, 27,* 25–50.

Houck, N., & Tatsuki, D. H. (Eds.). (2011). *Pragmatics: Teaching natural conversation.* Alexandria, VA: TESOL Publications.

Houtkoop-Steenstra, H. (1991). Opening sequences in Dutch telephone conversation. In D. Boden & D. Zimmerman (Eds.), *Talk and social structures: Studies in ethnomethodology and conversation analysis* (pp. 232–250). Cambridge: Polity Press.

Huth, T. (2006). Negotiating structure and culture: L2 learners' realization of L2 compliment-response sequences in talk-in-interaction. *Journal of Pragmatics, 38,* 2025–2050.

Huth, T., & Taleghani-Nikazm, C. (2006). How can insights from Conversation Analysis be directly applied to teaching L2 pragmatics? *Language Teaching Research 10,* 1–27.

Hymes, D. (1974). *Foundations in sociolinguistics.* Philadelphia: University of Pennsylvania Press.

Kasper, G. (1985). Repair in foreign language teaching. *Studies in Second Language Acquisition, 7,* 200–215.

Kasper, G. (1997). "A" stands for acquisition. *The Modern Language Journal, 81,* 307–312.

Kasper, G. (2006). Speech acts in interaction: Towards discursive pragmatics. In K. Bardovi-Harlig, C. Felix-Brasdefer, & A. S. Omar (Eds.), *Pragmatics and language learning, 22,* 281–314.

Kasper, G., & Kim, Y. (2007). Handling sequentially inapposite responses. In Zhu Hua, P. Seedhouse, Li Wei, & V. Cook (Eds.), *Language learning and teaching as social inter-action* (pp. 22 – 41), Basingstoke: Palgrave Macmillan.

Kasper, G., & Wagner, J. (2011). A conversation-analytic approach to second language acquisition. In D. Atkinson (Ed.), *Alternative approaches to second language acquisition* (pp. 117–142). New York: Routledge.

Kidwell, M. (2005). Gaze as social control: How very young children differentiate 'the look' from a 'mere look' by their adult caregivers. *Research on Language and Social Interaction 38,* 417–449.

Kidwell, M. & Zimmerman, D. H., (2006). Observability in the interactions of very young children. *Communication Monographs 73,* 1–28.

Kidwell, M. & Zimmerman, D. H., (2007). Joint attention in action, *Journal of Pragmatics 39,* 592–611.

Koshik, I. (1999). *Practices of pedagogy in ESL writing conferences: A conversation analytic study of turns and sequences that assist student revision.* Unpublished doctoral thesis, University of California, Los Angeles.

Koshik, I. (2005). *Beyond rhetorical questions and assertive questions in everyday interaction.* Amsterdam: John Benjamins.

Krashen, S. D., (1985). *The input hypothesis: Issues and implications*, New York: Longman.
Kurhila, S. (2006). *Second language interaction*, Amsterdam: John Benjamins.
Larsen-Freeman, D. (1980). *Discourse analysis in second language research.* Rowley, MA: Newbury House.
Lave, J., & Wenger, E. (1991). *Situated learning. Legitimate peripheral participation*, Cambridge: University of Cambridge Press.
Lazaraton, A. (1992). *A qualitative approach to the validation of oral language tests.* Unpublished doctoral thesis, University of California, Los Angeles.
Lerner, G., & Zimmerman, D. H. (2003). Action and the appearance of action in the conduct of very young children. In P. Glenn, C. LeBaron & J. Mandelbaum (Eds.), *Studies in language and social interaction* (pp. 441–457). Mahwah, NJ: Lawrence Erlbaum.
Lerner, G. H., Zimmerman, D. H., & Kidwell, M. (2011). Formal structures of practical tasks: A resource for action in the social life of very young children. In C. Goodwin, C. LeBaron & J. Streek (Eds.), *Embodied interaction: Language and body in the material world.* Cambridge: Cambridge University Press.
Lindstrom, A. (1994). Identification and recognition in Swedish telephone conversation openings. *Language in Society, 23,* 231–252.
Lindstrom, A. (2009). Projecting non-alignment in conversation. In J. Sidnell (Ed.), *Conversation analysis: Comparative perspectives* (pp. 159–186), Cambridge: Cambridge University Press.
Long, M. (1983). Linguistic and conversational adjustments to non-native speakers. *Second Language Acquisition, 5,* 177–193.
Macbeth, D. (2004). The relevance of repair for classroom correction. *Language in Society, 33,* 703–736.
Markee, N. (1988). *An appropriate technology model of communicative course design.* Unpublished doctoral dissertation, University of California, Los Angeles.
Markee, N. (1994). Towards an ethnomethodological respecification of second language acquisition studies. In E. Tarone, M. Gass, & A. Cohen (Eds.), *Research methodology in second language acquisition* (pp. 89–116). Hillsdale, NJ: Erlbaum.
Markee, N. (1995). Teachers' answers to students' questions: Problematizing the issue of making meaning. *Issues in Applied Linguistics, 6,* 63–92.
Markee, N. (2000). *Conversation analysis.* Mahwah, NJ: Erlbaum.
Markee, N., & Kasper, G. (2004). Classroom talks: An introduction, *Modern Language Journal, 88,* 491–509.
Maynard, D. (2003). *Bad news, good news: Conversational order in everyday talk and clinicial settings.* Chicago: University of Chicago Press.
Moerman, M. (1988). *Talking culture.* Philadelphia: University of Pennsylvania Press.
Mondada, L., & Pekarek Doehler, S. (2004). Second language acquisition as situated practice: Task accomplishment in the French language classroom. *Modern Language Journal, 88,* 536–550.

Mori, J. (2002). Task design, plan, and development of talk-in-interaction: A study of small group activity in a Japanese language classroom. *Applied Linguistics, 23*, 323–347.

Mori, J. (2004). Negotiating sequential boundaries and learning opportunities: A case from a Japanese language classroom. *The Modern Language Journal, 88*, 536–550.

Mori, J. (2007). Exploring the intersection of second language acquisition, conversation analysis, and foreign language pedagogy, *The Modern Language Journal, 91*, 847–860.

Mori, J. (2009). Language learning, cognition, and interactional practices: An introduction. *International Review of Applied Linguistics, 47*, 1–9.

Mori, J. (2010). Learning language in real time: A case study of the Japanese demonstrative pronoun *are* in word search sequences. In G. Kasper, H. t. Nguyen, D. R. Yoshimi, & J. K. Yoshioka (Eds), *Pragmatics and Language Learning, (Vol. 12),* (pp. 13–40), Honolulu: University of Hawai'i, National Foreign Language Resource Center.

Nguyen, H. t., & Kasper, G. (Eds.), (2009). *Talk-in-interaction: Multilingual perspectives.* Honolulu: National Foreign Language Resource Center.

Ochs, E. (1984). Clarification and culture. In D. Schiffrin (Ed.), *Meaning, form, and use: Linguistic applications* (pp. 325–341). Georgetown Roundtable on Language and Linguistics, Washington, DC: Georgetown University Press.

Ochs, E. (1991). Misunderstanding children. In N. Coupland, J. Wieland, & H. Giles (Eds.), *Miscommunication and problematic talk* (p. 44–60), Newbury Park: Sage.

Ochs, E., Schegloff, E. A., & Thompson, S. (Eds.). (1996). *Interaction and grammar.* Cambridge: Cambridge University Press.

Olsher, D. (2004). Talk and gesture: The embodied completion of sequential actions in spoken interaction. In R. Gardner & J. Wagner (Eds.), *Second language conversations* (pp. 221–245), New York: Continuum.

Olsher, D. (2011). Responders. In N. Houck & D. Tatsuki (Eds.), *Pragmatics: Teaching natural conversation*, Alexandria, VA: TESOL Publications.

Richards, K., & Seedhouse, P. (Eds.). (2005). *Applying Conversation Analysis,* Basingstoke: Palgrave.

Riggenbach, H. (1989). *Non-native dialogue versus monologue speech: A microanalytic approach.* Unpublished doctoral thesis, University of California, Los Angeles.

Sacks, H., Schegloff, E. A., & Jefferson, G. (1974). A simplest systematics for the organization of turn-taking for conversation. *Language, 50,* 696–735.

Schegloff, E. A. (1979). The relevance of repair to syntax-for-conversation. In T. Givon (Ed.), *Syntax and semantics, Volume 12: Discourse and syntax* (pp. 261–286). New York: Academic Press.

Schegloff, E. A. (1986). The routine as achievement. *Human Studies, 9,* 111–151.

Schegloff, E. A. (1997). Practices and actions: Boundary cases of other-initiated repair. *Discourse Processes, 23,* 499–545.

Schegloff, E. A. (2000). When "others" initiate repair. *Applied Linguistics, 21,* 205–243.

Schegloff, E. A. (2006). Interaction: The infrastructure for social institutions, the natural ecological niche for language, and the arena in which culture is enacted. In N. J., Enfield & S. C. Levinson (Eds.), *Roots of human sociality: Culture, cognition and interaction*, London: Berg.

Schegloff, E. A. (2007). *Sequence organization*. Cambridge: Cambridge University Press.

Schegloff, E. A. (2009). One perspective on *Conversation Analysis: Comparative perspectives*. In Sidnell, J. (Ed.), *Conversation Analysis: Comparative perspectives* (pp. 357–406). Cambridge: Cambridge University.

Schegloff, E. A., Jefferson, G., & Sacks, H. (1977). The preference for self-correction in the organization of repair in conversation. *Language, 53*, 361–382.

Schegloff, E. A., Koshik, I., Jacoby, S., & Olsher, D., (2002). Conversation analysis and applied linguistics. *Annual Review of Applied Linguistics, 22*, 3–31.

Schwartz, J. (1977). *Repair in conversations between adult second language learners of English*. Unpublished master's thesis, University of California, Los Angeles.

Schwartz, J. (1980). The negotiation of meaning: Repair in conversations between second language learners of English. In D. Larsen-Freeman (Ed.), *Discourse analysis in second language research*, (pp. 138–153). Rowley, MA: Newbury House.

Seedhouse, P. (2004). *The interactional architecture of the language classroom: A Conversation Analysis perspective*. Malden, MA: Blackwell.

Sidnell, J. (2007). Comparative studies in conversation analysis. *Annual Review of Anthropology, 36*, 229–244.

Sidnell, J. (Ed.). (2009). *Conversation analysis: Comparative perspectives*. Cambridge: Cambridge University Press.

Swain, M. (1985). Communicative competence: Some rules of comprehensible input and comprehensible output in its development. In S. Gass & C. Madden (Eds.), *Input in second language acquisition* (pp. 235–253). New York: Newbury House.

Taleghani-Nikazm, C. (2002). A conversational analytic study of telephone conversation openings between native and nonnative speakers. *Journal of Pragmatics, 34*, 1807–1832.

Tarone, E. (1977). Conscious communication strategies in interlanguage. In H. D. Brown, C. A. Yorio, and R. C. Crymes (Eds.), *On TESOL '77: Teaching and learning English as a second language: Trends in research and practice*, (pp. 194–203). Washington, DC: Teachers of English to Speakers of Other Languages.

Tarone, E. (1981). Some thoughts on the notion of communicative strategies. *TESOL Quarterly, 15*, 285–295.

Tatsuki, D., & Houck, N. (Eds.). (2010). *Pragmatics: Speech acts*, Alexandria, VA: TESOL Publications.

Thompson, S. A., & Hopper, P. J. (Eds.). Discourse and Grammar, special issue of *Text 14.4.*

van Lier, L. (1988). *The classroom and the language learner*. London: Longman.

Vygotsky, L. (1978). *Mind in society*. Cambridge, MA: Harvard University Press.

Waring, H. Z. (2005). Peer tutoring in a graduate writing center: Identity, expertise and advice resisting, *Applied Linguistics, 26,* 141–168.

Waring, H. Z. (2007a). Complex advice acceptance as a resource for managing asymmetries. *Text and Talk, 27,* 107–137.

Waring, H. Z. (2007b). The multi-functionality of accounts in advice giving. *Journal of Sociolinguistics, 11,* 367–369.

Waring, H. Z. (2008). Using explicit positive assessment in the language classroom: IRF, feedback, and learning opportunities. *Modern Language Journal, 92,* 577–594.

Waring, H. Z. (2009). Moving out of IRF: A single case analysis. *Language Learning, 59,* 796–864.

Waring, H. Z., & Hruska, B. (2011). Getting and keeping Nora on board: A novice elementary ESOL student teacher's practices for lesson engagement. *Linguistics and Education, 22,* 441–455.

Wong, J. (1984). *Using conversational analysis to evaluate telephone conversations in English as a second language textbooks.* Unpublished Master's thesis, University of California, Los Angeles.

Wong, J. (1994). *The token "yeah" in same turn repair and delayed next turn repair initiation in native/nonnative speaker English conversation.* Unpublished Doctoral thesis, University of California, Los Angeles.

Wong, J. (2000a). Delayed next turn repair initiation native/non-native speaker English conversation. *Applied Linguistics 21,* 244–267.

Wong, J. (2000b). The token "yeah" in native/non-native speaker English conversation. *Research on Language and Social Interaction, 33,* 39–67.

Wong, J. (2000c). Repetition in conversation: A look at "first and second sayings." *Research on Language and Social Interaction, 33,* 407–424.

Wong, J. (2002). "Applying" conversation analysis in applied linguistics: Evaluating dialogue in English as a second language textbooks. *International Review of Applied Linguistics, 40,* 37–60.

Wong, J. (2007). Answering my call: A look at telephone closings. In H. Bowles & P. Seedhouse (Eds.), *Conversation analysis and language for specific purposes,* (pp. 271–304). Bern: Peter Lang.

Wong, J. (2011a). Pragmatic competency in telephone conversation openings. In N. Houck & D. Tatsuki (Eds.), *Pragmatics: Teaching natural conversation,* (pp. 119–134). Alexandria, VA: TESOL Publications.

Wong, J. (2011b). Pragmatic competency in telephone conversation closings. In N. Houck & D. Tatsuki (Eds.). *Pragmatics: Teaching natural conversation,* (pp. 119–134). Alexandria, VA: TESOL Publications.

Wong, J. & Olsher, D. (2000). Reflections on conversation analysis and nonnative speaker talk: An interview with Emanuel A. Schegloff. *Issues in Applied Linguistics, 11,* 111–128.

Wong, J. & Waring, H. Z. (2009). "Very good" as a teacher response. *ELT Journal, 63,* 195–203.

Wong, J., & Waring, H. Z. (2010). *Conversation analysis and second language pedagogy: A guide for ESL/EFL teachers*. New York: Routledge.

Wu, R.-J. (2004). *Stance in talk: A conversation analysis of Mandarin final particles*. Amsterdam: John Benjamins.

Wu, R.-J. (2009). Repetition in the initiation of repair. In J. Sidnell (Ed.), *Conversation analysis: Comparative perspectives* (pp. 31–59). Cambridge: Cambridge University Press.

Zimmerman, D. (1999). Horizontal and vertical comparative research in language and social interaction. *Research on Language and Social Interaction 32*, 195–203.

Expanding Resources for Marking Direct Reported Speech

Eric Hauser
University of Electro-Communications, Japan
University of Hawaiʻi at Mānoa

The application of conversation analysis (CA) to longitudinal data is used to investigate how the resources used by one adult novice speaker and second language learner of English to mark direct reported speech (DRS) change over a seven-month period. The data are drawn from audio-recorded meetings between this adult and the researcher. In order to understand the observed change, a distinction is drawn between practices people engage in when they produce DRS and resources used to accomplish these practices. It was found that some resources remained stable over time while new resources were added. These new resources were, first, the use of person reference and, later, the use of person reference and a verb of speech to frame DRS. By shifting from a longitudinal perspective to a locally-sequential perspective, the analysis also demonstrates the local emergence of these new resources and their increasing stability. Finally, this paper serves as a demonstration that an exogenous theory of learning, such as situated learning theory, may not be necessary in order to investigate learning within CA-for-SLA.

Introduction

This paper applies conversation analysis (CA) to longitudinal data in order to investigate adult second language learning. Specifically, it investigates how the resources one novice speaker/ESL learner uses to mark direct reported speech (DRS) expand over a seven-month period. A possible strength of using CA with longitudinal data is that the data can be analyzed from both a longitudinal perspective and a locally-sequential perspective. Through such a shift of perspective, this paper also demonstrates how participant orientations to the local interactional context and the work participants do to make themselves understood may be related to the local emergence of new resources.

The use of CA with longitudinal data does not have a long history, but there is a growing body of work in this area (e.g., Hellermann, 2006, 2008; Hellermann & Cole, 2009; Ishida, 2009). One issue within what is now being called "CA-for-SLA" (i.e., conversation analysis for second language acquisition; see Wong [this volume] for arguments against the use of the terms "CA-for-SLA" and "CA-SLA") is the extent to which, if CA is not or does not contain a theory of learning, an exogenous theory of learning is necessary in order to investigate language learning (Markee, 2008). In particular, one proposal for a theory to be utilized within CA-for-SLA which appears to have a good deal of support is situated learning theory (Lave & Wenger, 1991). Hellermann (2006, 2008; Hellermann & Cole, 2009), for example, makes use of this theory, and its key theoretical concepts of *legitimate peripheral participation* and *community of practice*, in longitudinal investigations of learning among adults of limited English proficiency and, for some participants, limited classroom experience, in ESL classes in the U.S. Hellermann presents ESL classes as a community of practice (Wenger, 1998) and learning as movement from more peripheral participation to fuller participation in classroom interaction (cf. Young, 2007, 2009). Hauser (2011) has critiqued this use of situated learning theory for 1) lack of clarity about what sort of community of practice participants are becoming members of and, more importantly, 2) conflating participation in interaction with participation in the work of a community of practice. Other longitudinal work within CA-for-SLA takes a different approach. Ishida (2009), for example, does not find exogenous theory necessary in her longitudinal study of one adult learner's development in the use of *ne* in L2 Japanese. An interesting point of comparison is with Wootton's use of CA with longitudinal data involving young children learning their first language (Wootton, 1997), in which he also does not find such a theory necessary. One purpose of the current study is to understand how the resources that one adult learner of English uses to mark DRS expand over time *without* recourse to the use of an exogenous theory of learning and, in particular, to situated learning theory. To the extent that this is successful, this study provides a demonstration that an exogenous theory of learning is not necessary within CA-for-SLA.

Reporting directly on what someone else has said is a common interactional practice and quoted talk—that is, DRS—has been the object of a great deal of research. Halliday (1985) states that the "idealized function" of DRS "is to represent the wording" (p. 232), as opposed to the meaning, of what someone has said. According to Coulmas (1986), DRS "evokes the original speech situation and conveys, or claims to convey, the exact words of the original speaker" (p. 2). However, as has often been pointed out (Clift, 2007; Coulmas, 1986; Holt, 1999; Tannen 1986, 1989), it is important to recognize that this exactness is illusory.

DRS presents what someone has said *as if* it were an exact repetition, and actually in many cases, such as using DRS to report an unspoken thought (Haakana, 2007), it simply cannot be an exact repetition. While in some languages, there does not appear to be a clear distinction between DRS and indirect forms of reported speech (Rumsey, 1990), in English this distinction is encoded in the syntax (Huddleston, 2002). Overall, DRS has been widely studied in a variety of fields, including CA (see for example, the collection edited by Holt & Clift, 2007). Even so, the choice of the expansion of resources for marking DRS as the object of study was not based on any prior interest on my part in DRS. Rather, this was chosen as the object of study because the learner, Nori (a pseudonym), often told stories within which he used DRS, and there were some noticeable changes in how he produced the DRS over time. Expansion of resources for the marking of DRS thus presented itself as a promising object of study for investigating how Nori's use of English developed over time.

Data

The data come from audio-recordings of interaction between Eric (the researcher) and Nori, made between February and September, 2001, in Eric's apartment in Honolulu. There were a total of nineteen recordings of about 45 minutes each. Nori was a first language speaker of Japanese and a novice speaker of English who had moved to Honolulu from Tokyo with his wife and two daughters a few months prior to the first recording. He worked in Honolulu as the assistant manager of a Japanese restaurant. Eric was a graduate student who also worked part-time as a teacher and whose wife worked in the same restaurant as Nori. He was a first language speaker of English and a proficient second language speaker of Japanese. The ostensible purpose of the meetings between Nori and Eric was to provide Nori with opportunities to practice English. The recordings were made, with Nori's permission, for possible future use by Eric for research, but were unrelated to any research project that Eric was involved in at that time.

These recordings are now being used for a research project in CA-for-SLA with the use of longitudinal data. However, they are still being transcribed and the current paper can thus be seen as a work-in-progress. As of September, 2010, at least part of each recording has been roughly transcribed, while the first ten minutes of recordings 1, 2, 4, 6, 9, 11, 12, 16, 18, and 19 have been finely transcribed. It is this smaller subset of the data which is used for this paper. Clear cases of DRS have been found in recordings 2, 4, 9, 11, 12, 16, 18, and 19, for a total of fifteen cases. It is likely, though, that more cases will be found as the process of making detailed conversation analytic transcriptions continues. Each case, the number of the recording, the date of the recording, and the line numbers in the relevant transcript are listed in Table 1. A transcript of each case can also be found in the appendix. Each transcript follows standard

CA transcription practices (Jefferson, 2004), with the added convention of using italics to indicate the use of Japanese. In the appendix, arrows (→) are used to indicate lines of transcript which contain DRS.

Table 1. Cases of DRS

case	recording #	date	lines
I	2	Mar 30	76–136
II	4	Apr 20	115–129
III	4	Apr 20	237–244
IV	9	Jun 1	178–184
V	11	Jun 22	124–160
VI	11	Jun 22	193–217
VII	12	Jul 6	150–154
VIII	12	Jul 6	373–410
IX	12	Jul 6	460–476
X	16	Aug 3	379–384
XI	16	Aug 3	388–402
XII	18	Sep 4	414–431
XIII	19	Sep 11	18–40
XIV	19	Sep 11	97–110
XV	19	Sep 11	414–453

For the purpose of explicating an important distinction between practices and resources, I also use data drawn from two telephone calls between former U.S. President Johnson (J) and certain subordinates. These telephone calls are available in a book/CD set compiled as a resource for historical research by Prados (2003). I have re-transcribed these telephone conversations according to CA conventions.

Practices versus resources

In order to make sense of how Nori marked some bit of talk as DRS and how this changed over time, I found it useful to make a distinction between *practices*, which are socially-shared ways of doing something, such as producing DRS, and *resources*, the means for accomplishing these practices. I did not bring this distinction to the data as a prior theoretical commitment, but rather as a distinction that helped me understand and demonstrate to others how Nori's marking of DRS changed over time. However, as I will attempt to show in the next section, and as supported by other research, the three practices that I argue Nori engages in when he produces DRS are shared by others who are temporally and physically separated from Nori. I have labeled the three practices *enactment*, *scene-setting*, and *framing*.

Enactment (Beach, 2000; Holt, 2007) involves the use of various resources to dramatically perform talk attributed to another or to oneself. It may also involve an exchange of turns within the performance. Such an exchange of turns can be seen, for example, in a work-story told by a person employed in a hospital emergency room analyzed by Tannen (1986, 1989). This can also be seen in extract 1, in which J is relaying to his National Security Advisor, McGeorge Bundy (B), an earlier conversation with a State Department official. Bundy apparently knows that this earlier conversation involved Johnson criticizing the official for talking to reporters. The talk that Johnson attributes to this official can be heard as a series of excuses or accounts for his actions.

Extract 1

```
01   J:   =I jes' said that no:w, if uh he said ↑well
02        I'm just tellin' 'em what the administration's
03        plans are.=.hh   [an'    I     [said [(yes)=
04   B:                    [he said that [to   [you?
05   J:   ='n' I said ↑how in the hell do you know if I
06        don't know. .hh well 'e said ↑I'm talkin' about
07        our planning I'm not talkin' about what we:
08        going to do: an' I said ↑well, .h ↓uh: ↑you
09        put me in position where I might near got to do
10        it if you go talkin' about our plannin'.=now I
11        wan' chew ((want you)) t' talk to me about the
12        plannin',='n' not the newspapers.
```

After some self-repair in line 01, in which Johnson replaces "I just said" with "he said," Johnson reports what the administration official said. However, he does not just report what was said, but dramatically enacts it, using pitch reset to change into the voice of the State Department official. Johnson also uses "well," a word commonly used at or near the start of a turn involving some sort of disagreement (Pomerantz, 1984), as the first word of what this official is reported to have said, which together with the use of "just" in the excuse that Johnson attributes to this official, makes the talk that Johnson is reporting sound defensive. Next, when Johnson reports his response to this official's excuse, in lines 05 to 06, he again uses a pitch reset, this time to enact his own voice in the earlier conversation, and performs the anger that he felt towards this official by including in his self-attributed DRS the expression "in the hell." As Johnson continues, he enacts this official's next excuse in lines 06 to 08 and then enacts his own response to the second excuse in lines 08 to 12. It is interesting to note that in this enacted response, Johnson does not give the State Department official an opportunity to respond at the first possible completion point—after the word "planning"—but rather enacts more talk of his own, thus enacting his prevention of this official from responding, for example, by offering a third excuse. Beyond simply reporting what he and the official said to each other, Johnson dramatically performs the verbal conflict that ostensibly occurred. There is much more that could be said about how this dramatic performance, or enactment, is constructed, but this should be enough to indicate what is meant by the term enactment.

Rae and Kerby (2007) show how a description of a person's action, which may include a report of what the person said, can be used to provide a context for the DRS which follows the description. This is similar to what I have labeled *scene-setting*, in which some context is given within which the talk that is reported ostensibly occurred. This can be seen in extract 2, from a telephone call in which Johnson is berating a State Department official for talking to the press on behalf of the administration. (Later the same day, Johnson related this conversation to McGeorge Bundy, part of which is shown in extract 1.)

Extract 2

```
01   J:   .h Elie Abel, night before la:st, went on
02        television, en bee see ((NBC)), over the nation.
03        .hh an' 'e says thet thee administration's very
04        crue:l t' the poo::r (.) .h unassuming reporter=
05        because the administration calls 'im in an'
06        tells 'im we're going to war in North Vietnaem
07        then Johnson says I didn't say any such thing.
```

The DRS occurs in lines 03 to 07, from "the administration's" to "any such thing." Prior to this, Johnson sets the scene through a person reference in line 01, "Elie Abel," a time reference in the same line, "night before last," and a description of the medium through which the to be reported speech occurred, in lines 01 to 02, "on television, NBC, over the nation." He thus provides information about who the DRS can be attributed to, when it is said to have occurred, and how Johnson himself, as well as possibly millions of others, came to hear it.

Finally, I use the term *framing* to refer to overtly marking, intra-sententially, some stretch of talk as quoted and/or as attributed to a particular person. This terminology may be somewhat confusing, as the term *frame* is used in other ways as well (e.g., Goffman, 1974; Tannen, 1993), but my use of the term framing is not completely idiosyncratic (see for example, Holt, 2007). Tannen (1986) uses the term *introducer* to refer to such things as "he says" in extract 2, but this is less than satisfying as it implies that whatever is being used to overtly mark the talk as quoted comes prior to the DRS, which is not always the case in English and may never or almost never be the case in other languages, such as Japanese (Coulmas, 1986). A common resource for framing in English is person reference and a verb of speech, most commonly a form of "say" (Tannen 1986, 1989). This can be seen in line 03 of extract 2, "he says," and line 07 of the same extract, "Johnson says," where this is actually DRS embedded in DRS. While it is apparently common to use the past tense of "say," as Johnson does in extract 1, note that this is not obligatory, as Johnson in extract 2 uses the historical present and attributes its use to the person he is quoting. Also note that framing is not obligatory in English (Holt, 2007; Tannen, 1986, 1989; see also Besnier, 1995, in relation to a dialect of Tuvaluan in which the non-use of framing is characteristic of sermonic discourse).

Resources for accomplishing enactment, scene-setting, and framing

As will be demonstrated in this section, Nori uses various resources to accomplish the practices of enactment, scene-setting, and framing. The use of some of these resources is stable over time, while other resources are added.

Nori engages in the practice of enactment in almost all cases of DRS found in the data, except for cases XIII and XIV. One of the major resources for accomplishing enactment is *prosody* (see also Beach, 2000; Holt, 2007; Tannen, 1986, 1989). Changes in prosody are found in all the cases that involve enactment and, indeed, it is through changes in prosody that Nori can be heard as engaging in the practice of enactment. Extract 3, part of case V, contains some pertinent examples.

Extract 3   Case V, #11, June 22

```
139 N: yeah=yes yes=yes mechanic. mehk
140    (0.7)
141 N: .t (.) ↑eighteen hundred. (1.0) wuh (1.1)
142    ↑one hundred ↑eighty? (2.2) eigh- eighteen
143    hundred. (0.4) ↑heh (0.4) tuh (0.3) one hundred
144    eighty? one thousand ↑eighty hundred? hh (0.7)
145 E: hmh
146    (0.5)
147 N: ↑okay okay (0.5) please please fixed. (0.6)
148    ↑really? hh (0.6) heh? (0.9) ↓okay. (0.2)
149    ↑one hundred (.) eighty dollars? (0.3) ↓n:o.
150    (0.9) ↑eighteen hundr(h)ed dollars. (1.1)
151 E: m.
152    (1.4)
153 N: ↑one thousand eighty hundred? hoo hoo (0.6)
154    ↓yes yes. .hh oh hoh hoh ↑n(h)o no fi(h)x.
155    [n(h)o fix.
156 E: [heh heh heh huh huh huh huh
```

This case, which can be seen in its entirety in the appendix, involves Nori telling a story about a telephone conversation with a mechanic who was fixing the air conditioning in Nori's car. The story is about how it would cost $1,800 to fix the air conditioning and how long it took Nori to understand what the expression "eighteen hundred" meant. In line 141, as Nori reports the price that the mechanic ostensibly told him, he resets to a higher pitch than he used in line 139. This reset makes what he says, "eighteen hundred," hearable as an enactment of another's talk. In addition, the falling intonation at the end of the price makes what the mechanic is reported to have told Nori hearable as a simple informing. In line 142, Nori reports his response to what the mechanic told him, which was to check his understanding of the price. As he does this, he again resets his pitch at the start of "one hundred eighty," which makes this hearable as produced by a different person than the price that was stated in line 141. In addition, his change of pitch on "eighty" and the rising intonation at the end of "one hundred eighty" indicates that his response was not merely a check of his understanding of the price, but also a response that indexed his own uncertainty about this understanding.

A second resource that Nori uses for the accomplishment of enactment is the use of *non-lexical items* to index such things as surprise and lack of understanding. For example, in extract 3 above, Nori's reports himself as saying "wuh" in line 141 and "heh" in line 143 to index his lack of understanding of the price that the mechanic has reportedly told him. While he may or may not have actually used such non-lexical items in comparable sequential locations in his telephone conversation with the mechanic, by using them here Nori is able to enact a display of his difficulty in understanding the meaning of "eighteen hundred." This use of non-lexical items as a resource to accomplish enactment can be found in cases I, II, V, VI, VII, VIII, XII, and XV.

A third resource that Nori has available for the accomplishment of enactment is *temporal iconicity*. When Nori enacts talk which includes at least one exchange of turns, the order in which the DRS occurs in his talk is hearable as the order in which the ostensibly original talk occurred. Enactment of an exchange of turns, and temporal iconicity as a resource for its accomplishment, can be seen in cases I, II, III, V, VI, VIII, IX, and XII. Extract 3 above again provides an example. In line 141, Nori first reports the price the mechanic ostensibly told him, "eighteen hundred." After a one-second pause, Nori reports the first part of his reaction, the sound "wuh." In line 142, Nori then reports the second part of his reaction, which was to check his understanding of the price by saying, with rising intonation, "one hundred eighty." In lines 142 and 143, Nori next reports the mechanic's ostensible response to this understanding check, which was to repeat the original price, "eigh—eighteen hundred." Nori then continues by reporting his following response to the mechanic, which indexed his on-going lack of understanding with "heh" and "tuh" followed by two (incorrect) candidate understandings of the meaning of "eighteen hundred." Basically, something the mechanic ostensibly said is reported first, followed by Nori's response, followed by the mechanic's response to Nori's response, followed by Nori's response to the mechanic's response to his response.

Scene-setting is another important practice for Nori because he often engages in it when other features of the context do not provide information about who the participants are in the reported speech event. A major resource that Nori uses to accomplish this practice is *person reference plus action ascription*— Nori refers to a person and states what he or she did or was doing prior to or during the reported speech event. As this often involves stating what someone was doing prior to the reported talk, temporal iconicity can be understood as a second resource for accomplishing scene-setting. The use of person reference plus action ascription can be seen in cases III, V, VII (no reference to self), VIII, and possibly XII. Part of case III is shown here as an example.

Extract 4   Case III, #4, April 20

```
237  N:    .hh Maki chan: (0.5) look
238  E:    yeah.
239  N:    ° kimochiwar'i:°
```

In line 237, Nori refers to a person, "Maki-chan," and ascribes an action to her of "look"ing at some sort of swelling on a visible part of Nori's body that Eric and Nori have been talking about. In line 239, Nori says "*kimochi warui*," or, loosely translated, "disgusting." With the prior person reference and action ascription, this talk can be heard as a report of what the person referred to said when she saw the swelling.

One resource through which Nori occasionally accomplishes the practice of framing is through the use of a Japanese *quotative* (typically *to* or *tte*) following the DRS, as it does in Japanese (Coulmas, 1986). In the cases listed in the appendix, this can be seen in case I (lines 119 (possibly), 127), possibly VI (line 205), IX (line 475, where the DRS is in Japanese), possibly X (line 382), and XIV (line 100).

A later resource he uses to accomplish framing is *person reference* immediately prior to the DRS, in IV and IX. Part of case IX is shown here as an example.

Extract 5   Case IX, #12, July 6

```
467  N:    yeah ↑my daughter (0.3) ↓uh: (0.2) ↑are you
468        lonleyt? (0.7) ° ↓I (say)° (0.3) ↑not. heh heh
```

The meeting between Nori and Eric from which this extract is drawn occurred at a time when Nori's wife and children had returned to Tokyo for summer vacation. He is telling a story about talking to his family on the telephone. In line 467, he uses person reference, "my daughter," and then, after a brief pause, produces the non-lexical item "uh." After another brief pause, he produces the question "are you lonely?" (He actually produces a "t" sound at the end of "lonely," but neither Eric nor Nori orient to this as problematic.) The person reference, though it is missing the verb of speech that typically follows the person reference in English, can be heard as an introducer (Tannen, 1986) that grammatically frames what follows as DRS, in this case the question. With the question hearable as DRS attributed to Nori's daughter, especially since Nori next reports his answer to the question, the preceding "uh" becomes somewhat ambiguous—it could belong to Nori, or it could be part of the reported speech.

Once he starts using person reference, Nori begins using a more refined version of this resource for framing *person reference plus verb of speech* immediately prior to the DRS. This is found in cases VI, IX (a possible interpretation), X, XI, XII ("I" is missing), XIII, and XV. Case X is shown here as an example.

Extract 6   Case X, #16, August 3

```
379  N:    .h la- last day an↓o (0.7) teacher s say ↑my
380        younger (0.6) younger daughter,
381  E:    mhm,
382  N:    no speak Japanes:e. ts h .hh h    [.hh huh=
383  E:                                      [really?
384  N:    =yea(h)h .hh heh .hh school.
```

In line 379, Nori produces a person reference, "teacher," followed by the verb of speech, "say." In line 382, he reports what the teacher ostensibly said, "no speak Japanese." Actually, this example is a bit more complicated than person reference plus verb of speech followed by DRS; Nori inserts a second person reference, "my younger...younger daughter," between the verb of speech and the DRS, which indicates the ostensible recipient of the reported talk, as well as the person who most likely related this incident to Nori.

The verb of speech in case VI is "speak," but from case X (and also possibly from case IX), Nori uses "say" and his use of this verb stabilizes. While he does not inflect "say" for tense, aspect, or person, with this particular resource for framing of person reference plus verb of speech, Nori is able to produce a version of what, according to Tannen (1986), is the most common introducer in American English conversation, that is, person reference plus a form of the verb "say."

Table 2 displays Nori's use of resources across time. His resources can be seen as expanding as earlier resources (prosody, non-lexical items, temporal iconicity, person reference plus action ascription, Japanese quotatives) are not abandoned, while new resources for framing (person reference and person reference plus verb of speech) are added. Perhaps these latter framing resources can be seen as developing from the use of person reference alone, to person reference with a verb of speech (not necessarily "say"), to person reference with the verb "say" as a stabilized pattern. One caveat is that the distinction between scene-setting and framing is not always clear. Perhaps the later two resources for framing are best understood as developing from person reference plus action ascription used for scene-setting.

Table 2. Nori's use of different resources

	recording#|date							
	2|3/30	4|4/20	9|6/1	11|6/22	12|7/6	16|8/3	18|9/4	19|9/11
prosody enactment	I[a]	II,III	IV	V,VI	VII,VIII,IX	X,XI	XII	XV
non-lex. item enactment	I	II		V,VI	VII,VIII		XII	XV
tmp. iconicity enactment	I	II,III		V,VI	VIII,IX		XII	
person reference +action ascription scene		III		V	VII[b], VIII		(XII)[c]	
Japanese quotative framing	I			VI	IX	(X)		XIV
person reference framing			IV		IX			
person reference +speech verb framing				VI, *speak*[d]	(IX), *say*	X, *say* XI, *say*	XII[b], *say*	XIII, *say* XV, *say*

[a] Roman numerals refer to cases.
[b] No reference to self.
[c] Parentheses indicate uncertain transcription.
[d] Verb of speech in *italics*.

Repairs and re-doings

While attention to interactional details, as provided by CA, may be necessary for the analyses in the previous section, a CA framework may not be. They could also be made within, for example, some sort of functional linguistic framework. However, when CA is used with longitudinal data, the data can be analyzed from both a longitudinal perspective and a locally-sequential perspective. This allowance for a shift in perspective is a major strength of using CA with these sorts of data. In this section, I will shift to the latter perspective as I look at a few particular cases of repair and re-doing that are relevant for the resources that Nori uses to mark DRS.

First, even though he often uses Japanese in these meetings with Eric, Nori displays an orientation to English as the proper language to use in these meetings. This can be seen in his limited use of Japanese quotatives. For example, in case I (see appendix), he uses them in lines 119 (possibly) and 127 (possibly twice). There are several other places, though, where he could use them but does not, namely, after each of the other remaining instances of DRS in this segment. This orientation can also be seen the first time Nori uses person reference to frame DRS, in case IV, shown in the next extract.

Extract 7 Case IV, #9, June 1

```
179  N:   ko- (1.2) .hh ↑my daughter ↑I want to this
180       shoes.
```

In line 179, Nori produces self-initiated self-repair (Schegloff, Jefferson, & Sacks, 1977), initiating the repair by cutting off "*ko*," possibly the start of the Japanese word "*kodomo*" (child/children), and completing the repair by replacing what he was going to say with "my daughter." The person reference comes to be done in English as an outcome of the repair and illustrates Nori's orientation to English as the proper language to use in these meetings. This orientation also gives him a reason to refrain from using Japanese quotatives to frame DRS, and can thus be seen as providing Nori with a reason to find new, non-Japanese resources for framing.

In case VI, reproduced in part in the next extract, the local emergence of the use of person reference plus a verb of speech to frame DRS is visible as part of a repair sequence.

Extract 8 Case VI, #11, June 22

```
198  N:   .hh ano- ((sniff)) ↑ne (0.7) ° ↓u°
199       ↑eighteen (0.9) ↑one eight zero zero ↑point
200       ze(h)ro ze(h)ro. .h oh (0.5) one ↑eight
201       zero zero ↑point ↑zero(h) ze(h)ro?
202  E:   mhm,
203       (0.6)
204  N:   ah=oh ho ho ho ho okay .h okay (that case)
205       one thousand .hh ↓point to (wakannakatta).
206       (0.8)
207  E:   point=
208  N:   =>dakara< ((sniff)) eigh- eighteen wuh- (0.3)
209       kaiwa ga oh↑: nan da? (0.3) Jeff ↓J [eff=
210  E:                                       [mhm
211  N:   =speaking speak (.) uh one eight (.) zero
212       zero (.) point (.) ze(h)ro ze(h)ro.
```

That Eric does not understand what Nori has said in lines 199–201 and 204–205 is indicated by the gap in line 206 and Eric's repetition of a word used three times in these lines, without any other sort of uptake. In response, Nori produces self-repair in lines 208–209 and 211–212. As part of the repair, he uses a person reference, "Jeff," and a verb of speech, "speak," which is itself repaired within the same turn, changed from "speaking" to "speak." This then frames the following DRS. The work that Nori undertakes to make himself understood to Eric can be seen as leading him to deploy a new resource for marking DRS.

Finally, while it does not seem to be repair, in case XI Nori re-does the DRS attributed to his daughter's teacher that he did in case X (see appendix).

In both cases, he says "teacher say," an indication of the stability that "say" has obtained by this time as a resource for framing DRS.

Conclusions

A common stereotype of the Japanese learner of English is that he or she is quiet, shy, and concerned about making mistakes. During these meetings, Nori was very different from this stereotype (regardless of how accurate or inaccurate this stereotype actually is in general). In spite of fairly limited proficiency in English, he was talkative and often, but not always, unconcerned about making mistakes. As indicated above, a major reason I chose to look at his development of resources for marking DRS is simply that he told a lot of stories, often about people that Eric had either firsthand or secondhand knowledge of, which contained DRS. His approach to these meetings was not only as opportunities to practice English, but more specifically to tell stories, mostly about familiar people, in English. Given that he functioned almost exclusively in Japanese at both home and work, it is unlikely that Nori had many other opportunities to tell stories in English. His developing ability to mark DRS can be seen as closely related to his use of these meetings with Eric for story-telling. This study thus provides evidence that the course of language development is bound up with the context of language use. It could be argued that the expansion of resources for marking DRS is not so much an indication of Nori's growing proficiency in English, but rather an indication of his growing proficiency at a particular language game Wittgenstein (1953) in English and that it was only through his use of these meetings to play this language game that his proficiency to do so did, indeed, grow.

Admittedly, this study is based on a very limited set of data, consisting of only fifteen clear cases of DRS, as described above. It is also limited in that the data consist of audio-recordings rather than video-recordings, so that Nori's use of gesture and gaze as he produces DRS is unavailable for analysis. It is perhaps most limited in terms of generalizability, as the study is based on only one person's language development, a person who is in some ways quite different from the stereotype of others with whom he may be classified in terms of culture and first language. I do not claim that DRS marking will develop in the same way for all ESL learners, or for all Japanese ESL learners, in the same way as it did for Nori. However, I do argue that understanding language development requires careful examination of the resources that language learners/participants have available to them, of how they use these resources, and of how use of these resources changes over time. While gaining a *general* understanding of how people learn to interact in a second language is important, if it is not to be mere speculation, such a general understanding must be constructed through *particular* understandings of specific cases of language development.

As mentioned with regard to extract 7, Nori shows a strong orientation to English as the proper language to use in these meetings, even when he also uses a good deal of Japanese. This orientation can be seen as one reason that he seeks new resources for marking DRS. It leads him to refrain from using one resource that he can easily draw on—Japanese quotatives—and thus creates a need for a new resource. It should be noted that the resource which he refrains from using (Japanese quotatives) and the new resource that he comes to use in a relatively stable manner (person reference plus the verb of speech "say") are both resources for the same practice of framing. Along with the work Nori does to make himself understood, this orientation helps to push Nori's language development.

Finally, as mentioned in the introduction, it is sometimes argued that using CA with longitudinal data in order to investigate learning requires the combination of CA with an exogenous theory of learning, such as situated learning theory. In this study, I have tried to demonstrate that such an exogenous theory is not necessary. Nori's learning how to mark DRS, in particular his learning to use person reference plus "say" to frame DRS, involves an expansion of the interactional resources that he has available to draw on. It does not, however, involve movement from more peripheral to fuller participation in the interaction that he and Eric engaged in at these meetings. From the very first meeting, Nori participated fully in the interaction. Not only was an exogenous theory of learning unnecessary to investigate the expansion of resources that Nori had available to mark DRS, but the particular theory of learning which seems to have the most support within CA-for-SLA, situated learning theory, provides a model for learning which does not fit how Nori actually participated and learned. I would like to suggest that a theory of learning within CA-for-SLA should be seen as more of a *possible* outcome of longitudinal CA research on language learning. A central element of such a theory, if one comes to be developed, is likely to be language learners'/participants' expanding and changing use of various resources as they participate in interaction. Another element is likely to be how participants' orientations to such things as the proper language to use and to making themselves understood may influence the resources they use. In addition, such a theory may contain a distinction between practices and resources, such as the one made above. It should be emphasized, though, that such a theory of learning within CA-for-SLA would be an outcome of research, rather than a prerequisite.

References

Beach, W. A. (2000). Inviting collaborations in stories about a woman. *Language in Society, 29*, 379–407.

Besnier, N. (1995). *Literacy, emotion, and authority: Reading and writing on a Polynesian atoll*. Cambridge: Cambridge University Press.

Clift, R. (2007). Getting there first: Non-narrative reported speech in interaction. In E. Holt & R. Clift (Eds.), *Reporting talk: Reported speech in interaction* (pp. 120–149). Cambridge: Cambridge University Press.

Coulmas, F. (1986). Direct and indirect speech in Japanese. In F. Coulmas (Ed.), *Direct and indirect speech* (pp. 161–178). Berlin: Mouton de Gruyter.

Goffman, E. (1974). *Frame analysis*. New York: Harper and Row.

Haakana, M. (2007). Reported thought in complaint stories. In E. Holt & R. Clift (Eds.), *Reporting talk: Reported speech in interaction* (pp. 150–178). Cambridge: Cambridge University Press.

Halliday, M. A. K. (1985). *An introduction to functional grammar*. London: E. Arnold.

Hauser, E. (2011). On the danger of exogenous theory in CA-for-SLA: A response to Hellermann and Cole (2009). *Applied Linguistics, 32(3)*, 348–352.

Hayashi, M. (2004). Discourse within a sentence: An exploration of postpositions in Japanese as an interactional resource. *Language in Society, 33*, 343–376.

Hellermann, J. (2006). Classroom interactive practices for developing L2 literacy: A microethnographic study of two beginning adult learners of English. *Applied Linguistics, 27*, 377–404.

Hellermann, J. (2008). *Social actions for classroom language learning*. Clevedon: Multilingual Matters.

Hellermann, J., & Cole, E. (2009). Practices for social interaction in the language—learning classroom: Disengagements from dyadic task interaction. *Applied Linguistics, 30*, 186–215.

Holt, E. (1999). Just gassing: An analysis of direct reported speech in a conversation between employees of a gas supply company. *Text, 19*, 505–537.

Holt, E. (2007). 'I'm eyeing your chop up mind': Reporting and enacting. In E. Holt & R. Clift (Eds.), *Reporting talk: Reported speech in interaction* (pp. 47–80). Cambridge: Cambridge University Press.

Holt, E., & Clift, R. (Eds.). (2007). *Reporting talk: Reported speech in interaction*. Cambridge: Cambridge University Press.

Huddleston, R. (2002). Content clauses and reported speech. In R. Huddleston & G. K. Pullum (Eds.), *The Cambridge grammar of the English language* (pp. 947–1030). Cambridge: Cambridge University Press.

Ishida, M. (2009). Development of interactional competence: Changes in the use of *ne* in L2 Japanese during study abroad. In H. Nguyen & G. Kasper (Eds.), *Talk-in-interaction: Multilingual perspectives* (pp. 351–385). Honolulu: University of Hawai'i, National Foreign Language Resource Center.

Jefferson, G. (2004). Glossary of transcript symbols with an introduction. In G. H. Lerner (Ed.), *Conversation analysis: Studies from the first generation* (pp. 13–31). Amsterdam: John Benjamins Publishing Company.

Kasper, G., & Wagner, J. (2011). A conversation-analytic approach to second language acquisition. In D Atkinson (Ed.), *Alternative approaches to second language acquisition* (pp. 117–142). London: Routledge.

Lave, J, & Wenger, E. (1991). *Situated learning: Legitimate peripheral participation.* Cambridge: Cambridge University Press.

Markee, N. (2008). Toward a learning behavior tracking methodology for CA-for-SLA. *Applied Linguistics, 29*, 404–427.

Nguyen, H. t., & Kasper, G. (Eds.). (2009). *Talk-in-interaction: Multilingual perspectives.* Honolulu: University of Hawai'i, National Foreign Language Resource Center.

Pomerantz, A. (1984). Agreeing and disagreeing with assessments: Some features of preferred/dispreferred turn shapes. In J. M. Atkinson & J. Heritage (Eds.), *Structures of social action: Studies in conversation analysis* (pp. 57–101). Cambridge: Cambridge University Press.

Prados, J. (Ed.). (2003). *The White House tapes: Eavesdropping on the president.* New York: The New Press.

Rae, J., & Kerby, J. (2007). Designing contexts for reporting tactical talk. In E. Holt & R. Clift (Eds.), *Reporting talk: Reported speech in interaction* (pp. 179–194). Cambridge: Cambridge University Press.

Rumsey, A. (1990). Wording, meaning, and linguistic ideology. *American Anthropologist, 92*, 346–361.

Schegloff, E. A., Jefferson, G., & Sacks, H. (1977). The preference for self-correction in the organization of repair in conversation. *Language, 53*, 361–382.

Tanaka, H. (1999). *Turn-taking in Japanese conversation: A study in grammar and interaction.* Amsterdam: John Benjamins.

Tannen, D. (1986). Introducing constructed dialogue in Greek and American conversational and literary narrative. In F. Coulmas (Ed.), *Direct and indirect speech* (pp. 311–332). Berlin: Mouton de Gruyter.

Tannen, D. (1989). *Talking voices: Repetition, dialogue, and imagery in conversational discourse.* Cambridge: Cambridge University Press.

Tannen, D. (Ed.). (1993). *Framing in discourse.* Oxford: Oxford University Press.

Wenger, E. (1998). *Communities of practice: Learning, meaning, and identity.* Cambridge: Cambridge University Press.

Wittgenstein, L. (1953). *Philosophical investigations.* Malden, MA: Blackwell Publishing.

Wootton, A. J. (1997). *Interaction and the development of mind.* Cambridge: Cambridge University Press.

Young, R. F. (2007). Language learning and teaching as discursive practice. In Z. Hua, P. Seedhouse, L. Wei, & V. Cook (Eds.), *Language learning and teaching as social inter-action* (pp. 251–271). New York: Palgrave MacMillan.

Young, R. F. (2009). *Discursive practice in language learning and teaching.* Malden, MA: Wiley-Blackwell.

Appendix: Cases of DRS found in the data

N: Nori; E: Eric
→ before lines with probable DRS

```
Case I, #2, March 30, 76~136
76      N:   .h ↑two time (0.3) uh: (1.4) ↑morning,
77      E:   mhm
78      N:   uh:: s:even o'clock. (0.9) check in.
79      E:   mhm
80   → N:   m. (.) ↑come back uh: (0.5) ↑after: one
81   →      o'clock,
82           (0.2)
83      E:   [yeah
84   → N:   [come back (again/okay).
85           (0.4)
86      N:   nde ↑one o'clock (.) n (.) (itte) go to
             then                          (go)
87           (0.3) de ↑waiting.
                    then
88      E:   yeah
89           (1.2)
90      N:   thirty time. (0.3) one hour. (0.5) one hour
91           thirty?
92           (0.4)
93      N:   long ti- (0.6) zutto waiting.
                             long-time
94   → N:   de (1.0) uh:: ↑sorry (0.4) my dri- road
             then
95   →      test?
96      E:   mhm,=
97   → N:   =(take) ano::: ac- appoint (.) t wuh- one
                    SF
98   →      o'clock.
99      E:   yeah
100  → N:   yeah moo (0.4) outside waiting (0.8)
                  already
101  →      one hour thirty waiting.
102     E:   [mhm
103     N:   [(x)
104          (0.8)
105  → N:   (letter/later).
106          (0.7)
107  → N:   ↑leh- letter? huhh hh wha(h)t?
108          (1.2)
109  → N:   come back u- one o'clock,
110          (0.3)
111  → N:   huh? ↓>de one o'clock come backu< (1.5)
                   then
112          n: ↓nan to yuu n da.
113     N:   nto.
114     (1.0)
```

```
115  → N:  ↑one more check in.
116         (0.3)
117    E:  yeah=
118  → N:  =no.
119  → N:  ↑no: no check in. ° ↓(tte itta).°
                                  (QT said)
120         (0.7)
121  → N:  ↑n(h)o n(h)o check in? ((!))  [.hhh
122    E:                                [oh: so
123         when you come [back at one o'clock you were=
124    N:                 [yeah:
125    E:  =supposed to  [check in again.]
126  → N:                [mo- ↑morning   ] ti(h)me
127  →      che(h)ck in(h) ↓tte itta. .h ↑no ts (0.6)
                            QT said
128  →      afta: afternoon,  [(.)  [one o'clock, (0.2)=
129    E:                     [m    [hm
130  → N:  =more one more check in.
131    E:  [mhm
132  → N:  [no- no one more check in.
133    E:  oh you have to check in [(one more time)?
134    N:                          [huh hoh hoh hoh .h
135         heh huh (maybe) (x(h)x(h)xx). .h ni kai .h u:
                                              two times
136         uke sasete° morawanakatta.°
            take let allow-NG-PST
```

Case II, #4, April 20, 115~129
```
115    N:  =yeah ↑mail? .h uh ↑certified mail?
116    E:  yeah.
117  → N:  certified mail please. .hh ↓n: d ↑no
118  →     un- (0.3) ↑oka:y, (0.3) paper
119  →     paper wr(h)ite(h),
120    E:  yeah
121  → N:  ↑paper? (0.4) wuhh?° heh huh° (.) nuh-
122  →     number three paper write,
123    E:  ye [ah
124  → N:     [nuh- number three? (0.2) ah. .h ° >atta
                                                be-PST
125         atta atta.<°  [° (x)°
            be-PST be-PST
126    E:                 [yeah then you gotta
127         [fill that out.
128  → N:   [o(h)ka(h)y. .hh zenzen [wakannakatta.
                             at-all understand-NG-PST
129    E:                           [right,
```

Case III, #4, April 20, 237~244
```
237    N:  .hh Maki chan: (0.5) look
                     DIM
238    E:  yeah.
239  → N:  ° kimochiwar'i:°
           disgusting
240    E:  hih hih hih hih hih hih hih hih hih [hih hih
241  → N:                                     [° okay.
242  →     okay.° (0.8) ° m:° okay tomorrow, m Maki chan
                                                    DIM
```

```
243 →      home (.) ↓go (0.2) °(xxx) (tsukete kite)° .h
                                      (spread around)
244        huh .h huh .h huh .h huh

Case IV, #9, June 1, 178~184
178              (0.2) ((start of sound of turning pages))
179 → N:         ko- (1.2) .hh ↑my daughter ↑I want to this
                 chi-
180 →            shoes.
181    E:        oh your daughter [wants these shoes?
182    N:                         [yeah
183    N:        ↑no (1.2) n- (0.4) ↓ah (.) (uttena(h)i n(h)a).
                                         (sell-NG IP)
184              (2.3)

Case V, #11, June 22, 124~160
124    E:   yeah >y' c'n say< one thousand eight hundre:d,
125         (.) ↑or ↓eighteen hundred.
126    N:   oh=oh=oh=oh=oh.=
127    E:   =right
128    N:   eighty-=.h soo soo.=[.h    eh=oh↑: eighteen=
                  yes yes
129    E:                       [(yeah)
130    N:   =hundred yeah. ((sniff))
131    N:   a:no ↑Jeff?
            SF
132    E:   yeah.
133    N:   ↓Jeff ↑telephone talking.
134         (0.3)
135    E:   who's Jeff.
136    N:   jeh- uh Jeff uh:: (0.6)
137    E:   a mechanic?
138         (0.9)
139    N:   yeah=yes yes=yes mechanic. mehk
140         (0.7)
141 → N:    .t (.) ↑eighteen hundred. (1.0) wuh (1.1)
142 →       ↑one hundred ↑eighty? (2.2) eigh- eighteen
143 →       hundred. (0.4) ↑heh (0.4) tuh (0.3) one hundred
144 →       eighty? one thousand ↑eighty hundred? hh (0.7)
145    E:   hmh
146         (0.5)
147 → N:    ↑okay okay (0.5) please please fixed. (0.6)
148 →       ↑really? hh (0.6) heh? (0.9) ↓okay. (0.2)
149 →       ↑one hundred (.) eighty dollars? (0.3) ↓n:o.
150 →       (0.9) ↑eighteen hundr(h)ed dollars. (1.1)
151    E:   m.
152         (1.4)
153 → N:    ↑one thousand eighty hundred? hoo hoo (0.6)
154 →       ↓yes yes. .hh oh hoh hoh ↑n(h)o no fi(h)x
155 →       [n(h)o fix.
156    E:   [heh heh heh huh huh huh huh
157         (0.5)
158    N:   .hhh ↓oh:: teh ten ten minute talking. h huh
159         heh huh [huh .h h .h
160    E:           [yeah
```

```
Case VI, #11, June 22, 193~217
193    E:   so one thousand three hun [dred. (or) (.)]=
194    N:                              [one thou- yes.]
195    E:   =↑thirteen hundred.
196    N:   ah: (.) 'kay
197         (0.4)
198    N:   .hh ano- ((sniff)) ↑ne (0.7) ° ↓u°
                SF                 IP
199 →       ↑eighteen (0.9) ↑one eight zero zero ↑point
200 →       ze(h)ro ze(h)ro. .h oh (0.5) one ↑eight
201 →       zero zero ↑point ↑zero(h) ze(h)ro?
202    E:   mhm,
203         (0.6)
204 → N:    ah=oh ho ho ho ho okay .h okay (that case)
205 →       one thousand .hh ↓point to (wakannakatta).
                                      (understand-NG-PST)
206         (0.8)
207    E:   point=
208    N:   =>dakara< ((sniff)) eigh- eighteen wuh- (0.3)
                therefore
209         kaiwa ga oh↑: nan da? (0.3) Jeff ↓J [eff=
            conversation SB what CP
210    E:                                       [mhm
211 → N:    =speaking speak (.) uh one eight (.) zero
212 →       zero (.) point (.) ze(h)ro ze(h)ro.
213    E:   mhm
214         (0.8)
215 → N:    okay. okay. [no f(h)ix. .h no f(h)ix.
216    E:               [hih hih hih hih hih
217         (0.6)

Case VII #12, July 6, 150~154
150    E:                       [you went there by
151         your[self?
152 → N:        [yeah .h mitete (0.3) ↑heh? (0.7) finish
                          watch
153         (0.5) ↓de moo ka:eroo to omotte. ↑back home
                    then already go-home QT think
154 →       m- (0.9) buhbohm (.) ↑wah hoo hoo hoo .hhh

Case VIII, #12, July 6, 373~410
373    N:   .hh a lo:: lo- local local no uncle=u:
                                        GEN
374         (.) .h uh: (.) ↑side tree (0.3) punch.
375         (1.8)
376    E:   hm?
377    N:   suh ano ↑side (no) ↑tree,
                SF        (GEN)
378    E:   yeah
379    N:   yeah?
380    E:   he was hitting the tree?
381    N:   yeah yeah yeah. (.) sore o ano golf club de,
                                 that  O that            PP
382    E:   with a gulf club=
383    N:   =yeah.
384    E:   yeah=
385    N:   =puh- (0.3) punch (dashita) ↑punching.
                               (released)
386         (0.2)
```

Expanding resources for marking direct reported speech 49

```
387    E:    he was hitting the tree with a gulf [club?
388    N:                                        [y:
389          ↑yeah yeah.
390    E:    oh=
391    N:    =de ↑na:ni shite n da koitsu ↓to omottara
             then what do N CP this-person QT thought
392          .hh (0.6) fruits.
393    E:    yeah=
394    N:    =little fruits. .hh nuh- Hawaiia:n nan
                                                 what
395          toka Hawaiian (0.3) nan to apple.
             or-something       what QT
396    E:    ↑oh o:kay.
397  → N:    yeah very sweep.
398    E:    mou- [mountain apple.
399  → N:         [eat
400    N:    ah ↑mou(h)ntain app(h)le. [.hh
401    E:                              [yeah
402  → N:    ↑very sweep. ↑eat.
403          (0.4)
404  → N:    heh: ↑: tabe(h)ru? hh .hh h
                     eat
405    E:    yeah=
406  → N:    =kore (daijobu)? (.) ↓demo kotoware
             this (okay)           but refuse-can
407  →       nai kara ↑okay. ↑thank you. okay.
             NG because
408          (0.9)
409  → N:    ↑oh↓: [sweeps.
410    E:          [yeah (.) ↑but it duh-

Case IX, #12, July 6, 460~476
460    E:    you're not lonely?
461          (0.8) ((N sips coffee))
462    N:    mp. (0.4) ((swallows coffee)) no (not) lonely.
463          ↑(ne)
              (IP)
464    N:    .hh >(dakedo)< (0.3) ↑last day ↓ano ↑Japanese
                  (however)                      SF
465          telephone?
466    E:    yeah
467  → N:    yeah ↑my daughter (0.3) ↓uh: (0.2) ↑are you
468  →       lonleyt? (0.7) °↓I (say)° (0.3) ↑not. heh heh
469          heh heh [.h .h
470    E:            [oh you asked your [daughter?
471    N:                                [y: y::eah. daughter
472    E:    [y' daughter said no?
473    N:    [daughter. n.
474    E:    hih hih=
475  → N:    =nihon tanoshii tte. heh heh huh .hh moo kaette
             Japan fun QT                         again go-home
476  →       konai yo. (da tte) .hh
             come-NG IP (COP QT)
```

```
Case X, #16, August 3, 379~384
379   N:  .h la- last day an↓o (0.7) teacher s say ↑my
                            SF
380       younger (0.6) younger daughter,
381   E:  mhm,
382 → N:  no speak Japanes:e. ts h .hh h   [.hh huh=
383   E:                                   [really?
384   N:  =yea(h)h .hh heh .hh school.

Case XI, #16, August 3, 388~402
388   E:  do other student speak Japanese at school?
389   N:  yeah.
390       (0.5)
391   N:  .h ((sniff)) (no/north) ano:: (0.9) n-
                                    SF
392       ↑younger daughter no friend?
                              GEN
393   E:  y [eah.
394   N:    [Ja- Japanese friends.
395   E:  yeah.=
396   N:  =uh: talking speak uhs (0.4) Japanese?
397   E:  yeah.
398       (0.2)
399 → N:  yeah. ↑teacher say (.) no. ↑no ↑no speak
400 →     Japan(h)ese. .h
401   E:  [mhm
402 → N:  [only English(h).

Case XII, #18, September 4, 414~431
414   N:  ja, de, (0.8) [ah
          well then
415   E:                [but maybe ih- maybe it was
416       jus'[food poisoning. [h hih
417   N:      [e:
418   N:                       [my my wife
419 →     (so/thought) (.) ↓ano: say (.) Makiko last
                            SF
420 →     week last week Friday ma kimochiwarui tte.
                                kind-of feel-nauseous QT
421   E:  °n°
422 → N:  back home ↓tte.
                    QT
423       (0.5)
424 → N:  ↑ma sore wa are ja nai? (0.5) baby dekita
          well that TP that CP NG        conceived
425 →     n ja nai? (0.4) ↑oh [(0.5) ohho soo kamo na.=
          N CP NG                          that maybe IP
426   E:                      [so then- maybe maybe morning
427       sickness.
428   N:  =huh huh huh huh huh
429   N:  .hh [soo (d)
               yes
430   E:      [that's what they thought but (0.6) naw
431       it was jus' food poisoning. hih
```

Case XIII, #19, September 11, 18~40
```
18      E:  you were wa[tching tee vee?
19      N:              [watch t(h)ee v(h)ee .h
20              [hih .hh
21      E:  [oh so you get any sleep last nigh[t?
22      N:                                    [yeah.
23              .h de ano (1.2) nan ↑da, °n:° ↓nan da.
                   then SF      what CP        what CP
24              (2.6) ((sips coffee during pause)) ano (0.3)
                                                   SF
25   →          ↑newscaster s[ay: .h (.) other airpla:ne=
26      E:                   [mhm
27   → N:       =(.) attacku ano (1.6) ↑Pentagon.
                              SF
28      E:  yeah the Pentagon.
29      N:  yeah mada .h ((sniff)) m: (.) ↓°nan da° ts-
                  still                      what CP
30              (0.6) >dakara.< >moshikashitara.< if ano
                      therefore  if-so                SF
31              (.) live eigh- livu (1.1) l: live scene?
32              (0.2)
33      E:  yeah
34      N:  (xxx °xxxxxx°) ((Japanese))
35              (0.4)
36      E:  °yeah°
37      N:  °m°
38              (1.0)
39      E:  an' the World Trade Center (.) towers
40              collapsed.
```

Case XIV, #19, September 11, 97~110
```
97      E:  until they find out what's happening.
98              (1.2) ((N sips coffee))
99   → N:   dakara othe- other plane wa doo suru
            therefore               TP  how do
100  →          ka (0.3) itta kana: to.
                Q        said wonder QT
101     E:  oh
102             (0.6)
103     E:  where did you hea- (.) oh somebody asked
104             the question?
105     N:  n.
106             (0.3)
107     E:  °oh°
108             (0.5)
109     N:  °(doo) wakannai na:°
                (how) understand-NG IP
110             (1.2)
```

Case XV, #19, September 11, 414-453
```
414    N:    n? .h soo. wasureta(h). (0.3) last wee-
                 yes forgot
415          last week [u::
416    E:              [mm hm,
417          (0.4)
418    N:    suh say?
419          (0.3)
420    E:    yeah?
421    N:    yeah I am (.) understand?
422          (0.8)
423    E:    yeah.
424    N:    yeah itte kureta  [Ma- Maki chan.
                  said for-me       DIM
425    E:                     [(you- you) understand.=
426 →  N:    =↑yeah you understand. ↓you understand.
427    N:    [.h   [mistake Tomoko.
428    E:    [yeah [but
429    E:    oh really?
430    N:    Tomoko Tomoko.
431    E:    oh what did Tomoko say.=
432    N:    =yeah Tomoko mistake.
433    E:    ah
434    N:    I understand. .h huh huh huh .h heh heh huh
435          (0.4)
436    E:    yeah I told Makiko I thought you understood.
437          [but
438    N:    [n
439          (0.4)
440    N:    soo soo.
             yes yes
441    E:    she didn't think so.
442          (0.2)
443 →  N:    .h Maki chan say (0.7) ↑Nori san no no
                  DIM                    TL
444 →        uh- no understand.
445 →  N:    ↑oh (.) hhh (.) [you- understand=
446    E:                    [° heh heh heh°
447    N:    =but m m Tomoko mistake. ↓mistake.
448    E:    heh heh [hih hih heh heh heh
449    N:            [heh huh
450    N:    .hh
451    E:    ah so ↑Tomoko didn't think you understood.
452    N:    yeah
453    E:    ° m:°
```

Abbreviations in transcripts are adapted from Nguyen & Kasper, 2009, p. xiv, unless otherwise noted.

- C   copula
- DI   diminuitive (not in Nguyen & Kasper)
- GE   genetive particle (Hayashi, 2004; Tanaka, 1999)
- I   interactional particle nominalizer
- N   negative morpheme object marker
- P   postposition (not in Nguyen & Kasper)
- PS   past tense morpheme (not in Nguyen & Kasper) question marker
- Q   quotative
- S   subject marker
- S   sentence filler
- T   title (Hayashi, 2004)
- T   topic marker

Prioritization: A Formulation Practice and Its Relevance for Interaction in Teaching and Testing Contexts

Yusuke Okada
Ritsumeikan University, Japan

When we engage in interaction, there are numerous ways to formulate a referent, whether through words or behavior. Some recent conversation analytic (CA) studies (e.g., Bilmes, 2008, 2009a, 2009b, 2011; Deppermann, 2011a; Hauser, 2011; Stivers, 2007) have demonstrated the tactical nature of members' word selections and the reflexivity between a particular formulation choice, the local sequential context, and macro-level contexts. This chapter aims to illustrate a practice of formulation done by particular members in two specific types of interaction, namely the practice of prioritization by teachers and interviewers in EFL classroom talk and OPI role-play tasks. The analysis of 38 target cases from a corpus of nine EFL classroom conversations and 71 OPI role-plays indicates that the teachers and the interviewers prioritize actions (such as the acts of questioning, explanation for correction, and repair-initiation) to achieve the institutionally programmed aims of the interaction in the most effective manner. The study concludes with a discussion of the values of prioritization as an analytic lens for understanding the practices of language teaching and testing and as a strategic way of teaching and testing language in and through interaction.

Introduction

When we engage in interaction, there are numerous ways to formulate a referent with words. For example, one can refer to the same person as "Professor Kingsfield," "Charles," or "that guy on the second floor." Although the person these expressions refer to is the same, they have different connotations by virtue of the words used for them: each expression indicates the relationships between the speaker and hearer and the referred-to person (Sacks, 1992, pp. 502–503). For another instance, one can ask another person to open a window by saying, "I was wondering if you could open the window," or by saying "Open the window." In addition to these expressions, non-verbal behavior can also be used for formulating the same action: indeed, simply pointing to the person and then to the window might be sufficient to formulate the request through embodied action. Each of these formulations can be seen as an indication of a level of politeness because of the conventional understanding of the words and the behavior. Schegloff argues that choosing a particular formulation is a matter of social members' efficient use "of language as a resource in interaction" (1972, p. 117). Social members' practices for formulating referents are, therefore, a proper object of study for conversation analysis (CA), an approach whose project Heritage (1984) sums up as "describing and explicating the competencies which ordinary speakers use and rely on when they engage in intelligible, conversational interaction" (p. 241).

A number of CA studies have in fact investigated the issue of members' formulation practices. For example, Schegloff (1972, 1996), Sacks and Schegloff (1979), and Levinson (2007) investigate person and place references; Pomerantz (1986), Edwards (2000), and Sidnell (2004) account for extreme case formulations such as "best," "always" or "nothing;" and Heritage and Raymond (2005) and Heritage (2012) address the issue of epistemic displays in formulation. Some recent studies focus on methodical aspects of members' selection of a particular formulation over other alternatives, such as *marking* in person reference (Stivers, 2007); *generalization, specification, contrast* and *co-categorization* in choosing expressions (Bilmes, 2008, 2009a, 2009b, 2011); *generalization* of membership categories (Hauser, 2011); and *notionalization* (Deppermann, 2011a). By investigating not only *what* is achieved by the practices of formulation but also *how* they are practiced, these studies reveal the tactical nature of the speakers' selections and the reflexivity between a particular formulation choice, the local sequential context, and macro-level contexts such as identities and genres of talk (Deppermann, 2011b).

The current study aims to demonstrate one practice of formulation utilized by particular groups of members in two specific types of interaction, namely teachers' and interviewers' *prioritization* in English as a Foreign Language (EFL) classroom talk and oral proficiency interview (OPI) role-play. In the investigation, I will discuss both *how* a particular formulation is selected (or prioritized) and *what* is accomplished by that practice. In so doing, the study suggests the generality or context-freeness of the practice and its context sensitivity or reflexivity (see Sacks, Schegloff, & Jefferson, 1974, p. 699) to the situational contexts, and also points out some potential implications for second language (L2) teaching and testing. After reviewing the literature on formulation practices and explaining the notion of priority, instances of formulation will be analyzed in detail. The chapter will conclude with a discussion of formulation practices in relation to teaching and testing language.

Studies on formulation

First of all, it is necessary to be clear about the definition of *formulation* in the current study. Within CA and ethnomethodology, the term *formulation* has been given different meanings: on the one hand, formulation refers to what is achieved by a participant's *re-*formulation of what has been said by others in interaction (Garfinkel & Sacks, 1970; Heritage & Watson, 1979). However, in the current study, the term formulation is used to refer to a particular way of putting a referent (e.g., an object, a concept, a state of affairs, an act) into words or behavior (Bilmes, 2011), which covers both an *original* formulation and any subsequent *re-*formulation. A whole turn-at-talk can be a formulation if it is considered as a signification of a single referent; at the same time, a certain part of a turn can also be said to be a formulation if it performs a certain action or actions. The practice of formulation is meant to denote "a choice from among a number of alternative ways of identifying or describing the referent or producing the conversational action" (Bilmes, 2011, p. 134). Accordingly, it is necessary to consider what speakers accomplish by selecting a particular formulation instead of other alternatives. To address this issue, "structural techniques of comparing selected options with possible alternatives" (Deppermann, 2011b, p. 115) are required because "properties of formulations can only be grasped when [selected formulations are] compared to 'possible alternatives,' which are equally correct in truth-conditional terms" (ibid., p. 120). The following studies adopt such a comparative approach in order to examine members' practices of formulation.

Stivers (2007) investigated the practice of *marking* in formulating person reference. Studies on person and place reference (e.g., Schegloff, 1972, 1996; Sacks & Schegloff, 1979; Levinson, 2007; Stivers, 2007) reveal that there is a preference for recognitionals. When referring to a person, if the name of the referred-to person (e.g., Charles) is shared by the participants in the conversation, the name is normatively preferred for use and is therefore *unmarked* in comparison to some other description composed of multiple expressions, such as "the guy on the second floor," in that the former is more understandable for the hearer. If the speaker were to select the referent "the guy on the second floor," the choice would be less efficient than the name and would therefore be *marked*. However, if the name of the referred-to person is not shared, then "the guy on the second floor" is preferred over the name "Charles." The recipient design in terms of the recognizability of the reference comes before the preference for minimization or using a reference form composed of minimal expression (Sacks & Schegloff, 1979) and it (i.e., the recipient design) suggests what is the marked or unmarked reference form. Stivers demonstrates that when a speaker chooses a marked form of reference when an unmarked form is available, the marked choice makes relevant certain (often negative) inferences about the referred-to person available.

Deppermann (2011a) analyzes the practice of professionals' re-formulation of a lay persons' multi-unit, multi-turn description of an object into a single noun phrase in order to make the lay-persons' lengthy descriptions fit the talk constructed within sequential and situational contexts. For example, a patient's description of how his partner's illness caused him trouble was re-formulated into "fear about the partner" by a therapist (p. 160), and this notionalization clarified the patient's psychological state with the term fit for the therapist's work of describing the patient's symptoms.

Hauser (2011) investigates a practice for reformulating membership categories (Sacks, 1992), such as when a speaker rephrases "Fukushima people" to "people who speak dialects" (pp. 192–193). This generalization "initiates and performs repair and implicitly challenges what [one of the participants] says [i.e., "Fukushima people"] as distinctive of the speakers of the regional dialect of Fukushima Prefecture" (Hauser, 2011, p. 195). Through this and three other conversational segments, Hauser uncovers the generality and tactical nature of generalization and its use for challenging previous talk.

In a series of recent studies, Bilmes (2008, 2009a, 2009b, 2011) has explicated the practices of (re)formulating a referent in terms of specificity of descriptions and categorization direction. Bilmes (2009b) explores how the vertical relationship (i.e., generalization and specification) and the horizontal relationship (i.e., co-categorization and contrast) between formulations (including both actual and plausible) logically implicate certain connotations about the formulation through his (re)analysis of a telephone conversation between a social worker and a man who has been involved in a family altercation that resulted in police involvement, which was originally analyzed by Sacks (1992). By tactically choosing vertical and horizontal levels of alternative action verbs, the man and the social worker negotiate their description of the act as less violent but as a sufficiently adequate warrant for the man to be in trouble with the police. For example, the referent chosen to describe a given action can be generalized as "move" as well as specified as "shove." In addition, the formulation "shove" can be co-categorized with "hit" under the category of "violent act" and at the same time "shove" and "hit" can be used to denote a contrastive relationship. While "shove" can be generalized to "move," which may not be an act of violence, "hit" cannot be a specification of "move." Instead, "hit" can imply more specific violent acts such as "smack" or "punch." The formulations "move," "shove," "hit," and "smack" were actually used; on the other hand, "punch" and other words that could logically belong to a collection of "violence acts" were suggested by Bilmes as additional plausible word choices that make clear what is implied by the members' taxonomical arrangement of formulations.

The studies above suggest that the practice of formulation is tactical: a particular formulation is selected in order to assert certain connotations or rhetorical forces (Edwards, 1997), such as complaints, clarifications, challenges, or evading responsibility. Such meanings are implicated by the relationship between both (1) formulations that actually appear in the participants' talk and (2) plausibly selectable formulations of the same referent. These studies also indicate the necessity of employing cultural knowledge, such as the relationship between the participants and the referred-to person, the setting of the talk, knowledge about the people and regions of a country, and conventional semantic knowledge of words. However, a question arises here: how and to what extent should such cultural knowledge be incorporated in the analysis of formulation practices?

Schegloff (1991) proposed applying the notion of *procedural consequentiality* to demonstrate the relevance of such cultural knowledge for the interaction. In other words, cultural knowledge should be considered relevant to the interaction only when a participant orients to such knowledge and invokes it within interaction in a visible manner as a feature of turn or sequential organization. Depperman (2011a), Hauser (2011), and Stivers (2007) limit the use of background information about the members and situations in their data, preferring instead to restrict their account to what the members actually display in their orientations. On the other hand, Bilmes' use of invented alternatives (2008, 2009a, 2009b, 2011) along with taxonomical representations in a diagram may be seen as a rather *etic* (analyst's perspective) means of accounting for the meaning of the members' practices (Maynard, 2011). So, while I concur with the findings of Bilmes' work, I follow Schegloff's (1991) approach of relying on procedural consequentiality to establish the relevance of cultural knowledge to the interactional data, and call on background information for the analysis only when it is demonstrably oriented to by the members themselves.

The studies reviewed in this section have suggested some answers to the question of *why and how a particular formulation is selected instead of other possible formulations*. However, there will be other practices of formulation which social members use to exert a certain rhetorical value. *Prioritization*, the practice of formulating a referent according to its rank against other possible referents, provides another answer to the question of how formulations are selected.

(Response) priority and preference

Priority is a concept explicated by Bilmes in his 1993 paper as *response priority*. The proposition of response priority is as follows: "when one is going to commit an act that is one of a series of acts of a certain type, the most extreme act in the series gets first priority mention" (p. 391) and what should be the first priority mention in a series of acts is "proposed on the spot for present interactional purpose" (p. 391). Therefore, it is suggested that "[i]f X is the first priority response, then any response other than X (including no response) implicates (when it does not explicitly assert) that X is not available or is not in effect, unless there is reason to suppose that it has been withheld" (p. 391). In short, one is normatively expected to give the first priority choice when it is available. Take the following example: a person is invited to dinner by a friend but he wants to refuse the invitation for two reasons, "his brother's funeral" and "the friend's house is a bit far." In this case, the extreme choice (the brother's funeral) should be mentioned. If he selects "the friend's house is a bit far," then he would be implying that no stronger or better excuses are available (Bilmes, 1988). Consider also the following example. In an argument when one is accused of something, denial is the first priority, since being silent may indicate that one accepts the accusation or has no ability to argue against it. As seen from these scenarios, response priority explains the differences in terms of implications between formulations of responsive acts and what consequence is drawn from a specific formulation.

It should be made clear that the notion of (response) priority is different from the CA concept of preference, an idea that is occasionally explained as an interactional practice for the maintenance of social solidarity (Heritage, 1984, 2008). Giving an affiliative response to an offer is preferred because it works to maintain social solidarity between the answerer and the person who presents the offer. On the contrary, a rejection is dispreferred as it holds the potential to damage social solidarity and therefore hesitation (in the forms of a gap of silence and certain interactional markers such as 'well,' 'uh:') or an excuse are employed in order to mitigate the impact of the rejection to the offer (Pomerantz, 1984). The idea of preference for maintaining social solidarity is also applicable to the act of repair. Schegloff, Jefferson and Sacks (1977) demonstrate that self-repair (i.e., correction of a component of the speaker's own turn) is preferred over other-repair (i.e., repair of a component of the other conversationalist's turn). According to Lerner (1996), preference organization in the act of repair relies on members' face-work (Goffman, 1967) not to threaten one's self either as the author or the animator (Goffman, 1981) of a turn.

While the idea of preference is based on members' orientation to maintenance of social solidarity, (response) priority represents a scale which members share about the variety of forms an action could take in a specific sequential context of a particular discourse environment. By virtue of that type of intersubjectivity in interaction, members can estimate what is the extreme form of an act and what is not. The denial of an accusation given by another in an argument normatively gets the first priority because the lack of a denial allows for the inference that it is not available and then somehow indicates an admission of guilt. Although Heritage (1984) tries to interpret giving a contradiction after an accusation as a form of social solidarity because "an admission may announce a rift between the accused and others" (p. 269), it is hard to pursue the solidarity argument here. Bilmes (1988) writes:

> A rift is avoided by an admission in the form of an apology. The apologizer maintains a solidarity relation by becoming simultaneously a guilty actor and a true self who rejects that actor (Goffman, 1972). The case is, of course, even clearer with denials of nonaccusatory attributions. Here, too, denials are preferred, but it can hardly be argued that such denials are more solidarity-promoting than confirmations. (pp. 174–175)

In short, this example clearly shows the difference between priority and preference. Giving a contradiction after an accusation is not the member's orientation to maintaining social solidarity—it is his/her orientation to avoiding an unfavorable implication by taking other actions, such as being silent. Like the idea of adjacency-pairs, the notion of priority "account[s] for how what they do provides resources and constraints for other participants [in interaction]" (Bilmes, 1988: p. 173).

While Bilmes limited the notion of priority only to responsive acts and did not apply it to other general acts in interaction, this notion seems to have potential value in explaining member's formulation practices of any acts (not only those that are responsive but also initiating acts in interaction). To this end, the current study examines whether the concept of priority can be a procedure that members use in formulating not only the second pair part of an adjacency pair, but also acts in general in interaction.

Data

The sequences of talk on which we will base our observations are taken from two distinct data sets—teacher-student talk in an EFL classroom and the role-play section of an OPI test. The EFL corpus is composed of audio-recordings of 810 minutes of classroom interaction in nine EFL classrooms at a Japanese university. The teacher of the six classes, Derek (a pseudonym), is a first language (L1) English speaker who has ten years of English teaching experience in Japan and possesses a high level of Japanese competency. The teacher of the other classes, Ethan (again, a pseudonym), is also an L1 English speaker, and has 30 years of English teaching experience in Japan. The students are all L1 Japanese speakers. In each classroom, the teachers are expected to use English as the medium of the instruction. The teaching approach in all the classrooms can be said to be communicative. In every class, I observed the activities in the classrooms and took detailed ethnographic notes.

The role-play corpus is comprised of recordings of role-play tasks from a series of English oral proficiency interviews conducted in Japan for the purpose of testing the candidates' general English-speaking ability.[1] The oral interviews are authentic high-stake tests whose results are used by corporations for decisions on employees' career advancement and overseas posting. The candidates were all adult first language speakers of Japanese. Fifty were female and 21 were male. The eight interviewers (three females and five males) were all first language speakers of English who were certified after being trained by the administrator of the OPI. The aim of the role-play task was to gather evidence about pragmatic and interactional aspects of the candidate's English-speaking proficiency that were difficult to observe via the interviewing section of the test. In each role-play, the interviewer and the candidate took on roles specified on a task card to ad lib a variety of real-world communicative scenarios. The interviewer selected a card and then told the candidate what to do. Instructions were written in both English and Japanese, and after the interviewer read out the instructions on the card, the card was passed to the candidate.

The data were transcribed according to standard CA conventions (Schegloff, 2007) and the glossing abbreviations described in Nguyen and Kasper (2009).

Analysis and discussion

A total of 38 cases that included the formulation practice of priority were found in the two corpuses; 28 in the EFL data set and ten in the OPI role-play corpus. I present several selected excerpts transcribed from the data as perspicuous examples of formulation priority (see ten Have, 2007 on the notion of specimen perspective). Throughout the analysis in this section we will empirically explore how prioritization becomes relevant for the way participants formulate their turns in questioning sequences and instructional interaction.

When the teacher formulates a first pair part action

We will begin by considering how prioritization works as a pedagogical resource when classroom teachers formulate sequences of first pair part actions. The first segment we will examine is from an intermediate communication and writing class. Derek (D) is the teacher. Prior to this segment, he had asked the students to think about their impressions of Barack Obama, who had just become the 44th President of the United States at the time this interaction was recorded. One of the students responded that Obama is good because "there is force in what he says."

Segment 1 [TCWT5W7] ('D' for Derek [teacher], 'K' for Kenji)

```
1   D:  nice English. force in what he says. ((writing
2       "force in what he says" on the blackboard))
3       yes you can.
4       (0.9)
5       right?
6       (0.9)
7→D:  ((to the whole class)) ↑WHO WATCHED (0.3)
8→    Obama's speech,
9       (0.9)
10→D: <who watched,> (.) his speech.
11      (0.5)
12→D: ano  enzetsu o  mita,
        that speech  TP watch-past
        did you watch the speech?
13      (1.0)
14  K:  ((raises his hand))
15  D:  yeah? (.) it was so: good.
16      (0.5)
17  D:  if you wanna study good English, (1.4)
18      go internet. get a copy. good English
19      not so difficult.
```

After providing a positive assessment of the student's response and writing the response on the blackboard in line 2, Derek invokes one of Obama's famous political catchphrases, "yes you can," which was widely reported in the Japanese media at the time. Upon receiving no uptake from the students to his reference to the phrase, Derek initiates a confirmation check in line 5, which is followed by another gap in line 6. Derek then asks the students three versions of the same content at lines 7–8, 10, and 12. The first formulation of the question at lines 7–8 is produced at a normal speed. Again the students fail to respond, so Derek modifies his formulation at line 10 by repeating part of the question ("<who watched>") at a slower pace. After his modified question is again met with silence, eventually at line 12 he resorts to re-formulating the question in Japanese, the students' L1. In line 14, one of the students finally reacts to the question after Derek has been waiting for one second, which is a longer gap compared to the prior two in lines 9 and 11. Derek expands the sequence with an assessment of Obama's speech and a recommendation for the students. In terms of prioritization, the point to note here is that it appears the teacher is orienting to an ordering of questioning acts—one that favors "natural" English over carefully pronounced English or Japanese. While the first version of the question is emphasized in terms of the speech volume, the utterance speed is natural, so the modification of reducing the speed of the delivery enhances the recognizability of the question. The most recognizable form of the question is when it is formulated in the students' L1, but this was kept as a last resort, even though it was available from the beginning of the interaction.

A similar ordering pattern can be found in Segment 2, which is taken from an intermediate English communication class. The teacher, Ethan, is providing feedback to a pair of students who have just taken an in-house speaking test in which the students spoke to each other about set topics.

Segment 2 [STPS07529-H2] ('E' for Ethan [teacher], 'S' for Shugo, 'K' for Keisuke)

```
1  E:   uh: ONE MORE CHANGE. what do you like season?
2→      change English.
3       (1.0)
4→E:    what do you like season. change.
5       (0.3)
6  K:   change?
7       (2.1)
8  E:   what do you like season.
9       (1.2)
10 S:   mm: (fall).
11→E:   no change it. change the sentence.
12      (0.8)
13→E:   how do you change, what do you like season.
14      (1.0)
15→E:   what, do you like, season.
16      (0.8)
```

```
17  S:  un.
18  K:  what do you like season? ((to Shugo))
19      (0.5)
20→E:   [douiu-
         how say-
         What kind of-
21  S:  [what season do you like.
22  E:  yes Shugo so what season do you like.
```

In line 2, Ethan orders the students to "change English" or correct a certain error that Shugo made in the test. Mixing a quote of the student's erroneous utterance with the metalinguistic directive in minimal form ("change" instead of "you need to change that sentence," or something to that effect) initiates form-focused error correction and as such orients to the complementary activities of L2 teaching and learning. On seeing the students' non-reaction to his request, Ethan re-poses the error and again asks for the correction with the simple formulation "change" in line 4. However, the students display that they do not understand what the teacher is asking: Kensuke's "change?" in line 6 does a repair-initiation and this along with Shugo's answer "Fall" in line 10 shows their lack of comprehension at this point. After a brief negation ("no") which addresses the inappropriateness of Shugo's just-prior response ("fall" in line 10), Ethan rephrases what he is asking by saying "change it. change the sentence" in line 11. Then, following another gap of silence, he again changes the form of his action, this time to "how do you change, what do you like season," which syntactically formulates it as a question. While this rewording may have been designed to help the students to understand the required action, the question fails to get an answer from students until line 19. Finally Ethan resorts to using the Japanese language, formulating his cut-off turn in line with 20 with "douiu."[2] However, he stops there because Shugo overlaps his turn to provide an answer to what has been asked. In line 22, immediately after Shugo's answer, Ethan explicitly accepts the answer. While the sequence starts with a request for the students to correct an error, the request is subsequently turned into a question format prompting the students to speak about how they would correct the error and finally formulated into a Japanese question.

In the two segments so far, the teachers both displayed their orientations to an ordered sequence for formulating their first pair part actions or actions which make a responsive act from the students conditionally relevant (Schegloff, 1968): (1) a target language (TL) original action, (2) a modification or an increment in the TL, and (3) a subsequent version of the question formulated in the students' L1. The teachers' orientation to the priority ordering in formulating the same content first pair part action is reflexive to their pursuing the pedagogical values of such an action in a language classroom where the use of the TL as the medium of instruction is required. In such an environment, the use of the TL itself is considered as teaching the TL in that it requires the students to use their linguistic knowledge to understand the teacher's action. At the same time, the use of such a first pair part action is also instructive in that it enables the teacher to engage in pedagogical work at the position after the student's answer (Lee, 2007), as exemplified in Segment 1 by the teacher's giving an assessment of Obama's speech and recommending it as a good resource for studying English.

In order to achieve both of these pedagogical benefits, any first version of a first pair part action has to be initiated in the TL, meaning the use of the TL for questioning is prioritized. Subsequent modification or incremental additions in the TL (such as slowing the speed of the utterance, omitting a word or a phrase in the original question, and supplementing concrete objects to the indexical in the original question) are reasonable considering the teachers' orientation to the pursuit of the pedagogical aim of the first pair part action. While these modifications may weaken the first pedagogical benefit, they do not totally eliminate it. The use of the L1 is the least prioritized, as it does not require the student to use his or her knowledge of the TL and only achieves the second of the two pedagogical values (i.e., taking the third-position to initiate further pedagogical work), despite the fact that it accomplishes that goal more efficiently than does an action in the TL.

The following segment shows another manifestation of the prioritization of first pair part action: on receiving no response from the students at the turn after a question, the teacher poses possible answers to the non-answered question.

Segment 3 [TCWT5W5] ('D' for Derek, 'A' for Atsushi)
```
 1 D: what about now,
 2    (0.3)
 3 A: teacher
 4    (0.3)
 5 D: ↑teacher ((writing "teacher" on the blackboard))
 6    teacher is good very good job.
 7    (0.3)
 8 D: ↑what teacher¿
 9    (0.5)
10→D: high school junior high school elementary?
11    (1.0)
12 A: high school.
13 D: high school. ((writing "high school" on
14    the blackboard)) high school, (.) kids are
15    very (0.3) very nice.
```

In line 1 Derek initiates a question[3] which Atsushi answers with a simple one word response "teacher" (line 3). After receipting the response through repetition and an assessment, Derek initiates a topically related question, "what teacher" in line 8. Receiving no immediate response, he formulates a 3-part list of possible answers to the question in line 10. After a 1-second gap, Atsushi selects from the list to answer "high school," thereby accomplishing an incremental specification to his earlier response. One could expect a range of different responses when asking a post-expansion question like "what (sort of) teacher;" Derek could just have easily meant "a teacher of what subject," to which an appropriate answer might be something such as "PE teacher." By presenting possible answers, Derek retrospectively narrows the intent of his question and also prospectively suggests a class of answers: Atsushi could have answered, "I want to be a high school teacher," but he follows the suggested class of answer and formulates his response as simply "high school." This is receipted through repetition and embodied action by Derek, who then briefly extends it into a topically related assessment in the next turn constructional unit.

By proffering candidate responses the teacher does not deviate from the priority in formulating his question. Although it suggests possible answers, the list in line 10 is done in a question form with rising intonation and the students orient to it as a multi-part question, rather than as the answer. This sort of list is another interactional resource that teachers in FL classrooms use to simplify questions during post-expansion sequences. Using a prioritized hierarchy of formulations allows them to teach their students linguistic features of the TL as they interact.

Error correction and explanation

First pair part actions such as questioning are not the only pedagogical actions that teachers carry out in FL classrooms. They also frequently engage in the activity of giving an explanation for why an answer is correct. The following segment is an example of one such formulation of explanation by a teacher. As part of an extended sequence in which the teacher has been having the students correct mistakes they made in an earlier speaking test, Ethan repeats one of Maki's earlier grammatical errors as an attempt to elicit a self-correction from her.

Segment 4 [STPS07529-C2] ('E' for Ethan [teacher])

```
28       (0.4)
29 E:    I want to buy my pet
30       (2.0)
31 E:    I want to bu:y, (0.4) ei pet.
32       (1.0)
33→E:    jibun no: pet (wa)/(o) kaou to omoimasu.
         I     LK  pet  TP/ O   buy  QT  think
         I want to buy my pet.
34→      in Japanese okay, but in English it's strange.
```

After the teacher poses the error in line 29, there is a 2 second gap of silence in which Maki does not self-select, which leads the teacher to give the correct form at line 31. The turn is designed as a correction of the erroneous syntactic form by emphasizing the indefinite article (Hauser, 2010). A turn formulated in the students' L1 is then produced in line 33 after there has been no further acknowledgement or uptake of the correction from the students. The use of the students' L1 is a part of the turn that gets extended to line 34 where an account of why "my pet" cannot be appropriate in this context in English. This turn constitutes the act of explaining the error correction and the teacher's use of the students' L1 works to help the students understand the point. That being the case, why did the teacher choose to formulate the referent in Japanese, instead of other possible formulations in English? Actually, the same teacher uses a different approach to correction in the TL in other situations. The following segment is an example.

Segment 5 [STPS07529-F1] ('E' for Ethan, 'R' for Ryo)

```
50  E: so what is (0.4) famous for Osaka? change,
51     (1.4)
52  R: ↑ah:   sou     ka.
       oh     so      IP
       oh I got it.
53  E: <what is> (0.4) <Osaka famous for.>
54     (1.3)
55→ E: what is famous for Osaka? no. (.) what famous
56→    your hometown? no. (0.2) what is your hometown
57→    famous for,>so it's kind of a< word order
58→    problem.
```

This segment of interaction took place in a feedback session after the same speaking test with a different group of students. As was the case in the previous segment, the teacher requests the student to "change" his mistake (line 50). After one of the students makes public his claim to a new state of understanding (line 52), the teacher provides the correct form (line 53). In lines 55–58, the teacher re-poses the students' errors[4] and provides the correction again, then finally stipulates the type of the error ("it's kind of a word order problem") in the TL. The teacher does not give any explicit account of why the error is an error. However, the practice of contrasting the errors with the correct forms implicitly suggests what constitutes the errors and the stipulation "word order problem" followed by the upshot marker "so" (Raymond, 2004) in line 57 works to help the students understand why the error is an error. Therefore, while it is not explicit, the turn in lines 54–58 is considered as a type of explanation.

The different explanation formulations in Segments 4 and 5, one in Japanese and the other in English, are reflexive to the teacher's orientation to the error types. The nature of the student's mistake in Segment 4 is a case of negative transfer, that is, the interference of L1 knowledge on an incorrect L2 form. Therefore, posing an L1 version and saying, "in Japanese okay, but in English it's strange" will be more effective in assisting the students to understand the point than other formulations in L2, such as, "you cannot say I want to buy my pet in English, you should say a pet." This is supported by second language acquisition literature on the role of correction for learning L2 (Gass, 2003; Long, 1996). On the other hand, the mistake in segment 5 is a word-order problem, so it is sufficient for the teacher to contrast the error and correct form, as the contrast accounts for what part of the error is wrong.[5]

Within formulations of the action "explanation after error correction" practiced by the teachers who have good command of the students' L1, there is a priority: when a correction is made in the case of L1 interference, a formulation posing the interfering L1 grammar will get the first priority. However, when corrections of non-L1 related mistakes are required, an explanation in the TL is the first priority. The use of students' L1 violates the rule of the use of the TL as the medium of instruction; however, if the programmatic relevance (Bilmes, 1993) of the EFL classrooms is taken into account, the formulation with the students' L1 can be seen as a normative action, which orients to the aim of these classrooms. In a specific context, certain matters are *programmed*, or normatively supposed to be mentioned or implemented. While the use of the TL as the medium of communication is programmatically relevant, the most primary matter in any language classroom is that "*the teacher will teach the learners the L2*" (Üstünel & Seedhouse 2005, p. 310, original emphasis). Therefore, teaching the TL in the most effective way is also programmatically and primarily relevant in the EFL classrooms.

The educational goals of such classrooms (i.e., effective teaching of the TL and the use of the TL) seem to be nested, and oriented to as such by the teacher. In Segment 4, the teacher does not formulate the explanation in the L1 completely; instead the L1 is used only for a possible Japanese translation, and the differences between the Japanese grammatical system and that of English is explained in the TL. So, by minimizing the use of the students' L1, the teacher displays his orientation to the communicative norms of the EFL classroom. By prioritizing formulations that are determined to be effective for teaching the TL while minimizing the use of the L1, the teacher is teaching the TL to the students.

OPI interviewer's formulation of question and repair-initiation

We now turn to some cases of formulation in the OPI role-play task. The aim of this task is to elicit samples of speech that are likely to occur in various everyday occasions, such as requesting someone to do something, or negotiating with someone over a schedule. The interviewers use a variety of interactional techniques to manage the role-play interaction (Okada, 2010). Naturally, questioning is one of the main techniques employed by the interviewers.

The importance of questioning that was shown in teaching contexts above also holds for OPI role-plays: it enables the interviewers to gather evidence about the candidate's linguistic and interactional competencies. As this questioning is an essential and prevalent tool for the interviewers, it has to be designed carefully so that the interviewers can collect "ratable" speech samples in the form of replies in a valid and reliable way. The interviewer's prioritization of questions in the following segment displays her orientation to questioning as a means of eliciting an extended response from the candidate. The task in this role-play requires the candidate to act as a traveler who has a broken camera. She has to ask a camera store clerk (played by the interviewer) to repair the camera.

Segment 6 [58a025RP] ('I' for interviewer, 'C' for candidate)

```
31   I:          [↑okay? yes, good morning¿ can I help
32        you?
33   C:   .hhh uh:m (.) my camera is broken, so: .hh
34        uhn:: .hh (0.2) oh would you repair it?
35   I:   yes, (.) oh (.) what happened?
36        (0.6)
37   C:   .h[hh
38   I:     [what's the problem?
39        (0.7)
40   C:   uh: (1.1) ↓uh::: (0.9) it was (0.4) fallen?
41        (0.4)
42   I:   uh-huh-huh so, .hhh ↓uh:: <when did that
43        happen>
44        (1.4)
45   C:   uh::m (0.3) £yesterday£
46→ I:    yes, so, .hh where did you drop- (.) where did
47        you drop it¿
48        (0.2)
49→ I:    did you drop it on the ↑ground on the car↑pet, or
50        (0.2)
51   C:   uh::: .hhh (0.9) uh- uhm: on the ↑concrete.
52   I:   ↓uh::m [concrete. uh::: .hhh so, (.) we-=
```

The sequence starts with the interviewer's greeting and a formulaic offer of assistance that casts herself in the institutional role of shop assistant and therefore helps initiate the transition from interviewer explanation of the task instructions to the commencement of the role-play proper (lines 31–32). The candidate (in the role of customer) accepts the offer and asks the clerk to repair her camera (lines 33–34), which is the focal task of the role-play. In next turn, the interviewer agrees to comply with her request ("yes") and initiates a post-expansion sequence in which the topic becomes the details of the problem with the camera. In this part of the sequence, the interviewer initially asks, "what happened" (line 35) and then when no response is forthcoming from the candidate she rephrases this into "what's the problem" (line 38). After the candidate eventually answers the question ("it was fallen" in line 40), the interviewer initiates another follow-up question, "when did that happen" in lines 42–43 and the candidate gives the response "yesterday" in the next turn. After that, the interviewer asks one more question, "where did you drop it" in lines 46–47. The interviewer's subsequent question in line 49 proffers candidate answers with a turn-final "or" ("did you drop it on the ground on the carpet, or"), which signals an incomplete list and provides an opportunity for the candidate to fit a taxonomically-related item into the open slot (Stokoe, 2010). The candidate picks up on the proffered format and gives the response "on the concrete" in next turn. The interviewer repeats the key element "concrete" with falling intonation, which demonstrates her receipt of the candidate's answer.

This sequence of talk shows that the interviewer employs the strategy of proffering candidate answers to pursue a suitable response in order to keep role-playing when a reply is not forthcoming after the original questions. Reformulating the original question with this strategy makes it easier for the interviewers to get a response. However, this does not satisfy the objectives of the role-play interaction as part of an oral test which aims to obtain and evaluate ratable speech samples. Proffering possible answers gives too many hints to the candidates in that it tells them the expected category of answer and clarifies the propositional content of the question in detail. For that reason, it limits the chance to test the candidates' competence in discursive practical reasoning (i.e., to understand what is being asked by the question and what will fit the expected category of answer, as well as how to provide a response to fit that category). Therefore, a question that provides a possible answer is given the least priority: it is the interviewer's last resort in pursuing an answer due to the constraint of the OPI context and its institutional aims.

What the interviewer in the segment above did, however, is not a simple confirmation check to a proffered answer; she put forward a list of possible answers and gave the candidate a chance to complete it by attaching "or" at a turn-final position, which makes it possible to collect a speech sample provided in the candidate's own words. That is to say, while the interviewer's subsequent question formulation limits its institutional value for collecting ratable speech samples, it does not totally eliminate it. Therefore, the interviewer prioritizes the question formulations to maximize the chance of obtaining ratable speech samples: the first formulation choice is a question without any sample responses, the second is a question with a number of type-related answers plus "or," and the last possible resort is a confirmation check to the proffered answer.

In the following segment, I will examine another case of priority in formulating an action that orients to the interviewer's knowledge of the task, and therefore seems more specific to the role-play situation—the interviewer's formulation of repair initiation. In this instance, the candidate and the interviewer are role-playing as co-workers at an office. The situation is that they are about to go to lunch, but the candidate realizes that he does not have his wallet. The task requires the candidate to ask the interviewer if he can borrow some money to go to lunch. Although the scenario entails a candidate-initiated request sequence, the test-taker evidently misunderstands the task and therefore does not make the request, leading the interviewer to produce a series of increasingly on-record prompts, which serve as interactional slots where the candidate can begin the request.

Segment 7 [48a083RP] ('I' for interviewer, 'C' for candidate)

```
21  I:   O↑KA:↓Y it's lunch ↑ti:me. .hh uh:m I made a
22       reservation at a really nice French restaurant.
23       (0.2)
24  C:   °oh [(we will)°
25  I:       [shall we go?
26       (0.3)
27  C:   yes
28→     (0.2)
29  I:   okay?
30       (0.8)
31  C:   °that sounds very nice.°
32  I:   oka:y,
33→     (1.3)
34  I:   uh::m=
35  C:   =so: (0.4) uh::m (0.5) ↑where is it.
36       (0.2)
37  I:   .hh uh: the restaurant is actually gonna (.)
38       be a taxi ri:de,
39       (0.2)
40       but [it's just across the town by the Harbor=
41           [hm.
42  I:   =Bridge.°so° very very exclusive it's kind be a
43       little bit expensive is that okay?
44  C:   yeah, no problem.
45  I:   no problem?
46  C:   no problem.
47→     (0.4)
48  I:   o- ↑o:[kay,
49  C:         [°just moment.° (0.2) °I check° (2.0) ↑oh
50       (0.8) oh (.) I forgo(h)t(h)o bri(h)ng huh
51       m(h)y wa(h)llet.
52  I:   you forgot [your ↑wallet?
```

The interviewer begins the sequence with an announcement that it is lunch time in line 21 and a subsequent invitation to lunch in line 25, which the candidate accepts (line 27). The candidate's acceptance can be taken as a deviation from the task requirement, in that he has been instructed to borrow money before he goes to lunch—in other words, at this point he is expected to initiate an insertion sequence to carry out a request before formulating an acceptance of the interviewer's invitation. After being silent for 0.2-seconds (line 28), the interviewer initiates a confirmation to the candidate's acceptance in line 29, with a question-intoned "okay?," which can be considered as a repair-initiation to the candidate's action. Then, after a 0.8-second gap, in line 31 the candidate confirms his action. While the interviewer acknowledges the candidate's confirmation in line 32, his "okay" is prolonged, which might display his uneasiness with the candidate's action. After being silent for another 1.3 seconds, the interviewer takes a turn in line 34, but his "uh::m" is a form of delay, which indicates the interviewer's reluctance to progress the talk due to some sort of interactional trouble (Schegloff, 2010). In this case, the problem is that the candidate is deviating from the task instruction.

The candidate then takes a turn to ask a question concerning the location of the restaurant in line 35. The interviewer replies they need to take a taxi (lines 37–38), and seeing the non-reply to that from the candidate he characterizes the restaurant as an exclusive and expensive one and asks if the candidate is okay to go there (lines 42–43). The candidate confirms this with " yeah, no problem." in line 44. The interviewer immediately initiates a confirmation check with "no problem" emphasizing "no" in line 44, which is a repair-initiation strongly suggesting that "no problem" is the trouble source. However, the candidate again gives an affirmation with the repetition of "no problem" (line 46). The interviewer remains silent for 0.4-seconds (line 47) and then further seeks confirmation with rising intonation "o—↑o:kay," Finally, however, overlapping the confirmation check, the candidate initiates the action he is required to perform in lines 49–51. The interviewer receipts the candidate's turn through repetition emphasizing "forgot" and "wallet," which works to topicalize the candidate's forgetting his wallet in the following interaction.

The OPI interviewers are instructed to avoid any prompting that would lead to specific action from the candidate: therefore, they should refrain from initiating repair that identifies the trouble-source.[6] Silence does not inform the candidate what the trouble is and does not amount to "coaching" since it does not even specify which party (i.e., interviewer or candidate) has produced the problem but only implies that some sort of interactional trouble is going on in the talk. In the segment above, the interviewer initiates repair through a combination of silence and explicit repair-initiations, but the silence comes first and the confirmation checks are initiated only after the candidate fails to adequately deal with the trouble in the unfilled response slots. Through the prioritization of repair-initiation, the interviewer tries to observe the instruction and to provide an opportunity for the candidate to understand what the trouble-source action is and perform the required action while avoiding direct instruction. The interviewer's prioritization is a method for achieving the institutional aims of the OPI in the most effective manner out of the possible ways available at the moment of formulation.

Conclusion

The purpose of this study has been to explicate a procedure that members use in formulating an action in interaction through the analysis of two types of interaction, namely EFL classroom interaction and OPI role-play. The analysis revealed that the teachers and the interviewers formulated actions, such as the acts of questioning, explanation after error correction, and repair-initiation to achieve the programmed aims of these two types of interaction in the most effective manner out of the possible ways available at the moment of formulation. The practice of prioritization, which is aimed here at maximizing the pedagogical benefits for the recipients as language learners and test-takers, is *recipient-designed* (Sacks, Schegloff, & Jefferson, 1974) in that it makes relevant the co-participants' (i.e., recipients') situated, institutional identities as EFL learners and test takers.[7] Therefore, in addition to the interactional detail, we also need to investigate the "context" of interaction, the aim of the interaction as well as the relationship between the speaker/actor and the recipient, in order to understand why a given formulation is selected at a particular moment in the talk.

The findings seem to offer support to the argument for the use of the students' L1 by teachers in FL classrooms. Thus far, studies on this issue have focused on the reasons why they do so (Cook, 2001; Kim & Elder, 2005; Rolinlanziti & Brownlie, 2002; Turnbull, 2001). What is missing in such studies is an explication of the teachers' complex orientations to the context of FL classrooms when they execute a code-switch from the TL into the students' L1. The reason for the switch is not simply that maintaining a pedagogical focus at a particular moment of interaction is preferred (Üstünel & Seedhouse 2005); code-switching is just one formulation with which to do so. What the current study has shown is that teachers orient to priorities in multiple formulations of actions to teach the TL in the classroom.

Concerning OPIs, this study suggests the importance of paying close attention to each interviewer's testing procedure. OPIs are required to be valid and reliable in testing candidate's proficiency in TL speaking, since they have consequences for the real-world. The results of OPIs have been used for high-stake decision-making such as job promotion and hiring and even assigning citizenship. If an interviewer's testing procedure is different from other interviewers, the consistency could be called into question (Brown, 2004). By the same token, the construct of the candidate's proficiency could also be cast into doubt, because if it is co-constructed by the interviewer's actions, the performance would vary from interviewer to interviewer. Accordingly, the interviewers' collection method has to be understood as a potentially misleading element of the assessment. This is even more serious in the role-play section of the OPI, since it is conducted in accordance with a set of specific instructions (Okada & Greer, in press). Therefore, it is important to analyze the way each interviewer formulates questions in order to develop a standardized procedure so that role-play tasks can be more valid and reliable.

As we have seen in the examples above, prioritization of formulation is a method for doing a certain type of interaction. Thus, in addition to being an analytic lens, it can be taught as a strategic way of teaching and testing in and through interaction. Considering what is programmatically relevant and what prioritization will be normatively expected can help inform the professional training of language learning practitioners. As the teachers of the EFL classroom data demonstrated through their use of the students' L1, the resource for formulation that a participant has is critically related to achieving the objectives of the interaction he or she engages in. It is suggested that future studies examine other procedures of formulation in these types of interaction so that we can strive for better language teaching and language testing practices.

Notes

1. Due to the confidentiality of the test, the name and the details (e.g., the level of each task), which would lead to the disclosure of the test, cannot be specified.
2. The Japanese "douiu" alone means "how to say" or "in what way." However, since it is cut-off, it is assumed that Ethan was on the way to producing "douiu huu ni iimasu ka" or some similar Japanese expression that would translate as "How would you say X?"
3. Prior to this segment, the teacher asked the student (Atsushi) about what he wanted to be when he was a child. The question "what about now" in line 1 is therefore sequentially comprehensible as "what he wants to be now" by both the teacher and the student.
4. "What famous your hometown" is a student's mistake which the teacher corrected prior to this segment.
5. There are cases in which a word order problem is caused by negative transfer from the learner's L1; however, the point here is that the teacher does not treat the problem as a case in which he needs to resort to the students' L1, but that the contrast is sufficient as an implicit explanation for the error correction.
6. The testing manual instructs interviewers to avoid coaching and giving clues to the candidate even when the candidate asks for help so that the interviewer can collect any information that could influence final rating.
7. In addition, the L1 formulations are recipient designed to the students' transportable identities (Zimmerman, 1998) as L1 speakers of Japanese.

References

Bilmes, J. (1988). The concept of preference in conversation analysis. *Language in Society, 17*, 161–181.

Bilmes, J. (1993). Ethnomethodology, culture, and implicature: Toward an empirical pragmatics. *Pragmatics, 3*, 387–409.

Bilmes, J. (2008). Generally speaking: Formulating an argument in the US, Federal Trade Commission. *Text & Talk, 28*, 193–217.

Bilmes, J. (2009a). Kinship categories in a northern Thai narrative. In H. t. Nguyen, & G. Kasper (Eds.), *Talk-in-interaction: Multilingual perspectives* (pp. 29–59). Honolulu: University of Hawai'i, National Foreign Language Research Center.

Bilmes, J. (2009b). Taxonomies are for talking: Reanalyzing a Sacks classic. *Journal of Pragmatics, 41*, 1600–1610.

Bilmes, J. (2011). Occasioned semantics: A systematic approach to meaning in talk. *Human Studies, 34*, 129–153.

Brown, A. (2004). Discourse analysis and the oral interview: Competence or performance? In D. Boxer, & A. D. Cohen (Eds.), *Studying speaking to inform second language learning* (pp. 253–282). Clevedon: Multilingual Matters.

Cook, V. (2001). Using the first language in the classroom. *Canadian Modern Language Review, 57*, 402–423.

Deppermann, A. (2011a). Notionalization: The transformation of descriptions into categorizations. *Human Studies, 34*, 155–181.

Deppermann, A. (2011b). The study of formulations as a key to an interactional semantics. *Human Studies, 34*, 115–128.

Edwards, D. (1997). *Discourse and cognition.* London: Sage.

Edwards, D. (2000). Extreme case formulations: Softeners, investment, and doing nonliteral. *Research on Language and Social Interaction, 33*, 347–373.

Garfinkel, H., & Sacks, H. (1970). On formal structures of practical action. In J. C. McKinney, & E. A. Tiryakian (Eds.), *Theoretical sociology: Perspectives and developments* (pp. 338–366). New York: Appleton Century Crofts.

Gass, S. M. (2003). Input and interaction. In C. J. Doughty, & M. H. Long (Eds.), *The handbook of second language acquisition* (pp. 224–255). Malden, MA: Blackwell.

Goffman, E. (1967). *Interaction ritual: Essays on face-to-face behavior.* New York: Random House.

Goffman, E. (1972). *Relations in public.* New York: Harper & Row.

Goffman, E. (1981). *Forms of talk.* Philadelphia: University of Pennsylvania Press.

Hauser, E. (2010). Other-correction of language form following a repair sequence. In G. Kasper, H. thi Nguyen, D. Yoshimi, & J. K. Yoshioka (Eds.), *Pragmatics & Language Learning* (Vol. 12) (pp. 277–296). Honolulu: University of Hawai'i, National Foreign Language Research Center.

Hauser, E. (2011). Generalization: A practice of situated categorization in talk. *Human Studies, 34*, 183–198.

Heritage, J. (1984). *Garfinkel and ethnomethodology.* Cambridge: Polity Press.

Heritage, J. (2008). Conversation analysis as social theory. In B. Turner (Ed.), *The new Blackwell companion to social theory* (pp. 300–320). Oxford: Blackwell.

Heritage, J. (2012). The epistemic engine: Sequence organization and territories of knowledge. *Research on Language and Social Interaction, 45*, 30–52.

Heritage, J., & Raymond, G. (2005). The terms of agreement: Indexing epistemic authority and subordination in assessment sequences. *Social Psychology Quarterly, 68*, 15–38.

Heritage, J., & Watson, D. R. (1979). Formulations as conversational objects. In G. Psathas (Ed.), *Everyday language: Studies in ethnomethodology* (pp. 123–162). New York: Irvington.

Kim, S. H. O., & Elder, C. (2005). Language choices and pedagogic functions in the foreign language classroom: A cross-linguistic functional analysis of teacher talk. *Language Teaching Research, 9*, 355–380.

Lerner, G. (1996). Finding "face" in the preference structures of talk-in-interaction. *Social Psychology Quarterly, 59*, 303–321.

Lee, Y-A. (2007). Third turn position in teacher talk: Contingency and the work of teaching. *Journal of Pragmatics, 39*, 1204–1230.

Levinson, S. C. (2007). Optimizing person reference: Perspectives from usage on Rossel Island. In N. Enfield, & T. Stivers (Eds.), *Person reference in interaction: Linguistic, cultural, and social perspectives* (pp. 29–72). Cambridge: Cambridge University Press.

Long, M. H. (1996). The role of the linguistic environment in second language acquisition. In W. C. Ritchie, & T. K. Bhatia (Eds.), *Handbook of second language acquisition* (pp. 413–468). San Diego, CA: Academic Press.

Maynard, D. W. (2011). On "interactional semantics" and problems of meaning. *Human Studies, 34*, 199–207.

Nguyen, H. t., & Kasper, G. (Eds.). (2009). *Talk-in-interaction: Multilingual perspectives*. Honolulu: University of Hawai'i, National Foreign Language Resource Center.

Okada, Y. (2010). Role-play in oral proficiency interviews: Interactive footing and interactional competencies. *Journal of Pragmatics, 42*, 1647–1668.

Okada, Y., & Greer, T. (in press). Pursuing a relevant response in OPI role-plays. In S. Ross & G. Kasper (Eds.), *Assessing second language pragmatics*. Basingstoke: Palgrave.

Pomerantz, A. (1984). Agreeing and disagreeing with assessments: Some features of preferred/dispreferred turn shapes. In J. M. Atkinson & J. Heritage (Eds.), *Structures of social action: Studies in conversation analysis* (pp. 57–101). Cambridge: Cambridge University Press.

Pomerantz, A. M. (1986). Extreme case formulations: A way of legitimizing claims. *Human Studies, 9*, 219–30

Raymond, G. (2004). Prompting action: The stand alone "so" in ordinary conversation. *Research on Language and Social Interaction, 37*, 185–218.

Rolin-Ianziti, J., & Brownlie, S. (2002). Teacher use of learners' native language in the foreign language classroom. *Canadian Modern Language Review, 58*, 402–426.

Sacks, H. (1992). *Lectures on conversation, Volume I & II*. G. Jefferson (Ed.). Oxford: Blackwell.

Sacks, H., & Schegloff, E. A. (1979). Two preferences in the organization of reference to persons in conversation and their interaction. In G. Psathas (Ed.), *Everyday language: Studies in ethnomethodology* (pp. 15–21). New York: Irvington.

Sacks, H., Schegloff, E. A., & Jefferson, G. (1974). A simplest systematics for the organization of turn-taking for conversation. *Language, 50*, 696–735.

Schegloff, E. A. (1972). Notes on a conversational practice: Formulating place. In D. Sudnow (Ed.), *Studies in social interaction* (pp. 75–119). New York: Free Press.

Schegloff, E. A. (1968). Sequencing in conversational openings. *American Anthropologist, 70*, 1075–1095.

Schegloff, E. A. (1991). Reflections on talk and social structure. In D. Boden, & D. H. Zimmerman (Eds.), *Talk and social structure* (pp. 44–71). Oxford: Polity Press.

Schegloff, E. A. (1996). Some practices for referring to persons in talk-in-interaction: A partial sketch of a systematics. In B. A. Fox (Ed.), *Studies in anaphora* (pp. 437–485). Amsterdam: John Benjamins.

Schegloff, E. A. (2007). *Sequence organization in interaction: A primer in conversation analysis*. Cambridge: Cambridge University Press.

Schegloff, E. A. (2010). Some other "uh(m)"s. *Discourse Processes, 47*, 130–174.

Schegloff, E. A., G. Jefferson, and H. Sacks. (1977). The preference for self-correction in the organization of repair in conversation. *Language, 53*, 361–382.

Sidnell, J. (2004). There's risks in everything: Extreme case formulations and accountability in inquiry testimony. *Discourse and Society, 15*, 745–766.

Stivers, T. (2007). Alternative recognitionals in person reference. In N. J. Enfield, & T. Stivers (Eds.), *Person reference in interaction* (pp. 73–96). Cambridge: Cambridge University Press.

Stokoe, E. (2010) "Have you been married, or...?": Eliciting and accounting for relationship histories in speed-dating interaction. *Research on Language & Social Interaction, 43*, 260–282.

ten Have, P. (2007). *Doing conversation analysis (2nd ed.)*. London: Sage.

Turnbull, M. (2001).There is a reason for the use of L1 in second and foreign language teaching, but... *Canadian Modern Language Review, 57*, 531–540.

Üstünel, E., & Seedhouse, P. (2005). Why that, in that language, right now?: Code-switching and pedagogical focus. *International Journal of Applied Linguistics, 15*, 302–325.

Zimmerman, D. H. (1998). Identity, context and interaction. In C. Antaki, & S. Widdicombe (Eds.), *Identities in talk* (pp. 87–106). London: Sage.

Turn-taking Practices in Conversation-For-Learning

Tomomi Otsu
Tokyo University of Foreign Studies, Japan

Nathan P. Krug
Saitama University, Japan

> This study examines features of second language (L2) speakers' interactions in a conversation room within an English as a foreign language (EFL) institution in Japan. Formal language classrooms perpetuate distinctive sequential structures, such as initiation-response-feedback (IRF) patterns of interaction, and although such communication patterns are beneficial for language learning, they limit opportunities for L2 speakers to manage interactions for themselves, thereby reducing chances for the development of interactional skills. In marked contrast, the environment in the sorts of free-conversation lounges described in this study provides L2 speakers with opportunities to engage in a wider range of interactional practices. As such, conversation rooms are important learning environments, deserving closer scrutiny and analysis. Using conversation analytic (CA) techniques, this study investigates L2 speakers' talk in one such environment in Japan, focusing on turn-taking practices—especially on turn-allocation.

Introduction

It is often difficult for learners in English as a foreign language (EFL) environments to find opportunities to have an ordinary conversation in English. To solve this problem, many learning institutions have established free-access spaces or "conversation rooms" dedicated to English conversation—places where English learners are provided with opportunities to experience what

Kasper (2004) termed "conversation-for-learning." The overarching purpose of such conversation environments is to provide opportunities for second language (L2) learners to experience more ordinary-conversation-like talk with peers in EFL environments, and enhance their English fluency through target language practice.

Ordinary conversation is one significant site for language learning. It offers differing opportunities for language learning than classroom interaction (Markee, 2000). Unlike typical classroom environments, in ordinary conversation there are no fixed participant roles, hence the participants organize and structure such interactions on their own. In one sense, conversation rooms can help bridge the gap between the classroom and the 'real world' through what Hauser (2008) has called non-formal institutional interaction. Kasper (2004) argues that learning in conversation-type interaction is not limited only to the negotiation of meaning (such as talk that deals with communication difficulties); ordinary conversation can also be a productive environment for L2 learning. In the classroom, on the contrary, even if teachers conduct classroom activities that focus on meaning-and-fluency, the pedagogical agenda still places "outside" influences upon the interactions (see Okada, this volume). For example, due to restrictions upon topic choice, there can be minimal occurrences of topic initiation, shift or exit in such activities, and the freedom to enter or leave a given instance of interaction is reduced. Furthermore, Mori (2002) reveals that instructional design affects the ways in which L2 speakers construct their talk.

Learning institutions assume that conversation rooms serve the purpose of language learning well, and as a result such rooms or similar institutional facilities are becoming more common. However, to evaluate the educational effect of such arrangements and to expand and better understand the merits of conversation rooms, the interactional features of L2 conversation-room talk needs to be submitted to micro-analytic scrutiny. A number of recent studies have examined conversations arranged for language practice, and thus far have revealed how participants organize their interactions in conversation-for-learning in non-formal institutional settings, and how their organization of the interactions works to construct such talk. Kasper (2004) demonstrates how the interlocutors in her data orient to a variety of membership categories including target language expert and novice, and that the interaction develops in cycles of recurrent orientations to the interaction as conversation or as a language-learning event through the interlocutors' interactional conduct. Kasper and Kim (2004) also examine conversations designed for language practice outside of the formal language classroom, and reveal how third-position repair (Schegloff, 1992) is conducted by the target language expert in a covert manner which de-emphasizes the misalignment of question and answer sequences. Mori (2003) explores how interlocutors start topical talk in their initial encounters and organize their participation, pointing out how interculturality is used as a resource for organizing interaction. Jung (2004) examines repair as a language learning practice, and shows how L2 speakers learn L2 vocabulary in conversations with their conversational partners who are the target language experts. Mori and Hayashi (2006) provide a microanalysis of the practice of "embodied completion" (Olsher, 2004) in interactions between L1 and L2 speaking participants. They demonstrate how embodied completion is utilized to achieve intersubjectivity, and that it provides opportunities for presentation of refined linguistic expressions which capture the exact ideas originally expressed through gesture.

Following on from the above studies, the purpose of this study is to explore some of the interactional features of L2 speakers' conversations for language learning. We will focus on turn-taking practices in this chapter. According to Sacks, Schegloff, and Jefferson (1974), turn-taking in conversation is achieved through a system that is comprised of (1) a turn-constructional component (i.e., how the basic unit of turn is formulated) and (2) a turn-allocation component, including how to bring others into a conversation, how to take a turn at the right moment, and how to keep a conversation going. There are two reasons why we focus on turn-taking. Firstly, to better understand the nature of conversation-for-learning, it is necessary to have empirical research that investigates L2 speakers' turn-taking practices. As research on institutional talk shows, the institutional setting influences the turn-taking organization, and the way the participants organize turn-taking shapes the institutional talk (Drew & Heritage, 1992). Teacher-led classrooms have a distinct speech exchange system compared to ordinary conversation (Markee, 2000). The organization of turn-taking both in L2-classroom discussion (Hauser, 2009) and in conversation-room talk facilitated by an L1 speaker (Hauser, 2008) differs from that of ordinary conversation. Thus, it appears feasible that L2 speakers would organize turn-taking in student-run conversation rooms differently from that of formal classroom settings because of elements such as the purpose of the room and the absence of teachers or target language experts. Secondly, the ability to engage in turn-taking is a fundamental component of interactional competence, the ability to use verbal and nonverbal interactional resources and engage in L2 social interaction. The turn is a basic unit of conversation and a vehicle for other practices such as sequencing and structuring the overall conversation (Wong & Waring, 2010). This study seeks to better understand L2 speakers' interactional competence in relation to turn-taking practices.

Studies of L2 speakers' turn-taking so far have revealed how interlocutors with limited linguistic resources can achieve skillful interactions in their other language (Carroll, 2004, 2005; Gardner, 2007). According to Carroll (2004), for example, restarts at turn beginnings, observed in talk produced by novice Japanese speakers of English, have often been considered as indicative of L2 speakers' difficulty with speech production. However, similar phenomena have been observed in first language (L1) talk as well, in situations where there is clearly no difficulty with speech production (see, for example, Goodwin, 1980). Carroll revealed that L2 novice speakers employ (1) restarts to safeguard turn beginnings when their TCU-beginning might be obscured through overlap with another speaker, and (2) phrasal breaks to solicit the gaze of a non-gazing recipient. Carroll (2005) points out that these interlocutors can also utilize distinctly nonnative resources to accomplish sophisticated interaction. He found that vowel-marking, which is commonly observed in talk produced by novice Japanese learners of English, provides a little more time for the L2 speaker who initiates the repair to achieve self-repair. Furthermore, when vowel-marking occurs TCU-finally, it signals that there is more to come after the complete TCU. Vowel-marking is also employed as a means of re-establishing the right to speakership following overlap resolution. Gardner (2007) explores L2 speakers' turn-beginnings which are replete with a range of turn-delaying elements such as pauses, and points out that such broken starts are used to plan the turn, and then, the rest of the turn is delivered relatively smoothly. In addition, even during broken starts, L2 speakers confine silences to within a little more than just over a second, so that they can deflect potential incoming speakers, by employing other resources for slowing down the turn such as sound stretching and turn-holding tokens.

    The current study analyzes L2 speakers' organization of turn-taking in a conversation room within an EFL institution in Japan. The analysis here turns to what other interactional resources L2 speakers employ to organize turn-taking and achieve skillful interactions in their L2. Our focus is especially on how L2 speakers allocate turns among themselves; how they achieve the selection of other participants as the next speaker, and how they successfully self-select. In this chapter, we use conversation analytic (CA) techniques to explicate turn-taking practices. CA research is theoretically and methodologically grounded in the study of publicly observable phenomena, and the view of competence that CA supports is one of situated practices rather than psycholinguistic models that focus on learning processes or knowledge structures (Schegloff, Koshik, Jacoby & Olsher, 2002), offering a systematic means of understanding interactional competence. In an in-depth review of CA-informed studies conducted over the last decade, Seedhouse (2011) shows how the approach has been increasingly used to explore ways in which such competence is co-constructed by participants, and this in turn has led some language professionals to reconsider their perception of L2 speaker practices. As Firth and Wagner (1997) point out, if the bias of learner-as-deficient-communicator is eliminated, utterances that seemingly indicate an L2 speaker's disfluency can be reanalyzed as practices used to achieve other intricate interactional functions. In the same light, this study attempts to show some of the ways that L2 speakers construct interactional competence and achieve sophisticated interaction.

By examining short segments of group conversations conducted between intermediate-level EFL learners, it was found that L2 speakers achieve skillful turn-allocation, using a variety of linguistic and nonlinguistic resources, including those documented in previous CA studies of L1 talk. This chapter will show (1) how L2 speakers use the nonlinguistic resources of gaze and gesture to select the next speaker, (2) by employing the very same nonlinguistic resources, how a L2 speaker can construct a question to display that he or she is addressing multiple co-participants, and (3) how L2 learners draw co-participants' attention and negotiate next speakership.

Data

As outlined above, the data in this study were recorded in a conversation room situated within a university in Japan. The conversation room serves as a place for interested students to meet and practice English conversation skills in small groups. During operation, one member of the university's teaching staff is present in a teacher-as-facilitator role, assisting when required but not necessarily active in the conversation. Participation within the room does not lead to the accrual of academic credit for students, and students gather in the room whenever they desire. The students freely seat themselves in small groups and have conversations only in English. In this way, the discussions are not completely spontaneous, but are instead a semi-formal arrangement expressly designed for the purpose of facilitating the learning of English through learner-initiated target language practice.

Two video-recorded interactions (approx. 15 minutes each) were analyzed for this study. The excerpts that we examine in this paper were collected from a group of three intermediate-level EFL students: two men, Ryo (R) and Shun (S); and one woman, Emi (E). These three participants meet weekly in the conversation room with various other students. As such, the focal participants are acquaintances rather than close friends.

The data are transcribed according to CA conventions, although with some additional notation with regard to the participants' relative gaze direction and hand gestures (see Appendix for transcription conventions). The participants' gaze directions are marked below the turn notation tier. A solid line indicates at what point relative to the turn each participant begins his or her gaze, with the uppercase letter indicating who is gazing and the lowercase letter indicating at whom the gaze is directed. A lowercase letter "x" means a participant is not gazing at any co-participant, but is instead looking somewhere else, for example, at the surface of the table or at the wall. The starting point of a hand gesture is indicated by [H]. An example and explanation follows (based on an excerpt from Extract 2, which will be analyzed in detail later in this chapter).

```
Emi: how about   (.)  you.  huhuh
     Es_____[H]_____
     Rx_____Rs_____
     Sx_____Se_____
```

Figure 1. Gaze tier set and hand gesture notation

While Emi (E) is speaking, she is gazing at Shun (S), and after she utters "how about," she directs her hand [H] toward Shun around the micropause. Ryo (R) is not looking at anyone at the beginning of Emi's turn (as noted by the 'x' in 'Rx'), but he shifts his gaze to Shun around the micropause in Emi's turn. Shun is not looking at anyone either at the beginning, and he likewise shifts his gaze to Emi around the micropause.

Gaze transitions may occur as participants move their gaze from point to point, however such transitions are not considered in this study. Therefore, for readability, gaze transition is not differentiated from gaze maintenance in the extracts that follow. Readers should bear in mind that although the gaze line is fixed with clearly defined start and end points, there are also micro-moments when the participants are turning their heads to adjust their gaze direction.

Interactional resources for next-speaker selection: The set of "gaze direction plus hand gesture"

First of all, we observe aspects of next-speaker selection practices. We will limit our discussion to the first-pair part of adjacency pairs—those actions that project type-matched responding actions for next turn (for example, when an information-seeking query makes a type-matched answer relevant). Current speakers can select a next speaker by composing a turn with a sequence-initiating action (that is, the first-pair part of an adjacency pair). However, in multiparty talk, in order to explicitly select a specific next speaker, some form of address has to be present along with the sequence-initiating action. Sacks, Schegloff, and Jefferson (1974) propose that the most explicit method of addressing is accomplished by combining either (1) gaze direction or (2) an address term (such as calling the addressee by name) with a first-pair part. According to Lerner (2003), gaze direction explicitly demonstrates that an initiating action is being directed to a particular party. Hence, it shows that the participant who is gazed at is selected as the next speaker, and thus participants who are not gaze-selected are not expected to speak next. This method requires mutual gaze between the present speaker and the recipient. Therefore, in the case of its absence, mutual gaze is achieved through the utilization of resources such as restarts and pauses by the current speaker (Goodwin, 1979).

The following extract shows how a participant employs gaze as a method of addressing (Lerner, 2003).

Extract 1   (Lerner, 2003, p. 179: modified)[1]

```
01  Nancy:    You see all these (.) cars comin: (0.4) toward you with
02            the[r h e a d l i g h t]s
03  Vivian:      [Wul- thank Go][d there weren't that many. ]
04→Michael:                     ['Member the wah- guy we sa:]w?
05                      Vm-----Nm/Mn----------------------Sm-----
06            (0.2)
07  Nancy:    ehh↑(h)Oh(h)o he[e Y(h)a(h)a h ha ha ha ↑ha
08  Michael:                  [huh huh
```

In line 4, Michael gazes at Nancy as he begins speaking. Nancy, the recipient, can see that he is speaking to her. Vivian, who has been gazing at Michael, can also see that he has now turned to Nancy. Shane (who is indicated by S in line 5) also turns toward Michael at "sa:w?" in line 4, and sees Michael is directing his utterance to Nancy. Thus, Michael's gaze can demonstrate explicitly to the co-participants that this question is being directed to Nancy.

We found that L2 speakers employed gaze practices to successfully achieve next-speaker selection just as L1 speakers have been shown to do; they secure the co-participants' gaze, and then, gaze-select the next speaker. However, the L2 speakers in our study also often accompanied this with a range of hand gestures. This set of "gaze direction plus hand gesture" was used to designate specifically who was being primarily addressed.

In Extract 2, we can see that Emi utilizes the combination of gaze direction and the raised palms of both hands to select Shun as the next speaker at point [H] in line 8. Before this extract, Ryo initiated a sequence of talk by asking Emi about the difficulty of the teachers' employment test, to which Emi provided a lengthy explanation over several turns. Lines 1–4 show the ending of that explanation.

Extract 2

```
01  E:   I'm going to be a (.)
02       junior high school's teacher.

03       °so° (1.3) I study: (1.3) all over (1.3)
         Er      Es_Er       Es_Er
         Re                          Rx((nodding))
         Se              Sx      Se

04       new things (.) [°y e a h.°
```

```
05   R:                [.h h h h
                       Rx_____
                       Se_Sr_Sx((nodding))
                       Es_____


06   S:    <okay.>
           Sx____
           Rx____
           Es____


07   R:    hh oh:[: ((lifting up a cup at the same time))
           Rx_____
           Sx_____
           Es_____


08→ E:           [how about (.) you. huhuh
                 Es_____[H]_____
                 Rx_____Rs_____((drinking))
                 Sx_____Se_____

09         upcoming (.) spring.=what're you going to do:.
           _____
                                   Re_____Rs_____
           _____


10   S:    oh (.) I, (0.8) I just want to pre- pare
           Sx_____
           Rs_____
           Es_____


11         for my, (0.8) toefl english test.
           _____Se___
           _____
           _____


12   E:    ↑mmm.↓
           Es___Er
           Rs___
           Se___
```

In lines 1–4, Emi ends her explanation of how difficult the teachers' employment test is. After Emi says "all over" at line 3, Ryo acknowledges this by nodding, but without establishing eye contact with Emi. From this moment, Ryo appears to completely withdraw from the conversation, looking down at the table or displaying a fixed middle-distance gaze, and even raising a coffee mug near his mouth at line 7, indicating momentary unavailability.[2] Meanwhile, Shun is gazing at Emi at the TCU ending "new things" in line 4, but he averts his gaze from Emi when Emi nods and directs her gaze to him at line 4. When Emi recompletes her speaking turn with "yeah." at line 4, Shun glances at her, briefly making eye contact at line 5. Shun simply says "okay." without looking at Emi at line 6. Shun's nodding at line 5 and vocalized acknowledgement at line 6 make public the fact that he knows that he has been addressed, but rather than significantly advancing the talk, he continues looking at the table and does not speak further. As a result, at line 8, Emi proceeds to explicitly select Shun as the next speaker. At lines 8 and 9, Emi asks Shun about his plan for the spring vacation by saying "how about (.) you. huhuh upcoming (.) spring.=what're you going to do:.." When she poses the question, Emi is looking at Shun, thus explicitly selecting him as the next speaker. In addition, by making use of a micro-pause between "how about" and "you" in line 8, she secures the gaze from Shun. At around the point when Shun actually shifts his gaze over to Emi, Emi moves her hands—which had been momentarily resting on the table—bringing them toward Shun, just before she says "you," as shown in Figure 2. As Lerner (1996, 2003) argues, the recipient reference term "you" can indicate that someone has been selected as the next speaker among a group of co-participants, but does not necessarily in itself determine who has actually been addressed. In this extract, however, Emi clearly demonstrated that she is selecting Shun as next speaker even before saying "you," by directing her gaze towards him, securing his gaze, and using an accompanying hand gesture. According to Greer and Potter (2008), in order to make sense of the question "How about you?," it is necessary to understand which of the previous questions it references. Because the vacation plan topic[3] occurred some time ago in the interaction, Shun fails to provide immediate uptake, perhaps indicating that he does not follow what she means by the question "how about (.) you.." Accordingly, Emi adds an increment "upcoming (.) spring." at line 9, and initiates self-repair with "what're you going to do:.." Finally, at lines 10 and 11, Shun is able to provide his answer—the second pair part to Emi's question as selected next speaker.

```
                            08→E: [how about (.) you. huhuh
                            09    upcoming (.) spring.=what're you going to do:.
```

Figure 2. Explicit addressing with the set of gaze direction and hand gesture

Addressing a question to multiple co-participants with the set of "gaze direction plus hand gesture"

The set of "gaze direction plus hand gesture" also happens when questions are addressed to multiple co-participants. As mentioned in the preceding section, when a question includes the reference term "you," it usually indicates that one person among a group of co-participants has been selected as the next speaker. However, "you" can also be used to address multiple recipients, and it was observed that the L2 speakers in this study utilized the "gaze direction plus hand gesture" embodied action to direct a question that includes the reference term "you" to all of the co-participants, and therefore display that they were interested in receiving responses from *all* of the co-participants, not solely from one of them. The conversation from which Extract 3 is derived occurred a few weeks prior to the spring vacation of the participants' university. Ryo brought up a new topic, which was concerned with that upcoming spring vacation.

Extract 3

```
01   R:    mmmm

02         (.)
           Re[H]
           Sx___
           Ex___

03→R:  what di- >ah what will you< do (.) in your (.)
                  Rs[H]         Re[H]        Rx[H]
           Sx   Sr_____
           Er_____
```

```
04         spring vacation.
                       _____Re_____
             Sr_____Se__
             Er_____

05         (1.4)
06   E:    what did I do?
07   R:    yah
08         (0.2)
09   R:    will you do. (.) [spring vacation.
10   E:                     [°a:h.    will you do°.
```

At lines 3 and 4, Ryo asks a question by saying "what di- >ah what will you< do (.) in your (.) spring vacation.." However, just before that, at line 2, Ryo directs his gaze at Emi and moves his left hand toward her, and when Emi returns her gaze to him, Ryo starts the question at line 3. Therefore, we can see this question was firstly designed to address Emi. However, just after Ryo starts his question, he also secures Shun's gaze.[4] Then, Ryo cuts off, and directs his gaze and a similar hand gesture to Shun, while he initiates self-repair by saying ">ah what will you< do (.)" and restarts the question from the beginning. Up to this point, then, Ryo has used gaze direction and hand gesture, to show that he is addressing the question to both Emi *and* Shun. In other words, he is publicly displaying that he is eliciting a response from Shun as well as Emi.

While Ryo is conducting repair, his gaze and hand gesture move from Shun to Emi as shown in Figures 3 and 4. At the timing of his production of ">ah what will" in line 3 his gaze is at Shun and he is holding his left hand toward Shun. Then, he moves his gaze direction and left hand, and by the time he says "you< do (.)" his gaze and left hand are both completely directed at Emi.[5] Subsequently, Ryo continues to shift his gaze and left hand direction, and while he is saying "in your (.)," his gaze is paused in the space between Shun and Emi, and his left hand is likewise set in the middle position (Figure 5). At this point too, it appears Ryo is still addressing the question to both Shun and Emi.

Finally, at the end of Ryo's utterance, just as he says "vacation," Ryo directs his gaze at Emi again, and completes his question (Figure 6). Because Ryo's gaze is on Emi at this point, it appears he has selected Emi as the next speaker. Shun, who is not selected, also directs his gaze at Emi—displaying his understanding that Emi has been selected as the next speaker. Emi herself also initiates repair to clarify if Ryo is asking her about the last spring vacation or this coming one, at line 6, to answer Ryo's question.[6]

Though Ryo selects Emi as the next speaker in the end, in the process of constructing his question, he clearly displays that he is addressing both Shun and

Emi—showing he is open to hearing each co-participant's upcoming vacation plan.[7] In this way, Ryo utilizes gaze direction and hand gestures as interactional resources and sophisticatedly manages this moment of the interaction.

Figure 3. Ryo first looks and points at Shun

Figure 4. Ryo shifts his gaze and speaker-selection gesture to Emi

Figure 5. Ryo pauses his gaze and gesture in the middle position

Figure 6. Ryo shifts his gaze and gesture back toward Emi a second time

The negotiation of next speakership

This study also examined how the L2 speakers in our data drew co-participants' attention and obtained a turn. In this section, we discuss the L2 speakers' emergent movement for establishing upcoming speakership in multi-party conversation.

According to Sacks, Schegloff, and Jefferson (1974), the self-selector who gets the turn is the one who starts as early as possible at a transition-relevance place. In order to achieve this early start and finely coordinate a timely entry into talk, a range of practices can be implemented, including pre-starts like "well" and "so," recycled turn beginnings, nonverbal starts like facial expressions and in-breaths, and so on (Sacks, Schegloff, & Jefferson, 1974; Schegloff, 1987, 1996). In addition, Mondada (2007) describes how actions such as head movements, gaze directions and pointing gestures take place in pre-initial turn positions, that is, before the completion of the current speaker's turn, and therefore strongly project the beginning of a possible next turn.

It is important for learners to know how to jump into a conversation, or they will potentially lose opportunities for participation and learning. Though self-selection is probably the most challenging for L2 speakers, to enhance their chances of becoming the next speaker, we found that, like L1 speakers, L2 speakers can negotiate next speakership in the turn-initial position or even before the completion of the current speaker's turn. In this section, we focus on two such practices that possible next-speakers utilize to attract their co-participants' attention and thereby obtain the next turn at talk. The next-speaker negotiation techniques we will discuss are (1) displays of listening before the completion of the current speaker's turn, and (2) the abrupt "AHH!"-token at the turn-initial position.

Display of listening

In Extract 4, we can see that Emi uses various receipt tokens to show that she is listening during Ryo's talk and thus attracts his attention—a public display which results in Emi successfully obtaining a turn and starting to talk. At the opening of the extract, Ryo is discussing his need to take the TOEFL test.[8] Midway through his explanation, Emi aligns as a recipient by carrying out displays of uptake, and eventually obtains a turn to become the next speaker.

Extract 4

```
01  R:   I need a: (0.8) toefl score (.) over (0.7)
         Rx             Rs                 Rx
         Sr
         Er   Ex   Er


02→E:    mmm?
         Er
         Rx
         Sr


03  R:   nine(.)ty::: (.) w- >I don't know< (.) because
         Rs             Rx              Rs Rx
         Sr
         Er


04       I've never (0.5) I've never taken the exam?
                                    Rs        Re




05→E:    °mmhm°=
         Er
         Re  Rs
         Sr


06  R:   taken toefl (0.7) but (.) hehe
         Rs            Rx
         Sr
         Er
```

```
07         [.hh do-]

08→E:      [oh are-] are you going to study abroad?
           Er_____
           Rx_____Re_____
           Sr_____Se___Sr


09         (0.8)
10  R:     yeah: I want to go: [abroad
11  E:                         [Mmm?
12  R:     so (.) I need toefl scores.
```

While Ryo talks about his need to take the TOEFL test and the required score at line 1, he is gazing and addressing his talk to Shun, not actually to Emi.[9] Elsewhere in the data set, when the talk is not directly addressed to her, Emi quietly listens. For example, while Shun was discussing his plan before the talk shown here, Emi was listening quietly without providing any receipt tokens. However, in this extract, even though the talk is not directly addressed to her, at line 2, Emi vocalizes "mmm?," displaying that she is interested and listening. This does not immediately result in Ryo's gaze being directed to Emi because this response token happens at a moment when Ryo averts his gaze from Shun, looks at the table, and is "doing thinking," at the end of line 1. In addition, at lines 3 and 4, Ryo is initiating forward-oriented repair, which makes publicly available to the other participants that he is conducting a solitary word search (Goodwin & Goodwin, 1986), trying to recall the necessary test score. He is directing and redirecting his gaze between Shun and other places, such as the surface of the table. However, when Ryo says "exam?" in "I've never taken the exam?" at line 4, he shifts his gaze from Shun to Emi, and directs the talk to her. Immediately following that, at line 5, Emi again displays that she is listening by saying "°mmhm°." Then, at line 6, when Ryo has trouble continuing his sentence and laughs, at line 7, Emi takes this as a permissible point of entry into the talk. Even though there are micro-pauses and a short pause at lines 3 and 4, due to a variety of prosodic features in the delivery, including the continuing intonation before the pauses, the prolonging of the final vowel sound in "nine (.) ty:::," and the abrupt cut-off in "(.) w-," it is hearable that Ryo is still attempting to self-initiate repair, which involves maintaining the turn at talk. Therefore, at line 5, Emi merely produces a receipt token rather than taking a fuller turn. However, when Ryo's repair does not reach completion and the complete figure of the test score is not delivered in line 8, Emi finely co-ordinates her timely entry into the talk by adopting self-selection techniques that have been found in L1 talk, such as progressional overlap (Jefferson, 1983), overlap-absorption by the turn-entry device "oh" (Sacks, Schegloff, & Jefferson, 1974, p. 719) and a recycled turn beginning "are-] are you" (Schegloff, 1987, p. 80). In short, Emi employs a display of listening while her co-participant is speaking in order to draw the current speaker's attention. Then she waits for an appropriate point of entry, utilizes self-selection techniques for making an early start, and successfully obtains a turn at talk.

The abrupt "AHH!" token

In Extract 5, we can see that Ryo uses an abrupt "AHH!" token to become the next speaker. Emi says she plans to become a schoolteacher, and Shun asks how long she plans to continue studying. As Emi directs her answer to Shun, and they look at each other and nod, Ryo abruptly says "AHH!" (line 6). By doing so, Ryo secures a display of recipiency from his co-participants in the form of gaze before his actual turn beginning, and is thereby able to carry out an early start.

Extract 5

```
01   E:   I think I'll (1.8) study (0.9) to be a teacher?
              Er_____Es___Er_____
              Re_____Rx_____
              Se_____Sx

02        (1.2)

03   E:   mmmm
              Es__
              Rx__
              Sx((nodding))

04   S:   until graduating? or [(   )
              Se_____
              Rx___Rs_____
              Er___Es_____

05   E:                         [yeah
                                 Es((nodding))
                                 Rs___
                                 Se((nodding))
```

```
06→R:    AHH! (0.6) do [you-
         Rs___Re[H]_____
         Se_ Sr_____
         Es_ Er_____

07  E:              [yeah=
                    Er____
                    Re____
                    Sr____

08  R:   ahh (.) do you have any (0.8)
09       >how can I say< the (0.5)
10       jo:b (0.7) <in the> (.) next (.) years.
11  E:   I've justa got a (0.6)
12       °I've° just got a call?
```

At line 4, Shun directs a question to Emi, asking if she plans to continue studying to become a teacher until she graduates, and Emi responds at line 5. While responding, Emi is gazing at Shun and nodding, and even after her vocalized affirmation "yeah," she continues to move her head up and down slightly while her gaze is directed at Shun. Meanwhile, Shun is also looking at Emi, and he keeps nodding in a similar manner. In contrast, at line 4 Ryo shifts his gaze direction to Shun, and then keeps it on Shun. At precisely the point where the fifth stroke of Emi's head movement finishes in line 5, Ryo takes it as a permissible point of entry into the talk, and at line 6, he starts speaking. At the beginning of his turn, Ryo produces an "AHH!" at a volume that is noticeably higher than the surrounding talk. Tokens such as "oh" in English and "ah" in Japanese are epistemic markers that signal a change of knowledge state (Heritage, 1984; Nishizaka, 1999, 2001). Therefore, it appears that with this token, Ryo displays that he has suddenly noticed something in the just-prior talk, and subsequently initiates a new question, directing it to Emi after a short pause.

This turn-initial "AHH!" token does two kinds of interactional work; it draws all of the co-participants' attention, and it also works as a turn-entry device. Firstly, it is an attempt to establish the availability of a recipient so that the actual forthcoming turn beginning will be properly attended to. Just prior to "AHH!" at line 6, Shun and Emi have been looking at each other and nodding, so Ryo needs to attract their attention at the turn beginning. Immediately after producing "AHH!," the other two co-participants' both shift their gaze to Ryo. Then, having secured their displays of recipiency, during a 0.6-second pause, Ryo shifts his gaze from Shun to Emi with an accompanying pointing hand gesture, and he displays that he is addressing his question to Emi. Emi also responds to Ryo's cut-off ("do you-") and aligns as the recipient of the question, by uttering "yeah" at line 7 while looking towards Ryo—showing her attention.

Secondly, "AHH!" is employed as a turn-entry device, realizing Ryo's early start at line 6. Because there is a gap in the talk after Emi produces "yeah" at line 5, Ryo's "AHH!" might not look precisely positioned relative to the prior turn. However, note that it is precisely timed relative to Shun and Emi's nodding after Emi's "yeah." Turn-entry devices make it possible to begin a turn without projecting the constructional features of the turn. So, before either Shun or Emi started speaking, Ryo was able to start his turn. Even though he might not be completely ready, once he takes a turn at line 6, Ryo selects Emi as the next speaker through nonverbal addressing during the 0.6-second pause and holds the turn through the employment of a variety of interactional practices at lines 8–10. After Ryo restarts with "do you" to compensate for the overlapped turn beginning with Emi's talk at line 7, he successfully holds the turn while conducting an overt word search featuring self-addressed questioning (">how can I say<"), a prolonged vowel sound ("jo:b"), and other intonational features.

It appears then Ryo utilizes the "AHH!" token as an interactional practice which helps establish him as next speaker before the actual beginning of a TCU, combining it with other practices such as a restart and vowel elongation. Ryo might sound rather awkward here, but this practice works in attracting his co-participants' attention and allows him to accomplish a timely entry into the talk. He also combines this practice with other interactional resources to participate skillfully in the unfolding interaction.

Conclusion

In this chapter, we have examined several short segments of group conversations conducted between EFL speakers in a university conversation room in Japan, focusing on turn-taking practices. Through observing the interactions, the study explicated one aspect of the organization of conversation room interaction. We showed how L2 speakers achieved skilled turn-allocation, using a variety of interactional resources, including those documented in previous CA studies of L1 talk.

Firstly, in our data, we examined the participants' speaker-selection practices and found that they employed gazing as an addressing technique, a method which L1 speakers also use. The L2 speakers in our data characteristically combined hand gestures with gaze direction—utilizing this set of "gaze direction plus hand gesture" to designate specifically who it is that is being addressed. Secondly, it was found that the set of "gaze direction plus hand gesture" also happens with questions addressed to multiple co-participants. The speaker directed the set of "gaze direction plus hand gesture" to both of the other co-participants with a question which included the reference term "you," displaying that the speaker was interested in hearing responses from both the co-participants, not only from one of them. In short, they oriented to the set of "gaze direction plus hand gesture" as a situated resource in the management of conversational interaction. This also points to the open nature of some questions typically found in language conversation rooms, where topics are frequently raised in order to extend the talk and keep participants involved in the communication. Embodied speaker selection practices such as these help flag the question as potentially serial (Hauser, 2008), since it makes clear that a later version of the question will be available to whichever recipient does not respond first.

Thirdly, we examined the L2 speakers' emergent movement for establishing upcoming speakership, and found that interlocutors drew co-participants' attention and obtained a turn through the use of displays of listening, and through the use of an abrupt delivery of the change-of-state token "AHH!," combining both with other interactional resources. The participants openly displayed that they were listening prior to the completion of the current speaker's turn, and thereby drew their co-participants' attention for the purpose of successfully obtaining a turn and starting to talk. They also used the "AHH!" token as a turn-entry device, drawing co-participants' attention and finely coordinating their timely entries into talk.

As is clear from the above discussion, L2 speakers can display their interactional competence as equal participants in talk in conversation rooms, without any intervention from teachers by organizing and structuring these interactions on their own. This points to one of the greatest pedagogical values of such conversation rooms; they offer the opportunity to experience interactions that are similar to ordinary conversations. Ideally L2 speakers should have access to both traditional classrooms *and* conversation rooms as sites for learning. The classroom is a place where teachers organize interaction carefully so that students can learn the target language efficiently, while conversation room interaction offers L2 speakers the opportunity of experiencing the management of talk-in-interaction on their own. This is especially significant in EFL environments where it is often difficult for L2 speakers to participate in ordinary conversation on a regular basis. If institutions recognize the value of conversation-for-learning and facilitate it through conversation rooms, free-access spaces and so forth—in conjunction with classroom-based language instruction—it is extremely beneficial, if not ideal, for language learners. As researchers, we need to continue our investigation into what kinds of interactional practices occur in conversation rooms so that institutions can make better use of such learning environments.

Acknowledgements

The authors would like to express sincere thanks to Professor Gabriele Kasper, Dr. Tim Greer, and the anonymous reviewers for their helpful suggestions and guidance during the preparation of this chapter. This work was supported by JSPS KAKENHI Grant Numbers 22720198 and 24720250.

Notes

1. Line 5 shows at what points, relative to lines 3 and 4, each participant begins his or her continuing gaze, with the lower-case letters identifying at whom they are gazing.
2. According to Laurier (2008), drinking can be an interactional resource, which affects the talk organization.
3. Just prior to this extract Emi was talking about her spring vacation plan. This topic evolved into her future plan to be a schoolteacher, and subsequently, the required teachers' employment test.
4. As can be seen in Figure 3, Ryo is also holding a coffee mug in the hand he gestures with.
5. Because the spring vacation plan was a new topic introduced by Ryo's question, the time frame ("in your (.) spring vacation.") was necessary to understand Ryo's intention. Therefore, this point (after ">ah what will you< do (.)") is not hearable as the completion.
6. Ryo's question at lines 3 and 4 might have been problematic because he started his question with "what di-." Most probably he was going to say "what di(*d you do?*)," and this would explain Emi's request for clarification.
7. Chronologically, Extract 3 precedes Extract 2 in the raw data. Perhaps, Ryo's topic initiation of spring vacation plans in Extract 3 is related to why Emi asks Shun what his spring vacation plan was in Extract 2 in the previous section.
8. The Test of English as a Foreign Language (TOEFL) is administered by Educational Testing Service (ETS), a nonprofit educational testing and assessment organization headquartered in New Jersey (USA). It is quite common for Japanese students to take this test before embarking on study abroad programs (typically to the USA).
9. Ryo is primarily addressing his talk to Shun because he is treating both Shun and himself as co-examinees. Before this segment of talk occurred, the topic centered on Shun's plan to prepare for the TOEFL test. The topic involved a question from Ryo to Shun, asking when he would take the test—and the discussion lasted for an extensive number of turns. After Shun finished talking about his preparation schedule for the test, Ryo started to explain that he also needed to take the TOEFL test in line 1.

References

Carroll, D. (2004). Restarts in novice turn beginning: Disfluencies or interactional achievements? In R. Gardner, & J. Wagner (Eds.), *Second language conversations* (pp. 201–220). London: Continuum.

Carroll, D. (2005). Vowel-marking as an interactional resource in Japanese novice ESL conversation. In K. Richards, & P. Seedhouse (Eds.), *Applying conversation analysis* (pp. 214–234). Basingstoke/New York: Palgrave.

Drew, P., & Heritage, J. (1992). Analyzing talk at work: An introduction. In P. Drew, & J. Heritage (Eds.), *Talk at work: Interaction in institutional settings* (pp. 3–65). Cambridge: Cambridge University Press.

Firth, A., & Wagner, J. (1997). On discourse, communication, and (some) fundamental concepts in SLA research. *Modern Language Journal, 81*, 285–300.

Gardner, R. (2007). 'Broken' starts: Bricolage in turn starts in second language talk. In Zhu Hua, P. Seedhouse, Li Wei, & V. Cook (Eds.) *Language learning and teaching as social inter-action* (pp. 58–71). Basingstoke/New York: Palgrave.

Goodwin, C. (1979). The interactive construction of a sentence in natural conversation. In G. Psathas (Ed.), *Everyday language: Studies in ethnomethodology* (pp. 97–121). New York: Irvington Publishers.

Goodwin, C. (1980). Restarts, pauses, and the achievement of a state of mutual gaze at turn-beginning. *Sociological Inquiry, 50*, 272–302.

Goodwin, C., & Goodwin, M. H. (1986). Gesture and coparticipation in the activity of searching for a word. *Semiotica, 62*, 51–75.

Greer, T., & Potter, H. (2008). Turn-taking practices in multi-party EFL oral proficiency tests. *Journal of Applied Linguistics, 5*, 297–320.

Hauser, E. (2008). Nonformal institutional interaction in a conversation club: Conversation partners' questions. *Journal of Applied Linguistics, 5*, 275–295.

Hauser, E. (2009). Turn-taking and primary speakership during a student discussion. In H. t. Nguyen, & G. Kasper (Eds.), *Talk in Interaction: Multilingual perspectives* (pp. 215–244). Honolulu: University of Hawai'i, National Foreign Language Resource Center.

Heritage, J. (1984). A change-of-state token and aspects of its sequential placement. In J. M. Atkinson, & J. Heritage (Eds.), *Structures of social action: Studies in conversation analysis* (pp. 299–345). New York: Cambridge University Press.

Jung, K (2004). L2 vocabulary development through conversation: A conversation analysis. *Second Language Studies, 23*, 27–55.

Kasper, G. (2004). Participant orientations in German conversation-for-learning. *Modern Language Journal, 88*, 551–567.

Kasper, G., & Kim, Y. H. (2004). Handling sequentially inapposite responses. In Zhu Hua, P. Seedhouse, Li Wei, & V. Cook (Eds.), *Language learning and teaching as social inter-action* (pp. 22–41). Basingstoke/New York: Palgrave.

Laurier, E. (2008). Drinking up endings: Conversational resources of the cafe. *Language & Communication, 28*, 165–181.

Lerner, G. H. (1996). On the place of linguistic resources in the organization of talk-in interaction: "Some person" reference in multi-party conversation. *Pragmatics, 6*, 281–294.

Lerner, G. H. (2003). Selecting next speaker: The context-sensitive operation of a context-free organization. *Language in Society, 32*, 177–201.

Mondada, L. (2007). Multimodal resources for turn-taking: Pointing and the emergence of possible next speakers. *Discourse Studies, 9*, 195–225.

Markee, N. P. (2000). *Conversation analysis.* Mahwah, NJ: Lawrence Earlbaum Associates.

Mori, J. (2002). Task design, plan, and development of talk-in-interaction: An analysis of a small group activity in a Japanese language classroom. *Applied Linguistics, 23*, 323–347.

Mori, J. (2003). The construction of interculturality: A study of initial encounters between Japanese and American students. *Research on Language and Social Interaction, 36*, 143–184.

Mori, J., & Hayashi, M. (2006). The achievement of intersubjectivity through embodied completion: A study of interactions between first and second language speakers. *Applied Linguistics, 27*(2), 195–219.

Nishizaka, A. (1999). Kaiwa bunseki no renshuu: Soogokooi no shigen toshiteno iiyodomi [An exercise in conversation analysis]. In H. Yoshii, H. Yamada, & A. Nishizaka (Eds.), *Kaiwa Bunseki e no Shootai [An Introduction to Conversation Analysis]* (pp. 71–100). Tokyo: Sekai Shiso Sha.

Nishizaka, A. (2001). *Kokoro to kooi: Esunomesodorojii no shiten [Mind and Activity: From an Ethnomethodological Point of View].* Tokyo: Iwanami Shoten.

Olsher, D. (2004). Talk and gesture: The embodied completion of sequential actions in spoken interaction. In R. Gardner, & J. Wagner (Eds.), *Second language conversations* (pp. 221–245). London: Continuum.

Sacks, H., Schegloff, E. A., & Jefferson, G. (1974). A simplest systematic for the organization of turn-taking for conversation. *Language, 50*, 696–735.

Schegloff, E. A. (1987). Recycled turn beginnings: A precise repair mechanism in conversation's turn-taking organization. In G. Button, & J. R. E. Lee (Eds.), *Talk and social organization* (pp. 70–85). Clevedon: Multilingual Matters.

Schegloff, E. A. (1992). Repair after next turn: The last structurally provided defense of intersubjectivity in conversation. *American Journal of Sociology, 97*, 1295–1345.

Schegloff, E. A. (1996). Turn organization: One intersection of grammar and interaction. In E. Ochs, E. A. Schegloff, & S. A. Thompson (Eds.), *Interaction and grammar* (pp. 52–133). Cambridge: Cambridge University Press.

Schegloff, E. A., Koshik, I., Jacoby, S., & Olsher, D. (2002). Conversation analysis and applied linguistics. *Annual Review of Applied Linguistics, 22*, 3–31.

Seedhouse, P. (2011). Conversation analytic research into language teaching and learning. In E. Hinkel (Ed.), *Handbook of research in second language teaching and learning* (pp. 345–363). Abingdon: Routledge.

Wong, J., & Waring, H. Z. (2010). *Conversation analysis and second language pedagogy.* New York, NY: Routledge.

Appendix: Transcription conventions

[	Point of overlap onset
]	Point of overlap termination
=	Latched utterances
(1.4)	Interval between utterances (in seconds)
(.)	Very short untimed pause (0.2 seconds or less; a micropause)
e:r the:::	Lengthening of the preceding sound
-	Abrupt cutoff
?	Rising intonation, not necessarily a question
!	Animated or emphatic tone
,	Low-rising intonation, suggesting continuation
.	Falling (final) intonation
CAPITALS	Increased volume relative to surrounding talk
do you	Underlining of (part of) an utterance is used to indicate some form of stress or emphasis, either by increased loudness or higher pitch
↑ ↓	Marked shifts into higher or lower pitch in the utterance following the arrow
° °	Utterances between degree signs are noticeably quieter than surrounding talk
< >	Talk enclosed within angle brackets is produced more slowly or more drawn out than neighboring talk
> <	Talk surrounded by reversed angle brackets is produced more quickly than neighboring talk
( )	A stretch of unclear, inaudible or unintelligible speech
→	Marks features of special interest
((nodding))	Non-speech activity or transcriptionist's comment(s)
R:	Identified speaker (participant identifier)
Es	Gaze identifier (the uppercase letter indicates the participant doing gazing; the lowercase letter indicates at whom the gaze is directed)

Rx	A lowercase 'x' following a participant identifier indicates that the participant is gazing at something other than an interactant (typically at the wall or down at the surface of the table)
Es_Er	The underline following (and between) gaze identifiers marks continuation of gaze
[H]	Starting point of a hand gesture
▽	An inverted white triangle in the figures indicates the precise point in the talk at which that particular screen grab was taken

Working Through Disagreement in English Academic Discussions Between L1 Speakers of Japanese and L1 Speakers of English

Noël Houck
California State Polytechnic University Pomona

Seiko Fujii
The University of Tokyo, Japan

In this chapter, we investigate disagreement sequences in academic discussions between pairs consisting of a first-language speaker of English and a first-language speaker of Japanese, speaking English (EE-JE pairs). Discussions were analyzed to determine how these pairs work through disagreement to resolution. In particular we considered what types of interactional responses encouraged or discouraged discussion, and by whom a specific type of interactional behavior was employed. Using conversation analytic resources and incorporating a 3-Turn disagreement sequence as the basic interactional sequence for extended academic disagreements (Fujii & Houck, 2011), we identified verbal and nonverbal interactional behaviors in the EE-JE pairs that maintained or expanded on points of disagreement or that brought about abandonment of the disagreement.

Background

Over the last 30 years, research on the interactional features of disagreements has burgeoned. Working from a conversation analytic (CA) perspective, researchers have produced detailed descriptions of the sequential characteristics of disagreement in English conversation. Their work builds on recognition of disagreements as a dispreferred response, with pre-disagreement delays such as inter-turn gaps, pro-forma agreements, anticipatory accounts (Pomerantz, 1984; Schegloff, 2007), repair initiation (Mori, 1999), and the like.

In a separate thread, work on verbal disputes has treated disagreements as social interactions for which a sequence of stages or rules can be established, with a number of studies concentrating on the turns subsequent to disagreement – turns that take into account the participants' orientation to their contrasting positions. These post-disagreement turns have been the focus of research on argumentation in discourse. Within this strand attempts have been made to describe the moves or discourse acts available to the participants using an extended version of speech act theory (van Eemeren, Grootendorst, Jackson, & Jacobs, 1993) or a series of pair parts (Coulter, 1990). Using conversation analytic techniques and concepts, Coulter described the turn structure of family disputes as a 3-turn sequence, which he referred to as an "argument sequence." This sequence consists of an assertion by A (referred to henceforth as a claim), a disagreement by B, and a third turn response by A.

1st A: Declarative assertion (or claim) — assertion designed to make a point rather than to state a simple fact
2nd B: Disagreement — counter-assertion, challenge (including pre-disagreement tokens)
3rd A: Response to B Disagreement — including
   a. Backdown (modification of A's original claim)
   b. Reassertion (expansive recycling of A's original position)
or c. "New assertion" (essentially, topic shift or change)

While these are not strictly sequential turns, they represent a series of closely related actions, with the 2nd directly responsive to the 1st, and the 3rd a recognizable "next" action given the 1st and 2nd. As described by Coulter, the 3rd turn may take two general directions. Disagreement may be immediately resolved through agreement or abandonment of the issue through topic shift, or further discussion of the points can ensue. The resulting episodes may be described as *activity types* (Levinson, 1992), "discursive goal-oriented entities which comprise more than two turns and display structural properties which constrain the functions and interpretations of verbal contributions occurring in their course" (Gruber, 1998, p. 476).

For the most part, research on "argument sequences" has been limited to those contexts in which the disagreeing turn is expressed relatively explicitly, with little or no mitigation, and has then examined how the interaction evolved. Coulter (1990) provides for backing down or changing the topic after a disagreement or counter-assertion by B, as well as for continuing the argument in the third-turn "opportunity space" (p. 189). In those instances in which A continues the discussion by questioning B's 2nd or by defending A's own 1st (the original claim), there is consensus among most researchers that preference organization generally shifts, and disagreement in the discussion that follows is treated by participants as preferred, that is, produced with minimal delay and mitigation (Bilmes, 1991; Gruber, 1998; Kotthoff, 1993).

Disagreement sequences

A great deal of work has gone into describing *argument sequences*, with disagreement defined as an orientation to the nature of a recipient's response to an assertion; however, what constitutes a disagreement in an argument sequence is still under discussion. Thus, while researchers such as Coulter (1990), Bilmes (1991), and Gruber (1998) define *argument* as a series of relatively direct types of disagreements, less confrontational *disagreement sequences* may have different interactional characteristics. Building on the idea that the relevant absence of a preferred action allows the inference that some other possibility is "covertly present" (Bilmes, 1988, p. 166), some investigators have included less direct forms of resistance in their accounts. For instance, in addition to a contradiction, challenge, or claim of irrelevance, Muntigl and Turnbull (1998) added counterclaim – a contrasting claim that does not directly contradict A's claim. Likewise, Mori (1999), describing disagreements in Japanese, noted the occurrence of partial disagreement (indicated by, for example, exceptions and qualifications), as well as accounts pleading lack of knowledge or the complexity of the issue under discussion.

Thus, some interactions with recognizable divergence of the participants' positions may not be accurately characterized as argument sequences. As Mori (1999) observes, "Most disagreeing responses ... fall somewhere in between complete agreement and direct opposition" (p. 93). A wide range of responses can be perceived as disagreement, suggesting that a post-disagreement preference for disagreement may be dependent on the involvement and cooperativeness of the interlocutors themselves (Gruber, 1998). Since we will be discussing instances that do not necessarily involve direct expressions of disagreement, we will refer to these interactions as disagreement sequences. While these disagreement sequences are not strictly argument sequences, they have been shown to follow a similar trajectory (Fujii & Houck, 2011).

Disagreement among language learners

Studies of naturally occurring disagreement sequences have, until recently, been based on conversations between speakers from the same speech community. In the last decade, however, investigation into disagreement and argumentation has been extended to discussions of opinions on familiar, often controversial, topics in second language and foreign language classrooms. In 2004, Bardovi-Harlig and Salsbury analyzed disagreements in group discussions by learners of English in a university ESL classroom. Examination of data collected over a year revealed a sequence of developmental stages in learners' strategies for initiating disagreement. More recently, in cross-sectional studies contrasting disagreements by students at different levels of foreign language study, Dippold (2011) and Pekarek Doehler and Pochon-Berger (2011) observed recorded interactions of university learners of German in England (GFL) and secondary school learners of French in Switzerland (FFL), respectively. In both studies learners at higher levels of proficiency displayed a wider range of strategies for accomplishing disagreement and for extending disagreement sequences. These strategies included linguistic and discursive resources (e.g., post-disagreement accounts and examples), as well as a greater variety of conversational structures.

In contrast, in a study of low proficiency learners that tracked verbal and nonverbal behavior in small group discussions among first year college students in an English course in Japan, Fujimoto (2010, 2012) found that, given sufficient time and support, even students with very limited fluency were able to carry out disagreement sequences in English with highly complex expressions of and responses to disagreement. Meanwhile in a study of contrasting opinions by advanced language learners, Sharma (2012) described the resolution of disagreements in interactions by groups of graduate students in a university ESL writing class, focusing particularly on the practices used in concession sequences.

Thus, over the last decade, close analysis of classroom discussions has resulted in a detailed description of disagreement sequences by language learners at a range of proficiency levels.

Focus of the chapter

In this chapter, we extend the investigation of what we will refer to as disagreement sequences to the exchange of ideas common in academic discussions between members of pairs consisting of a first language (L1) speaker of English speaking English (EE) and an L1 speaker of Japanese speaking English (JE). The result is a set of interactions in which the disagreements are less rancorous or polarized than in most three-turn arguments, but which are realized in sequences in which contrasting positions are conveyed. We examine sequences that evolve after some form of non-agreement, concentrating on how disagreement sequences are negotiated by JE participants interacting with EE partners and how EE participants respond to their JE partners' contributions. In particular we analyze sequences terminating with both participants clearly accepting the same position or explicitly acknowledging an unresolvable divergence of positions and those culminating in weak agreement or lacking explicit resolution; we then attempt to account for moves by participants that lead to a mutually acceptable resolution or to abandonment of a position.

This study differs from previous investigations of disagreement in that the disagreements involve positions on cognitively challenging academic questions (but see Sharma, 2012), rather than opinions on issues familiar to the participants. In addition, the discussions took place not between two language learners or between speakers from the same speech community, but between colleagues, one from Japan and one from an English-speaking country. Both were graduate students in the same class at an American university in Japan, and both were speaking English, the language of instruction at the university and the first language of one member of the pair.

Data

The data reported in this chapter are part of a larger project involving dyadic interactions between 1) English speakers speaking English (EE), 2) Japanese speakers speaking Japanese (JJ), and 3) English speakers speaking English and Japanese speakers speaking English (JE). For the analysis reported in the present chapter, the participants were seven EE-JE pairs, all of whom were enrolled in a program with a minimum TOEFL score of 575 required for admission. EE-JE pairs were chosen for the analysis in the hope of gaining insight into how discussions between members with different L1s and different experiences/backgrounds in academic discussion would resolve differences of opinion.

With that in mind, it should be noted that the EE students were residents of Japan, most of whom had lived in Japan for five years or more and several of whom were fluent in Japanese. The JE participants had learned their English primarily in Japan, with only short-term, if any, experience in an English speaking country. Most of the EE and JE students in the study were employed as English teachers at the time of the data collection.

The data were collected during a course in second language acquisition. The course was one of the final required classes, so students had over a year of experience with graduate level reading, writing, and discussion. In the data examined in this chapter, each of the pairs is discussing an academic article by the linguist Robert Bley-Vroman (1987), in which he argues that second language (L2) acquisition resembles general skill learning, but has little in common with L1 acquisition. He presents 10 dimensions along which he suggests that obvious differences between L1 and L2 acquisition and similarities between L2 acquisition and general skill learning exist. A task sheet was provided listing the ten categories and the three types of learning discussed (see Appendix A). Participants were instructed to discuss each of Bley-Vroman's 30 claims (i.e., 30 points on which they could agree or disagree) and to decide jointly whether or not they accepted each claim.

The article was selected because its claims were (and still are) controversial, and because many of the terms are not clearly defined (e.g., *general failure*, *negative evidence*, *general skill learning* – which is not defined in the article, but only exemplified). Students were not required to agree; on the other hand, since the goal of the task was to familiarize them with a variety of complex questions related to L2 acquisition, they were encouraged to attempt to resolve differences and clarify ambiguities through discussion. Students were told to review the task sheet beforehand, as they were not permitted to bring the article to the discussion with them. Lack of access to the article forced them to rely on their recall of the author's claims and his characterization of each dimension, thus adding another level of potential disagreement to the discussion. Pairs were given one copy of the task sheet.

The discussions lasted approximately 20 minutes. With the exception of one discussion, all were audio—and video-taped and transcribed, and 28 disagreement sequences were analyzed. Conversation analytic techniques were used to identify the stages in the disagreement sequences. Thus, we identified a) a position-taking by one of the participants regarding one of the task questions (A's claim); b) disagreement—a nonagreeing move by B; and then c) occurrence of a 3rd Turn non-agreeing response by A. Once 1st, 2nd, and 3rd turns were ascertained, the sequence was analyzed turn by turn to its resolution.

Expressing and advancing disagreement

Disagreements during discussion of an assigned text often differ from those among disputants with strongly held positions. They generally revolve around the interpretation of a text and assessment of the author's claims. In the disagreement sequences analyzed in this chapter, students often spent much of the time discussing terminology, comparing interpretations, and assessing the applicability of a set of claims.

In this context, the claims under consideration involved the nature of L1 acquisition, L2 acquisition, and general skill learning. The point of the discussion was a deeper understanding of the issues, so disagreements and 3rd turn responses were generally in service of a congenial comparison of views through attempts to express students' own views and understand positions contrary to their own.

Thus, a discussion that developed beyond an initial disagreement had the potential to stimulate deeper exploration of the assigned question. At the same time, as with any disagreement sequence, after each disagreeing turn (and accompanying delays and accounts), an opportunity generally presented itself to pursue a contrasting point of view or instead to either agree or to withdraw from the disagreement (a move which would most likely be viewed as conceding).

In the following sections, we examine how disagreements were maintained and how their elaboration was encouraged, and, in some cases, how they were abandoned without clear resolution. The discussion explores in particular the nature of JE participants' perseverance in disagreement, the interactional resources they employed to develop their point of view, and how they withdrew from disagreement. In focusing on the JE participant, we in no way wish to detract from the role played by the EE partner in bringing about the sequences under consideration. Nor do we wish to claim that these are resources employed in academic disagreements exclusively by JE students. What we are saying is that these behaviors were found frequently in the EE-JE interactions we observed.

Discussions involving disagreement can be maintained through the use of mutually recognized or accommodated interactional resources. On the part of a participant wishing to express or even to delay disagreement, these may involve nonverbal displays or responses that do not recognizably address the prior claim. On the other hand, elaboration of a disagreeing position can be elicited through the use of restatement and questioning. Or it may be advanced by the disagreeing partner through creation of opportunities to complete the disagreeing turn – a strategy that offers the original claimant an occasion to either align with or oppose the contrasting position before it has been fully articulated.

Expressing disagreement nonverbally

One means of expressing disagreement rarely mentioned in discussions of disagreement episodes is the use of nonverbal resources to convey nonacceptance. While significant research has been devoted to gaze and the importance in establishing and maintaining hearer gaze during a turn at talk – both by speakers speaking their L1 (C. Goodwin, 1981; Goodwin & Goodwin, 1992) and by L2 speakers (Carroll, 2004), little has been reported on the effect of withholding gaze. Two notable exceptions are work on the lack of gaze and nonalignment of posture by children resisting parental directives in English and Swedish families (Goodwin & Cekaite, 2013) and Fujimoto's (2012) study on group discussions by novice English learners in which gaze avoidance was associated with disagreement or rejection of an invitation to speak. Thus, mutual gaze is an important behavior in communicating not only attentiveness, but availability to respond and even acceptance of the action of the prior talk.

In Excerpt 1, nonacceptance at a point of anticipated agreement is expressed through posture and gaze. Prior to the extract, Hiro and Stu are attempting to determine whether individuals experience what Bley-Vroman referred to as a "general lack of success" in learning a skill. Prior to the discussion reported in Excerpt 1, Stu has claimed that individuals do not suffer a lack of success in learning a skill (1st), and Hiro has disagreed with a qualifying 2nd ("sometimes yes, sometimes no"). After a long discussion about what is involved in the acquisition of a skill, both agree on the characteristics (it is cognitive, not "domain-specific" – a term used in the article, and it involves activities such as figuring out a puzzle and driving). The key area of disagreement is one that is never dealt with explicitly in the article – whether acquisition of a skill refers to skill learning by an adult or by a child. After extensive disagreement on what constitutes a skill, the resolution begins in Extract 1 with a recycling of Stu's original claim (a recycled 3rd). Pseudonyms are used for all participants.

Excerpt 1 (EJEM5 1c)

```
1        Stu:              [and so it would] be
2   3rd             something pertaining to adults, ((looking
3                   at Hiro)) °I believe.°
4   4th             (1.7) ((looks at Hiro))
5                   ((Hiro looks down at clasped hands))
6        Stu:       ((looking at Hiro, points at him)) >you,
7                   th- you say< both though?
8                   (0.6)
9        Stu:       >we could put,< (.) ((chuckles softly))
10                  okay, both,
11                  (1.0)
12       Hiro:      [u:h
13       Stu:       [>we could put<] ((begins writing))
                    writing--------------------------------
14       Stu:       Hiro:, (0.5) both, (0.3) [Stu,
15       Hiro:                               [°huh°
16                  ((moves paper))
17                  (0.8) ((Hiro reading))
18       Stu:       um, (0.2) adults only,
```

In lines 1–3, Stu states, that "it" (general skill learning) would be "something pertaining to adults," with a mitigating "I believe" (a reformulation of his original claim). Stu raises his eyes to Hiro, who sits still and looks down at his hands with no change in facial expression (lines 4–5) during a 1.7-second pause. Looking at Hiro, Stu recognizes his stance as not only non-agreeing (e.g., a simple turn pass without a commitment to agreement), but disagreeing, a resistance to giving up his original 2nd turn claim. Stu displays recognition of Hiro's position with his response ("you say both though?" lines 6–7). Thus, without a word Hiro has conveyed his non-acceptance of Stu's justification of his point of view. At this point Stu offers a compromise: they can enter different answers under each of their names on the task sheet.

A participant may also delay taking a position by simply not addressing the claim set forth by his partner. In a separate interaction with Stu, Hiro displays his reluctance to accept Stu's position through a series of reflective repetitions. In Excerpt 2, a discussion as to whether people learning a general skill experience general failure reveals differences in the participants' understanding of general skill learning.

Excerpt 2 (EJEM5 2c)

```
                          reading aloud--------------
1            Hiro:        general skill learning,
2            Stu:         [y:es]
                          reading aloud----------------------
3            Hiro:        °[gen]eral- general failure?°
                                       reading aloud-------
4            Stu:         g- oh, general failure,
5                         (0.4)
6            Stu:         <general> [failure,]
                                    reading-----
7            Hiro:                  [failure.] (0.2) °general,
8                         failure,°
9                         (0.4)
10           Stu:         ((looking at Hiro)) g- [does] that mean
11   1st     Hiro:                               [no.]
12           Stu:         everybody fails (.) at everything?
13                        (0.3)
                          reading aloud---------------
14   1st     Hiro:        general skill learning, no. °I would say.°
15                        ((looking at Stu)) cognitive, (0.6) skill.
16                        (1.7)
17           Stu:         ((looks at Hiro)) [well general refers to=
18           Hiro:                          [((whispers as he reads
19                                            to himself))
20           Stu:         =cognitive stuff, usually,
21                        (0.4)
22           Hiro:        ah huh huh huh,
23           Stu:         cognitive e[quals,
24           Hiro:                   [uh-huh, general [failure.
25           Stu:                                     [general,
26           Hiro:        general skill learning. general skill,
27                        general skill learning.
28                        (0.5)
29           Stu:         GENeral failure,
30                        (1.9) ((both looking at paper))
31           Stu:         um.
32                        (0.9) ((both looking at paper))
33   2nd     Stu:         I would say y:es. ((looks at Hiro))
34                        (0.9) ((Stu looking at Hiro))
35           Stu:         very few adults become perfect at
36                        ((establishes eye contact)) (0.3) anything.
37                        (3.7) ((Hiro puts down pen, sits back in
38                        seat, and rubs his neck))
39           Hiro:        °hm:, general failure, general failure.°
40                        (0.9)
```

```
41      Stu:   it's difficult to master, ((looks at Hiro))
42             (.) something like ((makes motion of
43             playing a piano)) playing the piano, you
44             can can always get better,
45      Hiro:  mhm,
46      Stu:   ((looking at Hiro)) but with language,
47             (0.2) we all, (1.1) become, (1.7) uh
48             fluent, and (1.2) accurate speakers.
49             (0.5) ((Hiro points at paper))
50      Hiro:  b- e:h, this item is eh, not talking about,
51             (0.6) L1. (.) nor L2. (.)((points at
52             paper)) L1, L2. (.) This, ((looks at Stu))
53             language.(0.5)
54      Stu:   ((eye contact)) y:es. (.) right.
55      Hiro:  °uhuh°
56      Stu:   general matters,
57      Hiro:  >°general matters.°< (.) [so]
58      Stu:                              [some]thing like,
59             (1.2) playing the- ((looks at Hiro and
60             gestures toward him)) what 's your hobby.
61             (0.2) do you have a hobby?
62             (1.7)
               (8 turns discussing hobby)
71      Stu:   I think the terms ((points to two spots on
72             paper)) are a little va:gue.
73      Hiro:  vague, yeah.
74      Stu:   what does ((points at paper)) general
75             failure mean.
76      Hiro:  °general failure,°
77      Stu:   d- does it mean everybody fails,
78      Hiro:  fails yes, °>general skills,<°
79             (0.5)
80 3rd  Hiro:  ((points at paper decisively)) no. ((sits
81             up with chin up and looks at Stu))
82             (1.5) ((Stu picks up pen and pulls paper
83             toward him))
                     writing----------------------------------
84      Stu:   °okay.° (0.4) general failure, (1.1) n:o?
85      Hiro:  °no.° ((leans over to see writing))
                     writing----------------------------------
86      Stu:   (0.8) okay, (0.5) and uh (.) I'm gonna put
                     writing----
87             a °slash,° ((looks at Hiro))
88             (0.2)
89      Hiro:  okay. ((laughs))
                     writing----------------------------------
90      Stu:   (0.3) <and,> (0.8) with a ((looks at Hiro))
91             question[mark.]
```

```
92    Hiro:            [yeah!] ((laughs))
93    Stu:    that's (.) my fault. ((looks at Hiro and
94            raises his hand)) question mark. I'm
95            confused.
```

In line 11, in response to the question of whether people generally fail at learning a skill, Hiro says "no," followed in line 14 by a complete reassertion and an audibly lower hedge ("no °I would say°"). Stu replies not with his own opinion but with statements about the relationship between general skill and cognitive learning, preceded by *well*, a common indicator of nonagreement (line 17). In lines 17–30 Stu then explains that *general* refers to "cognitive stuff usually, and cognitive equals general failure" – a claim collaboratively completed by Hiro in line 24 (pauses, repetitions deleted). Throughout Stu's review of the meaning of general skill learning, Hiro consults the task sheet (lines 18–19), agrees with Stu's assertions (line 22), and displays his understanding by accurately completing Stu's utterance ("general failure," in line 24), which Stu himself concludes in line 29, with an emphasis on "GENeral." At this point, after a 2.8-second period of relative silence (during which he and Hiro both look at the task sheet), Stu states in line 33 that he would say yes (i.e., people generally fail at learning a skill).

It would seem that Stu's review of the terms has led him to his counterassertion of Hiro's claim. However, despite the fact that Hiro has followed Stu's explanation and displayed what could be taken as agreement, he does not express agreement with Stu. Stu continues his explanation. However, Hiro's occasional attention to the task sheet, alternating with leaning back looking at Stu (and in one case rubbing the back of his neck) convey the impression of someone attempting to solve a problem. In this case, Hiro's problem is perhaps that of reconciling Stu's assertions with his own point of view. He attends to Stu's explanation of general skill learning, and requests clarification when it conflicts with his understanding (lines 50–53). In lines 63–70 (omitted) Stu uses Hiro's experience with a hobby to clarify his point. They return to the question in line 71, with Stu admitting that the terms are vague and posing the question at the heart of the disagreement, "what does general failure mean" (lines 74–75), and "does it mean everybody fails" (line 77). Hiro treats this as a non-rhetorical question, repeating his original claim, lines 78–80, "fails yes, general skills no" (i.e., general failure means everybody fails, and thus it does not apply to general skill learning). They resolve the issue with Stu entering a "no" for Hiro on the task sheet and a question mark for himself.

This rather long discussion is notable for what initially appears as an unyielding position by Hiro, but which, on closer inspection, reveals Hiro's keen involvement in the discussion through his constant reference to the task sheet and clear positions with regard to Stu's explanations (e.g., indicating essential agreement with Stu's characterization of general skill learning, questioning of Stu's reference to language in the context of the discussion). Thus, Hiro extends a discussion which could have ended in presumed agreement (e.g., particularly line 36) by withholding any signal of concession, instead sitting back and rubbing his neck in a display of thoughtful reflection (lines 37–38), followed by repetition of the term under discussion (line 39). This display of involvement, coupled with the JE participant's reluctance to concede, serves to extend the discussion. Hiro is thus able to maintain his position while Stu lays out details of the terminology on which agreement or disagreement rests. The behaviors of both participants conspire to produce a discussion (albeit an awkward one) during which each maintains his own point of view.

Developing disagreement through questioning

Questioning is another interactional behavior that can affect involvement by a partner who may be withdrawing from the fray since it can be used to draw out the evidence or arguments underpinning a position. Excerpt 3 illustrates how extensive use of questions can lead to a fully articulated argument, which in this case terminates in an explicit concession. The topic is whether language learners require "negative evidence" (input indicating that some aspect of their production is ungrammatical).

Excerpt 3 (EJEM5 9b)

```
1    1st Hiro:  ((moves pencil to middle category))
2               yes.
3               ((nods))
4               (0.6)
5   → Stu:      is it? ((looks at Hiro))
6               (0.3) ((Stu nodding))
7      Hiro:    yeah. (.) >eh but, negative evidence<
8               ((eye contact)) without negative e-
9               evidence, you know, uh, (.)
10              ((puts hand up to mouth)) L2 learner
11              learner, (0.4) u:h, sometimes, has a
12              chance to, (0.4) eh ((hand gesture))
13              fossilized.
14              (1.3) ((eye contact))
15     Hiro:    eh:, ((looking at Stu))
16              (0.9)
17  → Stu:      without negative evidence,
18     Hiro:    uhuh,
19  → Stu:      ((eye contact)) L2 ((holds up two
```

```
20              fingers)) learner?
21      Hiro:   (>ye- t- w-<) you- and- >negative,<
22              negative evidence means, (.) negative
23              feedback.
24              (0.6)
25      Stu:    [oh  okay,   okay. ]
26      Hiro:   [like when an adult] makes an ((hand
27              gesture)) [error,]
28      Stu:                      [right,]
29      Hiro:   nowa would, (0.3) eh, correct him.
30              (0.7)
31      Stu:    right.
32              (0.6)
33      Hiro:   so= ((picks up pen to write))
34      Stu:    =yeah.
35              (0.5)
36  →   Stu:    ((looks at Hiro)) [did you say Noah?
37      Hiro:                     [I
38              (0.4) ((Hiro pauses))
39      Stu:    ((quietly chuckles)) no one. ((stops
40              smiling)) oh, no one, yeah,
41      Hiro:   uhuh. ((nods))
42              (1.4)
43  1st Hiro:   I think yes. ((writes))
44              (1.7)
                                    reading aloud---------
45      Hiro:   ((pointing at paper)) the importance of
                reading---
46              negative, eh negative ev- feedback is
47              necessary.
48  2nd Stu:    °hh he wasn't ((points at paper)) very
49              sure  about that, was he. ((looking at
50              Hiro))
51              (2.6) ((Hiro looking at paper. Stu
52              looking at Hiro))
53      Hiro:   I ye- ((looks up, nods))
54      Stu:    he disCUSSED it,
55              (0.7)
56      Stu:    and, ⌊uh,
57      Hiro:       [eh, >but he mentioned< ((taps
58              paper, both look at it)) that negative
59              feedback ((looks at Stu)) is necessary.
60              (1.2) ((Stu looking at paper))
61      Stu:    ↑did ↓he, ((looking at Hiro, nodding))
62              (0.3) ((Hiro nods))
63      Stu:    he said it's absolutely °necessary?°
64              ((raises eyebrows))
65      Hiro:   ((looking away)) e:h I- I'm not sure. with
```

```
66  3rᵃ          absolutely, but, eh, negative
67               feedback ((looks back at Stu)) is
68               °necessary°.
69               (0.4)
70  Stu:         hm:. ((looks at paper))
71               (0.2)
72  Hiro:        for the L2 ((points at paper)) learner.
73               (2.6) ((Stu looking at paper. Hiro
74               looking at Stu))
75  Stu:         hu:h. (0.5) okay.
76               (0.9)
77  Hiro:        >uh d-< [u:h, ((points at paper))
78  Stu:                 [okay, ((looks at Hiro)) if y-
79               you're
80  Hiro:        ok.
81  Stu:         you ((nodding, points at Hiro))
82               seem to be  pretty sure, so that's okay,
83               we'll go with that.
```

In this excerpt, Hiro responds to the implied question on the task sheet (whether negative evidence is necessary for L2 acquisition) with a simple "yes," followed by a nod. Stu's response is a series of questions – initially repair initiations that are treated as comprehension checks (lines 5, 17, 19, arrowed) and in line 36 a questioning of a misheard pronunciation of "no one," which Stu resolves in lines 39–40. At the end of the series of questions, which have resulted in a more detailed statement of his original claim as well as an explanation of the term *negative evidence*, Hiro repeats his initial claim, expressed as a complete clause, that negative feedback is necessary (lines 46–47), referencing the paper by pointing.

At this point, Stu's questions take on the form of challenges, asking whether the author was very sure about this claim (lines 48–49) and then stating "he disCUSSED it,"(line 54), implying that the author did not actually accept the claim. Hiro replies that the author did mention that negative feedback is necessary (lines 57–59). In lines 61 through 64, Stu again challenges Hiro by saying "did he? (0.3) he said it's absolutely necessary?" and raising his eyebrows, emphasizing his skepticism. Hiro backs down by saying "I'm not sure. with absolutely," and then restates his claim "but eh negative feedback is necessary for the L2 learner" (lines 65–68, 72).

While Stu's questioning does not elicit a detailed explanation of Hiro's point of view, it does manage to convey Hiro's commitment to his position, which Stu acknowledges as he accepts Hiro's claim (beginning with "if y—you're" in lines 78–79, then self-repaired to "you seem to be pretty sure, so that's okay, we'll go with that," lines 81–83).

Providing opportunities for displays of understanding and stance

For the participant whose position is not elicited through focused questions, opportunities for drawing out displays of understanding or alignment can be created during an explanation of his point of view by delaying completion of an utterance in progress. In Excerpt 4, taken from a different pair discussing the same article, Ichi develops a position that is challenged by Andy. While explaining his point of view, Ichi pauses frequently, an act that provides Andy with opportunities to express a contrasting opinion or to voice support. As has been shown in previous examples, a recipient may choose to bypass opportunities to provide a substantive contribution during the expression of a contrasting point of view by his or her partner. However, the opportunities referred to here occur not necessarily at a point at which a response might be anticipated, but even before grammatical completion of the turn in progress.

Andy and Ichi are discussing whether L2 learners vary in course and strategy, that is, whether learners follow different paths of development and use different strategies in acquiring a second language.

Excerpt 4 (EJEM7 3b)

```
1   1st Ichi:   mm I STRONGLY feel
2              that uh:: (1.2) adult foreign learners (.)
3              ((looks at Andy))((Andy nods)) have various
4              kinds of (1.0) course of studying [the=
5       Andy:                                    [yeah.
6       Ichi:  =strategies.
7              (1.2) ((Andy looking at Ichi))
8       Ichi:  especially u::h, (2.0) lear- adult
9              learners?
10             (0.3) ((eye contact))
11      Ichi:  u::h, for living (1.4) in the country where
12             the- target lan- language is not spoken,
13             (0.4)((looks at Andy))
14      Ichi:  not used,
15      Andy:  mm. ((nods))
16             (0.4)
17      Ichi:  u:h,
18             (1.1) ((both look down))
19      Ichi:  have to have, (0.5) their own way,
20             (0.7)((eye contact, Andy nodding))
21      Ichi:  °o-° (.) °o-° (0.4) of those strategies,
22      Andy:  mm. ((nods))
23             (0.4) ((eye contact))
24      Ichi:  of studying (0.3) the target language.
25             (2.2)((both look down, Andy nodding))
```

```
26      Ichi:   so in this sense, (2.3) adult learners?
27              ((eye contact))
28              (0.6)((Andy nods))
29      Ichi:   of a foreign language. (3.6) ((Andy looking
30              at Ichi)) depend on (.) his own way.
31              (1.2) ((eye contact, Andy nods))
32 2nd  Andy:   do they?
33              (1.4) ((Andy smiling, Ichi looks at paper))
34      Ichi:   uh, course and strategy,
35              (1.2) ((eye contact))
36      Ichi:   which they- (.) which he or she has to
37              find. ((looks at Andy))=
38 2nd  Andy:   =do they depend on their own way? or do
39              they depend on what the teacher gives them.
40              (3.3) ((Andy looking at Ichi, Ichi looking
41              up))
42 3rd  Ichi:   m- at school, ((makes flat hand gesture
43              while looking at Andy))
44              (0.3)
45      Andy:   °yeah°=
46      Ichi:   =mm
47              (0.4)
48      Ichi:   they have to: follow. ((eye contact))
49              ((Andy nods)) (1.3)
50              °hh the wa:y the teacher use,
51              (1.1) ((eye contact, Andy nods))
52      Ichi:   uses but- (0.7) [uh (.) at home.
53      Andy:                   [hm.
54              (1.6) ((Andy looking at Ichi))
55      Ichi:   for example >Japanese< learner, ((looks at
56              Andy while Andy nods))(0.3) adult learner,
57              (1.6) use tape recorder? ((looks at Andy))
58              (0.8) ((Ichi looking at Andy))
59      Andy:   yeah. ((nods))
60              (0.7) ((Andy looking at Ichi))
61      Ichi:   or: (0.7) used radio, ((gestures holding a
62              radio))((Andy nods))(0.7) or=
63   →  Andy:   =in different to[pics, too.=
64      Ichi:                   [(tal- t-)
65      Ichi:   =yeah= ((nods))
66      Andy:   =yeah.((nods))
67              (0.6) ((both look at paper))
68   →  Andy:   they talk about n: ((pointing at paper))
69              [try to learn for different topics?]
70      Ichi:   [o::r (.) has u::h]
71      Andy:   n:
72              (0.3)
```

```
73    Ichi:  pen pal,
74           (0.8) ((Ichi looking at Andy))
75    Andy:  °yeah.° ((nodding))
76           (0.6) ((Ichi looking at Andy))
77    Ichi:  and to correspond wi:th, ((makes hand
78           gestures while looking at Andy))(0.8)
79           ((Andy nods)) h- him or her,
80           (1.0) ((Andy looking at Ichi, nodding))
81    Ichi:  through writing it.
82    Andy:  hm, ((nods))
83           (2.2) ((both look at paper))
84    Ichi:  so this is uh quite different from (0.6)
85           the second language learner, ((eye
86           contact)) (0.7) who have a lot of exposure,
87           ((eye contact, Andy nods)) (1.1) u::h in
88           daily lives. ((slightly lifts head))
89    Andy:  yeah. ((nods))
90           (1.7) ((Andy looking at Ichi))
91    Ichi:  so::, in this sense the foreign learners
92           have to, ((eye contact, Andy nods)) (1.2)
93           find, (1.1) their own style.
94    Andy:  ((coughs then nods))
95    Ichi:  for himself- (0.3) [for themselves.
96    Andy:                     [yeah,
97    Andy:  yeah. ((nods))
```

In the first few turns (not shown), Andy and Ichi decide that *variation in course and strategy* refer to whether L2 learners are taught or not (presumably a misinterpretation of "variation in course") and whether they use different strategies in learning English. Ichi launches the discussion with his strong opinion that foreign language learners have "various kinds of course of studying the strategies" (lines 1–6), a position with which Andy seems to agree ("yeah," line 5). Ichi continues by narrowing his assertion to countries in which the target language is not spoken. This occurs over several turns (lines 7–29), during which Andy passes up numerous opportunities to agree.

Finally, in line 32, Andy challenges Ichi's assertion ("do they?") and again does so in lines 38–39, with a more precisely formed challenging question ("do they depend on their own way? or do they depend on what the teacher gives them."). Ichi responds with an acknowledgment of Andy's point and an explanation of his position – when students get home from school they employ different strategies, which he starts listing (using tape recorder, radio), with pauses after each item. In lines 63 and 68–69 (arrowed) Andy adds to Ichi's list ("in different topics too," "they talk about n: try to learn for different topics?"), essentially aligning himself with Ichi's point that learners employ various strategies outside of school.

As Ichi restates his original position (lines 84–95), Andy responds not with minimal vocalizations, but with *yeah*, accompanied by nods (lines 89, 94, 96–97). Andy's co-construction of Ichi's list of various strategies is facilitated by Ichi's pauses, which provide opportunities for his partner to express a stance toward Ichi's argument. When Andy avails himself of the opportunity to supplement Ichi's list of examples supporting his position, he displays, at least at that point, an understanding, if not acceptance, of Ichi's position, which is reflected in his increasing use of *yeah* (often with nods) in response to Ichi's restatement. This is treated as agreement, and the two move on to the next topic.

This excerpt displays two behaviors that contribute to the development of a position. First, the use of a challenge (a particularly pointed question, conveying nonacceptance) is designed to elicit elaboration of a claim, which it does in this case. Second, alignment with Ichi's position is gradually forged as Andy contributes to the examples supporting Ichi's point, essentially co-constructing Ichi's explanation of his view. While this type of local support does not necessarily ensure agreement, the emergence of stronger signs of assent suggests a more general acquiescence (lines 89, 94, 96–97).

Just as Andy took advantage of the opportunity to contribute to a list of instances supporting Ichi, in Excerpt 5 the EE partner Tom is offered a number of opportunities to express a stance toward Jiro's position. Tom and Jiro are discussing whether L1 learners experience a general lack of success in acquiring their first language. In several instances Jiro pauses before grammatical completion of the explanation of his position, recycling clauses and leaving space for questions, comments, or position-taking by Tom (video for Excerpt 5 is unavailable).

Excerpt 5 (EJEM2 1a)

```
1          Jiro:  I think,
2                 (1.2)
3     1st  Jiro:  yes.
4                 (0.6)
5          Jiro:  I agree, (0.5) with °uh° a general lack of
6                 succ- success. I agree [°with him.°
7     →    Tom:                          [is for L1?
8                 (0.2)
9          Jiro:  yeah. L1 as well, (.) adult learners.
10                (0.7)
11         Jiro:  not children.
12                (1.9)
13    →    Tom:   °hh L[1] eh L1 would be a native speaker,
14         Jiro:       [m
15                (0.6)
```

```
16    Jiro:  yeah but uh (.) if native speaker (0.2)
17           you know? (.) u::h (0.5) >I mean< (0.3) >ya
18           know<, (0.5) when u:h some studen',
19           (0.4)
20    Tom:   hm.=
21    Jiro:  =emm (.) don't learn, (0.3) L1 as well.
22           (0.6)
23    Jiro:  for instance you know,=
24  → Tom:   =so you wouldn't learn Japanese.
25           (0.5)
26    Jiro:  yeah, because- i- no y- I mean >you know<
27           some children, (0.3) a:re you (0.4) u:h out
28           of society.
29           (0.6)
30    Jiro:  for a long time. or for instance, uh °you
31           know,°=
32    Tom:   =>okay.< in the rare excep[tion,
33    Jiro:                            [((laughs))]
34           yeah.
35    Tom:   in the rare excep[tion,=
36    Jiro:                   [yeah
37    Tom:   =I'll agree with you.
38           (0.6)
39    Jiro:  yeah, (0.2) okay,
40    Tom:   but for-
41    Jiro:  yeah [for ordinary=
42    Tom:        [for the majority
43    Jiro:  yeah ordinary children yeah
44    Tom:   I'd say no.
45    Jiro:  no. °yeah.°
```

The discussion begins with Jiro stating that he agrees with the idea of lack of success (lines 5–6). Tom responds by checking the scope of Jiro's claim (line 7, arrowed) and by reminding Jiro that they are discussing native speakers (line 13, arrowed). Jiro follows up with a defense of his position, qualifying his statement by specifying the special group of L1 learners he has in mind (lines 16–23), that is, those who have not had exposure to their L1 for a long time. Jiro's explanation that he is referring to children removed from their L1 never reaches grammatical completion. His entire utterance comprises an extended subordinate *when*-clause peppered with pauses, *I mean,* and *ya' know,* which Tom finally takes up as an opportunity to weigh in with "so you wouldn't learn Japanese" (line 24, arrowed), a question bordering on challenge. Again Jiro's answer in lines 26–31 consists of a *because* clause produced with frequent pauses. In line 32, before Jiro gets around to the consequence of the clause, Tom launches his response to Jiro's example (which he has inferred) with a strong qualification ("ok. In the rare exception, in the rare exception, I'll agree with you." lines 32, 35, 37). Tom and Jiro go on to agree that while Jiro has a point, in general the majority of children learn their L1 successfully.

In this instance, Jiro provides multiple opportunities for Tom to pose questions and express non-agreement. His use of extended subordinate clauses indicating cause allows Tom to respond to the implied result without Jiro ever articulating it.

Shutting down disagreement

Disagreement is not always resolved in clear agreement or mutual acceptance of each other's divergent positions. As Sharma (2012) has pointed out, concession and/or topic change can also end a disagreement sequence. One finding on argument sequences relates to their resolution, in particular the role of post-disagreement delay. Unlike delay preceding an initial disagreement, delay after the 2nd turn now becomes an indication of incipient concession – or at least of the inability to come up with a response (Bilmes, 1991; Kotthoff, 1993; Saft, 2001; Sharma, 2012). In a theoretical discussion of the preference structure of disagreement during arguments, Bilmes (1991) contends that lack of explicit disagreement leads to a strong presumption of agreement (reluctant or otherwise).

Data from actual disagreements provide details of negotiations of withdrawal from disagreement. Using dyadic discussions between Anglo-American and German students interacting with lecturers on a pre-designated topic, Kotthoff (1993) described how the shift from conflicting position to acceptance was achieved. Concentrating on the turns leading up to concession, Kotthoff identified precursors to the shift in position; these included reluctance markers, questions, and the absence of *but*, as well as elaboration on the concession. Additionally, Saft (2001) noted use of partial repetitions and *ahh* as displays of concession in faculty meetings at a Japanese university.

Likewise, in a study of concession that extended the analysis of argument exit patterns to groups of advanced international university students of English working jointly on a writing task, Sharma (2012) found that group members initiated concession gradually by claiming understanding, often preceding such claims with, for example, requests for confirmation. Sharma's data on learner arguments provide evidence that, for advanced learners of English, concessions in an academic context are achieved by the same moves as those of monolingual English speakers.

Thus, some paving of the way for acceptance of an opponent's position is expected, and its absence can have unfortunate consequences. In one such instance, a Chinese learner speaking German abandoned a dissenting position by abruptly agreeing. Günthner (1991, as cited in Kotthoff, 1993) observed that such concession without the appropriate preparation was grounds for complaint by the interlocutor. In contrast to gradual concession or sudden agreement, an interactant may abruptly withdraw from the discussion. For instance, Jones (1995) reported on an instance of a Japanese disagreement in the workplace in which the disputants physically withdrew from the conflict, leaving the issue unresolved and the participants' subsequent relationship damaged.

In addition, as suggested above, in most discussions of disputes-in-progress silence is taken as a sign that the disputant is unable to advance his or her point and is thus viewed as a preface to concession. However, there are various types of "silence," and withdrawal from disagreement can be managed quite subtly without involving clear concession. The following excerpts present instances of disagreements in which one participant withholds defense of her/his original position without accepting her/his partner's viewpoint. Excerpt 6 provides an example of disagreement in which the JE partner essentially withdraws from the disagreement, and in Excerpt 7, the JE participant explicitly refers to his inability to express his reasoning, at which point his EE partner shifts topic.

In Excerpt 6, Tess and Takako tackle the question of whether people learning a general skill employ different strategies.

Excerpt 6   (EJEF6 3c)

```
1         Tess:   [strat[egies,
2         Tak:    [mhm  [mhm
3                 (0.6)
4         Tess:   general skill [learning?
5         Tak:                  [°yes°
6                 (0.8)
7   1st  Tess:   °it's true:?° ((looks at Takako))
8                 (0.3) ((Takako looking at paper))
9         Tess:   don't we?
10        Tak:    mm::
11                (0.7)
12  2nd  Tak:    it depends,
13                (1.3) ((Takako looking at Tess))
14        Tak:    but do we? ((nods))
15                (1.0)
16  3rd  Tess:   ↑no I think s[o: ((looks at Takako))
17        Tak:                 [°yeah° ((nods))
18        Tess:   I think we [might (0.4) try to [do things=
19        Tak:               [°mm°                [°mhm°
20        Tess:   =[different [ways,
21        Tak:     [°mhm°     [°mhm°
22                (0.3)((Tess writing))
23        Tess:   use different strateg[ies,
24        Tak:                         [mm ((nods))
25                (2.5)
```

Tess begins with a proposal (spoken softly with rising intonation) that general skill learning involves different strategies. She ends with a tag, "don't we" (line 9), inviting agreement. Takako's response is rife with indications of disagreement, including delay ("mm::, pauses) and a clear qualification ("it depends,") in lines 10–12, followed with a disagreement marker "but" and a direct questioning of the claim "do we?" (line 14). Tess responds with a hedged "I think so," and a repetition of her position, again hedged and this time more completely expressed ("I think we might try to do things different ways, use different strategies," lines 19, 21, 23). Takako's noncommital *mm*s, *mm hm*s and nods (lines 22–24) essentially pass on the opportunity to expand on Tess's position, and after this Tess moves on to the next topic.

In Excerpt 6 the disagreement terminates with neither agreement nor explicit concession. Excerpt 7 presents a disagreement sequence that seems to be heading in the same direction as Excerpt 6, with no clear response to a disagreeing turn by the EE partner. However, in this excerpt, the 3rd Turn disagreement is expressed only after it is elicited by the EE co-participant, Andy. He and Ichi are debating whether someone learning a general skill will experience general failure. Although the Bley-Vroman article they are discussing characterizes general failure as lack of complete success, this is not referred to in the disagreement, which eventually turns on each of the participants' interpretation of general failure. In the first segment of this discussion (lines 81–88 omitted), Andy has talked about his own and his students' frustration speaking a foreign language. Throughout this explanation, Ichi has bypassed a number of opportunities to agree or to take the floor, but eventually, in line 89, he attempts to tie Andy's explanation of his experiences with language learning to the question.

Excerpt 7 (EJEM7 2c)

```
89      Ichi:   >so general< failure is y- ((pointing at
90              paper)) (0.7) generally speaking, (0.5)
91              adult learners, (0.9) fail, ((looks at
92              Andy))
93              (0.3)
94      Ichi:   ((making eye contact)) in eh acquiring
95              (1.1) a foreign language.
96              (1.8) ((Ichi looking at Andy))
97   1stIchi:   °yes.°
98              (1.2) ((both looking down))
99      Andy:   well-
100             (0.5) ((Ichi looking at Andy))
101     Andy:   yeah.
102             (2.1) ((Ichi looking at Andy))
```

```
103  2ⁿᵈAndy: ((eye contact)) but >I mean< people can
104            study. in what areas do they fail. ((Ichi
105            looks down)) I mean they may fail in the
106            native like accent [or native like grammar=
107     Ichi:                     [mm mm mm mm mm,
108            ((nods))
109     Andy: =but they don't fail in learn[ing the=
110     Ichi:                               [ahh, I see.
111            ((slightly raises head back))
112     Andy: =language.
113            (1.2) ((Andy looking at Ichi))
114     Andy  [I mean I learned- I started learning=
115     Ichi: [mm
116     Andy: =Chinese when=I was nineteen. I can speak
117            Chinese, [but I haven't=
118     Ichi:          [mhm,
119     Andy: =I don't have failure.
120            (0.4)
121     Ichi: yeah?
122            (0.6))
123     Andy: yeah but [um
124     Ichi:          [hmm,
125            (2.2)
126     Andy: but I have fairy- (0.2) failure in areas,
127            (0.2)
128     Ichi: °yes,° ((nods))
129            (0.9) ((both looking at paper))
130  2ⁿᵈAndy: but not- (.) I don't think general failure.
131            (0.8) ((Andy looks at Ichi))
132     Ichi: °yeah,°
133     Andy: °>you know<° unless you talk about native
134            like (0.7) accent. but is it so- (.) do you
135            think it's important?
136            (0.5) ((Andy looking at Ichi))
137  3ʳᵈIchi: ·hhh (.) yes? ((nods head))
138            (0.5)
139     Andy: why?
140            (0.5) ((Andy sits back, looking at Ichi))
141     Ichi: u::h ((looks down at desk))
142            (9.0) ((Ichi stares at desk)
143     Andy: ((looking at Ichi)) I think of failure, I
144            think it's so negative. (.) hh
145            (5.9)((Andy stares at Ichi))
146     Ichi: yes, failure itself ((eye contact)) is
147            negative, but uh °hh
148            (6.8)((Ichi looking down at desk))
149  → Ichi: sorry, I not ((Andy nods))(0.6) ex-
150            (1.0)
```

```
151    Ichi:  express what (.) (°>I can't<°) express what
152           I- I would like to say. ((smiles))
153           (0.7) ((eye contact))
154    Ichi:  I'm- I'm a little nervous today.
155           [((laughter))
156    Andy:  [okay,
157           (0.8) ((both lean forward and
158                  look at paper))
159    Andy:  (then)
160           (2.5) ((both looking at paper))
161    Andy:  yeah, well ((looking at Ichi)) it's nice we
162           had our last class.
```

Ichi summarizes Andy's contribution so far with the proposal that, generally speaking, adult learners fail in acquiring a foreign language (lines 89–95). After a 1.8-second pause, Ichi agrees with this position, with a soft °*yes*° (line 97). Andy responds with a nonagreement preface "well (0.5) yeah (2.1) but...," initiating his pre-disagreement account with the observation that people can study in those areas (lines 103–112). In lines 114–130, he goes on to assert that he started learning Chinese when he was 19, but he has not failed in Chinese, and that, although he does fail in some areas, he does not think that constitutes general failure. Until this point Ichi has been producing expressions of understanding ("ahh I see") and interest ("yeah?"), as well as minimal vocalizations ("*mm*," soft "°*yeah*°").

In the face of a lack of substantive response from Ichi, Andy goes on to add a hedge "unless you talk about native like accent" (lines 133–134). He then begins what appears to be the start of a general question as to the importance of accent, abruptly cutting himself off (line 134) and self-repairing, with an elicitation of Ichi's opinion ("do you think it's important?" lines 134–135). Ichi responds with a tentative ."hhh (.) yes?" Andy immediately requests an account ("why?" line 139). As Ichi hesitates, Andy elaborates, "I think of failure, I think it's so negative." (lines 143–144). Ichi begins an explanation (lines 146–147), but abandons it, explaining that he cannot express what he would like to say and pleading nerves (lines 149–154). Andy responds by shifting the topic to off-task talk (lines 161–162).

Several things seem to be going on here. First, Ichi does not avail himself of the opportunity to take a turn at relevant speaker transition opportunities during Andy's extended discussion of his opinion. Second, it is only when asked that Ichi voices his disagreement. Thus, it is questionable whether Ichi's lack of agreement would have arisen without Andy's elicitation. A number of possibilities exist as to why a discussant may decide not to pursue a disagreement in progress—lack of strong conviction, inability to muster a clear counterargument, or even an expectation that the speaker had not yet finished making his or her point. In this case, Ichi falters when faced with defending a position that implies that Andy has failed at learning Chinese (and thus threatens Andy's face). This excerpt raises the strong possibility that a discussion that terminates without an expression of alignment may represent a withholding of disagreement. Here, the disagreement by Ichi became evident only as a result of elicitation (see Houck & Fujii, 2006 for discussion of a similar case). Thus, while a partner may withdraw from a disagreement in progress, his behavior does not necessarily represent agreement with his interlocutor's point of view.

Conclusion

In this chapter we set out to determine how disagreement is managed – how it is maintained, expanded on, or shut down – in academic discussions between EE and JE co-participants. Disagreement may be extended through nonverbal and nonresponsive turns, suggesting the need for further reflection; or a partner may be drawn into a turn expressing disagreement with his position through opportunities to complete or extend the disagreement turn. On the other hand, withdrawal from disagreement may be effected by minimal responses that are taken as acceptance of the partner's position. None of these moves is particular to JE or EE partners. However their distribution in the data suggests JE participants' reluctance to expand on a disagreement unless encouraged by an EE partner (e.g., through questioning or co-construction). This has interesting implications for classroom discussions.

These interactions were carried out by students whose understanding of the material under discussion was comparable and in which the JE participant's position was generally reasonable and considered. The issue does not seem to be one of academic competence or of willingness to disagree with the EE partner (JE participants produced many of the initial disagreements), but of willingness to engage in pursuing a self-sustaining protracted defense of a position.

Thus, the interactions display not an inability by the JE interlocutor to express disagreement, but rather a tendency to concede or withdraw after opposition to his or her disagreement is suggested. Unless a question or a questioning challenge is issued, or the EE partner participates in constructing his explanation, the JE student may willingly proceed to the next point of discussion. Clearly, issues of culture and experience with academic oral discussion may play a role. However, these findings point to the possible advisability of monitoring university discussions – even by very advanced speakers of English – for opportunities to encourage and support expression of opposing points of view.

Acknowledgements

We would like to express our thanks to the editors and to two anonymous reviewers, who provided invaluable comments and suggestions.

References

Bardovi-Harlig, K., & Salsbury, T. (2004). The organization of turns in the disagreement of L2 learners: A longitudinal perspective. In D. Boxer, & A. Cohen (Eds.), *Studying speaking to inform second language learning* (pp. 199–227). Clevedon: Multilingual Matters.

Bilmes, J. (1988). The concept of preference in conversation analysis. *Language in Society, 17*, 161–181.

Bilmes, J. (1991). Toward a theory of argument in conversation: In F. van Eemeren, & R. Grootendorst (Eds.), *Proceedings of the second international conference in argumentation,* pp. 462–469., Amsterdam: SIC SAT.

Bley-Vroman, R. (1987). The fundamental character of foreign language learning. In W. Rutherford, & M. Sharwood Smith (Eds.), *Grammar and second language teaching* (pp. 19–30). Rowley, MA: Newbury House.

Carroll, D. (2004). Restarts in novice turn beginnings: Disfluencies or interactional achievements? In R. Gardner, & J. Wagner (Eds.), *Second language conversations* (pp. 201–220). New York: Continuum.

Coulter, J. (1990). Elementary properties of argument sequences. In G. Psathas (Ed.), *Interaction competence.* (pp. 181–203). Lanham, MD: University Press of America.

Dippold, D. (2011). Argumentative discourse in L2 German: A sociocognitive perspective on the development of facework strategies. *The Modern Language Journal, 95*, 171–187.

Fujii, S., & Houck, N. (2011). Trajectories of disagreement sequences in academic argument in English by native speakers of English and native speakers of Japanese. *Language Information Text, Vol. 18*, 15–31.

Fujimoto, D. (2010). Agreements and disagreements: The small group discussion in a foreign language classroom. In G. Kasper, H. t. Nguyen, D. R. Yoshimi, & J. K. Yoshioka (Eds.), *Pragmatics & Language Learning* (Vol. 12), (pp. 297–325). Honolulu: University of Hawai'i, National Foreign Language Resource Center.

Fujimoto, D. (2012) *Agreement and disagreement: Novice language learners in small group discussion.* Unpublished doctoral dissertation, Temple University Japan.

Goodwin, C. (1981). Restarts, pauses, and achievement. *Sociological Inquiry*, 272–302.

Goodwin, C., & Goodwin, M. (1992). Context, activity, and participation. In P. Auer, & A. Di Luzio (Eds.), *The contextualization of language* (pp. 77–99). Philadelphia: John Benjamins.

Goodwin, M., & Cekaite, A. (2013). Calibration in directive/response sequences in family interaction. *Journal of Pragmatics (46)*1, 122–138.

Gruber, H. (1998). Disagreeing: Sequential placement and internal structure of disagreements in conflict episodes. *Text, 18*, 467–503.

Houck, N., & Fujii, S. (2006). Delay as an interactional resource in native speaker-nonnative speaker academic interaction. In K. Bardovi-Harlig, C. Felix Brasdefer, &

A. Omar (Eds.). *Pragmatics and language learning,* (Vol. 11), (pp. 29–55). Honolulu: University of Hawai'i, National Foreign Language Resource Center.

Jones, K. (1995). Masked negotiation in a Japanese workplace. In A. Firth (Ed.), *The discourse of negotiation: Studies of language in the workplace* (pp. 141–158). Oxford: Pergamon.

Kotthoff, H. (1993). Disagreement and concession in disputes: On the context sensitivity of preference structures. *Language in Society, 22,* 193–216.

Levinson, S. (1992). Activity types and language. In P. Drew, & J. Heritage (Eds.). *Talk at work: Interaction in institutional settings* (pp. 66–100). Cambridge: Cambridge University Press.

Mori, J. (1999). *Negotiating agreement and disagreement in Japanese* (Chapters 4–6) Philadelphia: John Benjamins.

Muntigl, P., & Turnbull, W. (1998). Conversational structure and facework in arguing. *Journal of Pragmatics, 29,* 225–256.

Pekarek Doehler, S., & Pochon-Berger, E. (2011). Developing 'methods' for interaction: A cross-sectional study of disagreement sequences in French L2. In J. K. Hall, J. Hellermann, & S. Pekarek Doehler (Eds.), *L2 interactional competence and development* (pp. 206–243). Bristol: Multilingual Matters.

Pomerantz, A. (1984). Agreeing and disagreeing with assessments: Some features of preferred/dispreferred turn shapes. In J. M. Atkinson & J. Heritage (Eds.), *Structures of social action: Studies in conversation analysis* (pp. 57–101). Cambridge: Cambridge University Press.

Saft, S. (2001). Displays of concession in university faculty meetings: Culture and interaction in Japanese. *Pragmatics, 11,* 223–262.

Schegloff, E. (2007). *Sequence organization in interaction: A primer in conversation analysis, Vol 1.* Cambridge: Cambridge University Press.

Sharma, B. K. (2012). Conceding in disagreements during small group interactions in academic writing class. *Classroom Discourse, 3,* 4–28.

van Eemeren, F., Grootendorst, R., Jackson, S., & Jacobs, S. (1993). *Reconstructing argumentative discourse.* Tuscaloosa: The University of Alabama Press.

Appendix A: Task sheet

L1=L2 QUESTION (Exercise developed by R. Ellis)

This task gives you an opportunity to check Bley-Vroman's claims about the nature of L2 acquisition using your own experience and intuition.

Complete the table below by making notes about whether each characteristic of learning applies to a) L1 acquisition, b) foreign language acquisition, and c) general-skill learning.

CHARACTERISTIC	AREA		
	a) L1 acquisition	b) foreign lg. acquisition	c) general skill learning
1) General lack of success			
2) General failure			
3) Variation in course and strategy			
4) Variation in goals			
5) Correlation of age and profi- ciency			
6) Fossilization			
7) Indeterminate knowledge			
8) Importance of instruction			
9) Importance of negative evidence			
10) Role of affective factors			

Appendix B: Transcription conventions

Conventional spelling is used, with a few exceptions; utterances do not begin with capital letters

At the end of a word, phrase, or clause

?	Question mark indicates high rising intonation.
.	Period indicates falling intonation.
,	Comma indicates nonfinal intonation – no strong movement in intonation; it is heard as unfinished.
↑↓	Arrows indicate shifts in intonation into especially high or low pitch.
	No punctuation at clause end indicates transcriber uncertainty, often flat intonation.
LOU	Capital letters represent increase in volume.
raised pitch	Underlining represents a spike in pitch (sometimes accompanied by an increase in volume.
°soft speech°	Degree marks indicate that speech is softer than the surrounding speech.
[ ]	Brackets indicate overlapping speech; a left bracket marks the point at which overlap begins; a right bracket marks the point at which overlap ends.
=	Equal signs indicate no break or gap (latching).
(.)	A dot within parentheses indicates a brief pause (less than 0.2 seconds).
(1.5)	Numbers within parentheses indicate length of lapsed time in seconds.
(?)	A question mark within parentheses indicates an incomprehensible word or phrase.
(all right)	A word or phrase within parentheses indicates transcriber uncertainty about the word or phrase.
h	A series of 'h's indicates an out breath.
°	A series of 'h's preceded by a degree sign indicates an in breath.
a-	A hyphen after an initial sound indicates a cut-off.
a::	Colons indicate the stretching of a sound or syllable.
< >	Open angle brackets indicate that the bracketed phrase is spoken at a slower rate.

`> <`	Closed angle brackets indicate that the bracketed phrase is spoken at a faster rate.
`reading aloud--`	"Reading aloud" italicized, in 8-point font followed by a series of hyphens indicates that the text below (in italics) was read aloud.
`reading`	Indicates text that is read aloud
`writing--`	"Writing" italicized, in 8-point font followed by a series of hyphens indicates that the speaker is writing during the pause or text below it.
`((laugh))`	Double parentheses indicate nonlinguistic occurrences such as laughter.
`((eye contact))`	"Eye contact" within double parentheses indicates that both participants look at each other.
`((Andy looks at Ichi))`	One "looks at" another within double parentheses indicates that one turns gaze toward other, but the gaze is not returned.

Collaborative Creation of Spoken Language Corpora

Michael Haugh
Griffith University, Australia

Wei-Lin Melody Chang
Griffith University, Australia

Analysing authentic interactions at progressively greater levels of complexity is one means of promoting deeper engagement with pragmatic phenomena amongst L2 learners. However, effective analysis often requires a greater amount of data than learners can feasibly gather. It is proposed here that encouraging students to collaborate through the creation of a corpus of spoken interactions is one potentially effective way to help them engage with a much richer set of interactional data than they might normally encounter. Here we report on a corpus created through "crowdsourcing" the collection and transcription of recordings of spoken interactions, the Griffith Corpus of Spoken Australian English (GCSAusE), which was then made available to L1 and L2 students to use in analysing pragmatic aspects of spoken interaction. In this way, the students had the opportunity to be both creators and users of the corpus, and see how it results in the real and ongoing accumulation of knowledge about language use. The degree of engagement of students with the corpus was assessed through their research projects, a written survey, and a focus group conducted with a number of students who took the course.

Introduction

Research indicates that awareness of L2 pragmatic norms is not acquired through simply being immersed in an L2 environment, but requires sustained attention and effort from students to learn (Kasper & Rose, 2002). In this respect, it has been found that the development of pragmatic competence can be facilitated by explicit instruction, where learners are not only exposed to contextualised input, but are also encouraged to engage in (meta)pragmatic analysis of relevant phenomena (Ishihara, 2010; Ishihara and Cohen, 2010; Kasper, 2001; Rose, 2005). While there is some controversy as to which particular teaching approaches are more effective (Jeon & Kaya, 2006; Rose & Ng, 2001; Takimoto, 2008), having students analyse authentic interactions in their L2 at progressively greater levels of complexity appears to be one effective means of promoting deeper engagement with pragmatic phenomena. However, effective analysis of pragmatic aspects of interaction presupposes not only access to authentic interactions, but a greater amount of data than learners could feasibly gather themselves. It is thus proposed here that encouraging students to collaborate through the creation of a relatively large collection—or what is often termed a corpus—of spoken interactions is one potentially effective way of helping them engage with a much larger and more detailed set of interactional data than they might normally encounter. A corpus is generally defined as a relatively structured or targeted collection of samples of spoken (or written) data that is machine-readable, which means that large amounts of spoken interaction or texts can be searched according to specified parameters (Peters, 2009, pp. 1–2). Alongside the data itself, corpora also generally contain "meta-data," namely, information about the participants, time and place of recording and so on. Here we report on the development of a corpus, the Griffith Corpus of Spoken Australian English (GCSAusE), which was collaboratively created by students in order to collect and transcribe recordings of naturally occurring spoken interactions, a process termed "crowdsourcing" (Howe, 2006).

We begin by first outlining the case that has been made for drawing from authentic interactions in instructional pragmatics. The potential synergy between those who advocate applying results from studies in conversation analysis (CA), and those who have applied results from studies in corpus linguistics (or more specifically, corpus pragmatics), is also explored. One drawback of both approaches that emerges from this discussion is how to readily gain access to relevant datasets of authentic interactions. We next propose that recent developments in corpus building may offer at least one solution to this impediment to realising the promise of instructional pragmatics. After introducing the principles of cyclical and collaborative corpus creation, which allow for the progressive building of a corpus by multiple contributors, we next outline the implementation of these principles in the development of the GCSAusE, and discuss some of the practical problems that emerged in the course of building this corpus. The use of the corpus by advanced L2 and L1 students in a third-year university course in English pragmatics is then examined through multiple evaluative perspectives including: (1) analysis of research projects they conducted based on data from the corpus, (2) the results of a survey conducted with all the students in the course, and (3) a focus group conducted with a mixture of L1 and L2 speakers from that course. We conclude with a brief discussion of the promise that such an approach offers for instructional pragmatics more broadly, along with some of its limitations.

Authentic interactions in the teaching of L2 pragmatics

The view that we should be emphasizing the use of authentic interactions in teaching L2 pragmatics is now generally advocated by many if not most applied linguists. There are, however, differences in what is considered authentic and/or interaction. The teaching of L2 pragmatics has traditionally used data generated through discourse completion tests (DCTs), or alternatively examples constructed through native speaker intuition. One key problem with using such data, however, is that it "affords somewhat idealized versions of social interaction" (Huth & Taleghani-Nikazam, 2006, p. 54). Such idealised sociopragmatic norms may be incongruent with what actually occurs in interaction, as amply demonstrated by both conversation analysts (Kasper, 2006; Huth & Taleghani-Nikazam, 2006), and those working in corpus pragmatics (Adolphs, 2008; Geluykens & Kraft, 2008; Vine, 2004, 2009; cf. Schauer & Adolphs, 2006).

A second problem is that such data isolate the analysis of pragmatic phenomena from their sequential environment. As Kasper (2006) argues, traditional approaches based on speech act theory do not fully account for the "indexical character of situated action and especially its sequential environment" (p. 297). This is because speech acts are often not accomplished through a single turn at talk, but can be co-constructed over multiple turns (Huth & Taleghani-Nikazam, 2006, p. 63). Moreover, the temporal structure of actions in turns can also be critical to the analysis of various pragmatic phenomena (Kasper, 2006, p. 297). Such phenomena include meaning beyond what is said (what is presupposed, implied, or referred to through what is said), social actions (both those that form a part of members' conscious metapragmatic awareness and those are a part of only their interactional competence), and the evaluation of persons and relationships in conversational interaction (encompassing im/politeness, facework, humour, relational identity and the like) (Haugh, 2012).[1] In taking the position that meanings, actions and evaluations are interactionally and situationally achieved, that is, they are "constituted not only *in* but *through* social interaction" (Kasper, 2006, p. 282; see Arundale, 1999, 2005, 2010 for further discussion), it is clear that in order to fully understand pragmatic phenomena we need to be drawing from authentic interactional data situated in their sequential context.

Nevertheless, no matter what stance one ultimately takes on the issue of what counts as authentic interaction, there are numerous challenges facing any teacher wanting to introduce such data into the classroom. One key problem that emerges from an examination of studies that have strongly advocated the use of authentic interactions is just how one can obtain sufficient data for use in the classroom. Here we focus our discussion on challenges facing those advocating the use of CA (Barraja-Rohan, 1997; Félix-Brasdefer, 2006; Huth & Taleghani-Nikazam, 2006; Kasper, 2006; Koester, 2009; Wong & Waring, 2010), or corpus pragmatics (Geluykens & Kraft, 2008; Holmes, 2009; Jiang, 2006; Koester, 2002; Marra, 2008; Newton, 2004; Usami, 2005) in teaching L2 pragmatics, as these two disciplines are most directly relevant to the approach to corpus creation we advocate here.

A number of studies have illustrated the potential for detailed analyses of authentic interactions in the CA tradition to contribute to the teaching of L2 pragmatics. Huth and Talgehani-Nikazm (2006), for instance, argue that guiding learners through contrastive analyses of the opening sequences of telephone calls amongst speakers of American English and those between Germans provides them with more than just a "blueprint" for this particular conversational action sequence. It also enables learners to identify key differences that do not figure in standard textbook accounts (see also Wong, 2002), as well as raising awareness amongst language teachers about the folk or pre-scientific understandings of pragmatic phenomena that dominate textbooks (cf. Yates, 2010, p. 129). There are, however, some natural limitations to this approach, at least as framed by scholars thus far. Firstly, the way in which pragmatic phenomena are selected for teaching seems somewhat opportunistic, in the sense that the teacher here is actually directly drawing from his or her role as researcher. Félix-Brasdefer (2006), for example, draws from his broader (2008) study of refusals in American English and Mexican Spanish, while Huth and Taleghani-Nikazm (2006) draw from their earlier research on telephone openings in German (Taleghani-Nikazm, 2002). Secondly, the range of pragmatic phenomena selected for teaching seems to be limited in the literature thus far to the core concerns of CA, namely, turn-taking, adjacency, topic management, story-telling, openings and closings, repair, and a limited number of social actions (see, for instance, Wong & Waring, 2010). While such concerns are indeed important, pragmatic competence encompasses a broader range of phenomena some of which lie outside the direct purview of CA, such as interpersonal evaluations (including, e.g., im/politeness, face practices etc.). An over-reliance on CA-based materials thus potentially limits the scope of what is taught.[2] Thirdly, CA datasets are for the most part closed, in the sense that while transcripts are available for inspection, the original recordings are generally not made available beyond select groups of researchers, let alone to groups of L2 learners. This is not meant as a criticism of CA research per se, as researchers have legitimate reasons why audio and visual data cannot be made be widely available, often relating to the conditions imposed by the participants in the recordings. Some important exceptions to this trend include Schegloff's website, where he makes available audio/visual files, which feature mainly speakers of American English, alongside his published work, as well as Talkbank, which provides access to an increasing number of CA transcriptions and audiofiles.[3] However, at present learners do not generally have the opportunity to listen to accompanying recordings, except when the teacher is also the researcher in question. The problem is that exposing learners to CA transcripts without the opportunity to listen to original recordings not only makes it difficult for those learners to interpret and understand those interactions in the first place (but cf. Wong and Waring 2010), it is also inconsistent with the insistence of CA practitioners that the data for analysis ultimately reside in the recording not the transcript.

A parallel move towards using authentic interactions in the teaching of L2 pragmatics has emerged in applications of methodologies in corpus linguistics to pragmatics, or what has recently come to be known as corpus pragmatics (Jucker, Schreier & Hundt, 2009; Romero-Trillo, 2008; Rühlemann, 2010). Pedagogical applications of corpus pragmatics have advocated going beyond teaching lists of speech act phrases or syntactic structures to considering the relative frequency of different syntactic structures as well as illocutionary force (Kasper 2006) in different registers and genres (Jiang, 2006, Koester, 2002; Usami, 2005). The importance of exposing learners to recordings and transcriptions of authentic interactions is also argued by those advocating corpus-based approaches to teaching pragmatics. A corpus-based approach also allows for the examination of frequency of particular collocations in different contexts as well as common sequential structures underlying speech acts. Such an approach can thus be used to assist in the identification (Wulff, 2010), and teaching of formulaic or conventional expressions (Chambers, 2007; O'Keefe, McCarthy & Carter, 2007; Schmidt, 2004), the use of which is often avoided by L2 learners (Bardovi-Harlig, 2006, 2009, 2010, this volume).

However, while such studies demonstrate the great potential for corpus linguistics to contribute to the teaching of L2 pragmatics, there are also some natural limitations in the research published thus far, particularly in regards to spoken interaction. Firstly, transcripts in spoken corpora generally lack sufficiently detailed paralinguistic, nonverbal and contextual information (Geluykens & Kraft, 2008). This means more detailed analyses of the interactional accomplishment of pragmatic actions is difficult (Adolphs & Carter, 2007; Haugh, 2009). In some spoken corpora certain features of spoken interaction, like overlap, pauses, or laughter, are included in transcripts, such as in the case of the spoken components of the British National Corpus or International Corpus of English (Crowdy, 1993, 1994). However, the level of detail in the transcriptions is minimal. In other corpora, such details are completely absent. The Corpus of Contemporary of American English, for example, which features 85 million words of spoken text, draws from transcripts of what is said only (Davies, 2009). A related problem is that the primary focus of analysis in spoken corpora has always been textual transcriptions of audio (visual) recordings, with the original recordings themselves not traditionally being considered the focus of analysis, and so these are generally not made widely available (Wichmann, 2008, p. 189). One exception to this, at least in relation to English, is the Santa Barbara Corpus of Spoken American English, where audio files are made available alongside more detailed transcriptions.[4] Spoken corpora are thus almost always closed in the sense that audio recordings are not accessible, except to select researchers. Thirdly, the lack of direct correspondence between linguistic forms and pragmatic phenomena means the applications of linguistic corpora to instructional pragmatics are still somewhat limited (Ishihara, 2010), with phraseology, backchannels, and discourse markers receiving the most analytical attention in corpus pragmatics thus far (Rühlemann, 2010). While there have been recent attempts to study other pragmatic phenomena using corpora, including speech acts (Adolphs, 2008; Ramírez-Verdugo, 2008; Schauer & Adolphs, 2006; Vine, 2004), humour (Vaughan, 2008), and im/politeness (Clancy, 2011; Culpeper, 2011; Taylor, 2009, 2011), all of these studies draw from spoken corpora that are not accessible to teachers or learners. The corpora are either private collections of the researchers themselves, or are closed corpora (i.e., not made available beyond select groups of researchers), such as the Cambridge and Nottingham Corpus of Discourse in English (CANCODE) (Schauer & Adolphs, 2006), or the Language in the Workplace Corpus (Newton, 2004).

In summary, then, both CA-based and corpus-based approaches to instructional pragmatics advocate using authentic interactional data, albeit using quite different methods of representing and analysing such data. However, their call to arms is clearly attenuated by the simple fact that such materials, in particular, original audio (visual) recordings, are not widely available, either to language teachers or to L2 learners. This problem is, of course, not limited to those advocating CA-based or corpus-based approaches to teaching pragmatics, but is a challenge facing all those who advocate communicative language teaching more broadly. It appears, then, that the very real promise of using authentic interactional data in teaching L2 pragmatics is being hampered by the issue of where to source such materials.

In the following section, we suggest that cyclical and collaborative corpus creation, where the learners themselves are involved in the process of gathering and analysing spoken interactions, offers one potential solution to this data bottleneck in instructional pragmatics, particularly for more advanced L2 learners. It is also suggested that such a process enables language teachers to build on the relative strengths of CA in regards to the level of detail in transcription, on the one hand, and corpus pragmatics, which enables targeted search across relatively large datasets, on the other.

Cyclical and collaborative corpus creation

Spoken corpora have traditionally been very time-consuming and expensive to build. While building a representative collection of spoken interactions in the order of the ten million word spoken component of the British National Corpus is clearly not called for in teaching L2 pragmatics, a certain minimal amount of data is nevertheless required for analysing pragmatic phenomena. The problem is that even constructing a fairly limited or specialised corpus of spoken interaction involves collecting a greater amount of data than individual teachers or learners could feasibly gather on their own. Yet, as most of the corpora of spoken interaction that have been created to date are not readily accessible, it appears that collecting one's own data remains necessary if we are to realise the promise of an instructional pragmatics that is grounded in authentic interactional data.

One alternative to the traditional approach to building spoken corpora, however, is to employ a cyclical and collaborative model of creation. Instead of attempting to create a complete spoken corpus in its entirety before it can be used (i.e., traditional sequential corpus creation), a cyclical process model is proposed as a more realistic model in the context of teaching L2 pragmatics. This collaborative and cyclical model involves two key stages:

Stage 1: Crowdsourcing the recording and transcription of spoken interaction.
Stage 2: Query-driven, progressive annotation of relevant pragmatic features in those spoken interactions.

The first stage involves asking multiple contributors to record and transcribe one or two interactions each (i.e., crowdsourcing), thereby building a large collection through strength in numbers. The second stage refers to a bottom-up approach to adding pragmatic information (i.e., annotations) about the interactions based on the interests of the students themselves (i.e., query-driven) rather than being top-down or theory-driven. This model draws from Brinckmann's (2009) crowdsourcing model of transcription, and Voormann and Gut's (2008) Agile Corpus Creation Theory, which are discussed in further detail in sections 3.1 and 3.2 respectively.

It is worth reiterating at this stage that the term corpus can actually be used to refer either to a "structured collection of texts sampled from various types of [spoken] discourse" (Peters, 2009, p. 1), which "aim[s] for as broad, balanced and comprehensive coverage of spoken language data as possible that can later be used for many types of balanced and representative research" (Čermák, 2009, p. 114), or a largely ad hoc assemblage of spoken texts often associated with a particular research project (Peters, 2009, p. 1). The model proposed here begins by creating a corpus in the second more ad hoc sense, with the view to eventually creating a corpus in the first more structured and representative sense.

It is also worth noting that this model assumes a distinction between transcriptions and annotations, both of which are made in order to allow for the search and analysis of pragmatic phenomena in audio (visual) recordings. Transcriptions, which are fundamental to CA, and have been commonly used in building traditional spoken corpora, involve the representation of speech in textual form, including what is said, syntactic and lexical units, prosodic features, as well as (sometimes) nonverbal aspects of interaction. Annotations, on the other hand, are machine-readable, text-based pointers to such features in the audio (visual) files, themselves. They can be used to identify a broader range of pragmatic phenomena than transcriptions, however, as they also include descriptors of longer sequences, such as speech acts or activity types, for instance. However, regardless of whether one chooses to create transcriptions or annotations, the same issue arises, namely, that both transcribing and annotating spoken interaction is largely a manual and time-consuming process (Allwood, 2008; Brinckmann, 2009; Thompson, 2004). The cyclical and collaborative model of spoken corpus creation is proposed here as a way of sharing the load, as it were.

Crowdsourcing recording and transcription

Crowdsourcing refers to outsourcing a task to a large, sometimes undefined, group of people. It may also take advantage of Web 2.0 technologies. In regards to the creation of spoken corpora, both the gathering of recordings and their transcription can be crowdsourced.

Brinckmann (2009) makes reference to the PHATT speech database of German teenage speech (collected primarily for phonetic analysis), where examples of read and spontaneous speech were recorded by participants on their PCs with an Internet connection, as an example of how this principle can be put into practice. The recordings themselves were prompted via a web-based speech recorder (now part of WikiSpeech: http://wikispeech.org), which uploaded the recordings to a central server. In this way, the participants themselves were able to carry out the recordings without a researcher or technician being present (Brinckmann, 2009, p. 68). There is, however, another potentially less technologically-constrained way of crowdsourcing the collection of spoken recordings, which draws from a source readily available to language teachers, namely, students. In this case, one can ask a group of students to go out and make such recordings as part of their coursework. It is the latter approach which was utilised in the creation of the Griffith Corpus of Spoken Australian English (GCSAusE).

The transcription process can also be crowdsourced. Brinckmann (2009) cites the example of the "German Today" speech project where a system was set up to enable efficient crowdsourcing of transcription. This system is represented in Figure 1.

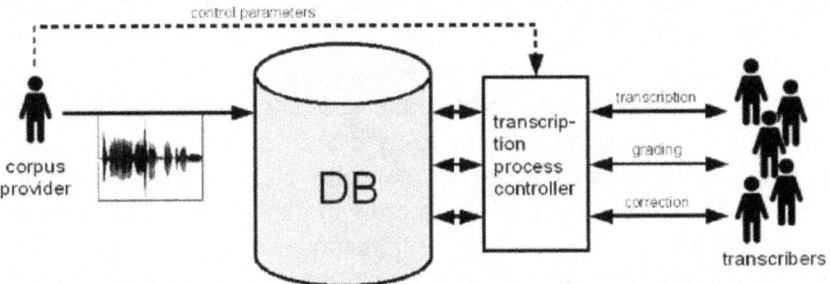

Figure 1. Simplified architecture for system for crowdsourcing transcription (Brinckmann, 2009, p. 172)

The above system consists of six key components:
1. A database of speech files and metadata
2. Task definition (including conventions for transcription, grading and correcting tasks)
3. Process control
4. Database of human transcribers
5. Transcription process (initial transcription, grading, correction)
6. Rewards (grades, lists of top transcribers etc.) (Brinckmann, 2009, pp. 170–171)

In this system, contributors may transcribe recordings they themselves have made, or others provided by the teacher. The system of transcription can vary, of course, with standard CA transcription conventions (Jefferson, 2004) being more suited to advanced level learners, while less advanced learners might use a more simplified transcription system. There are three modes of presentation of transcriptions (or annotations): the "vertical mode" is generally employed by those who use text-processing software like Word to create transcriptions, while the "partiture mode" (which is similar to an orchestral score) or the "column mode" are utilised in specialised annotation editors, such as EXMARaLDA, ELAN, CLAN or Transana (Rohlfing et al., 2006). One problem with the fairly widespread practice of creating vertical transcriptions in programs like Word is that such documents are not readily machine-readable, nor are they easily time-aligned with the original recordings (Haugh, 2009, p. 80). The use of specialised annotation editors, on the other hand, allows the researcher to create machine-readable annotations with varying degrees of interoperability across different software systems. However, specialised annotation programs may not be feasible in language classrooms, as it can take some time to learn how to use such software. Moreover, the software and thus the annotations it generates may become outdated or no longer supported (Deppermann & Schütte, 2008, p. 198). The creation of traditional vertical CA transcriptions in Word thus remains a practical compromise for the moment, although it does limit the addition of further pragmatic information, such as speech act descriptors and the like.

After a transcription is completed and submitted, it can be graded by the teacher (or alternatively peer-reviewed) and then sent back to the learner for correction. This process of correction can also be useful from a pedagogical perspective as it allows the teacher to draw the learner's attention to features that he or she did not notice in the first instance, or to their "mishearings" of certain parts of the recording.

In order for the crowdsourcing of the recording and transcription of spoken interaction to be successful, Brinckmann (2009) suggests that three general principles be followed:

Focus Every task should be described as clearly as possible together with a set of rules.
Filter Use the crowd and experts to extract the best answers.
Reward Reward can be money, recognition or fun. (pp. 169–170)

In the case of language classrooms, these three principles can be realised as follows: (1) the focus of the task should be carefully outlined, with prior training of the learners or students before they go out to record and transcribe the spoken interactions; (2) careful filtering of the recordings and transcriptions needs to be undertaken by the teacher, although peer-review of transcriptions is another pedagogical and practical means of sharing the load to ensure accurate transcriptions enter the corpus; and (3) the reward can be graded assessment, as well as the satisfaction gained from contributing to something both oneself and others are able to later collectively use.

Once an accurate transcription of the recording is available it can be added to the corpus together with the original recording itself, as well as metadata about the recording (e.g., when and where the recording took place, the background of the participants, etc.). At this point the corpus can be searched (or queried), and excerpts identified by both the teacher and learners. The ultimate use these excerpts are put to is dependent, of course, upon the pedagogical model employed in the classroom.

In order to add further value to the collection, however, additional annotation is necessary if learners are to readily identify examples of pragmatic phenomena in the corpus. In the cyclical model proposed here it is suggested that such pragmatic information can be progressively added in the form of annotations based on the interests of the learners themselves.

Query-driven progressive annotation

Traditionally in corpus creation, an annotation schema (i.e., a structured set of inter-related categories applied to different pragmatic phenomena) is first created and then applied to a set of data. In Agile Corpus Creation Theory (Voormann & Gut, 2008), however, it is proposed that the sequential process be replaced by a cyclic process model that is driven by queries from users of the corpus, as illustrated in Figure 2 below.

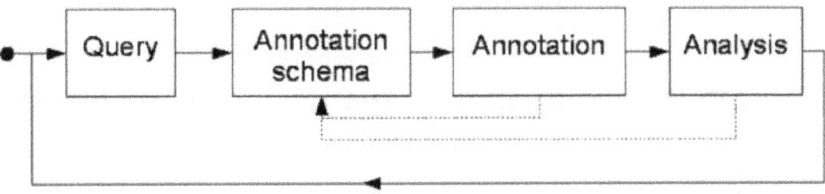

Figure 2. Query-driven corpus annotation process (Brinckmann, 2009, p. 175)

The annotation process starts with a query from the learner, which is then re-defined if necessary relative to a basic annotation schema, subsequently added as an annotation to the corpus, and finally fed back into the learner's analysis. Although allowing annotation to be progressively created in this way diverges from the traditional approach to corpus creation, a query-driven approach to corpus building is likely to yield a spoken corpus that can be put to work quickly, and also avoids inadvertently building early errors in the annotation process into the whole corpus (Voormann & Gut, 2008, p. 235). The aim of this approach is to allow "successive cycles [to] improve the annotation scheme and limit it to the elements necessary for the queries" (Brinckmann, 2009, p. 175).

While the employment of established standards is recognised as the ideal for most types of annotation (Haugh, 2009, p. 81), there is much less certainty in regards to adding pragmatic annotations for the simple reason that such annotations are essentially a kind of interpretative record, and thus are always embedded within a particular analytical and theoretical perspective (Archer, Culpeper & Davies, 2008, p. 637). This means a theory-driven pragmatic annotation system may inadvertently fail to identify important phenomena in the data. A query-driven approach to pragmatic annotation avoids this problem, at least to some extent, as it is driven through bottom-up analysis of the spoken data.

At a very minimum, pragmatic annotation can be used to create a record of social actions identified by learners in the spoken recordings. Some of these social actions are familiar to us through vernacular labels (e.g., requests), while others (e.g., reformulations) go beyond the metapragmatic awareness of ordinary members (Kasper, 2006, p. 305). Various pragmatic annotation schemas are available (Archer et al., 2008), which can offer a source of labels to consistently identify pragmatic phenomena in the corpus. A limitation of such annotation schemes, however, is they do not necessarily accommodate pragmatic phenomena that go beyond vernacular labels or particular theoretical models of language use.

In the following section, we outline how the Griffith Corpus of Spoken Australian English was created by implementing this cyclical and collaborative model, as well as briefly discussing some of the practical problems we faced in this process.

The Griffith Corpus of Spoken Australian English (GCSAusE)

The Griffith Corpus of Spoken Australian English (henceforth GCSAusE) is a progressively growing collection of audio recordings of face-to-face, interpersonal interactions between family members and friends conducted in homes and on university grounds in Brisbane, Queensland. The collection includes recordings made between 2007–2010 inclusively. The participants are Australian speakers of English, although not all are Australian-born, reflecting the demographic reality of Australia, where up to 25% of Australians are born overseas. These audio recordings are accompanied by transcriptions made using standard CA conventions (Jefferson, 2004), along with metadata outlining basic information about the participants themselves, their relationships to each other (held in separate metadata records), as well as the locations and occasions of the conversations (listed at the beginning of the transcripts). The corpus is managed in an institutional repository system, the Equella-based Research Data Management System, which makes metadata about the GCSAusE publicly available, but not the transcripts or audio files. The entry portal for the GCSAusE is illustrated in Figure 3.

Access to audio recordings and transcripts is currently restricted to staff and students at Griffith University due to administrative limitations in setting up an appropriate access control system to the repository system.[5] The 2010 version of the GCSAusE consists of 30 recordings of spoken interactions, each of which is approximately five minutes in length, along with transcripts and associated metadata. The metadata for each recording consist of a separate entry about the audio file itself, the transcript, and each of the participants. Pseudonyms are used in the transcripts and participant metadata records, while instances where the participants are explicitly named are muted in the audio recordings, in accordance with university ethics requirements. The corpus can be queried either through keyword search or by restricting searches according to participant-related criteria (for example, a search restricted by gender or age).

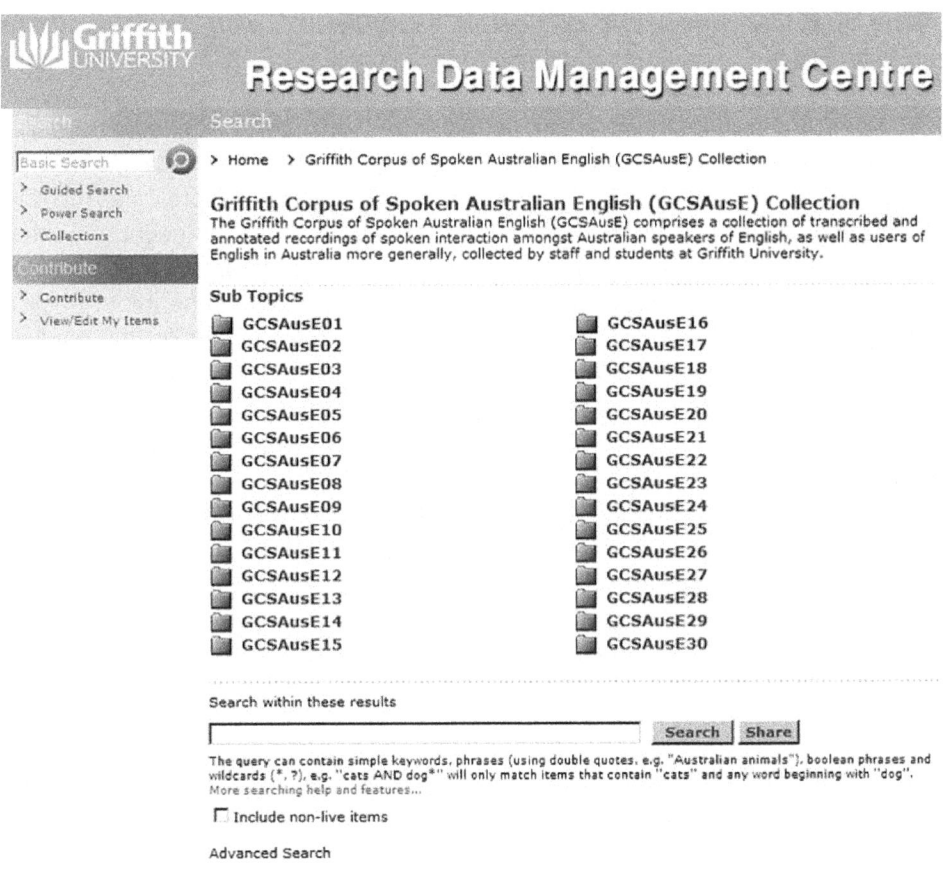

Figure 3. Screenshot of Griffith Corpus of Australian English entry portal

The crowdsourcing of the recording and transcription production was accomplished in a third year course in English pragmatics, in which both L1 and advanced L2 speakers of English were enrolled. All students in the course were required to collect and transcribe spoken data as part of their assessed coursework. All of the recordings and transcriptions were graded by the teacher (the first author) and necessary corrections indicated, with corrections also being suggested through peer review of the transcriptions. The contribution of their recordings and transcriptions to the GCSAusE was entirely voluntary, because it was dependent on gaining written consent from all the participants in the recordings themselves, as well as that of the student who made the recording in the first place. Roughly two thirds of the students offered to contribute their recordings and transcriptions in the 2009 and 2010 offerings of this course, although a small number of these were not accepted on the basis that transcriptions were not sufficiently accurate. Only audio recordings are included in the corpus. Although audiovisual recordings were sometimes made by students, inclusion of these in the GCSAusE was considered to be problematic, since ensuring anonymity for the participants is not possible in the case of audiovisual recordings.[6]

The requirement that transcriptions be consistent with standard CA conventions, and that the audio recordings be made available alongside the transcriptions means the GCSAusE differs from standard practices to date in building spoken corpora. In traditional spoken corpora, transcripts contain less detail about paralinguistic features of the interaction, for instance (Crowdy, 1994), and audio recordings are also not readily accessible. The importance of having a more detailed transcript and accompanying audio files for the analysis of pragmatic phenomena, however, has been firmly established through a multitude of studies in CA and pragmatics (Haugh, 2009; Kasper, 2006), although this is perhaps not yet fully appreciated amongst corpus linguists (cf. Adolphs, 2008; Rühlemann, 2010).

In the following excerpt from an interaction between two Australian male housemates, taken from the GCSAusE, one calls the other a "nobhead."

Excerpt 1. GCSAusE06: 1:03

```
23      N:      so you were born
24              on Sunday, (0.5) of the fir:st month, (0.5) of (.)
25              the twenty-seventh day of nineteen eighty three=
26      D:      =↑no:, not ↑February ma:n
27              (0.2)
28      N:      oh, yo:u're a nobhea:d.
29              (0.6)
30      D:      °what° (.) h ha ↑hehehehe .hhhh
```

Up until this point in the conversation, Nick has been showing David how his new mobile phone can be used to calculate the day of the week on which David was born, which turns out to be a Sunday (lines 23–25). The insult in line 28 is occasioned by David's slipup in thinking the first month of the year is February (line 26). David responds after a brief pause by delivering an open-class repair initiator (Drew 1997), ("what," which orients to Nick's insult in line 28), before displaying realization through his laughter that he has made a mistake. In this case, then, we have an instance of "jocular abuse," that is, a non-serious insult (Haugh, 2009, pp. 77–8). However, without access to this kind of detailed transcript and accompanying audio recording such an analysis could only be tentative at best.

One advantage of including detailed CA transcripts in the GCSAusE is that they can be adapted to create more simplified transcripts quite readily, while the reverse is not the case. The disadvantage of the traditional CA approach to transcription, however, is that these details are not generated in the form of machine-readable annotations.[7] The use of specialised transcription software, in particular, EXMARaLDA (Schmidt, 2004), was thus considered in a pilot study with a small number of users, but it was found to be very time-consuming to learn, and thus not appropriate in the context of a university course with limited contact hours.[8] The more traditional method of creating standard CA vertical transcriptions within Word documents was thus favoured despite its current limitations in regards to creating annotations. Students were, however, guided to use Audacity, a sound editor, to assist them in making their transcriptions.[9]

A number of practical problems were encountered in the course of crowdsourcing the creation of the GCSAusE. The first was that some students had difficulty producing completely accurate transcriptions. While one might expect that L1 speakers of English would be better placed to produce accurate transcriptions than L2 speakers, this was not in fact always the case. This is perhaps a reflection of their advanced level, as they were third year students taking the course in English pragmatics as part of an International English major specifically designed for L2 speakers. Nevertheless some of the L2 students did have difficulty producing completely accurate transcriptions. However, such difficulties occasioned opportunities for feedback from the teacher on aspects of spoken interaction they were unaware of or possibly mishearing, and so in that sense, what was a problem for building the corpus itself, represented an opportunity for learning on the part of students. A second issue was that many students had difficulty producing consistently formatted transcripts. The formatting of transcripts is important to ensure the accuracy of searches across data in the corpus. Some transcriptions were thus excluded from the GCSAusE for this reason, although peer review proved a useful means of improving the formatting of transcripts. A third problem was that students did not always provide sufficient details about the participants and the recording itself (i.e., the metadata), although this was more easily rectified by following up such details in class.

After its creation, the corpus was then made available to students to use in analysing pragmatic aspects of spoken interactions in Australian English in the 2010 offering of the course. At this point, queries were created by students that are seeding the development of further pragmatic annotation, in particular, for different kinds of social actions found in the corpus. Pragmatic tags generated included practices such as "asking socially sensitive questions" (GCSAusE19, GCSAusE29), "broaching emotionally-charged topics" (GCSAusE19), "ironic receipting of complainables" (GCSAusE09), and "occasioning self-talk through inquiring about others" (GCSAusE09, GCSAusE15). However, while such tags contain useful pragmatic information, they are largely ad hoc, meaning systematic search across these annotations remains difficult for the simple reason students do not always know what they can be searching for across the corpus. The ad hoc nature of these pragmatic tags reflects the more general problem that we currently lack widely agreed upon standards for pragmatic annotation (Archer et al., 2008). In the following section we discuss a further potential issue, namely, the degree of engagement by students with the corpus, in particular, the L2 speakers.

Using the corpus: a student-based perspective

The GCSAusE was created by students enrolled in a third year course in English pragmatics. These students include both L1 and advanced L2 speakers of English. The former take the course as part of a major in linguistics, while the latter take it as part of a major in International English designed for L2 speakers. A key feature of this course is that it employs a research-based learning paradigm. In other words, students learn through conducting analyses of authentic interactional data themselves. In that sense, this approach is clearly most suited to educational contexts where there are advanced L2 speakers who specialise in English at undergraduate or even postgraduate level. The degree of engagement of students with the GCSAusE was thus considered to be fundamental for the relative success of the course from a pedagogical perspective. Their degree of engagement was evaluated in multiple ways, including through (1) an examination of the actual research projects they produced using the corpus, (2) a written survey which all the students taking the course answered, and (3) a focus group conducted with a small number of students in that course.

In the research projects, students were required to first record and transcribe a short, spoken interaction, and then identify a pragmatic phenomenon (e.g., a particular social action, instances of anticipatory completions, or a face practice) of interest in their own dataset. They were also required to find other examples of the same phenomenon in other data held in the GCSAusE for inclusion in their final analytical report. As noted previously, a number of practices were identified by students in their own data and in other recordings in the corpus. For example, two different practices were identified by students in the same excerpt from the corpus (GCSAusE09). The first was glossed "occasioning self-talk through inquiring about others" (initially noted by the student in data from the corpus, GCSAusE15), and the second "ironic receipting of complainables" (initially noted in the student's own data which was not subsequently contributed to the corpus).

The practice of occasioning self-talk through inquiring about others was first noticed by the student (an L1 speaker) in another conversation from the corpus (GCSAusE15), where two male housemates are chatting at home. The practice involves cases, as seen in the short excerpt below, where speaker A's inquiry about what speaker B has been doing (line 4) is not reciprocated by speaker B (line 5), yet speaker A nevertheless goes on to topicalize what he/she has been doing in a subsequent telling (line 6).

Excerpt 2. GCSAusE15: 0:02

```
4    J:   been fishin' lately? (0.8)
5    N:   No: (0.6) I rea:lly wanna go fishin' actchally?
6    J:   been fishin' a fair bit down the coa:st (0.4)
```

In example (3) taken from GCSAusE09, the student identified the same practice appearing over the course of a longer sequence. The relevant excerpt from a conversation between two male undergraduate students chatting at university is reproduced below.

Excerpt 3. GCSAusE09: 0:00

```
1    B:   >so what did you do on the weekend<
2         (1.2)
3    A:   ah::: went and saw a friend and °ah:°
4         (0.6)
5    B:   ah ↑o↓kay, (1.8) >was it fun?<
6         (0.9)
7    A:   it wa:s okay we went and ate subway °a:nd° (1.2)
8         yeah just chatted about (0.2) world events
9         and [the     economies   ]
10   B:       [just >chilling out<]
11        (0.3)
12   A:   yeah
13        (1.0)
14   B:   cool (0.2) yeah I ah (1.0) >what did I do I just<
15        studied (0.2) >spent the whole weekend studying
16        did semantics on Saturday, (0.6) and di:d (0.2) CA
17        >conversation analysis< on ↑Sun↓day
18        (1.8)
19   A:   sounds like fun °there goes° the students life
20        HA ha [.hh hh .hh hh .hh ]
21   B:         [ah:: yes it was very] interesting
22        (0.8)
23   A:   um ↑hm
24        (3.3)
25   A:   °so yeah°
```

In the same way as we saw in example (2), speaker A's inquiry about what speaker B has been doing (line 1) elicits a telling about his weekend (lines 3–10), but the inquiry is not reciprocated by speaker B. After a gap of silence in line 13, speaker A launches his own telling through a self-directed inquiry (line 14: "what did I do"), before going on to talk about his own weekend's activities. The students labelled this interactional practice "occasioning of self-talk." The practice involves the speaker directing a question to the recipient, which subsequently furnishes grounds for the speaker to "tell an experience" (cf. Pomerantz, 1980, who describes the practice of "telling my side" as a fishing device, which involves the speaker "telling an experience" as a "possible elicitor of information" from the recipient, p. 187).

The practice of ironically receipting complainables was first noted by a student (an L2 speaker) in her own recording. The practice involves speaker A responding to a potential complaint from speaker B with ironic uptake. This occasions recognition on the part of speaker B of both the complainable import of his or her prior utterance, as well as the move by speaker A to a non-serious, ironic frame. This recognition is displayed by speaker B responding with a further ironic utterance subsequent to speaker A's initial ironic formulation. The student then found another example of the same practice in excerpt 3 from GCSAusE09 reproduced above. In lines 15–17, speaker B describes how he spent the whole weekend studying. This is treated as a complainable by speaker A, who responds with an ironic formulation in line 19 ("sounds like fun °there goes° the students life"). It is recognisably ironic as clearly speaker A does not mean studying all weekend is a fun thing to be doing, but rather that it is exactly the opposite, and thus something about which making a complaint is reasonable. It is also marked as being delivered within a non-serious frame as speaker A also initiates laughter (line 20). However, instead of reciprocating the laughter, speaker B responds with another ironic formulation in line 21 ("ah:: yes it was very interesting"), where he displays support for speaker A's previous stance.

According to the results of a brief written feedback survey about the corpus, which was distributed at the end of the course to the 24 students who were enrolled (see Appendix A), approximately 90% of the students accessed the GCSAusE online, with 82% of them going on to use data from the corpus in their analytical projects. While 82% of the students reported the corpus was easy to use, most of the students accessed data in the corpus through the browse function, with only 40% using a keyword or guided search.

In order to get more detailed feedback, an in-depth focus group was conducted with a smaller number of students. Three students took part in the focus group, two L1 speakers and one L2 speaker, with the second author facilitating the discussion. The second author was not involved in teaching or grading the course in order to minimize any possible conflicts of interest in conducting this evaluative focus group (see Appendix B for a list of the guiding questions). The discussion was recorded and transcribed, and then analysed independently and the findings subsequently compared by the two authors. Three key themes emerged from this analysis. First, the students emphasised the importance of having access to the original audio recordings, not just the transcripts. One L1 student, for instance, in response to being asked how she used the corpus said:

"I went into ones that had audio because I find it really hard to read the transcripts and just try and read it so I went through and found ones that had, so I just browsed and found ones that had audio and then I went through so yeah that's how I went through."

While CA transcripts are useful for detailed analysis, they can be challenging for students to interpret, particularly if no accompanying audio file is available, a point that was also reiterated by the L2 student.

A second theme that emerged was how getting access to other conversations, beyond the one they themselves recorded and transcribed, helped the students to not only appreciate the complex nature of conversational interaction, but also its ability to stir interest in learning more about it. In the following excerpt, an L1 student responded to the facilitator's question about the benefits of donating to or using the corpus (turn 24) by claiming she found examining other conversations piqued her interest in analysing conversational structure (turn 25).

24 A: And what benefits can you see for you from donating or using the corpus?
25 B: I think well immediately for other research projects but I guess it's really interesting to read them, like you go through and the little subtleties in the conversation I guess, I don't know it kind of opens up your eyes to what really happens in a conversation because even though I didn't think mine was that interesting, then when I kind of looked at others, I was like wow mine is kind of, it's really, I don't know, it kind of opens you up to what conversations are about, and I guess ...
26 D: Yeah at first you don't think it is interesting but then ...
27 B: Yeah.
28 D: But when you look in more details in every conversation you can find something.

This claim was supported by the L2 student, who said she did not find analysing the conversations interesting at first (turn 26), but later appeared to find some value in doing so (turn 28).

The third theme was that the students found the corpus useful in undertaking their projects, as they were given access to a greater amount of data than they could have feasibly gathered on their own. However, the students also recognised that the corpus could be used by the wider community, suggesting a sense of belonging to the university research community engendered through contributing to the corpus.

32 C: I think it's just the very practical way to like show people's work and data even if it's not just for assessment, like it's just sort of like the whole bringing together of like all the students and other people's research, I think that is very practical and it's like all in one area as well. Rather than having to go and search and find say for example we need to get Australian English examples to try

and search for that, like it's all sort of basically there for you, it's just all really practical.
33 B: I think it's good and like anyone that, even having it there and if you have another interest, if you take the course and think oh that's what I really want to do, you can kind of go back there and [...] it's good to have like the opportunity for Griffith students and then like the wider community to have them being able to research and use our stuff.
34 A: Okay
35 C: Sort of puts Griffith on show as well I think what's actually happening, so.

As can be seen in the excerpt above, one student mentions the practicality of the corpus (turn 32), while another points to the potential for wider use of the corpus by others outside of the university (turns 33 and 35). It appears that in having the opportunity to be both creators and users of the corpus, and seeing how it results in the real and ongoing accumulation of knowledge about language use, students gained a sense of having a place within the research community.

Concluding remarks

The Griffith Corpus of Spoken Australian English (GCSAusE) has been, and continues to be, created through a cyclical and collaborative model. In this way, students are both creators and users of the corpus. This approach is one possible means of overcoming the current bottleneck in readily accessing authentic spoken interaction for use in instructional pragmatics. It also forms part of the research-based learning paradigm implemented in this and other related courses in the International English program, where undergraduate students, both L1 and L2 speakers of English, have the opportunity to have their research projects published online.[10] While the corpus itself is created and used in an advanced level of course in which both L1 and L2 students take part, L2 students in other English courses are given access to the corpus as well. It is this latter use of the GCSAusE which means that such a model can benefit not only educational contexts where research-based learning is feasible, but also educational settings where access to "real life" interactional data is limited, since it contributes in a very real way to progressively increasing the amount of authentic interactional data available for use in ESL/EFL classrooms.

There are, of course, likely to be some limitations to the implementation of this kind of model, but we believe its basic principles can be at least partially adapted to other contexts. For instance, if students are at a lower level of proficiency in the L2 in question, they can be guided to produce less complex transcriptions. If access to recording authentic interactions in the target language is not readily available, Geluykens and Kraft (2008) propose that examples of spontaneous interaction can be found in new television formats such as "docusoaps" or "flyon-the-wall documentaries," which attempt to "simply record everyday events as they unfold, without any script or manipulation" (p. 101). The latter claim can be disputed perhaps, but it is clear that the Internet increasingly provides access to all kinds of spontaneous interactions across different languages. The model proposed here allows teachers and learners alike to systematically exploit this potential, whilst also building an ongoing resource for the institution where the learning takes place. In this way, students are able to learn through sharing the fruits of their efforts with others.

Notes

1. cf. Kasper, Nguyen, and Yoshimi (2010), who limit the scope of pragmatics to the "study of language-mediated social *action*" (p. 3, emphasis added), reflecting a more strictly CA-oriented approach to pragmatics.
2. Such limitations account for why Barraja-Rohan (1997) and Félix-Brasdefer (2006) suggest drawing from mainstream pragmatics as well as CA in the teaching of L2 pragmatics. However, such an approach is potentially fraught with problems, namely, that drawing conclusions using rationalistic theories of pragmatics within the context of a constructivist approach to data analysis arguably generates theoretical and methodological incoherence (Arundale, 2005, 2010; Haugh, 2010, pp. 372–3).
3. See: http://www.sscnet.ucla.edu/soc/faculty/schegloff/sound-clips.html, and http://talkbank.org/CABank/.
4. See: http://www.linguistics.ucsb.edu/research/sbcorpus.html
5. Further information about the GCSAusE, including detailed metadata can be found by logging in as a guest at http://equella.rcs.griffith.edu.au/research/logon.do. The corpus is also available to researchers and educators more widely through the Australian National Corpus, which has been established in a joint venture between Griffith University and Macquarie University with funding from the Australian National Data Service. For further information see http://www.ausnc.org.au. It is also going to be made available through Talkbank (www.talkbank.org).
6. To blur the face of the participants would defeat one of the main purposes of having audiovisual recordings in the first place, namely, to allow the analysis of gaze, facial expressions and so on. While the physical setting and posture and some gestures of the participants could be retained in this way, the extra effort involved was not considered worthwhile if only such restricted data could be made available.
7. A new type of specialized transcription software, FOLKER (Schmidt and Schütte, 2010), has since been released, however, which may prove more accessible to students. See http://agd.ids-mannheim.de/html/folker_en.shtml for further details.
8. Important work to rectify this problem has been undertaken at Talkbank (http://www.talkbank.org), where traditional CA transcripts have been "converted" into machine-readable ones. However, the software is relatively time-consuming to learn to use and so arguably not appropriate for use in a university course.

9   Audacity, a freely available sound editor is available for download from http:// audacity.sourceforge.net/.
10 See the online journal, *Griffith Working Papers in Pragmatics and Intercultural Communication*, available at http://www.griffith.edu.au/arts-languages-criminology/school-languages-linguistics/publications.

References

Adolphs, S. (2008). *Corpus and context. Investigating pragmatic functions in spoken discourse.* Amsterdam: John Benjamins.

Adolphs, S., & Carter, R. (2007). Beyond the word: New challenges in analysing corpora of spoken English. *European Journal of English Studies, 11*, 133–146.

Allwood, J. (2008). Multimodal corpora. In A. Lüdeling, & M. Kytö (Eds.), *Corpus linguistics: An international handbook. Volume 1* (pp. 207–225). Berlin: Mouton de Gruyter.

Archer, D., Culpeper, J., & Davies, M. (2008). Pragmatic annotation. In A. Lüdeling, & M. Kytö (Eds.), *Corpus linguistics: An international handbook. Volume 1* (pp. 613–642). Berlin: Mouton de Gruyter.

Arundale, R. (1999). An alternative model and ideology of communication for an alternative to politeness theory. *Pragmatics, 9*, 119–154.

Arundale, R. (2005). Pragmatics, conversational implicature, and conversation. In K. Fitch, & R. Sanders (Eds.), *Handbook of language and social interaction* (pp. 41–63). Mahwah, NJ: Lawrence Erlbaum.

Arundale, R. (2010). Constituting face in conversation: face, facework and interactional achievement. *Journal of Pragmatics, 42*, 2078–2105.

Bardovi-Harlig, K. (2006). On the fole of formulas in the acquisition of L2 pragmatics. In K. Bardovi-Harlig, J. Félix-Brasdefer, & A. Omar (Eds.), *Pragmatics and Language Learning* (Vol. 11) (pp. 1–28). Honolulu: University of Hawai'i, National Foreign Language Resource Center.

Bardovi-Harlig, K. (2009). Conventional expressions as a pragmalinguistic resource: recognition and production of conventional expressions in L2 pragmatics. *Language Learning, 59*, 755–795.

Bardovi-Harlig, K. (2010). Recognition of conventional expressions in L2 pragmatics. In G. Kasper, H. Nguyen, D. Yoshimi, & J. Yoshioka (Eds.), *Pragmatics and Language Learning* (Vol. 12) (pp. 141–162). Honolulu: University of Hawai'i, National Foreign Language Resource Center.

Barraja-Rohan, A.-M. (1997). Teaching conversation and sociocultural norms with conversation analysis. *Australian Review of Applied Linguistics Series, 14*, 71–88.

Brinckmann, C. (2009). Transcription bottleneck of speech corpus exploitation. In V. Lyding (Ed.), *Proceedings of the Second Colloquium on Lesser Used Languages and Computer Linguistics (LULCLII 2008)* (pp. 165–179). Bolzano/Bozen: EURAC.

Čermák, F. (2009). Spoken corpora design. Their constitutive parameters. *International Journal of Corpus Linguistics, 14*, 113–123.

Chambers, A. (2007). Integrating corpora in language learning and teaching. *ReCall, 19*, 249–251.

Clancy, B. (2011). Do you want to do it yourself like? Hedging in Irish traveller and settled family discourse. In B. Davies, M. Haugh, & A. Merrison (Eds.), *Situated politeness* (pp. 129–146). London: Continuum.

Crowdy, S. (1993). Spoken corpus design. *Literary and Linguistic Computing, 8*, 259–265.

Crowdy, S. (1994). Spoken corpus transcription. *Literary and Linguistics Computing, 9*, 25–28.

Culpeper, J. (2011). *Impoliteness: Using language to cause offence*. Cambridge: Cambridge University Press.

Davies, M. (2009). The 385+ million word *corpus of contemporary American English* (1990–2008+). *International Journal of Corpus Linguistics, 14*, 159–190.

Deppermann, A., & Schütte, W. (2008). Data and transcription. In G. Antos, & E. Ventola (Eds.), *Handbook of interpersonal communication* (pp. 179–213). Berlin: Mouton de Gruyter.

Drew, P. (1997). 'Open' class repair initiators in response to sequential sources of trouble in conversation. *Journal of Pragmatics, 28*, 69–101.

Félix-Brasdefer, J. (2006). Using the negotiation of multi-turn speech acts: using conversation-analytic tools to teach pragmatics in the FL classroom. In K. Bardovi-Harlig, J. Félix-Brasdefer, & A. Omar (Eds.), *Pragmatics and Language Learning* (Vol. 11) (pp. 165–198). Honolulu: University of Hawai'i, National Foreign Language Resource Center.

Félix-Brasdefer, J. (2008). *Politeness in Mexico and the United States: A contrastive study of the realization and perception of refusals*. Amsterdam: John Benjamins.

Geluykens, R., & Kraft, B. (2008). The use(fulness) of corpus research in cross-cultural pragmatics: Complaining in intercultural service encounters. In J. Romero-Trillo (Ed.), *Pragmatics and corpus linguistics* (pp. 93–117). Berlin: Mouton de Gruyter.

Haugh, M. (2009). Designing and multimodal spoken component of the Australian National Corpus. In M. Haugh, K. Burridge, J. Mulder, & P. Peters (Eds.), *Selected Proceedings of the 2008 HCSNet Workshop on Designing the Australian National Corpus: Mustering Languages* (pp. 74–86). Sommerville, MA: Cascadilla Press.

Haugh, M. (2010). Co-constructing what is said in interaction. In E. Nemeth T., & K. Bibok (Eds.), *The role of data at the semantics-pragmatics interface* (pp. 349–380). Berlin: Mouton de Gruyter.

Haugh, M. (2012). Conversational interaction. In K. Allan, & K. Jaszczolt (Eds.), *Cambridge handbook of pragmatics* (pp. 251–273). Cambridge: Cambridge University Press.

Holmes, J. (2009). Disagreeing in style: Socio-cultural norms and workplace English. In C. Ward (Ed.), *Language teaching in a multilingual world: Challenges and opportunities* (pp. 85–102). Singapore: SEAMEO Regional Language Centre.

Howe, J. (2006). The rise of crowdsourcing. *Wired, 14*, 1–5. Retrieved February 17, 2013 from http://www.wired.com/wired/archive/14.06/crowds.html.

Huth, T., & Taleghani-Nikazm, C. (2006). How can insights from conversation analysis be directly applied to teaching L2 pragmatics? *Language Teaching Research 10*, 53–79.

Ishihara, N. (2010). Instructional pragmatics: bridging teaching, research, and teacher education. *Language and Linguistics Compass, 4*, 938–953.

Ishihara, N., & Cohen, A. (2010). *Teaching and learning pragmatics: Where language and culture meet.* Harlow: Longman.

Jefferson, G. (2004). Glossary of transcript symbols with an introduction. In G. Lerner (Ed.), *Conversation analysis: Studies from the first generation* (pp. 13–23). Amsterdam: John Benjamins.

Jeon, E. H., & Kaya, T. (2006). Effects of L2 instruction on interlanguage pragmatic development: a meta-analysis. In J. M. Norris, & L. Ortega (Eds.), *Synthesizing research on language learning and teaching* (pp. 165–211). Amsterdam: John Benjamins.

Jiang, X. (2006). Suggestions: what should ESL students know? *System, 34*, 36–54.

Jucker, A. H., Schreier, D., & Hundt, M. (Eds.). (2009). *Corpora: Pragmatics and discourse.* Amsterdam: Rodopi.

Kasper, G. (2001). Four perspectives on L2 pragmatic development. *Applied Linguistics, 22*, 502–530.

Kasper, G. (2006). Speech acts in interaction: Towards discursive pragmatics. In K. Bardovi-Harlig, C. Félix-Brasdefer, & A. S. Omar (Eds.), *Pragmatics and Language Learning* (Vol. 11) (pp. 281–314). Honolulu: University of Hawai'i, National Foreign Language Resource Center.

Kasper, G., Nguyen, H. t., & Yoshimi, D. (2010). Introduction. In G. Kasper, H. Nguyen, Y. D. Rudolph & J. Yoshioka (Eds.), *Pragmatics and Language Learning* (Vol. 12) (pp. 1–14). Honolulu: University of Hawai'i, National Foreign Language Resource Center.

Kasper, G., & Rose, K. (2002). *Pragmatic development in a second language.* Malden, MA: Blackwell.

Koester, A. (2002). The performance of speech acts in workplace conversations and the teaching of communicative functions. *System, 30*, 167–184.

Koester, A. (2009). Conversation analysis in the language classroom. In S. Hunston & D. Oakey (Eds.), *Introducing applied linguistics: Key concepts and skills* (pp. 37–48). London: Routledge.

Marra, M. (2008). Recording and analysing talk across cultures. In H. Spencer-Oatey (Ed.), *Culturally speaking: Culture, communication and politeness theory* (pp. 304–321). London: Continuum.

Newton, J. (2004). Face-threatening talk on the factory floor: Using authentic workplace interactions in language teaching. *Prospect, 19*, 47–64.

O'Keefe, A., McCarthy, M., & Carter, R. (2007). *From corpus to classroom: Language use and language teaching.* Cambridge: Cambridge University Press.

Peters, P. (2009). The architecture of a multipurpose Australian National Corpus. In M. Haugh, K. Burridge, J. Mulder, & P. Peters (Eds.), *Selected Proceedings of the 2008 HCSNet Workshop on Designing the Australian National Corpus: Mustering Languages* (pp. 1–9). Sommerville, MA: Cascadilla Press.

Pomerantz, A. (1980). Telling my side: "limited access" as a "fishing" device. *Sociological Inquiry, 50*, 186–198.

Ramírez-Verdugo, M. D. (2008). A cross-linguistic study on the pragmatics of intonation in directives. In J. Romero-Trillo (Ed.), *Pragmatics and corpus linguistics* (pp. 205–233). Berlin: Mouton de Gruyter.

Rohlfing, K., Loehr, D., Duncan, S., Brown, A., Franklin, A., Kimbara, I., et al. (2006). Comparison of multimodal annotation tools—workshop report. *Gesprächsforschung—Online-Zeitschrift zur verbalen Interaktion, 7,* 99–123.

Romero-Trillo, J. (Ed.). (2008). *Pragmatics and corpus linguistics.* Berlin: Mouton de Gruyter.

Rose, K. (2005). On the effects of instruction in second language pragmatics. *System, 33*, 385–399.

Rose, K., & Ng, C. (2001). Inductive and deductive teaching of compliments and compliment responses. In K. Rose, & G. Kasper (Eds.), *Pragmatics in language teaching* (pp. 145–170). Cambridge: Cambridge University Press.

Rühlemann, C. (2010). What can a corpus tell us about pragmatics? In A. O'Keeffe, & M. McCarthy (Eds.), *The Routledge handbook of corpus linguistics* (pp. 288–301). London: Routledge.

Schauer, G. A., & Adolphs, S. (2006). Expressions of gratitude in corpus and DCT data: Vocabulary, formulaic sequences, and pedagogy. *System, 34*, 119–134.

Schmidt, T. (2004). *Transcribing and annotating spoken language with EXMARaLDA.* Paper presented at the LREC Workshop on XML based richly annotated corpora, Lisbon.

Schmidt, T., & Schütte, W. (2010). FOLKER: an annotation tool for efficient transcription of natural, multi-party interaction. *Proceedings of the Seventh conference on International Language Resources and Evaluation (LREC'10)* (pp. 2091–2096). Valletta: European Language Resources Association (ELRA).

Takimoto, M. (2008). The effects of deductive and inductive instruction on the development of language learners' pragmatic competence. *The Modern Language Journal, 92*, 369–386.

Taleghani-Nikazm, C. (2002). A conversation analytical study of telephone conversation openings between native and nonnative speakers. *Journal of Pragmatics, 34*, 1807–1832.

Taylor, C. (2009). Interacting with conflicting goals: Facework and impoliteness in hostile cross-examination. In J. Morely, & P. Bayley (Eds.), *Corpus assisted discourse studies on the Iraq conflict: Wordings of war* (pp. 208–233). London: Routledge.

Taylor, C. (2011). Negative politeness forms and impoliteness functions in institutional discourse: A corpus-assisted approach. In B. Davies, M. Haugh, & A. Merrison (Eds.), *Situated politeness* (pp. 209–231). London: Continuum.

Thompson, P. (2004). Spoken language corpora. In M. Wynne (Ed.), *Developing linguistic corpora: A guide to good practice* (pp. 59–70). Oxford: Oxbow Books.

Usami, M. (2005). Why do we need to analyse authentic materials in developing conversation teaching materials? In Y. Kawaguchi, S. Zaima, T. Takagi, K. Shibano, & M. Usami (Eds.), *Linguistic informatics. State of the art and the future* (pp. 279–294). Amsterdam: John Benjamins.

Vaughan, E. (2008). 'Got a date or something?': A corpus analysis of the role of humour and laughter in the workplace meetings of English language teachers. In A. Ädel, & R. Reppen (Eds.), *Corpora and discourse: The challenge of different settings* (pp. 95–115). Amsterdam: John Benjamins.

Vine, B. (2004). *Getting Things Done at Work*. Amsterdam: John Benjamins.

Vine, B. (2009). Directives at work: Exploring the contextual complexity of workplace directives. *Journal of Pragmatics, 41*, 151–160.

Voormann, H., & Gut, U. (2008). Agile corpus creation. *Corpus Linguistics and Linguistic Theory, 4*, 235–251.

Wichmann, A. (2008). Speech corpora and spoken corpora. In A. Ludeling, & M. Kytö (Eds.), *Corpus linguistics: An international handbook* (Vol. 1) (pp. 187–207). Berlin: Mouton de Gruyter.

Wong, J. (2002). "Applying" conversation analysis in applied linguistics: Evaluating dialogue in English as a second language textbooks. *IRAL, International Review of Applied Linguistics in Language Teaching, 40*, 37–60.

Wong, J., & Waring, H. Z. (2010). *Conversation analysis and second language pedagogy*. London: Routledge.

Wulff, S. (2010). *Rethinking idiomaticity. A usage-based approach*. London: Continuum.

Yates, L. (2010). Dinkas down under: Request performance in simulated workplace interaction. In G. Kasper, H. Nguyen, D. Yoshimi, & J. Yoshioka (Eds.), *Pragmatics and Language Learning* (Vol. 12) (pp. 113–140). Honolulu: University of Hawai'i, National Foreign Language Resource Center.

Appendix A: Survey of Griffith Corpus of Spoken Australian English (GCSAusE)

1. Did you access the GCSAusE online? Yes / No
2. Did you use data from the GCSAusE in your research project? Yes / No
3. Did you find the corpus easy to use? Yes / No
   Why or why not?

4. How did you use the corpus?
   a. Browse: Yes / No
   b. Keyword search: Yes / No
   c. Guided search: Yes / No
5. How do you think the corpus could be improved?

Appendix B: Focus group guiding questions

1. How are you using data from the corpus in your research project?
2. How did you find suitable data in the corpus (e.g., browse, guided search etc.).
3. Did you find it easy to locate suitable data? Why/why not?
4. Did you donate data to the corpus? Why/why not?
5. What benefits can you see for you from donating or using the corpus?
6. How do you think the corpus could be improved?

Acquisition of the Pragmatic Marker 'Like' by German Study Abroad Adolescents

Averil Grieve
University of Melbourne, Australia

This chapter focuses on the acquisition of the pragmatic marker 'like' by German adolescents on five- and ten-month exchanges to Australia. Their acquisition is compared to that of German adolescents on a five-month exchange, German teenagers learning English in Germany and Australian adolescent language. While a number of studies exist on 'like' in adolescent language, little attention has been paid to second language acquisition of 'like' during study abroad. This is surprising considering the importance of 'like' for the expression of adolescent identity and as an indicator of social integration. The data come from twenty-six German exchange students, twenty German non-exchange adolescents and thirteen Australian adolescents. Audio-recordings of unstructured informal conversations were collected before and at the end of the exchange. After transcription, their use of 'like' was coded for either its interpersonal or discourse function. Results show a statistically significant increase in use of 'like' by the exchange students, especially in the first five months of the exchange. This increase was not found in the non-exchange data. After ten months, exchange student usage did not always match native-speaker levels and there was a high degree of individual variation. This was linked to expected length of stay and success of local speech community integration.

Introduction

The pragmatic marker 'like' is perhaps one of the most socially maligned markers of adolescent speech. It is often seen as a marker of teenage vacuity and the language of airheadism, a worldview which is essentially about accepting the status quo, being lazy and shirking adult responsibilities (Gare, 2006). In the second language classroom, it may also be considered inappropriate or 'bad English.' After acquiring the pragmatic marker 'like' in Australia, one of the exchange students in this study had points deducted for each time she used it in school speaking assessments when she returned to Germany.

From a more positive viewpoint, 'like' is a marker of adolescent identity that contributes to establishing a sense of in-group membership and bonding (Andersen, 2001). 'Like' also assists in establishing coherent discourse that is easily comprehensible to the listener (Müller, 2005) and maintaining amicable, non-face threatening interaction (Terraschke, 2008). The functional range of 'like' and its role in indicating degree of group membership mean it is a key marker for understanding the relationship between study abroad, English language acquisition and successful integration into adolescent communities of practice.

This chapter begins with an overview of the acquisition of pragmatic competence during study abroad. It then discusses how pragmatic markers and 'like' are operationalized in this study. An explanation of the methodologies and coding system is provided before reporting and discussing the results of the acquisition of 'like' during five and ten month student exchanges to Australia. Comparisons are also made with native-speaker use of 'like.'

Study abroad, adolescent language and pragmatic competence

Study abroad provides language learners with an excellent opportunity to acquire pragmatic knowledge (Barron, 2003; Cook, 2008; Dewaele & Regan, 2001; Ishida, 2009, 2011; Kinginger, 2008, 2009; Schauer, 2007), including mastery of pragmatic markers (Grieve, 2010). However, students do not magically become fluent or native-like speakers (Ferguson, 1995; Isabelli-Garcia, 2006). Indeed variation in pragmatic competence within study abroad is much higher than that of learners who do not go abroad (Guntermann, 1995). In part, this is due to large differences in their experiences and the quantity and quality of language contact they have with native speakers. The latter is dependent on both the language learner and the discourse community's acceptance of the learner as an in-group member (Norton, 2000). This results in a learner's paradox. On the one hand, to be a group member, non-native speakers must learn the in-group language. However, their ability to learn that language is directly related to their degree of in-group membership (Bremer, Broeder, Roberts, Simonot & Vasseur, 1993).

In-group membership is of particular importance to adolescents, regardless of whether they are speaking their first or second language. Adolescents are preoccupied with developing a sense of identity that marks them apart from adult figures of authority (Chambers, 2000). Such boundary marking can be manifested linguistically, such as by prolific use of the pragmatic marker 'like' in English (Andersen, 2001; Gare, 2006; Tagliamonte, 2005). It follows that by studying the acquisition of 'like' among study abroad adolescents in Australia, we can gain further insight into the complex relationships between the acquisition of pragmatic competence, in-group membership and study abroad language learning.

Pragmatic marker 'like'

The pragmatic marker 'like' is notoriously difficult to classify due to its multifunctional nature (Terraschke, 2008). The focus of current debate is whether it has exclusively interpersonal or discourse functions, or both. Interpersonal markers are those that express the speaker's stance, attitudes and solidarity towards the proposition and interlocutors (Brinton, 1996; Halliday, 1973). Discourse markers focus primarily on the text or talk itself and help establish coherence in conversational structure (Fraser, 1999). Both interpersonal and discourse markers can also have an overarching politeness function, whereby their use concurrently expresses a desire to save the face of self or other (Jucker, Smith & Lüdge, 2003; Nikula, 1996).

Underhill (1988) maintains that 'like' is purely a marker of discourse focus. It highlights significant new information in narratives, questions and answers to questions, for instance a bookstore clerk responding to a request for a particular book: "You go *like* in the back room and they're *like* in the left corner," (p. 234). Under the functions of focus-'like,' Underhill includes the highlighting of information that: (1) is intended to impress (e.g., "The waves were *like* really big.," p. 238); (2) is considered to be unusual by the speaker (e.g., "Can I *like* nibble on your neck?," p. 241); or (3) includes stereotyped expressions (e.g., "That is *like* so not happening!," p. 242). Unusual information may include hyperbole, whereby the speaker marks the focused segment for "unreality" (p. 241) or "disbelief" (p. 242). Such highlighting of unusual notions and stereotyped expressions concurrently contain a politeness or hedging element, whereby "the speaker is distancing himself from the focused segment" (Underhill, 1988, p. 241), e.g., a college student talking to instructor in office: "I couldn't make it to class 'cause, well, *like*, I had this accident on the freeway" (p. 242). However, this means that such uses of 'like' provide implicit information about the speaker's covert thinking (Schourup, 1985), particularly his or her attitudes to the proposition and speaker. In other words, the primary function of 'like' is not necessary on a discourse level (i.e., focusing on new information), but on an interpersonal or attitudinal level (i.e., focusing on information that is unusual or intended to impress).

Miller and Weinert (1995) also maintain that 'like' has a predominately textual focus, especially in clause-initial and clause-medial positions, such as in "*like* that's how you go" and "right so I'm just *like* below the allotments just now" (p. 365). According to Miller and Weinert, there are two major focusing functions of 'like.' Clause-final 'like' is concerned with countering disbelief, objections and assumptions. For example, the final phrase plus 'like' in "my wee girl can swim you know – she has her wings *like*" (p. 389) ensures that the listener does not start to think the speaker is indicating the two-and-a-half year old girl can actually swim properly. Comparatively, 'like' in other syntactic positions is concerned with the elucidation of previous comments and is associated with instructing, aligning and checking in map-task dialogues. However, if clause-final 'like' is concerned with speaker-listener alignment, it must also have interpersonal rapport management functions and, therefore, does not necessarily only focus on the text or discourse.

In accordance with Underhill (1988) and Miller and Weinert (1995), Müller (2005) maintains that the marker 'like' only has discourse functions. These include:

1. searching for the appropriate expression; "and then... all of a sudden this...*like* a= [...] guy who just found th—... the money also" (p. 208)
2. marking an approximate number or quantity; "he got *like* I guess ten cents back" (p. 210)
3. introducing an example; "you know he started to order *like* coffee and other stuff" (p. 214)
4. marking lexical focus; "they walk around *like* a corner" (p. 220)
5. introducing an explanation; "and then there would actually be someone [...] playing the piano there. *like* a=long for the ac[companiment]." (p. 215)
6. various other functions, such as digressions and change of narrative focus, preceding a restart.

Numbers 1 to 4 and number 6 all tie in with functions that have previously been recognized in the literature, i.e., hesitation, approximation, exemplification and focus. According to Müller (2005), 'introducing an explanation' is a category that had not previously been recognised. However, it has many qualities of Miller and Weinert's (1995) and Underhill's (1988) clause initial focus-'like.'

While Müller (2005) maintains that 'like' is exclusively text-focused, her classification includes instances of 'like' to mark subjective stance and attitude towards the interlocutor. As she points out herself, approximator-'like' can be used to reduce the commitment of the speaker to the utterance, indicate "that the exactness of the information is not important for the speaker's purpose" (p. 212), and implicitly convey the feelings of the speaker. Similarly, lexical focus includes the use of 'like' for intensification. It may implicitly reinforce listener impressions of the speaker's attitude to the proposition (e.g., curiosity and displeasure) as well as highlight hyperbole. In all of these cases, the speaker shows an implicit and subjective stance towards the proposition, which moves the function of 'like' beyond a purely textual-focus.

Indeed, the core problem of Underhill (1988), Miller and Weinert (1995) and Müller (2005) is that they fail to take interpersonal and politeness functions of 'like' into consideration (Terraschke, 2008). Comparatively, Schourup (1985) and Andersen (2001) focus only on interpersonal aspects, without taking discourse functions into account. Schourup (1985) classifies 'like' as an evincive that links spoken discourse to the speaker's inner processes and, in doing so, highlights a "discrepancy between what the speaker is about to say and what the speaker feels ideally might or should be said" (Schourup, 1985, p. 42). This excludes the use of 'like' meaning 'approximately,' 'about,' 'around' or 'nearly,' but includes all cases where 'like' can be glossed with 'as it were' or 'so to speak.' Quotative 'like' is included as a pragmatic marker as it highlights a discrepancy between what the speaker reports as having occurred and what was actually said at the time, e.g., "she's *like* "Come in here (a)n(d) have a beer, y(o)u know?" (p. 43). Exemplification 'like' (e.g., "Because see I—a lotta people *like* in business or other – uh things like that," p. 49) is also classified as a pragmatic marker, especially in initial position, as it indicates that the following instance is an accurate but selective representation of something. Similarly, both sentence-initial-'it's like' (e.g., "Carmelita has a hot car. *It's like* the one that Cecil bought," p. 59) and hesitation-'like' (e.g., "They may not be nice – y(ou) know *like* – um so nice," p. 54) indicate the speaker's inability to formulate a more accurate or appropriate version of what they want to express (Schourup, 1985). This means that all instances of 'like' in Schourup (1985) are interpersonal as they function primarily to indicate the attitude of the speaker to the content of the utterance and the interlocutor.

In a similar vein, Andersen (2001) maintains that all uses of pragmatic marker 'like' share the core meaning of "non-identical resemblance between utterance and underlying thought" (Andersen, 2001, p. 233). By employing 'like,' the speaker implicitly expresses a subjective stance towards the utterance. Andersen (2001) suggests a three-tiered model for analyzing pragmatic devices and argues that 'like' functions primarily on the subjective and interpersonal, but not textual, levels of marker use.

Andersen (2001) recognizes that 'like' may fulfil textual functions such as approximation, exemplification, quotation and hesitation. However, he argues that while 'like' can also be used to focus on new and given information, the main role of focus-'like' is not textual, but metalinguistic. As a metalinguistic focus marker, 'like' highlights "lexical material which is from a foreign conceptual domain, sociolinguistically unfitting, stylistically marked, or which appears to involve a relatively high production cost on the part of the speaker" (p. 247). For example in "Did erm, did, Daniel just suddenly *like* ask you out or did someone get you together?" (p. 242), 'like' creates metalinguistic focus by creating a hedge on the expression 'ask you out.' However, such an analysis of 'like' is highly dependent on researcher interpretation and cannot be used to explain all instances of 'like' as a clause-medial focus-marker. Indeed, Andersen's (2001) classification does not include 'like' as an intensifier and fails to provide a clear and detailed account of its textual functions (Terraschke, 2008).

It also becomes increasingly difficult to argue that 'like' always retains a core meaning of approximation or inexactness. In Example 1 from the data collected for this study, it is difficult to argue that in prefacing 'Germany' with 'like' (line 33, LFO renders the term vague or distances herself from it. It is known to both speakers that the friend to whom LFO refers (Esther) moved from Peru to Germany and not to any other European country. It is equally difficult to argue that use of the term 'Germany' involves high production cost to the speaker. The most likely interpretation of 'like' in this particular instance is one of lexical focus, whereby LFO places particular emphasis on the most salient aspect of the sentence in relation to the message she wishes to express.

Example 1. (AES, 10-mth, interview)

```
27      LFO:    we visited friends that live in
28              hameln which is just outside of
29              berlin and I was like open space
30      AG:     yah (laughs)
31      LFO:    yah but um (.) esther had never
32              had that before + like because she
33              moved to (.)  **like** germany when
34              she was four or five + @ she @
35      AG:     @ yep @
36      LFO:    can only just remember peru +
37              so(.) she (.) basically is german
38              (.) but she's @ not (.) um (.) so @
```

Using Andersen's (2001) three-tier model for analyzing pragmatic marker functions, Hasund (2002, 2003) argues that 'like' functions on all three tiers. Firstly, 'like' can implicitly express the speaker's subjective attitude to the utterance. This could be a hedge expressing approximation or imprecision such as in connection with quotations, e.g., "Sing it like, *like* glow in the dark Embassy or something" (Hasund, 2003, p. 124). It could also be an intensifier expressing precision and focus, e.g., "And they're *like* so loud and high-pitched and then when they laugh" (Hasund, 2003, p. 174). Secondly, as an interpersonal politeness marker, 'like' can mark concern towards the listener, indicating an interest in ensuring the listener understands the utterance the way the speaker intended, as in a conversation between M1 and M2, M2 does not understand M1's question "Was that big at one time?" so M1 repeats the question as "Was a micro chip *like* really big at one time?" (Hasund, 2003, p. 179). Finally, textual or linking functions of 'like' include introducing an explanation or elaboration of a previously made point, as in "it gets to her head really quickly. (2) *Like* one, two glasses of wine, and she's off her trolley" (Hasund, 2003, p. 123). However, Hasund (2002, 2003) does not clearly distinguish between interpersonal and discourse focus, and the "interpersonal functions of 'like' seem to depend on its use in conjunction with one of the other functions, which makes it impossible to differentiate between them" (Terraschke, 2008, p. 139).

Terraschke (2008) argues that the interpersonal functions of 'like' discussed in Hasund (2002) are simply a by-product of its textual and subjective functions.

She laments the unclear distinctions and overlaps between functional areas in both Andersen (2001) and Müller (2005). Instead, she collapses the large number of functions they use into four distinct categories:

Discourse link "I did kind of like the politics stuff . *like* political philosophy and stuff" (p. 150)

Subjective stance marker "why are people writing in about first year you were all first years once which is *like* the most clichéd thing to say when refuting first years are dumb" (p. 144)

Quotative "the doctor came out and was just *like* oh you're done I was *like* oh okay ." (p. 153)

Hesitation marker "but the Red Squad were like the=the *like* um . the bovver boys of the police" (p. 158)

Discourse link-'like' encompasses all instances of 'like' which predominantly establish links between units or mark the discourse function of certain elements. Instances of link-'like' primarily "introduce additional information that relates to a previously made comment" (p. 149). This includes 'like' for explanations and clarifications, specifications, exemplifications and elaboration and the phrase 'it's like' (Example 2).

Example 2. (from Terraschke, 2008, p. 150)

```
I did kind of like the politics stuff .
**like** political philosophy and stuff .
but that's one of the   I mean that's
one of the good things about going to the States
```

The main function of Terraschke's (2008) subjective stance-'like' is to express the speaker's evaluation of the accuracy of the utterance. This includes cases where the degree of certainty is less than 100% (i.e., hedge) or more than 100% (i.e., intensification). Uses of 'like' for approximation are classified as subjective stance, as is employment of 'like' to introduce random examples, hyperbole, metaphor or jokes.

Quotative-'like' encompasses all instances where 'like' introduces reported speech of actual conversations or internal monologues. Hesitation-'like' includes 'like' in false starts, self-repairs, repetitions and phases of planning difficulty. However, it is not clear why these two functions are not simply sub-functions of 'like' as a discourse link, as both quotative-'like' and hesitation-'like' fulfil the defining characteristics of the discourse link category: namely, they establish links between units (e.g., restart or self-repair showing digression from previous talk) and/or mark discourse function (i.e., reported speech).

Unfortunately, Terraschke (2008) does not clearly explicate the difference between 'like' as a 'hedge' or as a 'politeness strategy.' She states that "instances of 'like' that belong to the subjective stance category often serve as politeness devices in that they help to soften or emphasize the illocutionary force of speech acts" (p. 143). Her use of 'often' indicates that 'like' may be used as a hedge without a concurrent politeness function. In her discussion, Terraschke (2008, p. 144) indicates that concurrent functions are possible, i.e., 'like' as a hesitation marker can concurrently have a hedging or approximation function. Underhill (1988, p. 241) also acknowledges that 'like' can function as both a focus marker and a hedge, whereby 'like' highlights new information and, at the same time, allows speakers to distance themselves from the assertion and lower their commitment to it.

Terraschke's (2008) classification of 'like' most closely resembles the system used for 'like' in this study. This is purely coincidental as the coding and classification system for this study was already set in place before Terraschke's dissertation was published.

Disregarding use of terminology, there are two core differences between the two classification systems. Firstly, in this study, hesitation-'like' and quotative-'like' are subcategories of 'like' as a discourse marker. Secondly, politeness-'like' is not integrated into subjective stance marking but is a separate overlaying function that can be applied to either discourse or interpersonal marking. For example, both hesitation-'like' and approximation-'like' may concurrently be marked for politeness, whereby they indicate respect for the face of self or other through hesitation and vagueness in a face-threatening situation. We now turn to a discussion of the methodologies and coding of 'like' in the current study.

Method

Participants

All non-native speakers were sixteen to seventeen year old adolescents who had just completed Year 10 at a German *Gymnasium* (high school) at the start of data collection. They were first introduced to formal classroom instruction of English in either Year 4 or 5 and had little experience (i.e., two weeks or less) of living in a target language environment. They all spoke high-German as their mother tongue and lived in Northern Germany.

They were divided into three groups. The first group consisted of fourteen students (eight female, six male) who went on a ten-month exchange to Australia (GES10). In the second group, there were twelve adolescents (eight female, four male) who participated in a five-month exchange (GES05). Finally, the third group was made up of twenty teenagers (fifteen females, five males) who did not go on exchange (GS).

While GES10 and GES05 were pre-existing groups of students who had successfully applied to go on exchange, GS students were recruited using a matched pair technique. Each participant in GES10 and GES05 was matched with a student of the same age, gender, English classroom and English grade in GS. Unfortunately, four such matched GS participants could not be found. By closely matching GES10 and GES05 with GS participants, use of 'like' as a pragmatic marker in the control group was highly comparable to that of experimental groups at the outset of the study. Indeed there were no statistical differences between the use of 'like' by GES10, GES05 and GS in the zero-month data.

Thirteen Australian native-speakers (ten female, three male) were also recruited to match the GES10 participants. They lived in the same region, were mainly of the same age and gender, and attended the same school or school type as the matched GES10 exchange student. Preference was given to native-speakers from the exchange students' direct Australian peer group. An overview of the participants is provided in Table 1.

Table 1. Participant overview

	GES10	GES05	GS	AES
research function	experimental	experimental	control	baseline
study abroad	10 months	5 months	0 months	0 months
group size	14	12	20	13
age	16–18 years	16–18 years	16–18 years	16–18 years
native language	High German	High German	High German	Australian English
pre-test proficiency	intermediate–advanced	intermediate–advanced	intermediate–advanced	native speaker

Data collection

As in similar studies (Aijmer, 2004; Marriott, 1995; Müller, 2005; Regan, 1995, 1998; Sawyer, 1992), semi-structured sociolinguistic interviews were used as data. The interviews were conducted by the researcher (AG), who is a native speaker of Australian English, and were held in informal, relaxed settings (e.g., the participants' homes, gardens or student common rooms). There were two to three data collection points for all non-native speaker participants (Table 2). As suggested by Matsumura (2001), all pre-exchange zero-month interviews (GES10, GES05, GS) were conducted in Germany within two weeks before GES10 and GES05 participants departed for Australia (June–July, 2005). GES10 and GES05 participants were interviewed after five months in Australia (i.e., at the end of GES05's exchange and halfway through the GES10 program in November 2005). The GES10 ten-month interviews were primarily conducted in Australia during April through May 2006. This was within two weeks of departing for Germany, although some were also conducted within one week of the student returning to Germany. No GS data was collected at five months due to the logistical difficulties of recording in Australia and Germany at the same time. Considering the low levels of acquisition of 'like' by GS participants over the entire ten month period, this was not detrimental to the analysis. The GS ten-month interviews were conducted in Germany within two weeks of the GES10 exchange-students' return. Finally, as there were no issues of acquisition in the native-speaker group, AES interviews were conducted only once per participant from November 2005 to June through July 2006 and not necessarily at the same time as the non-native participants.

The interviews were based on a general topic area (e.g., holidays, parties/celebrations and pastimes/hobbies), but no set schedule of conversation was followed and the speakers often diverged into a range of conversational themes. A natural flow of conversation was always given precedence over strict interview style or adherence to a set time limit. This meant that there were differences in interview length from one participant to the next. For this reason, analysis of pragmatic marker use was based on an average marker per minute use or percentage, rather than raw frequencies.

Table 2. Data collection overview

	2005		2006	
	June–July	November	April–May	June–July
GES10	holidays	festivities	free time	
GES05	holidays	free time		
GS	holidays			
AES		free time	free time	free time

Transcription and coding

The interviews were transcribed with minimal mark up due to the large amount of data (see Appendix). A concordancer was developed and used to extract all occurrences of 'like' and these were then coded for function according to the classification system shown in Figure 1.

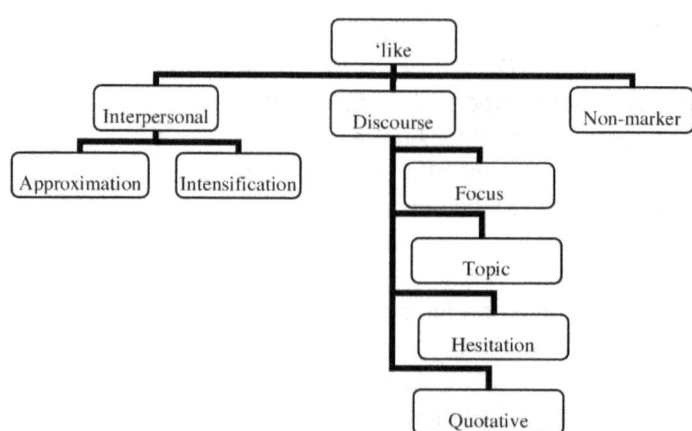

Figure 1. Functional coding of 'like'[1]

Interpersonal-'like'

'Like' was coded as an interpersonal marker when it signalled implicit attitudes, feelings or prejudices and highlighted a desire to establish a relationship between speaker, hearer and message. It did this by either marking approximation or intensification of the proposition.

Approximator-'like' highlighted use of vague terminology or rendered an exact term or quantity vague (Jucker et al., 2003). In doing so, it reduced the speaker's commitment to the literal truth of the utterance (Andersen, 2001). It implicitly conveyed the speaker's attitudes and emotions by indicating that not only might he or she not know a more precise expression or number, but that such precision was not necessary in the context of speaking (Östman, 1981). Additionally it implied shared interlocutor knowledge of vague concepts and categories (Channell, 1994).

Approximator-'like' was clause-medial and often accompanied by other vague markers. To differentiate it from use of 'like' for exemplification, it provided an example of a larger class of potentially relevant items that remained unmentioned (Terraschke, 2008). In Example 3 (line 186), MM prefaced 'sofas' with 'like' to indicate that it was a prototypical example of a wider range of items that would be useful for parties. In doing so, he indicated assumed mutual knowledge of such items. In this and many similar examples, approximator-'like' co-occurred with the general extender 'and stuff,' but could also appear without the general extender.

Example 3. (GES10, 5-mth, interview)

```
180    MM:   it's better for him to have it
181          outside because not so many things
182          get like smashed + or
183    AG:   yep
184    MM:   yeah so (.) / but it's sometimes
185          better inside because you have
186          **like** (.) um sofas and stuff +
187    AG:   yep
188    MM:   where you can (.) just relax on
189          + @ and @
```

Intensifier-'like' signalled emotional and attitudinal involvement in the subject matter (Biber & Finegan, 1989; Chafe, 1982) and subjective interpretation of salient information (Athanasiadou, 2007). Most commonly it highlighted information the speaker considered to be particularly surprising or interesting or use of hyperbole, sarcasm/irony or jokes. It was clause-medial and the focus of intensification was never a full clause. In Example 4 (lines 572 and 575), NS used 'like' to highlight use of hyperbole. It was clear to both AG and NS that the entire wall could not have actually been covered in DVDs nor could the friend have owned every DVD released, but by including 'like,' NS showed that he was intensifying the phrase for effect and that he believed it was an incredibly large number of DVDs.

Example 4. (GES10, 10-mth, interview)

```
571    NS:    he had like a whole (.) / a
572           whole wall was   **like** covered
573           in dvds+
574    AG:    yeah
575    NS:    and he had **like** everything
576           and he had all the simpsons episodes +
```

Discourse-'like'

'Like' was classified as a discourse marker when it focused primarily on reducing the hearer's processing load in utterance comprehension (Andersen, 1998). It was subdivided into four categories: focus, topic, hesitation and quotative. These were further subdivided into a range of functions (e.g., continuation of a topic, introducing an example or explanation, hesitation due to interruption by self or other). However, these sub-functions were not analyzed separately due to high levels of overlap (see Terraschke, 2008).

Focus-'like' drew attention to the most salient piece of information, highlighted contrasting elements or signposted information for increased coherence and comprehension. It was always clause-medial and could be differentiated from intensifier-'like' in that it highlighted elements for coherence and not affective purposes. In Example 5 (lines 409 and 414), LN prefaced 'for children' and 'deeper' with 'like' to focus on the main point of her argument, i.e., the film was, on the one hand, made for children but, on the other, more suitable to adults who could comprehend the depth of the story. Note that in both cases, 'like' was preceded by 'it's' but was not followed by a full clause, so could not be considered part of an 'it's like' phrase (Schourup, 1985).

Example 5. (GES10, 10-mth, interview)

```
406    LN:    yeah it's a kid's film but (1.0)
407           yeah it's pretty funny + @ but @
408    AG:    @ yeah + @
409    LN:    it's **like** for children + but
410           I don't think it's for children
411           because(1.0) it / if you are older
412           you can understand it a bit more +
413    AG:    yeah
414    LN:    it's **like** deeper +
```

Topic-'like' showed transitions and continuations between segments of speech. This included moves between topics, digressions, summaries, examples, explanations and links to previously discussed topics. It was always clause-initial or occurred in the clause-initial phrase 'it's like' + clause (Schourup, 1985). In Example 6 (line 538), RHI began the clause with 'so like' to show that there was a thematic relationship between her host family aunt's love for traveling and the aunt returning from Russia when RHI left for Australia.

Example 6.   (GES10, 10-mth, interview)

```
532    RHI:   she's thirty but still um (.)
533           yeah has / at the moment she has no
534           boyfriend + she has no (.) ah
535           children + @ and @
536    AG:    @ yep @
537    RHI:   ah yeah and she loves traveling
538           + so **like** she came back from
539           russia when I left um (.) germany +
```

Hesitation-'like' indicated difficulties in formulating speech. It invariably collocated with other markers of hesitation and often occurred near the truncation of a clause or intonation unit (Example 7, line 445). It included false starts, planning difficulties, word search and self-correction. Unlike topic-'like,' it did not necessarily occur in clause-initial position. Most commonly the clause position was difficult to determine due to the disjointed nature of the surrounding speech.

Example 7.   (GES10, 10-mth, interview)

```
445    LN:    oh (laughs) ok um it's  **like**
446           (2.0) um (.) what is it called in
447           English + (laughs) I forgot um (2.0)
448           I don't even know it in german
449    AG:    (laughs)
450    LN:    (1.0) I really don't know like
451           the big elephants with the big teeth +
```

Arguably a subsection of topic-'like,' quotative-'like' formed part of the construction verb + 'like' and was used to indicate approximate rendition of actual or assumed speech, thought or feelings (Müller, 2005). While 'be' was the most prevalent verb in quotative 'like' constructions, other verbs such as 'look,' 'think,' 'see' and 'ask' were also used (Müller, 2005). The item being reported was the speech, thought or feelings of the speaker or others (Example 8, line 358).

Example 8. (GES10, 10-mth, interview)

```
354   MAM:   and then the / and then the guy
355          comes +
356   AG:    hmhm
357   MAM:   and **he's** oh you want some
358          help + and I live here **like** this
359          is my (.) territory +
360   AG:    hmhm
361   MAM:   I know about it and then they
362          said ok so they drive with him
363          there+
```

Unlike Müller (2005) and Terraschke (2008), in this study quotative-'like' was classified as a discourse marker. This was mainly due to the fact that, in the data, quotative-'like' was syntactically optional, even when used in 'be' + 'like' constructions (Example 8, line 357) and syntactic position was not fixed (Example 9, line 348 and Example 10, line 197).

Example 9. (GES10, 10-mth, interview)

```
348   MAM:   and **like everybody's** oh we
349          left a light on and stuff +
350   AG:    yep
351   MAM:   and then the / and then the guy
352          comes +
```

Example 10. (AES, 10-mth, interview)

```
192   CM:    like one lady ran up to me
193          screaming (high voice) I want a
194          cappuccino like @ that @
195   AG:    @ (laughs) @
196   CM:    and I just [turned round]
197          **like** have you ever considered
198          decaf +
199   AG:    (laughs)
200   CM:    cause she was just hyped up and
201          she was just like laughing so much
202   AG:    (laughs)
```

Non-marker-'like'

Example 11. (GES05, 5-mth, interview)

```
53    AW:   yeah then it's just great and
54          hm: I don't know we have so much
55          time  together and we're / I don't /
56          I think because we are so
57          different that's why we   **like**
58          each other so much +
59    AG:   yeah
60    AW:   and it's interesting and always
61          funny yeah
```

Non-marker 'like' included all uses of 'like' when it is not used as a pragmatic marker. This includes 'like' as a verb, adjective, adverb, noun, preposition, suffix or conjunction and when it could not be omitted from the context without damaging syntactic and grammatical integrity (Example 11, line 57). If 'like' could not be coded due to incomplete syntactic structure (e.g., when the speaker was cut off by the hearer after using 'like'), it was coded as unclassifiable and not included (see Example 12, line 599).

Example 12. (GES10, 5-mth, interview)

```
598   ERM:  I didn't get lost (.) yeah but
599         I was **like**  / ah by the way I'd
600         realised that I was the only one
601         actually prepared for something like
602         that +
603   AG:   yep
604   ERM:  cause I had a fruit with me + I
605         had a towel with me + I had
```

Analysis

As the data did not fulfil more than one of the assumptions required for parametric statistical testing, nonparametric statistics were used for analysis. Significance levels were set at $p<.05$. If significance levels were reached, a Cohen's d effect size was calculated. If effect size was greater than 0.8, it was considered large (Cohen, 1988) and further detailed analysis was conducted.

Results

Interpersonal-'like'
GES10

Interpersonal-'like' was acquired within the first five months of a ten month exchange in both its approximation and intensification functions. As shown in Figure 2, approximator-'like' increased significantly with a medium to large effect size (p=.001, ES=.7) and intensifier-'like' increased significantly with a large effect size (p=.002, ES=1.2) from zero to five months. The slight decrease in use of both approximator-'like' and intensifier-'like' from five to ten months was not significant and was therefore not explored further.

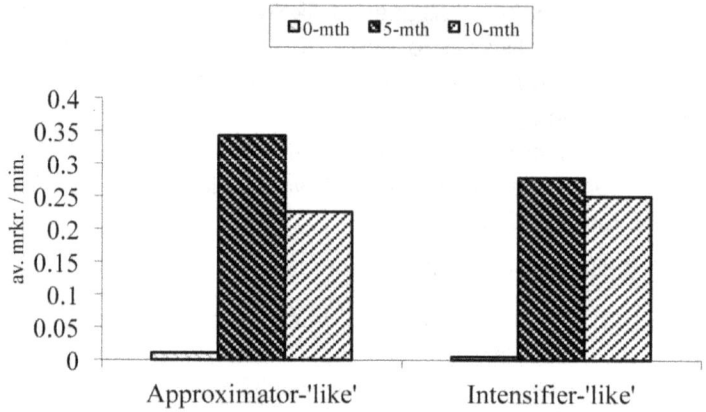

Figure 2. GES 10 Interpersonal-'like' (0–10mths)

GES10 vs. GS

While use of interpersonal-'like' was the same at the outset of data collection for GES10 and GS, after ten months it was used significantly more in GES10 than by GS participants who did not go on exchange (Figure 3 and Figure 4). Higher use by GES10 was significant and large for both approximator-'like' (p=.000, ES=1.0) and intensifier-'like' (p=.000, ES=1.4). This indicated that interpersonal-'like' was acquired through native speaker contact in a study abroad setting and not in the foreign language high school classroom.

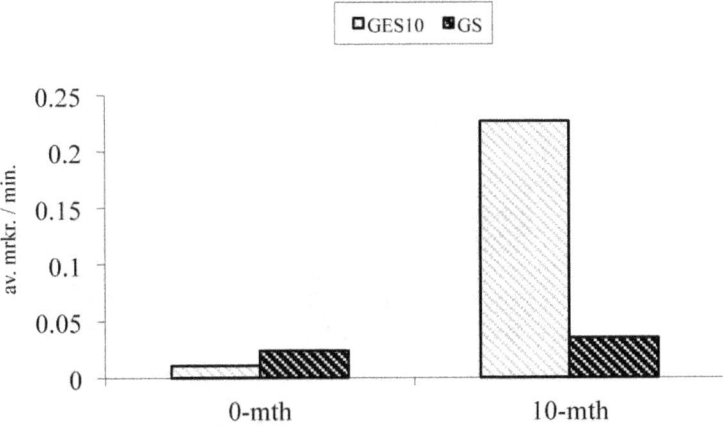

Figure 3. GES10 vs. GS approximator-'like' (0–10mths)

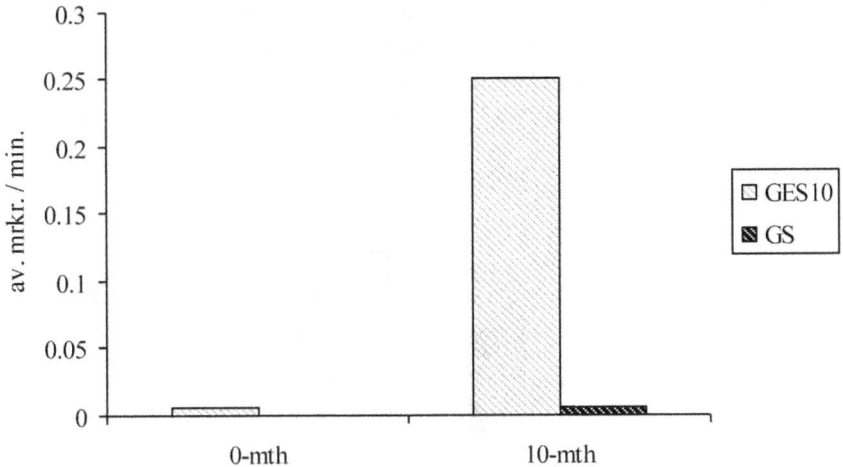

Figure 4. GES10 vs. GS intensifier-'like' (0–10mths)

GES10 vs. AES

As shown in Figure 5, higher use in AES compared to GES10 was significant and large for approximator-'like' (p=.000, ES=2.0) at zero months. After five months of the ten month sojourn, GES10's use of approximator-'like' remained lower than that of AES. While this difference was not significant at five months, it was both significant and large after ten months of living in the target culture (p=.005, ES=0.9). Indeed, use of 'like' by GES10 was higher at five months than at ten months. This may indicate that ten months was not enough time for GES10 participants to reach consistent native-like levels of approximator-'like.'

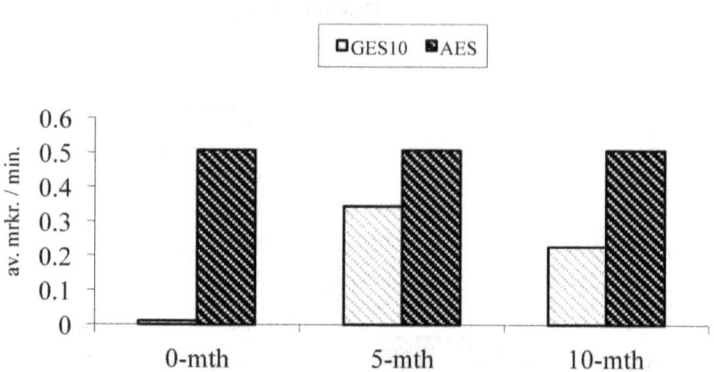

Figure 5. GES10 vs. AES approximator-'like' (0, 5 & 10-mths)

AES's higher use of intensifier-'like' was also significant and large at zero months (p=.000, ES=1.7). However, after five months of their ten-month study abroad, GES10's use of intensifier-'like' closely resembled that of native-speakers in AES and levels of usage remained similar after ten months (Figure 6). This may indicate that intensifier-'like' was learnt before or faster than approximator-'like.'

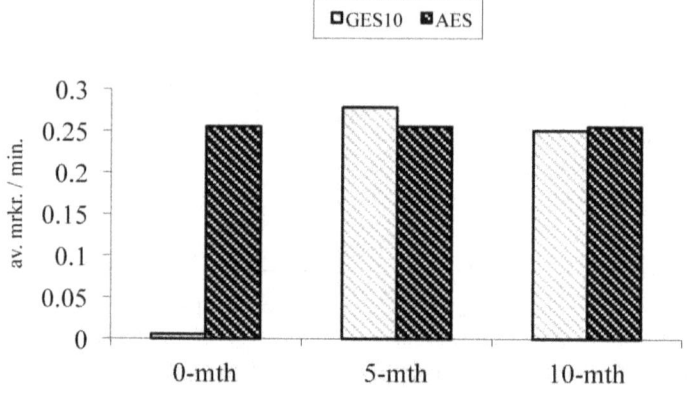

Figure 6. GES10 vs. AES intensifier-'like' (0, 5 & 10mths)

GES10 vs. GES05

Similar to the results for GES10, in GES05 use of interpersonal-'like' increased significantly with a large effect size (p=.028, ES=1.2) during the five months of their exchange. However, while there was a significant and large increase in intensifier-'like' (p=.018, ES=1.1) after five months, increased use of approximator-'like' was not statistically significant (p=.086). Indeed comparisons of the GES10 and GES05 data after five months of their respective exchanges showed that GES10 made significantly larger use of both intensifier-'like' (p=.000, ES=1.7) and approximator-'like' (p=.023, ES=.9) with a large effect size compared to GES05 (Figure 7 and Figure 8).

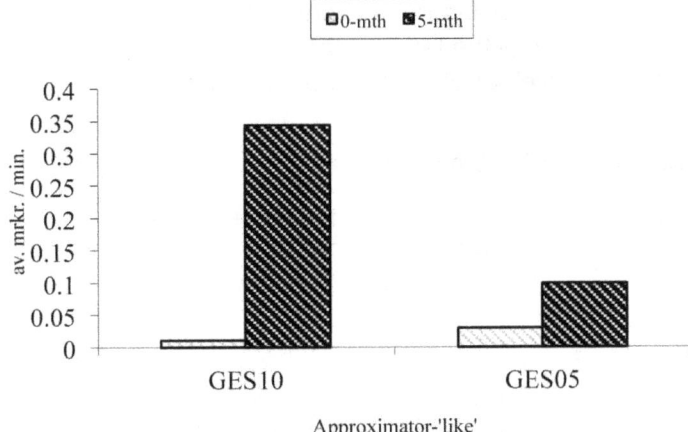

Figure 7. GES10 vs. GES05 approximator-'like' (0–5mths)

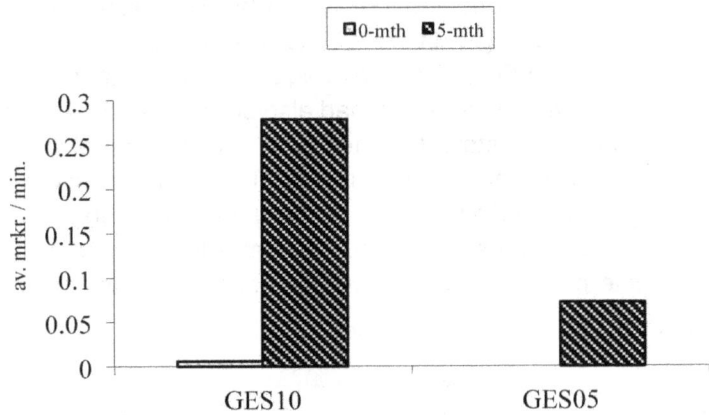

Figure 8. GES10 vs. GES05 intensifier-'like' (0–5mths)

Since both groups were statistically equivalent in their use of interpersonal-'like' at the outset of the exchange, the reason for this difference must lie in either the motivations of students who decide to go on a five or ten month exchange or the exchange experience itself. Questionnaire and interview content did not indicate any differences in motivation at the outset of the study. The students' decisions to go on a five rather than ten month exchange was mostly based on financial or logistical reasons (e.g., reintegration into the German school system). However, large differences in GES10 and GES05's individual motivations and experiences during the exchange were apparent. Based on interview content, conversations with the participants and questionnaire data, GES05 participants were less likely to invest in host family relations and adolescent friendships than GES10 participants. At the five-month data collection point, five of the twelve GES05 participants (42%) were unhappy with their host family, but had decided to put up with the family rather than initiate change (Example 13). Use of interpersonal-'like' for all of these participants was low (.14 average tokens/minute or below).

Example 13. (GES05, 5mth, interview)

```
34    AG:    have you got mixed feelings
35           about (.) going home +
36    LK:    no (laughs) I'm more like / I
37           don't know I'm happy to have this
38           week here +
39    AG:    yep
40    LK:    but I don't know I'm finished
41           with my host family (laughs) so
```

Comparatively, only one GES10 participant (7%) reported difficult family relations at five months. Despite extreme difficulties based on differences in religious beliefs, he had decided to invest in family relations rather than simply give up on communicating with them (Example 14). SJ's use of interpersonal-'like' was the lowest in GES10 (.04 average tokens/minute) closely followed by PN (.06 average tokens/minute). PN had also been very unhappy in his first host family, with whom he had stayed for the first 4.5 months before initiating a change in family through the exchange organization. They were an elderly Dutch couple without children and PN did not feel they were able to understand the social and emotional needs or interests of an adolescent. All other participants in GES10 made use of interpersonal-'like' on average at above 0.2 tokens/minute.

Example 14. (GES10, 5-mth, interview)

```
338   AG:    oh wow (.) yeah (.) then do you
339          / like with your mates around here +
340          do you usually sort of spend time
341          with them after school + and
342   SJ:    hm yeah I mean after school it's
343          (.) / there's / (.) yeah sometimes I
344          was running + I was ah practising
345          for the city to surf run + (.) um
346          (.) and ah (2.0) yeah but it's four
347          o'clock then + and (.) then they /
348          then I have to study a little bit +
349          and yeah and you do stuff with your
350          family because they come home and
351          you know
```

```
352   AG:   yep
353   SJ:   you want to do / do something
354         with them +
```

Difficult host family relations and a lack of desire to negotiate with the host family or organization meant the student's access to native-use of 'like' was limited. For example, one GES05 participant (MF) lived remotely and could not join in any organized activities with friends because she was not prepared to negotiate transport with host family members. This resulted in less quality adolescent language contact and integration, which was reflected in GES05's comparatively low acquisition of interpersonal-'like.' One of the GES10 participants (RHI) also lived remotely, but due to a positive relationship with her host family she was able to organize transport and sleepovers at friends' houses so that she could pursue her sporting and social interests. As such, she and a number of other GES10 participants were able to enjoy a wide range social activities after school and acquired high levels of interpersonal-'like.'

Discourse-'like'
GES10

GES10's increased use of discourse-'like' in the first five months (Figure 9) was significant and large for focus ($p=.011$, ES=1.3), topic ($p=.001$, ES 1.4), hesitation ($p=.001$, ES=1.7) and quotative ($p=.008$, ES=1.0). Slight increases or decreases from five to ten months were not significant. Hesitation-'like' replaced other hesitation-markers that were common to both German and English native-speakers (e.g., 'um,' 'er,' 'hm') or particular to German native-speakers (e.g., 'pf').

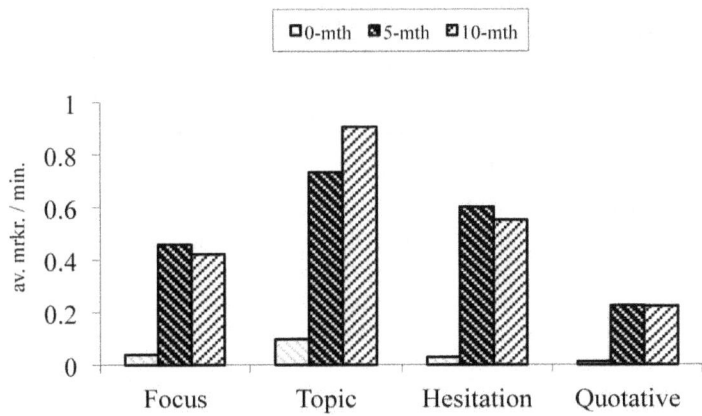

Figure 9. GES10 discourse-'like' (0–10mths)

GES10 vs. GS

Again, mirroring results found for interpersonal-'like,' little or no increase was found in the use of discourse-'like' among GS participants who did not participate in an extended exchange during data collection. There was no statistical difference between GES10 and GS's use of discourse-'like' at the outset of the study. However, as shown in Figure 10, at the ten month data collection, higher use of discourse-'like' in GES10 compared to GS was significant and large for focus (p=.000, ES=1.3), topic (p=.000, ES=1.5), hesitation (p=.000, ES=1.5) and quotative (p=.000, ES=1.1). This indicated that the large increases found in both GES10 and GES05 were due to differences in the language acquisition context (i.e., study abroad vs. foreign language classroom).

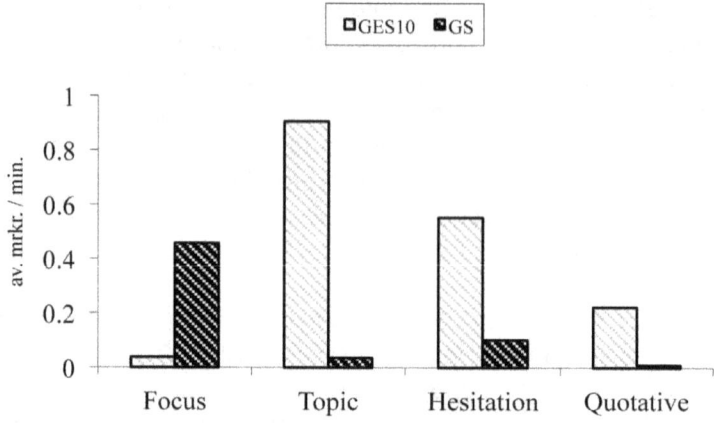

Figure 10. GES10 vs. GS discourse-'like' (0–10mths)

GES10 vs. AES

At the outset of the study, lower use of discourse-'like' by GES10 compared to AES was significant and large for focus (p=.000, ES=1.8), topic (p=.000, ES=1.7), hesitation (p=.000, ES=1.2), and quotative (p=.000, ES=1.1). After five and ten months, GES10 continued to use focus-'like' and, to a lesser extent, topic-'like' and quotative-'like' less than AES, but these differences were not statistically significant (Figure 11). Similarly, slightly higher use of hesitation-'like' by GES10 compared to AES at five and ten months was not statistically significant. This indicated that within five months, the exchange students acquired native-speaker-like levels of discourse-'like.'

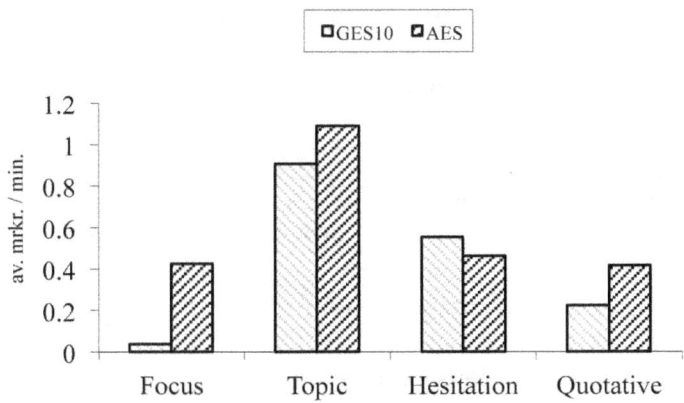

Figure 11. GES10 vs. AES discourse-'like' (10-mths)

GES10 vs. GES05

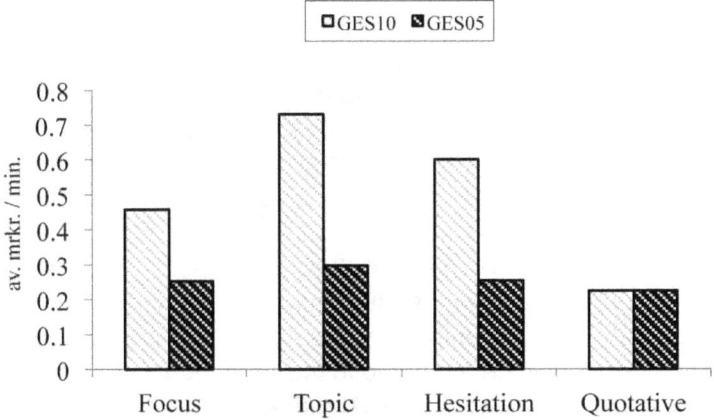

Figure 12. GES10 vs. GES05 discourse-'like' (5-mths)

Comparisons of GES10 and GES05 also strongly resembled results found for interpersonal-'like.' Significant and large increases were found from zero to five months in GES05 for focus (p=.003, ES=1.4), topic (p=.013, ES=1.0), hesitation (p=.041, ES=1.0) and quotative (p=.018, ES=.9). While levels of use remained below that of GES10 for focus, topic and hesitation (Figure 12), only lower use of topic (p=.015, ES=.9) and hesitation (p=.020, ES=.9) were significant and large. After five months, use of quotative-'like' was the same for GES10 and GES05. As levels of use in GES10 did not increase further from five to ten months and were the same as use in AES, quotative-'like' was acquired to native-speaker levels within five months of either a five or ten month exchange. However, all other functions were attained more quickly by students on a ten-month exchange than those on a five-month program. As was the case for comparisons in the acquisition of interpersonal-'like,' this was most likely due to lower levels of social investment and integration in GES05 than GES10. This is discussed further in the next section of this chapter.

Discussion

This study found that 'like' has interpersonal and discourse functions in the language of both native and non-native speakers of Australian English. A key marker of adolescent language, it was learnt in both its interpersonal and discourse functions within the first five months of a student exchange to Australia.

However, it is unfair to assume that the non-native speakers actually strived towards native-speaker levels of use. Considering the close connection between use of 'like' and the expression of self, it is possible that German adolescent exchange students were keen to maintain and express their German adolescent non-native speaker identities. Indeed, by not entirely emulating native speaker use of 'like,' the German exchange students could position themselves as being foreign or German or European, which might have granted them status, rights and privileges that the adolescent native-speakers did not possess. This is an area that remains open for further research.

'Like' also seemed to be indexical of social integration, whereby the more integrated exchange students felt in their host families and local adolescent communities, the more likely they were to acquire high use of 'like.' However, students who knew from the outset of the exchange that they would only be in Australia for five months seemed less likely to invest in host family relations and friendships than those exchange students on a ten month program. This was especially apparent when relations in the host family turned sour. Such lack of investment may not only be attributed to the exchange students, but also to their host families and potential peers. For all three of these players, a short length of stay may have meant they were less prepared to negotiate differences and invest in establishing and maintaining close contact.

Unfortunately, the scope of this study did not include the attitudes and beliefs of host families and potential peers. It did, however, clearly indicate the integral role of the host family to study abroad experiences (Knight & Schmidt-Rinehart, 2010). The more at home students felt in their host family environments, the more able they were to invest in relationships with other teenagers outside of the home and the higher their use of 'like' became. As interactions within the host family were not taken into account in this study, no assumptions can be made as to how often 'like' was acquired and used in this particular setting. The argument put forth here is simply that host family relations have a gate-keeping function in terms of integration and access to settings where adolescents interact outside of school. For example, if host family relations were not positive, the exchange student was less likely to request permission from host parents to attend extracurricular activities such as sporting events and parties where they could interact with other adolescents. Thus their access to use of 'like' by adolescents was restricted to interactions at school, which mostly took place during short recess and lunch breaks.

It is also tempting to discuss reasons for the slight reduction in the use of 'like' as an interpersonal and discourse marker by GES10 from the five to ten month collection points. For example, it could be argued that this was due to increased lexical knowledge and competency resulting in lower use of 'like' for hesitation or increased sociolinguistic competence in use of 'like' with a non-adolescent interlocutor. However, considering the fact that this decrease was minimal and by no means statistically significant, any of these arguments would be difficult to substantiate. Additionally, there is no correct level of use of 'like' as a pragmatic marker due to its inseparable link to the expression of identity. Identities are always multiple and the relative importance of marking one identity over another is by no means static, but can change from moment to moment, even within the same conversation.

Finally, the results of this study indicate a range of potential areas for further research. Using the coding system for this study, larger cohorts of both native and non-native speakers of a variety of Englishes could be conducted. With increased time and personnel, more detailed transcriptions could be made, allowing for increased sophistication in the recording, coding and analysis of 'like' (e.g., inclusion of paralinguistic features). Systematic and detailed collection of language contact experiences could also be included, such as interviewing friends and host families, including e-journals and observations of interactions at home and school.

While one-on-one sociolinguistic interviews with the same interlocutor ensured comparability of the data, other types of speech situations and interlocutor constellations could be trialled. Non-native participants' awareness of 'like' in adolescent language, as well as its relationship to the expression of their own non-native speaker identities could also be researched in detail. Further research would not only continue to unravel the multifunctional nature of the pragmatic marker 'like' in adolescent language, but also provide critical information for increasing the likelihood of success in exchange student program design.

Conclusion

'Like' can have both discourse and interpersonal functions. The results of this study indicate that study abroad is a primary opportunity for acquiring 'like' in both its interpersonal and discourse functions, especially for individuals on a ten-month or longer exchange program. Given the importance of 'like' for the expression of adolescent identity, differences in the acquisition of 'like' during study abroad may be indicative of integration into native-speaker adolescent communities. In turn, degrees of integration reflect the extent to which exchange students, host families and adolescent peers are prepared to invest in their relationships with each other. Clearly, the academic fields of pragmatics, second language acquisition and adolescent language benefit from these findings. Additionally, study of the acquisition of 'like' in study abroad contexts may have far reaching consequences for exchange student programs. This includes program design, the matching of students with host families and provision of support for students, families and schools in the host country.

Note
1   In addition to its interpersonal or discourse functions, 'like' could be used to boost or mitigate an utterance. These politeness functions of 'like' were not included in the analysis reported in this paper.

References

Aijmer, K. (2004). Pragmatic markers in spoken interlanguage. In K. Dollerup (Ed.), *Worlds of words: A tribute to Arne Zettersten. Nordic Journal of English Studies, Special Issue, 3*, 173–190.

Athanasiadou, A. (2007). On the subjectivity of intensifiers. *Language Sciences, 29*, 554–565.

Andersen, G. (1998). The pragmatic marker 'like' from a relevance-theoretic perspective. In A .H., Jucker, & Y. Ziv (Eds.), *Discourse markers: Descriptions and theory* (pp. 147–170). Amsterdam/Philadelphia: John Benjamins.

Andersen, G. (2001). *Pragmatic markers and sociolinguistic variation: A relevance—theoretic approach to the language of adolescents.* Amsterdam/Philadelphia: John Benjamins.

Barron, A. (2003). *Acquisition in interlanguage pragmatics: Learning how to do things with words in a study abroad context.* Amsterdam/Philadelphia: John Benjamins.

Biber, D., & Finegan, E. (1989). Styles of stance in English: Lexical and grammatical marking of evidentiality and affect. *Text, 9*(1), 93–124.

Bremer, K., Broeder, P., Roberts, C., Simonot, M., & Vasseur, M.-T. (1993). Ways of achieving understanding. In C. Perdue (Ed.), *Adult language acquisition: Cross—linguistic perspectives, Vol. II: The results* (pp. 153–195). Cambridge: Cambridge University Press.

Brinton, L. J. (1996). *Pragmatic markers in English.* Berlin/New York: Mouton de Gruyter.

Chafe, W. (1982). Integration and involvement in speaking, writing and oral literature. In D. Tannen (Ed.), *Spoken and written language: Exploring orality and literacy* (pp. 35–53). Norwood, NJ: Ablex.

Chambers, J. K. (2000). *Sociolinguistic theory* (2nd ed.). Oxford: Blackwell.

Channell, J. (1994). *Vague language.* Oxford: Oxford University Press.

Cohen. J. (1988). *Statistical power analysis for the behavioural sciences.* Hillsdale, NJ: Erlbaum.

Cook, H. M. (2008). *Socializing identities through speech style.* Bristol: Multilingual Matters.
Dewaele, J. M., & Regan, V. (2001). The use of colloquial words in advanced French interlanguage. *EUROSLA Yearbook, 1,* 51–67.
Ferguson, C. (1995). [Foreword]. In B. Freed (Ed.), *Second language acquisition in a study abroad context* (pp. xi-xv). Amsterdam/Philadelphia: John Benjamins.
Fraser, B. (1999). What are discourse markers? *Journal of Pragmatics, 31,* 931–952.
Gare, S. (2006). *The triumph of the airheads: And the retreat from commonsense.* Double Bay: Park Street Press.
Grieve, A. (2010) *Adolescent identity and pragmatic marker acquisition in a study abroad context.* Unpublished doctoral dissertation. University of Melbourne, Australia.
Guntermann, G. (1995). The Peace Corps experience: Language learning in training and in the field. In B. Freed (Ed.), *Second language acquisition in a study abroad context* (pp. 149–170). Amsterdam/Philadelphia: John Benjamins.
Halliday, M. A. K. (1973). *Explorations in the functions of language.* London: Edward Arnold.
Hasund, I. K. (2002). 'Congratulations, like! – Gratulerer, liksom!' Pragmatic particles in English and Norwegian. In L. E., Breivik, & A. Hasselgren (Eds.), *From the colt's mouth ... and others* (pp. 125–139). Amsterdam: Rodopi.
Hasund, I. K. (2003). *The discourse markers 'like' in English and 'liksom' in Norwegian teenage language: a corpus-based, cross-linguistic study.* Unpublished doctoral dissertation. University of Bergen and Agder University College, Norway.
Isabelli-García, C. (2006). Study abroad social networks, motivation and attitudes: Implications for second language acquisition. In DuFon, M., & Churchill, E. (Eds.), *Language learners in study abroad contexts* (pp. 231–258). Clevedon: Multilingual Matters.
Ishida, M. (2009). Development of interactional competence: Changes in the use of *ne* in L2 Japanese during study abroad. In H. t. Nguyen, & G. Kasper (Eds.), *Talk-in-interaction: Multilingual perspectives* (pp. 351–385). Honolulu: University of Hawai'i, National Foreign Language Resource Center.
Ishida, M. (2011). Engaging in another person's telling as a recipient in L2 Japanese: Development of interactional competence during one-year study abroad. In G. Pallotti, & J. Wagner (Eds.), *L2 learning as social practice: Conversation-analytic perspectives* (pp. 45–85). Honolulu: University of Hawai'i, National Foreign Language Resource Center.
Jucker, A. H., Smith, S. W., & Lüdge, T. (2003). Interactive aspects of vagueness in conversation. *Journal of Pragmatics, 35,* 1737–1769.
Kinginger, C. (2008). *Language learning in study abroad: Case studies of Americans in France.* Modern Language Journal Monograph, 92. Oxford: Blackwell.
Kinginger, C. (2009). *Language learning and study abroad: A critical reading of research.* New York: Palgrave MacMillan.
Knight, S. M., & Schmidt-Rinehart, B. C. (2010). Exploring conditions to enhance student/host family interaction abroad. *Foreign Language Annals, 43,* 64–79.

Marriott, H. (1995). The acquisition of politeness patterns by exchange students in Japan. In B. Freed (Ed.), *Second language acquisition in a study abroad context* (pp. 197–224). Amsterdam/Philadelphia: John Benjamins.
Matsumura, S. (2001). Learning the rules for offering advice: A quantitative approach to second language socialisation. *Language Learning, 51*, 635–679.
Miller, J., & Weinert, R. (1995). The function of 'like' in dialogue. *Journal of Pragmatics, 23*, 365–393.
Müller, S. (2005). *Discourse markers in native and non-native English discourse.* Amsterdam/Philadelphia: John Benjamins.
Nikula, T. (1996). *Pragmatic force modifiers: A study in interlanguage pragmatics.* Jyväskylä: University of Jyväskylä.
Norton, B. (2000). *Identity and language learning.* Essex: Pearson Education.
Östman, J. O., (1981). *You know: A discourse-functional approach.* Amsterdam/Philadelphia: John Benjamins.
Regan, V. (1995). The acquisition of sociolinguistic native speech norms: Effects of a year abroad on second language learners of French. In B. Freed (Ed.), *Second language acquisition in a study abroad context* (pp. 254–268). Amsterdam/Philadelphia: John Benjamins.
Regan, V. (1998). Sociolinguistics and language learning in a study abroad context. *Frontiers: The interdisciplinary journal of study abroad, Fall 1998*, 61–90.
Sawyer, M. (1992). The development of pragmatics in Japanese as a second language: The sentence –final particle 'ne'. In G. Kasper (Ed.), *Pragmatics of Japanese as a native and target language* (pp. 83–125). Honolulu: University of Hawai'i, Second Language Teaching and Curriculum Center.
Schauer, G. A. (2007). Finding the right words in the study abroad context: The development of German learners' use of external modifiers in English. *Intercultural Pragmatics, 4*, 193–220. [Special issue on acquisitional pragmatics].
Schourup, L. C. (1985). *Common discourse particles in English conversation.* New York/London: Garland.
Tagliamonte, S. (2005). So who? Like how? Just what? Discourse markers in the conversations of young Canadians. *Journal of Pragmatics, 37*, 1896–1915.
Terraschke, A. (2008). *The use of pragmatic devices by German non-native speakers of English.* Unpublished doctoral dissertation, Victoria University of Wellington, New Zealand.
Underhill, R. (1988). Like is, like focus. *American Speech, 63*, 234–346.

Appendix: Transcription conventions

+	rising intonation
@ xx @	overlapping speech
(.)	silence for less than one second
(2.0)	2 second pause (3.0 is a 3 second pause, etc)
x	emphatically marked speech
=	latching
/	repair (i.e., change of sentence started, resumption after a pause)
[X]	unclear (one word or syllable)
[XX]	unclear (two words)
[XXX]	unclear (more than two words)
~ xxx ~	non-English words
AG:	interviewer (Averil Grieve)

On Saying the Same Thing: Issues in the Analysis of Conventional Expressions in L2 Pragmatics

Kathleen Bardovi-Harlig
Indiana University

This chapter addresses issues in the analysis of conventional expressions in L2 pragmatics. With its fundamental concern for the role of context in language use, pragmatics provides an ideal framework for the investigation of the acquisition and use of conventional expressions. Approaching the analysis of conventional expressions using the characteristics identified by Myles, Hooper, and Mitchell (1998) for the analysis of formulas, this paper first addresses the issues of identifying conventional expressions in native speaker speech employing the criteria of recurrence of sequences, context dependence, and community-wide use. It then considers issues of analysis of learner production and approaches to evaluating the equivalence of expressions based on recurrence of sequences, phonological fluency, and volubility. It further discusses parameters along which native speaker and learner production may differ, and optimal coding for different research questions.

Introduction

This chapter addresses issues in the analysis of conventional expressions in L2 pragmatics. Conventional expressions (also referred to as *pragmatic routines, routine formulae,* and *situation-based utterances* in the pragmatics literature) include such strings as *No problem, Nice to meet you,* and *That'd be great,* which native speakers use predictably in certain contexts. In no other area of pragmatics is saying the same thing taken as literally as in the study of the acquisition and use of conventional expressions. Whether comparing native speakers to other native speakers, learners to native speakers, or higher-level learners to lower-level learners, most levels of analysis allow for some leeway. The same speech act or semantic formula may be realized in a variety of ways. Similarly, the same content may be encoded differently, and the same forms such as mitigators, downgraders, or upgraders may appear in very different utterances. However, for speakers to use the same conventional expression in the same context, the speech act performed, the semantic formulas used to perform it, the content encoded, and the form (the specific sequence of words) must all converge. This paper addresses the issues involved in determining what 'saying the same thing' means when evaluating learner production of target-language conventional expressions.

Conventional expressions are a social and linguistic construct. According to Coulmas (1981), they are

> highly conventionalized prepatterned expressions whose occurrence is tied to more or less standardized communication situations... Conversational routines are tacit agreements, which the members of a community presume to be shared by every reasonable co-member. In embodying social knowledge they are essential in the handling of day-to-day transactions. (p. 2–3)

House (1996) writes that routines "embody the societal knowledge that members of a given community share ... [and] routine formulas are thus essential in the verbal handling of everyday life" (pp. 227–228). Their social importance does not guarantee ease of acquisition, however, and Kasper and Blum-Kulka (1993, p. 9) observe that "one area where insufficient control of pragmalinguistic knowledge is particularly obvious is that of pragmatic routines." In light of Kasper and Blum-Kulka's observation, it is not surprising that mastery of conventional expressions often comes late and thus their use may characterize highly advanced learners (De Cock, 2000; Forsberg, 2009; Foster, 2001; House, 1996; Howarth, 1998; Scarcella, 1979; Schmitt & Underwood, 2004; Spöttl & McCarthy, 2004; Yorio, 1989).

Considering the current interest in formulaic language in L2 pragmatics and more broadly (e.g., Bardovi-Harlig, 2009, 2012a; Bardovi-Harlig et al., 2010; Barron, 2003; Edmondson & House, 1991; House, 1996; Kecskes, 2000, 2003; Roever, 2005), it is timely to consider the issues of coding conventional expressions in oral production data. Given the relatively fixed nature of conventional expressions, it may seem at the outset that identifying them in learner production should be straightforward. Yet, the fact that large-scale empirical investigations of conventional expressions based on production data are fairly recent means that scoring has not been widely discussed. Moreover, the dominant use of written data to represent oral conversation in interlanguage pragmatics has heretofore precluded the development of analyses of oral characteristics of speech. In addition, even with the growing interest in conventional expressions in L2 pragmatics, many studies have not investigated production, but rather have focused on interpretation (Kecskes, 2000, 2003), selection of an expression in a multiple choice task (Roever, 2005, 2006, 2007), recognition (Bardovi-Harlig, 2010), and comprehension (Taguchi, 2011).

Whereas conventional expressions for nonproduction tasks have been gathered by a number of means including previous literature, intuition, and observation, the identification of conventional expressions in connected language samples requires a principled approach. The classic definitions of conventional expressions give a strong sense of their social function, but do not provide a sufficient basis for their identification (this was also pointed out by Davies, 1987, who developed principles for crosslinguistic comparisons of politeness formulae). To that end, this study adopts the description advanced by Myles, Hooper and Mitchell (1998, p. 325). Although not designed expressly for research in pragmatics, their description provides an explicit framework for analysis. Conventional expressions are (a) at least two morphemes in length; (b) phonologically coherent (fluently articulated, nonhesitant); (c) used repeatedly and always in the same form; (d) situationally dependent; and (e) community-wide in use.[1] Characteristic (a), that conventional expressions are at least two morphemes in length, gives the most basic feature of a conventional expression (whether called a *formula, routine,* or *situation-based utterance*), otherwise we would be discussing a word. All the other characteristics follow from this one. Characteristics (b) through (e) will be discussed in the following sections.

The chapter is organized as follows: The first section will begin with native speaker data and consider (c) repeated use of the same form, (d) situational dependence, and (e) demonstrations of community-wide use. The next section will take up learner data and investigate what (c), repeated use in the same form means for learner data, and will then examine the phonological criteria in (b) for learner data. The chapter will conclude with a summary of the analytic issues.

The production data for this discussion are drawn from a previously analyzed corpus (Bardovi-Harlig, 2009; Bardovi-Harlig et al., 2010).[2] The issues considered here arose during the analysis of the 5,500 utterances collected from a large cross-sectional study in which 122 ESL students and 49 native speakers of American English participated. Participants responded orally to a computer-delivered DCT whose 32 scenarios were designed to elicit conventional expressions. The timed DCT gave learners 7 seconds to respond, simulating conversational turns.

The learners were enrolled in four levels of classes in an intensive English program, from low-intermediate at Level 3 to low-advanced at Level 6. Each level of instruction was seven-weeks long, with 135 to 165 hours of instruction. The learners represent 11 language backgrounds (Arabic: 54; Chinese: 12;[3] Japanese: 13; Korean: 28; Thai: 5; Spanish: 3; Portuguese: 2; Turkish: 2; and one each of Italian, Tibetan, and Kazakh). Native speakers were divided into native-speaker teachers and peers (undergraduates in the same age range as the learners). All participants lived in the same community and attended or taught at the same university, which is important because there are regional preferences for conventional expressions.

All responses were transcribed and checked by at least two researchers (Bardovi-Harlig et al., 2010). The 12 scenarios which produced the examples used in this chapter are provided in the Appendix. The first time a conventional expression occurs in the text, a short name which identifies the context in which it was produced will be given.

Towards an analysis of conventional expressions

Native speaker conventional expressions

There are at least three issues in analyzing native-speaker production of conventional expressions which forms the basis for the analysis of learner production: how to identify a string that is "always in the same form" (c), how to establish situational dependence (d), and how to operationalize concepts such as (e) "community-wide use" (Myles, Hooper, & Mitchell, 1998) and "tacit agreements" (Coulmas, 1981).

The identification of situational dependence has long been a strength of empirical pragmatics.[4] The use of the scenario—a short description of an environment, context, speakers, and motivation—has been used in a range of elicitation tasks in pragmatics, including most famously written DCTs (discourse completion tasks) and oral DCTs (also known as closed role plays), and open role plays. Language production, including conventional expressions, can easily be compared across different scenarios.

Identifying conventional expressions in native speaker usage begins with identifying the strings that occur repeatedly in specific contexts (Bardovi-Harlig et al., 2010). For example, a string such as *thank you* is a candidate expression. However, *thank you* occurs in many thanking contexts, and is not uniquely associated with specific situations. The next step is to identify the longest sequence of words that occurs repeatedly in a specific context. Consider, for example, the use of thanking expressions with *thank you/thanks* in two different contexts. In one context, participants responded to a professor offering them a chance to make up a test they had missed (Make-up Test) and in the second, participants provided a closing to an office hour appointment (Busy Teacher).

Make-up Test

You have been studying very hard for your test. But on the morning of the test, your alarm does not go off and you oversleep. You ask your teacher for a make-up test.

[participants hear] "Okay. I'll give you a make-up test this time, but don't let it happen again."

[silent screen prompt] You say:

Busy Teacher
You stop by your teacher's office to ask a question about the assignment. She takes time to answer your question. You know she is very busy, so before you say good-bye, you say:
[silent screen prompt] You say:

In response to Make-up Test, 89% of the NS undergraduates in our sample population said *Thank you so much!* In contrast, in response to Busy Teacher, 94% of NS undergraduates said *Thanks/Thank you for your* NP which included both *Thank you/Thanks for your time*, and *Thank you/Thanks for your help*. Thus, characterizing native speaker production included the initial identification of a repeated sequence, the empirically driven identification of a sequence of maximal length, and documentation of alternation or variability (as in the case of *time/help* above), and these are tied to specific contexts addressing situational dependence.

Variability is an intriguing aspect of conventional expressions, which are noteworthy for their sameness. Although some expressions exhibit more variability than others, it is widely accepted that variability in conventional expressions can take many forms (e.g., lexical, morphological, or syntactic; Nattinger & DeCarrico, 1992; Schmitt & Carter, 2004). For example, in Closing, at the end of a conversation with a friend whom the speaker had not seen for a long time, 71% of the undergraduates said either{*good/nice/ great/glad*}*to see you* or{*good/nice/great*}*seeing you,* the dominant choice being *Good to see you* (40%) followed by *good seeing you* (11%).[5] Such variation is taken into account by describing the expression as *Adj {to see/ seeing} you*.

The third issue is operationalizing the concept of "community-wide" use. Bardovi-Harlig (2009; Bardovi-Harlig, Rose & Nickels, 2008; Bardovi-Harlig et al., 2010) set the cut-off for community-wide use of conventional expressions at the rate of at least 50% use by one group of native speakers. The 50% minimum cut-off identifies a single dominant expression and at the same time acknowledges native-speaker variation in speech act realization, thus suggesting what level of consistency in production might be expected from learners. As Forsberg (2009, p. 177) explains: "It is *preferred*, that is *more frequent in a given context*, in *native speakers' production*, than a combination which could have been equivalent had there been no *conventionalization*" (original emphasis). Other studies have also reported a 50% mark: In Manes and Wolfson (1981), the most common compliment formula is found in 54% of the 686 compliments they collected, and in Culpeper (2010), a formula was considered to convey impoliteness only if 50% or more of the formula's occurrences had impolite readings.

The 50% density of use by at least one of two NS groups (college-age peers and teachers) is greater than the frequency definitions used by corpus studies. For example, Biber, Johansson, Leech, Conrad, and Finegan (1999, p. 990) considered multi-word units to occur frequently in a register if they occur 10 times per one million words; Biber, Conrad, and Cortes (2004, p. 376) set a higher frequency level with 40 occurrences per million words, with occurrence in multiple texts. This is much less frequent than the 50% level, and not restricted to the same context which is crucial for the study of conventional expressions in pragmatics. In addition, pragmatics studies are, at the time of this writing, better able to control context through scenario construction than corpus studies are as situations are often not comparable (see also Schauer & Adolphs, 2006).

Now that criteria for identification and analysis of conventional expressions in native speaker production have been outlined, the next section turns to the issue of determining whether learner production can be said to exhibit the same conventional expressions as native speakers. Equivalence is based on similarity of sequences which may include native and nonnative variation, co-occurrence of expressions with other expressions, and phonological fluency and other segmental and prosodic characteristics.

Assessing learner production of conventional expressions

In order to capture the development of conventional expressions, there need to be analyses that are both sensitive enough and generous enough to show development. If an analysis is not sensitive, and uses an "anything goes" approach including everything that approximates a conventional expression, the analysis will not reveal development because all production, regardless of nuanced differences, has been included. On the other hand, if an analysis is too strict and admits no interlanguage forms, then it is not generous enough to show development because everything except for exact matches will be excluded. The following sections consider some of the issues that researchers working in this area will encounter.

Identifying sequences: Binary coding

Identifying sequences in interlanguage follows the same procedure as identifying sequences in native-speaker production (i.e., identifying repeated strings that are contextually determined) with the exception of the criterion of establishing community-wide use. This criterion is replaced by the consideration of equivalence. The importance of how closely learner production matches native-speaker production depends on whether the coding is binary. Binary coding (providing yes/no scores) is used to answer research questions such as "Do learners use the same conventional expressions as native speakers?"

Learner variation that mirrors NS variation

The presence of native-speaker variation means that learners have some 'wiggle room.' Although some expressions, such as *Nice to meet you* show little or no variation in our corpus, others do. For example, in native-speaker expressions of thanking, *Thanks* and *Thank you* alternate. Other expressions show alternations of contracted and uncontracted copula (*I'm/I am*) or contracted and uncontracted *would* (*That'd/That would*). For example, native speakers said both *I'm so sorry* and *I am so sorry*. Although the full copula was restricted to this expression in our native-speaker data, it was found throughout the learner data in alternation with the contracted form, including *I'm so sorry* and *I am so sorry*, as well as other expressions such as *I'm just looking* and *I am just looking*. The principle of allowing all native speaker variation would count both forms as tokens of the target conventional expression (Bardovi-Harlig et al., 2010), although this is an extension of the native-speaker context. (See Bardovi-Harlig, in press, for a further discussion of variation.)

Learner variation that diverges from NS variation

Variations in morphology that do not occur in native-speaker production seem to change the utterance from a conventional expression to an innovative one. Barron (2003) documents an alternation in person in learner production. Whereas native speakers of German use an impersonal expression *Das ist nett* 'That's kind (of you),' learners personalize the expression *Sie sind nett* or *Du bist nett* 'You're kind.' Barron codes the learner production as a separate category, indicating that it was not treated as an equivalent to the conventional expression (Table 24, p. 191). One example of non-native variation which is found in our learner data is variation in tense. Disallowing variation not present in native-speaker production would exclude *Sorry I was late* as a realization of the conventional expression *Sorry I'm late*; likewise, *Sorry I forget* would not be treated as a realization of the conventional expression *Sorry I forgot*. This is not to say that these would not result in a felicitous contribution, just that a conventional form had not been used.

Capturing the development of conventional expressions

Where binary coding gives a yes/no rating, other analyses are more appropriate for addressing research questions with a developmental focus. Questions such as "Do learners attempt conventional expressions in appropriate contexts?" or "How do conventional expressions develop in L2 acquisition?" require a more nuanced analysis. Consider the following analysis of thanking expressions in Make-up Test where native speakers prefer *Thank you so much*. 86% of the native-speaker peers and 71% of the teachers use an intensifier with *thank you* (Table 1). As row 1 shows, 66% of the learners as early as Level 3 reply to the scenario with *thank you*, increasing to 92% by Level 6. However, the use of intensifiers, which are typical in native-speaker responses, builds more slowly, from a low of 29% in Level 4 to 60% in Level 6. Although learners prefer *very much* to the NSs' use of *so much* (Rows 3 and 4), the rise in the use of intensifiers nevertheless shows that learners increasingly recognize and respond to this scenario as a context in which the conventional response requires intensification of *thank you*.

Table 1. Distribution of thanking expressions in Make-up Test scenario

target expression	level 3 n=35		4 n=31		5 n=32		6 n=25		NS P n=35		NS T n=14	
	%	(N)	%	(N)	%	(N)	%	(N)	%	(N)	%	(N)
thank you (all expressions)	66	(23)	65	(20)	84	(27)	92	(23)	91	(32)	71	(10)
thank you + intensifier + much	40	(14)	29	(9)	34	(11)	60	(15)	86	(30)	71	(10)
thank you very much	26	(9)	13	(4)	22	(7)	36	(9)	6	(2)	7	(1)
thank you so much	14	(5)	16	(5)	12	(4)	24	(6)	80	(28)	64	(9)

The key words in the expression *Thank you so much* are *thank you*. The use of key words alone by learners cannot be said to constitute the conventional expression as shown above, but it can be used to support the claim that learners have developed an association of a particular lexical item and the context. In the case of the expression, *I'm just looking,* the key words are *just look*. In spite of the relatively simple grammar of the expression (present progressive with a contracted copula and an adverb), the cross-sectional production data show that learners build up their morphosyntax to be able to produce the string (Table 2). Only one-third of the learners in Levels 3 and 4 attempt the conventional expression, as do only one-half of the learners in Levels 5 and 6.

Table 2. Building an expression from a lexical core (number of responses)

emergent expression	level 3 n=35	4 n=31	5 n=32	6 n=25	NS P n=35	NS T n=14
just look			1			
I just look	1	2		1		
just looking		1			2	1
I just looking	3		2			
I'll just looking	1					
just I'm looking			1			
I am just looking	2	2	1	6		
I'm just looking	3	9	11	7	25	9
total	10	14	16	14	27	10

In contrast to *I'm just looking* where the key words *just* and *look* are contiguous, the key words in an expression may also be noncontiguous as in the case of *sorry...late* from the conventional expression (*I'm*) *sorry I'm late.* Learner attempts at *Sorry I'm late* (Example 1) reveal that the expression is sensitive to the development of complementation, as learners over-shoot the relatively syntactically simple conventional expression. (The code following the examples shows a learner's level, section, and computer number).

Example 1. Interlanguage production of *Sorry I'm late* (Late 5 Minutes)

I'm sorry for late (3AS6)
I'm sorry for I'm late (3CS5)
I'm sorry about late (3BS4)
I'm so sorry about my late (3CS7)
I'm so sorry to being so late (4CS13)
I'm sorry because I late. (5AS5)

In the cases discussed in this section, attempts at conventional expressions are identified by the recurring key words. While interlanguage forms would not, by most analyses, be considered examples of the conventional expressions, coding developmental forms contributes to our understanding of expressions and the relationship of expressions (pragmalinguistic knowledge) to context (sociopragmatic knowledge).

How much is enough? How much is too much?

In some cases learners and native speakers vary in the length of their contributions. In some contexts a primary expression seems to be accompanied by a secondary expression. For example, in response to *Have a nice day!*, 94% of native speaker undergraduates and 100% of native-speaker teachers used *You too!* as did 83–84% of the learners. Seventy-four percent of native speakers additionally used a thanking expression (*Thanks! You too!*); however, learners used this combination noticeably less, in only 29% of their responses. Fifty percent of all learners used *You too* exclusively, whereas only 18% of all native-speaker participants used the reciprocating expression exclusively.

A similar case occurs in the Shopping No Help scenario in which speakers declined help in response to an offer "Can I help you?" In addition to *I'm just looking,* 71% of the native-speaker peers and 64% of the teachers used another semantic formula realized by a thanking expression (*No thanks, I'm just looking* or <*Thanks*> *I'm just looking* <*thanks*>). Learners gradually add the thanking formula to the declining expression starting with 9% of the responses in Level 3, going to a high of 31% in Level 5 and 28% in Level 6, showing increased sociopragmatic sensitivity to the context.

Treating the thanking expression as separate from the reciprocal wishes (*You too!*) or from the explanation (*I'm just looking*) has a basis in the rates of use in native-speaker production in which the primary expression is much more frequent. Dividing expressions also captures interlanguage development. Learners seem to use the contextually more frequent expression first, and then add the second semantic formula.

Learners do not always say less than native speakers, however. In the Introduction scenario in which a friend introduces his new roommate (saying *This is my new roommate Bill*), native speakers produced the response *Nice to meet you* and then stopped, whereas learners typically responded, *Nice to meet you* and then introduced themselves as shown in Example 2.

Example 2. Use of addition semantic formulas in introduction

>   Nice to meet you. I'm NAME. (3BS9)
>   >Oh nice to meet you. My name is NAME.< (4AS6)
>   Hi Bill. Nice to meet you, my name is NAME (3AS13)

The learners' use of the additional semantic formula in response to Introduction is observed at all four levels, but is especially evident in Level 3. Whereas 63% of all native-speaker responses included only the target or the target with a greeting, only 42% of all learner responses included just these semantic formulas. In Level 3, for example, 54% of the responses also included a self-introduction.

In using the expression *I'm just looking* (in Shopping No Help), some learners used more words within the same semantic formula, as in Example 3. No native speaker, peer or teacher, used a complement for this expression whereas eight learners did, apparently not distinguishing between the conventional use of *I'm just looking* which takes no complement (and is conventionally used to decline help) and *I'm looking for* +NP which takes a complement (and is conventionally used to accept help; see Shopping Help).

Example 3.

>   No thanks, I'm just looking for... something... (6BS20)
>   Uh, that's Okay I'm just looking for some, t-shirts. (6BS21)

Examples 2 and 3 are somewhat different in that the responses in Example 2 complete the semantic formula exactly as native speakers do and then add another semantic formula, whereas in Example 3, learners add to the expression within a single semantic formula. In both cases, the learner productions use the same sequence, but have produced more when compared to the conventional use of the native speakers. In a similar finding, Tateyama (2001) observes that second language learners of Japanese may use what appear to be targetlike expressions to which they add unexpected and nontargetlike particles (e.g., *ne*). Taken together, these cases argue that use of a conventional expression does not guarantee a nativelike contribution.

Oral production

Given the dominance of written language samples in interlanguage pragmatics, the analysis of conventional expressions produced orally for conversation raises issues not previously addressed, but not necessarily unique to conventional expressions. This section considers Myles, Hooper, and Mitchell's (1998) criterion (b), that formulas be phonologically coherent (fluently articulated, nonhesitant) and also examines other attributes of oral production including pronunciation and prosody. In the cases considered in this section, learner sequences match those used by native speakers, but learner delivery is noticeably different from that of their native-speaker counterparts.[6] For example, (4a) and (b) (More Food) include the same contiguous words, but show different delivery in terms of pauses, resulting in a very different sounding refusal.

Example 4.

No thanks, I'm full. (NS)
No. Thanks. (.) I'm full. (5BS2)

Segmental features

Differences in segmental production occasionally occurred (Example 5). Some of the targets are relatively easy to identify given a context in which a particular conventional expression is expected. For example, the use of *[S]ank you* for *Thank you* seems to be easily recoverable for both listeners and coders. Pronunciations that show greater divergence or are less familiar to listeners could take more time to resolve or fail to convey the illocutionary force intended by the speaker.

Example 5. Segmental features

[S]ank you for your time (4AS3)
[S]ank you so much (4AS5)
I need your hel[f] (for *help*) (5AS3)
I'm so sorry I'm [perate] (for *late*) (5AS3)
No thank you, I'm [hull] (for *full*) (4AS2)

Prosody and voice quality.

Prosody affects the perception of the sincerity of an utterance and even the perception of the function of a contribution, or its illocutionary force. As in all other categories, some learners produced conventional expressions with the same prosody used by native speakers. In the production of "You too!" in the reciprocal closing following *Have a nice day!*, both native speakers and learners used an intonation that transcribers marked as "melodic," "sing song," and "intonation just like a NS."[7] Other productions of *You too* were labeled "robotic" or "monotone." Both House (1996) and Tateyama (2001) enlisted judges to evaluate learners' oral production. The judges reported that German learners of English often employed a "mechanical" delivery (House, 1996) and that American learners of Japanese exhibited a number of nontargetlike features (Tateyama, 2001). The American learners of Japanese were too smooth where hesitancy was required. Learner apologies were reported to be not apologetic sounding, abrupt, and to not have the expected intonation. Other instances of interlanguage prosody are found in Example 6.

Example 6.   Prosody and voice quality

Nó, thánk yóu. (evenly stressed and spaced words) (5AS12)
No, thank you! I am full! (exclamation) (5AS11)
So::rry::, °I'm late° (breathy) (5CS3)
°Oh no, thank you.° I'm full. (breathy) (4AS6)

In (6a) all the words received equal stress, while (b) is delivered as an exclamation. Both (c) and (d) are produced with breathy voice.

Hesitations, pauses and rate of speech.

One of the most convincing arguments that a recurring sequence of words is actually a unit is its nonhesitant, fluent production. Myles, Hooper, and Mitchell (1998, p. 325) use three descriptors: phonologically coherent, fluently articulated and non-hesitant. Learners at various levels of proficiency can and do produce nonhesitant conventional expressions as shown in Example 7. Following the transcription conventions of Jefferson (2004), right/left carats (> <) indicate speech that is faster than surrounding talk and left/right carats (< >) indicate speech that is slower than surrounding talk.

Example 7.   Phonologically coherent, fluently articulated, non-hesitant learner production

>No, thank you, I'm just looking< (5CS10)
>You too thanks< (3AS1)

Although many learner expressions are nonhesitant, others occur with pauses and hesitations located between compound expressions or at a constituent boundary within the expression. Whereas native speakers produce compound expressions such i) *No thank you,* ii) *I'm sorry I'm late,* and iii) *No thanks I'm just looking* as one prosodic phrase or breath group, learners often produce them in two parts. Examples (8)—(10) show hesitations in learner productions with two semantic formulas which are typically produced by native speakers as one breath group.

Example 8.   Learner productions of target *Sorry I'm late* with pauses

I'm so sorry (0.4) I'm late (4BS5)
I'm so sorry (1.0) I'm late (3CS2)

Oh↘ sorry. (2.79) I'm late. (4AS7)
Oh::↘ I'm so (1.68) late. (4AS10)

Example 9. Learner productions of target *No thanks, I'm just looking* with pauses

No! Thank you (0.5) > I'm just looking< (5CS6)
No thanks! (0.6) just looking (3AS6)
No: (.) I'm just looking (5AS1)
No, thank you (.) just looking (5AS10)

Example 10. Learner productions of target *No thanks I'm full/ You too, thanks!* with pauses

No:: thank you, I am full (5BS9)
No:: thanks (0.9) I'm full (3BS8)
No! (0.5) Thanks! (1.2) I'm full. (5BS11)
You too! (1.7) Thanks! (6CS18)

Within conventional expressions with single semantic formulas, learners may pause at a constituent boundary. The utterances in Example 11 show that learners often get as far as *for* and then begin a word search.

Example 11. Hesitations as word searches

Yes, I'm looking for::: (inhales .85) a::h shis [size] L (4CS11)
I'm looking fo:::r (1.38) party dress (4CS6)
Thank you for (1.1) respo:nsing (0.5) >my question< (5AS9)
Thank you very much (.) for your time (5AS5)
Thank you for (0.9) thanks you for (0.8) making (0.6) time for me (5AS10)

The hesitations after *thank you for* and *I'm looking for* suggest that the learners may not have quite worked the co-occurrence restrictions for the expressions.

Like native speakers, some learners use rate of speech expressively. For example, intermediate learners in Level 3 (the lowest proficiency learners to complete the task), used lengthening to express condolences in the Father Died context as shown in Example 12. This use of lengthening was not found in Level 6 (the highest proficiency learners to participate).

Example 12. Use of lengthening in condolences by intermediate learners

<O::h I'm so so::rry.> (0.8) It's sa:d. (3CS3)
O:↘:h <I'm so so::rry.> (3CS9)
<I'm so sorry.> (1.2) Okay. (1.2) I can wait. (3CS2)
<I'm sorry about that.> (3BS8)
O::h, I'm so:rry::.(3BS1)
O:::h, I am:::, so sorry about that. (3AS4)

In condolence contexts fast tempos were not expected, and only one instance was found (Example 13a). In Example 13b the learner performs a self-repetition, adding the intensifier *really* which is itself repeated as the tempo increases. This latter case seems to be a case of experimentation as much as self-repair.

Example 13. Use of rapid tempo in condolences by intermediate learners
a. [fast tempo] >I'm so sorry< You mu-, you should, you (must) to be sad. (3CS8)
b. (slow) O::h↘ <I'm so:rry about tha:t.> ((faster)) >Really really I'm sorry about that.< (3CS12)

One final observation is that these differences in NS and learner production may have a cumulative effect on a listener. The utterances in Example 14 differ by full and reduced forms (*thank you/thanks* and *I am/I'm*) and by lengthening (*No::* with elongated vowel vs. an unremarkable duration *No*).

Example 14. Multiple differences in production of conventional expressions

No thanks, I'm full
No:: thank you, I am full (5BS9)

An important consideration for any analysis is the extent to which these utterances would be perceived as interchangeable by a listener.

Summary of the issues

The previous sections have reviewed many of the issues that researchers will encounter in analyzing oral production of conventional expressions. This section summarizes those issues following the framework found in Myles, Hooper, and Mitchell (1998) and considers them in relation to previous and future research. Pragmatics research has a tradition of investigating context and context-use associations that are necessary for documenting the context-dependence of conventional expressions. Employing designs that use scenarios facilitates the documentation of rates of use. Similarly, it provides a means of documenting increased use by learners when a cross-sectional or longitudinal design is also employed. While mastery of the conventional expressions themselves is part of pragmalinguistic competence, linking expressions to contexts is part of sociopragmatic competence. Thus, the research traditions of empirical pragmatics are very well suited to the research of the use and development of conventional expressions.

Binary analysis of learner production requires a comparison of learner production with native speaker production. One way of conducting binary analyses is to treat learner variation that mirrors native-speaker variation as reflecting knowledge of the expression, even though the distribution of the variants is different. Developmental analyses identify the key words (which are different for every expression) and the linguistic contexts in which they are embedded.

The issue of co-occurring expressions is thought provoking. The interpretation of lack of co-occurring expressions which appear in most (but not all) native speaker production, the presence of co-occurring expressions where native speakers do not use them, and the augmentation of expressions may suggest that learners assign different pragmatic values to an expression (such as sufficient illocutionary force), but do not necessarily suggest that learners do not "know" the conventional expressions. However, volubility does present a challenge to the notion of 'saying the same thing.'

The final area for consideration was phonological fluency, with additional considerations of pronunciation and prosody. This might be included as part of a general concept such as oral fidelity: the ability to produce segments and their combinations so that words are recognizable, with stress and intonation that is consistent with the intended illocutionary force, without pauses or hesitations that interfere with that illocutionary force. Oral fidelity may be as much related to general oral proficiency (Taguchi, 2007) as it is to the production of conventional expressions and to pragmatics, and it is an inescapable fact of conversation. To my knowledge, few studies to date have dealt directly with oral fidelity in pragmatics, but judges who are asked to evaluate oral learner production may respond to it as part of a holistic evaluation of appropriateness, as indicated in comments from the judges who participated in the studies reported by House (1996) and Tateyama (2001). (See also Taguchi 2007 for the use of judges to evaluate oral speech act production.) Treerat (2012) uses judges to interpret sincerity of apologies with special focus on intonation. The criteria for judging equivalence of expressions—including equivalent sequences, length of contribution, and oral fidelity—could be given to judges who would then evaluate learner production as a supplement to transcription and analysis. Given a data-based framework, the use of judges could contribute to our understanding of what it means to say the same thing.

Careful comparison of conventional expressions produced by learners and native speakers shows that learners can and do acquire both the pragmalinguistics (the conventional expressions themselves) and the sociopragmatics governing their use. It further shows that conventional expressions show many signs of interlanguage development; they do not emerge in interlanguage fully formed. In order to be able to show how conventional expressions are used in L2 pragmatics, we need tools to describe development. I hope that this study will encourage more research on conventional expressions in different contexts and languages.

Notes

1. The psycholinguistic and developmental characteristics listed by Myles, Hooper and Mitchell (1998) are not included here.
2. Results are only discussed here as they pertain to the analytic issues raised in this paper. These data enabled us to address many questions about the acquisition of conventional expressions. Interested readers may find further reports on this data set as it relates to the recognition and production of conventional expressions (Bardovi-Harlig, 2009), length of turn and the use of conventional expressions (Bardovi-Harlig et al., 2010), influence of first language (Bardovi-Harlig, Rose & Nickels, 2009), the influence of proficiency, length of stay, and intensity of interaction (Bardovi-Harlig & Bastos, 2011), and variation (Bardovi-Harlig, 2012b).
3. First language information was collected by self-report. Students reported "Chinese" rather than a more specific designation such as "Mandarin."
4. Granger (1998) credits interest in formulas in part to the increase in research in interlanguage pragmatics. The fundamental interest in context in pragmatics makes it an ideal discipline in which to situate research on development and use of conventional expressions
5. Conventional expressions are given using standard linguistic notation. Curly brackets show alternation, and parentheses indicate optional elements: {*I'm/I am*} (intensifier) *sorry* may be realized as *I'm sorry, I am sorry,* or both, with the addition of *so* or *very*
6. In this case "noticeably different" means that two experienced transcribers indicated a difference in segmental production, or variations in prosody, tempo, loudness, or other characteristics which distinguished a portion of speech from a speaker's own general production. Each speaker had the opportunity to respond to 32 scenarios which forms the basis of the transcribers' assessments.
7. The transcribers' notes on prosody were impressionistic, as one reviewer pointed out. Although this is not uncommon in pragmatics (see House, 1996; Tateyama, 2001), a serious investigation of intonation requires measurement. However, the point here remains that a learner's intonation on a formulaic sequence may differ noticeably from a native speaker's, and that this in turn may influence a listeners' interpretation of that contribution. That is, a formulaic sequence delivered nonconventionally in terms of intonation may not constitute a conventional expression. The degree to which intonation and formulaic sequences compete in a listener's interpretation of a contribution is an empirical question.

References

Bardovi-Harlig, K. (2009). Conventional expressions as a pragmalinguistic resource: Recognition and production of conventional expressions in L2 pragmatics. *Language Learning, 59*, 755–795.

Bardovi-Harlig, K. (2010). Recognition of conventional expressions in L2 pragmatics. In G. Kasper, H. t. Nguyen, D. R. Yoshimi, & J. K. Yoshioka (Eds.), *Pragmatics and language learning* (Vol. 12) (pp. 141–162). Honolulu: University of Hawai'i, National Foreign Language Resource Center.

Bardovi-Harlig, K. (2012a). Formulas, routines, and conventional expressions in pragmatics research. *Annual Review of Applied Linguistics, 32*, 206–227.

Bardovi-Harlig, K. (2012b). Pragmatic variation and conventional expressions. In J. C. Félix-Brasdefer, & D. Koike (Eds.) *Variation in pragmatics.* Amsterdam/Philadelphia: John Benjamins.

Bardovi-Harlig, K., & Bastos, M.-T. (2011). Proficiency, length of stay, and intensity of interaction and the acquisition of conventional expressions in L2 pragmatics. *Intercultural Pragmatics, 8*, 347–384.

Bardovi-Harlig, K., Bastos, M.-T., Burghardt, B., Chappetto, E., Nickels, E., & Rose, M. (2010). The use of conventional expressions and utterance length in L2 pragmatics. In G. Kasper, H. t. Nguyen, D. R. Yoshimi, & J. K. Yoshioka (Eds.), *Pragmatics and language learning* (Vol. 12) (pp. 163–186). Honolulu: University of Hawai'i, National Foreign Language Resource Center.

Bardovi-Harlig, K., Rose, M., & Nickels, E. (2008). The influence of first language and level of development in the use of conventional expressions of thanking, apologizing, and refusing. In M. Bowles, R. Foote, S. Perpiñán, & R. Bhatt (Eds.) *Selected Proceedings of the 2007 Second Language Research Forum* (pp. 113–130). Somerville, MA: Cascadilla Proceedings Project. (also available: http://www.lingref.com/cpp/slrf/2007/index.html)

Barron, A. (2003). *Acquisition in interlanguage pragmatics: Learning how to do things with words in a study abroad context.* Amsterdam: John Benjamins.

Biber, D., Conrad, S., & Cortes, V. (2004). *If you look at ...*: Lexical bundles in university teaching and textbooks. *Applied Linguistics, 25*, 371–405.

Biber, D., Johansson, S., Leech, G., Conrad, S., & Finegan, E. (1999). *Longman grammar of spoken and written English.* London: Longman.

Coulmas, F. (1981). *Conversational routine: Explorations in standardized communication situations and prepatterned speech.* The Hague: Mouton.

Culpeper, J. (2010). Conventionalised impoliteness formulae. *Journal of Pragmatics, 42*, 3232–3245.

Davies, E. E. (1987). A contrastive approach to the analysis of politeness formulas. *Applied Linguistics, 8*, 75–88.

De Cock, S. (2000). Repetitive phrasal chunkiness and advanced EFL speech and writing. In C. Mair, & M. Hundt (Eds.), *Corpus linguistics and linguistic theory* (pp. 51–68). Amsterdam: Rodopi.

Edmondson, W., & House, J. (1991). Do learners talk too much? The waffle phenomenon in interlanguage pragmatics. In R. Phillipson, E. Kellerman, L. Selinker, M. Sharwood Smith, & M. Swain (Eds.), *Foreign/second language pedagogy research: A commemorative volume for Claus Færch* (pp. 273–287). Clevedon: Multilingual Matters.

Forsberg, F. (2009). Formulaic sequences: A distinctive feature at the advanced/very advanced levels of second language acquisition. In E. Labeau & F. Myles (Eds.), *The advanced learner variety: The case of French* (pp. 173–197). Oxford: Peter Lang.

Foster, P. (2001). Rules and routines: A consideration of their role in the task-based language production of native and non-native speakers. In M. Bygate, P. Skehan, & M. Swain (Eds.), *Researching pedagogical tasks: Second language learning, teaching and testing* (pp. 75–93). Harlow: Longman.

Granger, S. (1998). Prefabricated patterns in advanced EFL writing: Collocations and formulae. In A. P. Cowie (Ed.), *Phraseology: Theory, analysis, and applications* (pp. 145–160). Oxford: Clarendon.

House, J. (1996). Developing pragmatic fluency in English as a foreign language: Routines and metapragmatic awareness. *Studies in Second Language Acquisition, 18*, 225–252.

Howarth, P. (1998). The phraseology of learners' academic writing. In A. P. Cowie (Ed.), *Phraseology: Theory, analysis, and applications* (pp. 161–186). Oxford: Clarendon.

Jefferson, G. (2004). Glossary of transcript symbols with an introduction. In G. H. Lerner (Ed). *Conversation Analysis: Studies from the first generation* (pp. 13–31). Amsterdam/ Philadelphia: John Benjamins.

Kasper, G. & Blum-Kulka, S. (1993). Interlanguage pragmatics: An introduction. In G. Kasper, & S. Blum-Kulka (Eds.), *Interlanguage pragmatics* (pp. 1–17). Oxford: Oxford University Press.

Kecskes, I. (2000). Conceptual fluency and the use of situation-bound utterances. *Links & Letters, 7,* 145–161.

Kecskes, I. (2003). *Situation-bound utterances in L1 and L2.* Berlin: Mouton.

Manes, J., & Wolfson, N. (1981). The compliment formula. In F. Coulmas (Ed.), *Conversational routine: Explorations in standardized communication situations and prepatterned speech* (pp. 115–132). The Hague: Mouton.

Myles, F., Hooper, J., & Mitchell, R. (1998). Rote or rule? Exploring the role of formulaic language in classroom foreign language learning. *Language Learning, 48,* 323–363.

Nattinger, J. R., & DeCarrico, J. S. (1992). *Lexical phrases and language teaching.* Oxford: Oxford University Press.

Roever, C. (2005). *Testing ESL Pragmatics: Development and validation of a web-based assessment battery.* Berlin: Peter Lang.

Roever, C. (2006). Validation of a web-based test of ESL pragmalinguistics. *Language Testing, 23*, 229–256.
Roever, C. (2007). DIF in the assessment of second language pragmatics. *Language Assessment Quarterly, 4*, 165–189.
Scarcella, R. (1979). Watch up! *Working Papers in Bilingualism, 19*, 79–88.
Schauer, G. A., & Adolphs, S. (2006). Expressions of gratitude in corpus and DCT data: Vocabulary, formulaic sequences, and pedagogy. *System, 34*, 119–134.
Schmitt, N., & Carter, R. (2004). Formulaic sequences in action. In N. Schmitt (Ed.) *Formulaic sequences: Acquisition, processing and use* (pp. 1–22). Amsterdam: Benjamins.
Schmitt, N., & Underwood, G. (2004). Exploring the processing of formulaic sequences through a self-paced reading task. In N. Schmitt (Ed.) *Formulaic sequences: Acquisition, processing and use* (pp. 173–189). Amsterdam: Benjamins.
Spöttl, C., & McCarthy, M. (2004). Comparing knowledge of formulaic sequences across L1, L2, L3, L4. In N. Schmitt (Ed.) *Formulaic sequences: Acquisition, processing and use* (pp. 191–225). Amsterdam: Benjamins.
Taguchi, N. (2007). Task difficulty in oral speech act production. *Applied Linguistics, 28*, 113–135.
Taguchi, N. (2011). The effect of L2 proficiency and study-abroad experience on pragmatic comprehension. *Language Learning, 61*, 1–36.
Tateyama, Y. (2001). Explicit and implicit teaching of pragmatic routines: Japanese *sumimasen*. In K. Rose & G. Kasper (Eds.), *Pragmatics in language teaching* (pp. 200–222). Cambridge: Cambridge University Press.
Treerat, S. (2012). *Sincerity, intonation, and apologies: A Case study of Thai EFL and ESL learners*. Unpublished doctoral dissertation, Indiana University, Bloomington.
Yorio, C. (1989). Idiomaticity as an indicator of second language proficiency. In K. Hyltenstam, & L. K. Obler (Eds.), *Bilingualism across the lifespan* (pp. 55–72). Cambridge: Cambridge University Press.

Appendix: Oral production task (selected items)

See Bardovi-Harlig (2009) for complete task

Initiators. All scenarios are followed by a visual prompt on the screen that says *You say:*

item	name	scenario	conventional expression
I-4	Closing	You are in the library and you see an old friend who you have not seen for a long time. You talk for a little while and as you are leaving you say,	{good/nice/great/glad} {seeing/to see} you
I-9	Movie	You are in the theater. There is a group of young teenagers sitting behind you. They are talking so loudly that you cannot hear a word.	Be quiet
I-10	Busy Teacher	You stop by your teacher's office to ask a question about the assignment. She takes time to answer your question. You know she is very busy, so before you say good-bye, you say,	Thank you/ Thanks for your{time/help}

Replies: All scenarios are followed by an oral turn (given in quotation marks) and visual prompt on the screen that says *You say:*

item	name	scenario	conventional expression
R-4	Shopping Help	You go to a clothing store and you need to find a new shirt. A salesperson approaches you. You want the salesperson's assistance. "Can I help you?"	I'm looking for
R-6	*Have a Nice Day!*	You are in the supermarket. After you pay, you are ready to pick up your bags. The cashier says, "Have a nice day!"	You too!
R-7	Late 5 Minutes	You made an appointment with your teacher. Unfortunately you arrive five minutes late for the meeting. Your teacher says, "Hello. Come on in."	Sorry I'm late
R-8	Forgot Book	You borrowed a book from your friend, Kate. You promised to return it today. She needs it for her presentation in class tomorrow. However, you left the book at home. You meet her in class. "By the way, did you bring my book? I really need it for my presentation tomorrow.'	I'm sorry, I forgot.

R-12	Shopping No Help	You go to a clothing store and you need to find a new shirt. A salesperson approaches you. You don't want the salesperson's assistance. "Can I help you?"	*I'm just looking.*
R-15	Introduction	Your friend introduces you to his new roommate. "This is my new roommate, Bill."	*Nice to meet you*
R-16	Father Died	You go to ask your teacher if he will be having office hours tomorrow, and he tells you about his father. "I won't be having office hours tomorrow. My father died, and I have to go to the funeral."	*I'm* (intensifier) *sorry*
R-17	Make-up Test	You have been studying very hard for your test. But on the morning of the test, your alarm does not go off and you oversleep. You ask your teacher for a make-up test. "Okay. I'll give you a make-up test this time, but don't let it happen again."	*Thank you/ Thanks so much*
R-19	More Food	You are having dinner at a friend's house. Your friend offers you more food, but you couldn't possibly eat another bite. "Would you like some more?"	*No thanks/thank you, I'm {full/ stuffed}*

The Effects of Explicit Metapragmatic Instruction on EFL Learners' Performance of Constructive Criticism in an Academic Setting

Nguyen Thi Thuy Minh
Nanyang Technological University, Singapore

Pham Minh Tam
Vietnam National University, Hanoi, Vietnam

Cao Thuy Hong
Vietnam National University, Hanoi, Vietnam

Previous research has shown that second language learners can experience considerable difficulty when giving constructive criticism to peers in instructional settings (see Nguyen, 2005). The current study examines whether metapragmatic instruction facilitates the learning of this speech act set. The study is conducted in an attempt to address the need for further research on L2 pragmatic instruction (see Rose, 2005) and expand the range of speech acts under investigation, which is currently restricted to a small set of well-defined acts and excludes more complex speech act sets such as constructive criticism. Thirty Vietnamese high-intermediate-level learners of English as a foreign language were recruited for the comparison and treatment conditions. Over a 15 week semester, the treatment group received explicit instruction in constructive criticism in English while the comparison group did not receive any equivalent instruction. As pre- and post-tests, learners participated in oral peer-feedback sessions where they provided constructive criticism on peers' actual written assignments. The treatment group also completed a post-test discourse completion task for the purpose of triangulation and wrote a one-page essay to reflect on what they had learned. Findings show positive instructional effects on learners' pragmatic performance and raise issues about task effects on measuring L2 pragmatic performance.

Introduction

This exploratory study sets out to investigate the effects of explicit metapragmatic instruction on a group of EFL learners' performance of constructive criticism in institutional settings. More specifically, it examines whether explicit teaching helps to improve learners' use of pragmatic strategies for delivering constructive criticism and linguistic devices to compensate for the potential face-threat of the criticism. This study is part of a larger ongoing research project which aims to compare the relative effectiveness of implementing explicit and implicit pedagogical interventions in the pragmatic realm. It is conducted to address the need to further research on L2 pragmatics instruction (Jeon & Kaya, 2006; Kasper & Rose, 2002; Rose, 2005; Rose & Kasper, 2001), especially regarding under-represented speech act sets[1] such as giving constructive criticism to peers in the classroom context.

Previous L2 pragmatics research has indicated that non-native speakers can experience considerable difficulty when performing speech acts in the target language (TL) due to their incomplete L2 pragmatic knowledge, limited proficiency in the TL, and also because of the influence of their first language (L1) knowledge of pragmatics (see Ellis, 2008; Kasper & Rose, 2002 for reviews). Uninstructed learners in foreign language (FL) contexts might encounter even greater difficulty compared to those in second language (SL) contexts who are exposed to the TL use to a considerably greater extent (Kasper & Rose, 2002; Rose & Kasper, 2001). Learner difficulty with the pragmatics of another language can cause more problems than their difficulty with grammar when they participate in intercultural communication. This is because pragmatic errors are often perceived by native speakers (NS) as rudeness rather than a lack of competence in the L2 (Boxer, 1993; Thomas, 1983). Instruction at the pragmatic level is therefore important in helping L2 learners to communicate more appropriately in the TL.

Recent years have witnessed an increase in research interest in the instruction of different speech acts or speech act sets, including Olshtain and Cohen (1990) on apologies, Billmyer (1990) and Morrow (1995) on refusals and complaints, Kondo (2001) on refusals, Rose and Ng (2001) on compliments and compliment responses, Fukuya and Clark (2001), Safont (2003), Salazar (2003) and Takahashi (2001, 2005) on requests, and Martínez-Flor and Fukuya (2005) on suggestions. These studies have sought to address three important topics: the teachability of a particular speech act, the benefits of instruction versus exposure, and the relative effectiveness of different teaching approaches (Jeon & Kaya, 2006; Rose, 2005).

Overall, findings regarding the first and second topics have suggested that although certain L2 pragmatic areas remain difficult for learners, L2 pragmatics can be taught and instruction has a beneficial effect on pragmatic development. For example, Olshtain and Cohen (1990) found an increased use of intensifiers and a wider variety of apology strategies for instructed learners. Safont (2003) reported a marked increase in the use of request modifications after the participants received instruction in this area. Billmyer (1990) found that instructed learners generally enjoyed an advantage over their uninstructed peers in using compliments and compliment responses, especially with regard to frequency, spontaneity, appropriateness and adjectival repertoire. A meta-analysis by Jeon and Kaya (2006) that examined the efficacy of 13 instructed L2 pragmatics studies, many of which involved the teaching of speech acts, reported a medium effect size when comparing the performance of instructed and uninstructed learners, and a large effect size when comparing the performance of the instructed learners before and after interventions, also attesting to the benefits of L2 pragmatics instruction in general.

However, findings regarding the third topic have been more controversial. Although there seems to be evidence to suggest that explicit teaching has more effect than implicit teaching (Rose & Ng, 2001; Takahashi, 2001), Jeon and Kaya (2006) have warned against drawing premature conclusions because of the limited data available and a variety of methodological issues, including unequal treatment lengths for explicit and implicit groups and variation in the data collection methods. To achieve more conclusive research outcomes, this line of research should be continued and methodological issues should be addressed in future studies.

Another limitation of the existing body of research on instructed L2 pragmatics lies in its narrow scope of investigation. Despite the growing interest in this realm, much of the current research focuses on a rather restricted range of relatively 'well-defined' speech acts (see above). Thus, it remains to be seen whether instruction works for more complex speech act sets such as constructive criticism, which may cause even more problems for L2 learners and therefore require at least equally careful pedagogical attention (Nguyen, 2005, 2008a, 2008b).

Constructive criticism in general refers to negative assessment of an individual's work-in-progress with the aim of improving current or future performance (Nguyen, 2005).[2] In this sense, it includes giving critical feedback on task performance in the language classroom.[3] In an empirical study of constructive criticism given to peers by Vietnamese EFL learners and NSs of Australian English in writing feedback sessions, Nguyen (2005) found that criticism is made up of multiple components, none of which is the head act (Blum-Kulka & Olshtain, 1984)[4] and therefore may be better described as a speech act set rather than a single speech act. For example, criticism can be realized by means of any combination of the following: expression of disapproval, expression of negative evaluation, statement of problem, and advice for change. Because it involves a negative evaluation of the recipient's (R) work with the view of influencing R's future action, criticism may pose a threat to both the recipient's positive face (the desire to be approved or accepted by others) and negative face (the desire to be free from imposition from others) (Brown & Levinson, 1987). Therefore, this speech act set is often mitigated by means of various external and internal modifiers, such as compliments (i.e., positive remarks to preface the criticism), grounders (justifications for the criticism), hedges, and downgraders. (see Appendix 1 for definitions and examples of these categories).

Providing constructive criticism in institutional settings is normatively expected of teachers. However, delivering criticism from one peer to another is often tricky, not only because learners generally lack the knowledge required to give fair criticism, but also because they lack the pragmatic competence to express their criticism in an appropriate manner. Research has shown that while students from some countries may find giving constructive criticism that can improve a colleague's work to be a positive exercise, students from other cultures (particularly Asian cultures) are often uncomfortable expressing criticism of another student's work (Nelson & Carson, 1998). Other studies have indicated that learners of English may give constructive criticism very differently from native speakers, which may adversely affect their communication with NS peers. For example, Nguyen (2005, 2008a, 2008b) found that when commenting on peers' essays, Vietnamese EFL university students tended to soften their criticism less frequently and provided direct criticism more often than their fellow Australian L1 students. The L2 speakers also employed modal verbs such as *must, should,* and *have to* inappropriately and thus needed pedagogical assistance to improve their pragmatic competence.

Although to date a great deal of pedagogical effort has been devoted to orienting L2 learners to the content of peer assessment and the structure of peer assessment sessions (Liu & Hansen, 2002; Mendonca & Johnson, 1994; Rollinson, 2005), little attention has been focused on the language used to provide negative assessment. The present study aims to address some of the language problems that L2 speakers can have with constructive criticism and thus constitutes an attempt to expand the range of learning targets under investigation. It focuses on a group of TEFL (Teaching English as a Foreign Language) teacher-students who have had quite limited exposure to English use outside the classroom. It is argued that these students need training in how to give constructive criticism appropriately so that they can successfully transfer the acquired knowledge and skills to their future professional practices. Further, since their only regular source of TL pragmatic input seems to come from their formal English classes, some pragmatics-focused instruction is necessary to help them achieve a higher level of pragmatic competence in the TL.

The study defines explicit teaching as a pedagogical approach that combines metapragmatic generalizations (DeKeyser, 2003), output practice and explicit correction of forms and meanings. Multiple instructional strategies have been employed because it is believed this can produce more positive learning effects than the adoption of a single teaching strategy (Izumi, 2002; Martínez-Flor & Fukuya, 2005). In conceptualizing its pedagogical interventions, the present study draws on Schmidt's (1993, 1995) noticing hypothesis, Swain's (1985, 1995, 2005) output hypothesis, and Long's (1983, 1996) interaction hypothesis, which specify conditions for language learning as opportunities for input noticing, corrective feedback and output. In other words, it is believed that learners can benefit from a type of instruction that allows them to attend to linguistic forms and see the relationship between forms and pragmatic meanings, receive negative evidence about their output and modify their output accordingly.

In designing its teaching materials the present study draws on a resource for teaching constructive criticism developed by Nguyen and Basturkmen (2010). This resource included activities originally devised for a group of young Vietnamese EFL learners in an English for Academic Purposes program. The activities aimed to increase the learners' sensitivity to cultural issues involved in giving constructive criticism in peer assessment sessions, and to help them find socially appropriate language for performing this speech act set in academic contexts. Observations of the learners' constructive criticism after the implementation of these activities showed evidence of improvement. Details of the instructional implementation will be described in the section below. To evaluate the effectiveness of this instructional implementation, the present study aims to answer the following two research questions:

1. Do learners benefit from explicit instruction in constructive criticism in English?
2. Do some aspects of giving constructive criticism benefit more from explicit instruction than others?

Methodology

Study design and participants

The present study adopted a quasi-experimental, pretest-posttest design with a comparison group. Two intact EFL classes consisting of a total of thirty students were recruited for the study. At the time of the data collection, the students (1 male and 29 female) were pre-service EFL teachers majoring in their third year of English at a teacher training institution in Hanoi, Vietnam. In order to be admitted to this four-year teacher training program, the students had to sit for a nationwide university entrance exam on English grammar and reading comprehension (alongside math and literature). After the students passed the entrance exam, they took another English placement test which included all four language skills. The top fifteen students were placed on a fast-track program and the remaining cohort was randomly assigned to different classes in a mainstream program. The students stayed in the same class from Year 1 through to Year 4.

Two classes were randomly selected from among the mainstream classes and assigned to the treatment ($N=12$) and comparison ($N=18$) conditions. Although there was no official information on the students' English proficiency levels, according to the institution, the mainstream third year class was considered to be at the high-intermediate level. There were no notable differences between the two groups in terms of age range, lengths of English study and exposure to English outside the classroom. In both groups, the learners' ages ranged between 20 and 23 (average 21). Their lengths of English study ranged between 6 and 9 years. None of them had ever visited an English-speaking country. They all had limited exposure to English in their daily lives and little chance to use English for communication outside the classroom.

Treatment was incorporated into a writing syllabus where the students were taught how to write paragraphs and different types of academic essays in English. The writing class met for three class hours every week. Instruction on constructive criticism was implemented for the treatment group for one class hour (i.e., 45 minutes) every week over a 15 week semester between February and May, 2010. The second author taught the comparison group and the third author taught the treatment group. Both instructors were trained EFL teachers and had obtained master's degrees in English language education from English-medium institutions outside Vietnam. The two classes followed the same writing syllabus and schedule. The only difference was the additional instruction of language for giving constructive criticism for the treatment group. Other than the writing course, the students also took part in oral skills and reading courses as well as courses in English linguistics, English language teaching methodology, and the history and geography of English speaking countries.

Instructional procedures

Over the 15 week period, the treatment group received explicit instruction on the target forms, participated in productive activities (e.g., role-play, oral peer-feedback), reflected on their own output, and received explicit correction throughout the process. The comparison group, on the other hand, did not receive any equivalent instruction.

The target forms included two major strategies for delivering constructive criticism: (1) statement of problem and (2) giving advice for improvement, as well as two types of criticism modifiers: (1) external modifiers (compliments, grounders and disarmers) and (2) internal modifiers (past tense, modal verbs, modal adverbs, expression of uncertainty, hedges and downgraders) (see Appendix 1). These strategies and modifiers were selected as instructional foci because they occurred most frequently in NS criticism. They also constituted areas of difficulty for many learners of English (Nguyen, 2005; 2008a). The teaching activities for the treatment group were adapted from Nguyen and Basturkmen (2010) and are summarized in Table 1.

Table 1. Instructional procedure for the treatment group

week	focus and activities	description
1	• pre-test • reflection on experience	• Learners worked in groups to reflect on and share their experience of giving and receiving constructive criticism in equal-status academic encounters. They also reflected on the similarities and differences between their native language and culture and English in giving constructive criticism.
2	• strategies for giving criticism: awareness-raising activity • metapragmatic instruction on criticism strategies	• Learners were guided to identify criticizing strategies from authentic NS samples of speech. • Explicit instruction on two major strategies for delivering constructive criticism: (1) statement of problem and (2) giving advice for improvement. • Distribution of explanatory handouts.
3	• modifying criticism: awareness-raising activity • metapragmatic instruction on criticism modifiers	• Learners were guided to identify types of modifiers from authentic NS samples of speech. • Explicit instruction on two major types of criticism modifiers: (1) external (e.g., compliments and disarmers) and (2) internal (e.g., hedges, downgraders, etc.) • Distribution of explanatory handouts.
4	• practice: recognizing degree of softening	• Learners identified modifiers from samples and judged the relative degrees of softening of the given criticism, using their knowledge of criticism modifiers.
5	• practice: softening criticism using appropriate modifiers	• Learners added modifiers to samples to make given criticism more sociopragmatically appropriate.
6	• practice: role-play	• Learners paired up to write and act out on structured role-plays involving giving constructive criticism to peers in classroom situations.
7–15	• practice: oral peer-feedback on actual written assignments • reflection on own output • post-tests	• Learners paired up to give oral constructive criticism on peers' actual written assignments, then reflected on and evaluated their own output for sociopragmatic appropriateness and pragmalinguistic accuracy.

Data collection

The learners' use of constructive criticism before and after the treatment was measured by means of an oral peer-feedback task and a discourse completion task (DCT) (see Appendix 2). These two instruments were developed and validated by Nguyen (2005).

To elicit data on constructive criticism, Nguyen (2005) first asked the participants to write a 250-word argumentative essay on a controversial topic. They were then arranged into pairs to give oral constructive critical feedback on each other's essays.[5] The feedback was based on three main assessment criteria, namely the organizational structure of the essay, the quality of argumentation, and grammar and vocabulary. To triangulate this set of data, Nguyen devised a DCT consisting of four criticizing situations. These situations were constructed based on peer-feedback data taken from a pilot study with four dyads of learners and three dyads of NSs one month prior to the main study. The purpose was to make the situations as comparable to the peer-feedback task as possible.

Similar procedures for conducting the oral peer-feedback task were followed in the current study and the learners' feedback conversations were audio-taped and transcribed for later analysis. For the DCT task, learners were asked to give responses to four hypothetical situations involving giving critical feedback on a friend's writing assignment. These situations were taken from Nguyen (2005).

Pre-test data were collected in Week 1, at the onset of the study, and consisted of learners' oral peer-feedback conversations. Post-test data were collected in Week 15, at the end of the treatment period, and consisted of oral peer-feedback conversations for both groups plus DCT responses for the treatment group. In addition, learners from the treatment group were also required to write a reflection essay in English after the procedure, in which they commented on their learning experience in the course (see Appendix 2). Data from this source were then analyzed for instances of input noticing.

Data analysis

Data from one learner from the treatment group and two learners from the comparison group were excluded from statistical analysis because they did not participate in all pre- and post-tests. Therefore, out of the 30 learners, only 27 were considered for analysis. This included 11 learners in the treatment group and 16 in the comparison group. The data were coded independently into different types of criticizing strategies and modifiers, and then carefully cross-checked by two of the researchers, adapting the categorization scheme devised and validated by Nguyen (2008b) (summarized in Appendix 1). This procedure achieved an inter-rater agreement rate of 95%.

An analytical assessment was then conducted to assign scores to each learner for his or her use of constructive criticism in the tests, using a 10 point scale adapted from Martínez-Flor and Fukuya (2005). This scale consisted of two parts, allowing the researchers to assess both sociopragmatic appropriateness and pragmalinguistic accuracy in learners' constructive criticism (see Appendix

3). Each part was rated from 0 to 5, making a total score ranging from 0 to 10. Sociopragmatic appropriateness was assessed in terms of knowledge of what to say to a particular interlocutor in a particular context or situation and determined by the right choice of realization strategies and politeness devices. Pragmalinguistic accuracy was assessed in terms of the learners' knowledge of various expressions for conveying intentions and determined by the correct use of relevant linguistic structures.

Note that although the learners were assessed for both sociopragmatic appropriateness and pragmalinguistic accuracy, they were to be awarded scores in the latter area only when they were awarded scores in the former area. In other words, pragmalinguistic accuracy was scored only when sociopragmatic appropriateness had been achieved. Note also that scores were awarded only when the learners made use of one of the target forms which had been taught to them during the treatment (see Appendix 1). A learner's final score on a task was obtained by averaging the sum of the sub-scores that he or she achieved for each criticism made while performing the task. The scoring procedures were conducted independently and cross-checked carefully by two of the researchers, reaching an agreement rate of 98%.

Analysis of the data was based on both between-group (comparison vs. treatment) and within-group (pre-test vs. post-tests) comparisons. Statistical procedures for the former case included ANCOVA, which was to test the difference in means between groups while controlling pre-existing differences due to non-random selection of participants, and Chi-square tests for relatedness, which was to test the differences in frequencies. Statistical procedures for the latter case included one-way repeated measures ANOVA, which was to test differences in means among three test conditions (in the case of the treatment group) and Friedman, which was similar to repeated measure ANOVA but employed in the absence of a normal distribution of data. Where a significant difference was found, paired samples t and Wilcoxon were utilized respectively for *post-hoc* comparisons. These two procedures were also used to compare differences in means between two test conditions (in the case of the comparison group). The former was used when data were normally distributed and the latter was used when data were not. A modified Bonferroni procedure was conducted when multiple tests on the same set of data were run in order to reduce the chance of Type 1 error.

Results

This section reports the results for the treatment group with respect to their overall pragmatic scores, frequency of use of target forms, and use of modifiers after instruction. Reference to the comparison group will also be made in order to examine whether improvements (if any) observed for the treatment group resulted from instruction.

Table 2 summarizes the two groups' pragmatic performance as measured by their overall scores gained in the pre- and post-tests. First, comparisons were made between the treatment group's scores on the two post-tests with the comparison group's oral post-test scores. Results of ANCOVA tests showed that the treatment group gained higher scores when measured by both oral and DCT post-tests ($M=4.6$ and 5.9 respectively for the treatment group vs. $M=3.0$ for the comparison group), but significantly differed from the comparison group only when they were measured by the DCT post-test [$F(2, 24)=9.794$, $p=.005$, $d=1.37$, suggesting a very large effect size (see Cohen, 1988)]. The difference between their oral post-test and the comparison group's oral post-test was not found to be significant [$F(2, 24)=2.854$, n.s., at $p=.10$], although the effect size calculated for this comparison was considered relatively large ($d=.86$) following Cohen's (1988) recommendation, suggesting large-magnitude superiority of the treatment group over the comparison group.

Table 2. Means and standard deviations of the pre and post-test overall scores for the comparison and treatment groups

	comparison (n=18)		treatment (n=12)	
	M	SD	M	SD
pre-test	3.3	1.5	1.9	1.9
oral post-test	3.0	2.0	4.6	1.7
DCT post-test	n.a		5.9	2.2

Indeed, this superiority became more evident when it came to within-group comparisons, i.e., comparisons of the performance by the same group on different test conditions. Results of a paired samples t suggested that the comparison group did not score higher in their post-test [$t(15)=.682$, n.s., at $p=.51$]. However, the treatment group's scores on both their oral and DCT post-tests increased considerably after interventions (Table 2).

Results of a one-way repeated measures ANOVA showed a significant difference when comparing three sets of scores from the treatment group, pre-test, oral post-test and DCT post-test, suggesting a significant improvement for this group after 15 weeks of instruction [$F(2, 18)=7.864$ at $p=.004$]. Results of *post hoc* paired samples t with Bonferroni correction found that this improvement was evident when the treatment group's performance was measured by both the oral ($p=.025$) and DCT post-tests ($p=.002$) (Table 3). Effect sizes calculated for both of these analyses were considered very large (pre-test vs. oral post-test: $d=1.49$; pre-test vs. DCT post test: $d=1.94$).

Table 3. Results of *post hoc* paired samples *t* with Bonferroni correction for the treatment groups' pre- and post-test scores

	absolute value of t	P value	critical alpha
pre-test vs. DCT post-test	4.218	.002	.05/3=.017
pre-test vs. oral post-test	2.642	.025	.05/2=.025

Effects of instruction on the treatment group's pragmatic competence were also evident when examining their post-instructional improvement in those pragmatic features that caused them problems before the experiment. Table 4 shows the frequencies and percentages of "giving advice" categorized as target forms as used by the comparison and treatment groups in their pre-and post-tests. This strategy was selected for the analysis because previous research has shown learners of English often employed the modal verbs *must, should,* and *have to* inappropriately and rarely hedged their advice when giving constructive criticism to peers (Nguyen, 2005, 2008b). Initial screening of pre-test data also showed that "giving advice" seemed more problematic to learners than "statement of problems." Thus, it would be worthwhile knowing to what extent this area of difficulty responded to instruction. For the analysis below, an instance of advice-giving was categorized as "target-like" only when it corresponded to the pragmalinguistic features that had been taught to the learners in the experiment and contained the taught modifiers.

Table 4. Frequencies and percentages of "giving advice" categorized as target forms before and after instruction

	comparison (*n*=18)				treatment (*n*=12)			
	target		non-target		target		non-target	
	F	%	F	%	F	%	F	%
pre-test	15	29	36	71	7	12	52	88
oral post-test	6	25	18	75	14	50	14	50
DCT post-test	n.a.				34	72	13	28

As can be seen, the comparison group consistently made use of a high percentage of nontarget-like advice in both of the tests (71% and 75%, respectively; Table 4). Outcomes of a Chi square test revealed no significant difference for this analysis [$\chi^2(1, N=75)=.015$, n.s., at $p=.46$]. The treatment group, on the other hand, displayed a significant improvement in their use of target forms after instruction. Their rate of use of target-like advice increased from 12% in the pre-test to 50% in the oral post-test and 72% in the DCT post-test. Their use of non-target forms reduced accordingly from 88% in the pre-test to 50% in the oral post-test and 28% in the DCT post-test (Table 4). These differences were found significant by Chi-square test results (pre-test vs.

oral post-test: [χ^2(1, N=87)=13.070 at p<.001; pre-test vs. DCT post-test: χ^2(1, N=106)=37.830 at p<.001].

Below are some illustrative examples of how a learner in the treatment group employed the strategy of "giving advice" while carrying out constructive criticism with her peer in three areas (essay organization, ideas and grammar) as observed in her pre-test as well as in the oral and DCT post-tests. As can be seen, before receiving instruction on constructive criticism, she tended to draw heavily on the structure "*You should*" to advise her classmate how to make changes in the three areas. However, after the 15 week course she used more target-like structures such as *may* and the conditional clause.

Pre-test
Organization: I think you *should* change the way you arrange your writing.
Ideas: You *should* give a clear opinion about this [the topic].
Grammar: You make some mistakes. It makes the readers confused.

Oral post-test
Grammar: You use (read aloud) but I think *it could be* (read aloud).

DCT post-test
Organization: You *may* think of rearrange [rearranging] some ideas to make your writing easier to follow.
Ideas: You *may need to* focus on the topic and omit some irrelevant ideas.
Grammar: Your writing *would be* much better *if you* pay some attention to linking words to make the essay cohesive.

Similarly, another student learned to give advice in a more target-like manner by making use of modal structures such as "might" and "could" and conditional structure, which she did not employ before receiving instruction on constructive criticism.

Pre-test
Ideas: You *need to* improve your ideas to make your writing more effective.
Grammar: You *need to* improve the vocabulary.

Oral post-test
Organization: Your writing *would be* better *if you* can balance the length between different points.
Ideas: *It's better to* rewrite the [thesis] statement or illustrate it in another way, not repeat it.

DCT post-test
Organization: You *might* rearrange the paragraphs to make them clearer.

Ideas: *If you* could give more convincing supporting ideas, *you could* convince readers more successfully.

Grammar: You *could* use linking words to make your writing more cohesive.

In order to more closely examine whether instruction affects the treatment group's scores for sociopragmatic appropriateness or pragmalinguistic accuracy, their pre-test and post-test scores in these two aspects were also compared. Table 5 presents the mean scores for appropriateness and accuracy, standard deviations, and the results of the one-way repeated measures ANOVA run for these statistics. As can be seen, learners scored significantly higher for both aspects in the two post-tests. Their scores for appropriateness increased considerably from 1.5 in the pre-test to 3.2 in the oral post-test and 3.5 in the DCT post-test [$F(2, 18)=9.415$, $p=.002$]. There was a corresponding increase in their accuracy scores from 0.6 in the pre-test to 1.4 in the oral post-test and 2.4 in the DCT post-test [$F(2, 18)=5.083$, $p=.018$] (Table 5).

Table 5. Results of one-way repeated measures ANOVA for mean scores of appropriateness and accuracy

	M	SD	F	P value
appropriateness				
pre-test	1.5	1.1	9.415	.002
oral post-test	3.2	0.9		
DCT post-test	3.5	1.3		
accuracy				
pre-test	0.6	1.0	5.083	.018
oral post-test	1.4	2.1		
DCT post-test	2.4	1.0		

Results of *post hoc* paired samples *t* with Bonferroni correction indicated that the learners significantly improved their sociopragmatic appropriateness on both the oral and DCT post-tests (pre-test vs. oral post-test: $p=.005$, $d=1.69$; pre-test vs. DCT post-test: $p=.002$; $d=1.66$). However, significant improvement in the area of pragmalinguistic accuracy was evident only in the DCT ($p=.003$, $d=1.79$) and not in their oral post-test scores ($p=.22$, *n.s.*, $d=.48$) (see Table 6), although the effect size calculated for the latter analysis was considered medium (see Cohen, 1988).

Table 6. Results of post hoc paired samples *t* with Bonferroni correction for the treatment group's scores of appropriateness and accuracy

	absolute value of *t*	*P* value	critical alpha
appropriateness			
pre-test vs. DCT post-test	4. 238	.002	.05/3=.017
pre-test vs. oral post-test	3. 541	.005	.05/2=.025
accuracy			
pre-test vs. DCT post-test	3.840	.003	.05/3=.017
pre-test vs. oral post-test	1.304	.2	.05/2=.025

Instruction also seemed to affect the treatment group's frequency of use of modifiers to soften their constructive criticism. Table 7 presents the results of Friedman tests run for medians of modifiers produced per criticism by this group in three test conditions. Overall, the learners employed a notably greater number of modifiers in the two post-tests than in the pre-test (pre-test: $Mdn=.20$, oral post-test: $Mdn=1.0$, DCT post-test: $Mdn=1.0$, $x^2=11.870$ at $p=.003$). However, post hoc Wilcoxon analyses showed that although there were significant improvements for both the oral and DCT post-tests (Table 7), these improvements were regarding learners' use of internal modifiers (pre-test vs. oral post-test: $p=.020$; $d=1.24$; pre-test vs. DCT post-test: $p=.006$, $d=1.63$) rather than their use of external modifiers, although the effect size calculated for post-instructional improvement in external modifiers when measured in the oral post-test was rather large (pre-test vs. oral post-test: $p=.019$, n.s., $d=1.07$; pre-test vs. DCT post-test: $p=.20$, n.s., $d=.20$) (Table 8).

Table 7. Results of Friedman for mean scores of criticism modifiers

	mdn	x^2	*P* value
external modifiers			
pre-test	.20	10.255	.006
oral post-test	.95		
DCT post-test	.45		
internal modifiers			
pre-test	.00	9.814	.007
oral post-test	.20		
DCT post-test	.50		
total mean			
pre-test	.20	11.870	.003
oral post-test	1.0		
DCT post-test	1.0		

Table 8. Results of post hoc Wilcoxon for the treatment group's means of modifiers

	absolute value of z	P value	critical alpha
external			
pre-test vs. oral post-test	2.355	.019	.05/3=.017
pre-test vs. DCT post-test	1/247	.20	.05/2=.025
internal			
pre-test vs. DCT post-test	2.752	.006	.05/3=.017
pre-test vs. oral post-test	2.319	.020	.05/2=.025
total			
pre-test vs. DCT post-test	2.714	.007	.05/3=.017
pre-test vs. oral post-test	2.361	.018	.05/2=.025

Discussion

Research question 1

The present study has sought to address two research questions: (1) Do learners benefit from explicit instruction in constructive criticism in English? and (2) Do some aspects of giving constructive criticism benefit more from explicit instruction than others? With regard to the first question, a positive answer was supported by the findings that the instructed students generally outperformed their uninstructed peers and improved their pragmatic performance significantly compared to their pre-test results. They also employed more target-like advice and internal modifiers, which constituted an area of difficulty for them before receiving pedagogical intervention.

To interpret the relative effectiveness of the instructional approach employed in this study as compared to instructional approaches used in previous studies, effect sizes were calculated for both the between-group (i.e., treatment vs. comparison) and within-group (i.e., pre-test vs. post-test) analyses. These were compared with the corresponding figures reported by Jeon and Kaya (2006) in their meta-analysis of instructed L2 pragmatics studies, and Norris and Ortega (2000) in their meta-analysis of instructed L2 grammar studies. In the present study, the mean treatment-versus-comparison effect size ($d=1.12$), calculated by averaging the effect sizes for oral post-test contrast ($d=.86$) and DCT post-test contrast ($d=1.37$), was considered relatively large, following Cohen's (1988) recommendations. This was larger than both the mean effect size of .59 reported for pragmatic instruction by Jeon and Kaya (2006) and the mean effect size of .96 reported for grammar instruction by Norris and Ortega (2000) (see Table 9).

Table 9. A comparison of mean effect sizes for treatment-versus-comparison and pretest-to-posttest contrasts among three studies

	instructional foci	treatment vs. comparison	pre-test vs. post-test
present study	L2 pragmatics	1.12	1.71
Jeon & Kaya (2006)	L2 pragmatics	.59	1.66
Norris & Ortega (2000)	L2 grammar	.96	1.57

Similarly, the mean pretest-to-posttest effect size in the present study (d=1.71), calculated by averaging the effect sizes for oral post-test contrast (d=1.49) and DCT post-test contrast (d=1.94), was found to be larger than the corresponding figures reported in Jeon and Kaya (2006) and Norris and Ortega (2000) (see Table 9) and considered relatively large, following Cohen (1988). These results seem to suggest a greater magnitude of effects for the instructional approach employed in the current study.

Positive instructional effects were also evident in the learners' comments about their learning experience in end-of-course reflective essays. These effects, reported by all twelve learners from the treatment group, included heightened awareness of the politeness aspect of giving constructive criticism, enhanced metapragmatic knowledge, as well as knowledge of the linguistic devices used for expressing and softening their constructive criticism. For example, one learner wrote:

"Since the first year I've checked and given feedback to my friends. However, I did not have much knowledge about how to give feedback. I just focused on my friends' mistakes and gave feedback directly to their mistake without caring much about how my friends felt when receiving my feedback. Recently, I learn something about giving feedback. I suppose that the most important thing I learned is to give feedback that doesn't hurt my friends but still points out their mistakes by using mitigation."

The overall benefits of explicit metapragmatic instruction reported in the present study are consistent with the findings of previous studies (Billmyer, 1990; Bouton, 1994; Lyster, 1994; Martínez-Flor & Fukuya, 2005; Olshtain & Cohen, 1990; Safont, 2003; Yoshimi, 2001) and can be attributed to various factors. First, instructional activities such as guided discovery and discussion of metapragmatic rules served to draw the learners' attention to the targeted features and caused them to notice the relationship between form, meaning and use, thus aiding their acquisition of these features (Schmidt, 1993, 1995). Indeed, instances of input-noticing resulting from this learning process were reported in the learners' end-of-course reflective essays, adding further evidence about the noticing function of the above-mentioned instructional activities. For example, one learner wrote:

"One important thing about giving critical peer feedback I have learned in the last session is that I know how to soften criticism by using the modal verbs like *might, would,* etc. or uncertain structures like *I'm not sure* or *It seems.*"

Similarly, another learner commented:

"In terms of language, by learning about giving critical peer feedback, I know how to point out the mistakes without depressing or hurting my friends. For example, instead of saying straightly about the weak points, I can use mitigation devices, like 'I think this point is a little bit far from the topic in the way that....' to soften the comment."

Second, the learners also benefit from the explicit correction they received from their teachers, especially when the need to focus on form arose out of meaningful communication (e.g., giving constructive criticism in oral role-plays and oral peer-feedback tasks). Such interactional feedback causes learners to attend to problematic forms, notice the gap between their own output and the target form, and modify their output accordingly, which is believed to contribute to learning (Long, 1983, 1996; Swain, 1985, 1995, 2005). Similar learning benefits also result from learners' reflection on their own output after each peer-feedback session, which also provides opportunities for gap-noticing and modified output. Instances of gap-noticing were found in learners' reflective journals too. For example, one learner commented:

"I often directly give comments on what my friends do wrongly. However, now I usually give my friends' strong points first and then I comment on his/ her weak point so that my friends are not really disappointed and hurt."

Similarly, another student wrote:

"When it comes to giving comments, I usually use expressions such as *I think that you should* or *You should not,* which are direct and clear. However, sometimes I found my friends not really satisfying with my feedback due to its straightforwardness. Therefore, I have tried to soften it. In other words, I have attempted to make use of softeners such as *You might,* or *I'm not pretty sure* so that my friend can find it easier to receive the feedback. The result is that my peers take my comments more seriously."

Research question 2

With regard to the second research question, findings suggested that while instruction generally benefited the learners' performance of constructive criticism, it seemed to affect different aspects differently. For example, the learners' post-instructional improvement was more evident in sociopragmatic appropriateness than in pragmalinguistic accuracy. While the gains made in their sociopragmatic appropriateness scores were significant in both the oral and DCT post-tests, their gains in pragmalinguistic accuracy were significant only in the DCT post-test, where they were not under pressure to produce online speech and thus could plan their production more carefully.

Table 10. Pretest-to-posttest effect sizes for gains in sociopragmatic appropriateness and pragmalinguistic accuracy

	sociopragmatic appropriateness	pragmalinguistic accuracy
effect size for pretest vs. oral post-test contrast	1.69	.48
effect size for pre-test vs. DCT post-test contrast	1.66	1.79
mean effect size	1.67	1.13

Comparing pretest-to-posttest effect sizes for gains in these two aspects, it was found that the mean effect size for gains in sociopragmatic appropriateness (d=1.67) was larger than that in pragmalinguistic accuracy (d=1.13). This was because of the larger magnitude of effects on sociopragmatic appropriateness (d=1.69) as compared to effects on pragmalinguistic accuracy (d=.48) when both aspects were measured in the oral post-test condition but not when they were compared in the DCT post-test condition (d=1.66 for sociopragmatic appropriateness; d=1.79 for pragmalinguistic accuracy) (Table 10).

These results suggest some possible interplay between instructional effects and processing issues. Instructional effects were more evident in test conditions such as the written DCT, which allowed a greater amount of planning time and imposed relatively less processing demand. In other words, instructional effects presented themselves more obviously when learners were measured for what they could possibly do under controlled, pressure-free conditions than when they were measured for what they actually did under the pressure of real-time interaction.

On the one hand, these findings carry important implications for future studies in designing their outcome measures to capture instructional effects on different aspects of learners' pragmatic performance. Written DCTs may be effective in measuring what learners know about L2 pragmatics while oral, spontaneous production tasks are effective in measuring whether they can retrieve this knowledge for use in real time.

The findings also suggest pedagogical implications in fostering pragmatic fluency. In particular, the learners' lower accuracy in the oral post-test suggested that they did not achieve full control over pragmalinguistic forms due to a lack of fluency in the L2, with the result that they did not use these forms accurately when under time constraints, despite their knowledge of the forms. According to Nation (2011), fluency development requires not only plentiful and repeated communicative practice in which learners can work to avoid communication breakdown but also some pressure on learners to perform at a faster than usual speed. Although the instructional approach employed in the current study met the first condition, it fell short of the second. While it allowed the learners to be regularly engaged with meaning via communicative tasks such as role plays and oral peer-feedback, it did not require them to produce faster speech each time they delivered it. In the future, teachers should take timed practice into consideration when designing tasks to help improve learners' automaticity in using pragmalinguistic conventions. In addition, perhaps allowing plentiful time for pre-task planning may also compensate for this lack of pragmatic fluency.

Further, the instructional approach employed in the present study also seemed to produce different effects on learners' use of external and internal modifiers. Findings showed that instruction caused learners to use significantly more internal modifiers but not more external modifiers. The mean effect size calculated for improvements in internal modifiers ($d=1.43$) was twice as large as that calculated for improvements in external modifiers ($d=.63$). These results are worth noting, given the findings of earlier studies which suggest that internal modifiers tend to pose more challenges to L2 learning than do external modifiers because of their less noticeable pragmatic meaning and the possibility of adding to the structural complexity of the speech (Hassall, 2001; Nguyen, 2008a). Indeed, the findings of the present study indicate that learners generally preferred external modifiers to internal modifiers before pedagogical interventions (c.f.: $M=.3$ for external modifiers vs. $M=.02$ for internal modifiers). After receiving instruction, however, they preferred external modifiers only when they participated in the spontaneous, oral peer-feedback task ($M=1.5$ for external modifiers vs. $M=.2$ for internal modifiers). When they were given more processing time in the pressure-free, written DCT condition, they employed more internal modifiers ($M=.4$ for external modifiers vs. $M=.6$ for internal modifiers).

The above findings might be explained by the observation that unlike external modifiers, which learners already employed extensively before treatment, internal modifiers represented 'newer' knowledge to learners, i.e., something they were less likely to notice otherwise, and therefore attract more of their attention. Unfortunately, without conducting retrospective interviews with the learners, no definite answers can be provided at this point and obviously further investigation into the issue is required. All in all, the learners' considerable improvement in the area of internal modifiers is worth applauding and suggests the advantage of explicit instruction in raising the learners' awareness of forms and meanings which would have been far less salient to them without instruction.

Conclusion

Overall, like many previous studies (Jeon & Kaya, 2006; Rose, 2005), the findings of the present study indicate that as in the case of L2 grammar (Norris & Ortega, 2000), L2 pragmatic development can be enhanced through an appropriate pedagogical approach. More specifically, learning L2 pragmatics can benefit from opportunities for input noticing, meaningful output practice, corrective feedback and modified output. These findings thus lend support to second language acquisition theories which hold that part of learning must require consciousness and that input and output modified via meaningful communication can aid learning (Long, 1983, 1996; Schmidt, 1993, 1995; Swain, 1985, 1995, 2005). These findings also suggest that constructive criticism is teachable, despite the fact that it is a challenging speech act set which may require a relatively high degree of linguistic complexity as well as pragmatic sophistication. The findings thus make a strong case for teaching the language for delivering constructive criticism in peer assessment tasks in L2 classrooms. Such instruction is especially necessitated in EFL contexts where learners have limited exposure to sociopragmatic rules and pragmalinguistic resources in the TL.

The findings of this study also suggest some effects of test methods on learners' pragmatic performance, as pointed out in many previous studies (e.g., Bardovi-Harlig & Hartford, 1993; Beebe & Cummings, 1996; Hartford & Bardovi-Harlig, 1992; Hinkel, 1997; Jeon & Kaya, 2006; Johnston, Kasper, & Ross, 1998; Nguyen, 2005; Rose, 1992; Sasaki, 1997; Wolfson, 1989; Yuan, 2001). In this study, learners' superior performance in the DCT task, especially regarding their overall pragmatic scores as compared to their uninstructed peers, and gains in scores for pragmalinguistic accuracy as compared to gains in sociopragmatic appropriateness, might have been explained by the written nature of the DCT. More specifically, the task allows them more processing time, and thus is less imposing on their processing capacity, which enables them to attend to those forms which have not yet been automatized (Nguyen, 2005). In this way, the DCT provides useful information about learners' declarative knowledge of L2 pragmatics, or what learners *can* do under controlled conditions, in addition to their procedural knowledge, or what they *actually* do in real-time communication, which might be measured more faithfully by means of spontaneous interaction, e.g., the oral peer-feedback task (see Anderson, 1976, 1980, for further discussion of declarative and procedural knowledge).

These findings raise several issues for future research in designing data collection methods. Employing multiple and different modes of data collection would potentially help capture the subtle changes and differences caused by instruction. Comparing studies that employ elicited data exclusively with those employing both elicited and naturally occurring data, Jeon and Kaya (2006) found a larger effect size for the latter. However, they warn against any premature conclusion because of the limited number of studies available for their meta-analysis. Further systematic research might be conducted to address the relationship between observed instructional effectiveness and types of outcome measure so as to inform the methodology of future instructed L2 pragmatics studies.

The findings of the present study also carry important pedagogical implications. Bialystok (1993) assumes that the acquisition of pragmatic knowledge in the TL requires two separate cognitive processes: that of acquiring the knowledge and that of gaining automaticity in using this knowledge. Previous research shows that high proficiency learners sometimes learn grammatical forms but do not learn all their functions, with the result that they do not always put these forms to their correct pragmatic use (Hassall, 2001; Nguyen, 2005, 2008a). In other cases, difficulty does not arise from deviant knowledge of form-function mapping but from learners' inability to draw on this knowledge when they need it, as was the case with the treatment group in the present study. Therefore, pragmatic instruction should allow not only focus on attention to form-function mapping but also control over this attention so that learners can produce pragmatically appropriate and linguistically accurate speech acts in real time.

Finally, a word of caution is in order. Despite some interesting insights, the findings in this chapter are still exploratory and should not be generalized without careful consideration of the limitations of the study. These limitations included the employment of a small, nonrandomized, gender biased sample (with all but one of the students being female), which affects the representativeness of the findings. Further, the lack of a delayed post-test also made it impossible to measure the long-term retention of instructional effect on the learners. Therefore, while positive instructional effects were observed at the end of the intervention, one cannot conclude with confidence that these effects will be maintained beyond immediate post-interventional observations. What is more, the fact that the study employed two different instructors for the treatment and comparison groups may have also contributed to the differences in learning outcomes. In particular, although the instructors followed the specified instructional protocols, they might still have differed in their teaching styles, which could have affected the students' motivation to learn. Future studies need to include classroom observation in order to document how the instructors deliver the teaching and how the students participate in the activities under investigation.

Notes

1   A speech act set is composed of a range of strategies, any combination of which could perform it (Olshtain & Cohen, 1983) and was first used by these researchers to describe apologies.

2   Criticizing refers to the act of finding fault with another person (Tracy, van Dusen, & Robinson, 1987). It may involve criticizing another's work, ideas, or personal style (Tracy & Eisenberg, 1990). However, it should be noted that criticizing someone's work might be expected to be constructive and supportive in nature. Thus, the type of criticism under inquiry in the present study may involve a lower level of 'infraction'

than the more 'biting' types of criticism such as criticizing someone's appearance or behavior.
3   In many studies on workplace communication or communication for teachers in the context of mentoring, the terms 'criticism' and 'critical feedback' are used interchangeably (Tracy & Eisenberg, 1990; Wajnryb, 1993, 1995).
4   Although this concept was first mentioned in a published article by Blum-Kulka and Olshtain (1984), as they point out in that article, it was originally coined and used by Susan Ervin-Tripp and David Gordon in their coding manual for analyzing requests within the framework of their unpublished *Social Development and Communication Strategies* project.
5   The students were not told what counted as 'constructive criticism' but were instead simply asked to find points in their peer's essays they felt unsatisfied with and to comment on these points. The instruction also indicated that although the task required them to comment specifically on the points they were unsatisfied with, they might also comment on the good points (if any) in the essay (see Appendix 2).

References

Anderson, J. (1976). *Language, memory, and thought.* Hillsdale, NJ: Erlbaum Associates.

Anderson, J. (1980). *Cognitive psychology and its implications.* San Francisco: W. H. Freeman.

Bardovi-Harlig, K. & Hartford, B. (1993). Refining the DCT: Comparing open questionnaires and dialogue completion tasks. In L. Bouton, & Y. Kachru (Eds.), *Pragmatics and language learning* (Vol. 4) (pp. 143–165). Urbana-Champaign, IL: University of Illinois.

Beebe, L., & Cummings, M. (1996). Natural speech act data versus written questionnaire data: How data collection method affects speech act performance. In S. Gass, & J. Neu (Eds.), *Speech acts across cultures* (pp. 65–86). Berlin: Mouton de Gruyter.

Bialystok, E. (1993). Symbolic representation and attentional control in pragmatic competence. In G. Kasper, & S. Blum-Kulka (Eds.), *Interlanguage pragmatics* (pp. 42–57). New York: Oxford University Press.

Billmyer, K. (1990). I really like your lifestyle: ESL learners learning how to compliment. *Penn Working Papers in Educational Linguistics, 6*, 31–48.

Blum-Kulka, S. & Olshtain, E. (1984) Requests and apologies: A cross-cultural study of speech act realisation patterns (CCSARP). *Applied Linguistics,* 5, 196–213.

Bouton, L. F. (1994). Can NNS skill in interpreting implicature in American English be improved through explicit instruction? – A pilot study. In L. Bouton (Ed.), *Pragmatics and language learning,* (Vol. 5) (pp. 88–109). Urbana-Champaign, IL: University of Illinois.

Boxer, D. (1993). Complaints as positive strategies: What the learner needs to know. *TESOL Quarterly, 27,* 277–299.

Brown, P. & Levinson, S. (1987). *Politeness: Some universals in language usage.* Cambridge: Cambridge University Press.

Cohen, J. (1988). *Statistical power analysis for the behavioral sciences* (2nd ed.). Hillsdale, NJ: Lawrence Erlbaum Associates.

DeKeyser, R. (2003). Implicit and explicit learning. In C. Doughty, & M. H. Long (Eds.), *The handbook of second language acquisition* (pp. 313–348). Oxford: Blackwell.

Ellis, R. (2008). *The study of second language acquisition* (2nd ed.). Oxford: Oxford University Press.

Fukuya, Y., & Clark, M. (2001). A comparison of input enhancement and explicit instruction of mitigators. In L. Bouton (Ed.), *Pragmatics and language learning, (Vol. 10)* (pp. 111–130). Urbana-Champaign, IL: University of Illinois.

Hassall, T. (2001). Modifying requests in a second language. *International Review of Applied Linguistics in Language Teaching 39*, 259–283.

Hartford, B. & Bardovi-Harlig, K. (1992). Experimental and observational data in the study of interlanguage pragmatics. In L. Bouton, and Y. Kachru (Eds.), *Pragmatics and language learning* (Vol. 3) (pp. 33–50). Urbana-Champaign, IL: University of Illinois. Hinkel, E. (1997). Appropriateness of advice: DCT and multiple choice data. *Applied Linguistics, 18*, 1–26.

Izumi, S. (2002). Output, input enhancement, and the noticing hypothesis: An experimental study on ESL relativization. *Studies in Second Language Acquisition, 24*, 541–577.

Jeon, E. H., & Kaya, T. (2006). Effects of L2 instruction on interlanguage pragmatic development: A meta-analysis. In J. M. Norris, & L. Ortega (Eds.), *Synthesizing research on language learning and teaching* (pp. 165–211). Amsterdam: John Benjamins.

Johnston, B., Kasper, G., & Ross, S. (1998). The effect of rejoinders in production questionnaires. *Applied Linguistics, 19*, 157–182.

Kasper, G., & Rose, K. (2002). *Pragmatic development in a second language*. Oxford: Blackwell.

Kondo, S. (2001). Instructional effects on pragmatic development: Refusal by Japanese EFL learners. *Publications of Akenohoshi Women's Junior College, 19*, 33–51.

Liu, J. & Hansen, J. (2002). *Peer response in second language writing classrooms*. Ann Arbor, MI: University of Michigan Press.

Long, M. (1983). Native speaker/ Non-native speaker conversation and the negotiation of comprehensible input. *Applied Linguistics 4*, 126–141.

Long, M. (1996). The role of the linguistic environment in second language acquisition. In W. Ritchie, & T. Bhatia (Eds.), *Handbook of second language acquisition* (pp. 413–468). San Diego: Academic Press.

Lyster, R. (1994). The effect of functional-analytic teaching on aspects of French immersion students' sociolinguistic competence. *Applied Linguistics 15*, 263–287.

Martínez-Flor, A., & Fukuya, Y. J. (2005). The effects of instruction on learners' production of appropriate and accurate suggestions. *System, 33*, 463–480.

Mendonca, C. O., & Johnson, K. E. (1994). Peer review negotiations: Revision activities in ESL writing instruction. *TESOL Quarterly, 28*, 745–769.

Morrow, K. C. (1995). *The pragmatic effects of instruction on ESL learners' production of complaint and refusal speech acts.* Unpublished doctoral thesis, State University of New York at Buffalo.

Nation, P. (2011). Second language speaking. In Hinkel, E. (Ed.) *Handbook of research in second language teaching and learning* (Vol 2). (pp. 444–454). New York: Routledge.

Nelson, G., & Carson, J. (1998). ESL students' perceptions of effectiveness in peer response groups. *Journal of Second Language Writing, 7,* 113–131.

Nguyen, T. T. M. (2005). *Criticizing and responding to criticism in a foreign language: A study of Vietnamese learners of English.* Unpublished doctoral dissertation, University of Auckland, Auckland, NZ.

Nguyen, T. T. M. (2008a). Modifying L2 criticism: How learners do it? *Journal of Pragmatics, 40,* 768–791.

Nguyen, T. T. M. (2008b). Criticizing in a L2: Pragmatic strategies used by Vietnamese EFL learners. *Intercultural Pragmatics, 5,* 41–66.

Nguyen, T. T. M., & Basturkmen, H. (2010). Teaching constructive critical feedback. In N. Houck & D. Tatsuki (Eds.), *Pragmatics: Teaching speech acts* (pp. 125–140). Alexandria, VA: TESOL.

Norris, J. M., & Ortega, L. (2000). Effectiveness of L2 instruction: A research synthesis and quantitative meta-analysis. *Language Learning, 50,* 417–528.

Olshtain, E., & Cohen, A. (1983). Apology: A speech act set. In N. Wolfson, & E. Judd (Eds.), *Sociolinguistics and second language acquisition* (pp. 18–35). Rowley, MA: Newbury House.

Olshtain, E., & Cohen, A. (1990). The learning of complex speech act behavior. *TESL Canada Journal, 7,* 45–65.

Rollinson, P. (2005). Using peer feedback in the ESL writing class. *ELT Journal, 59,* 23–30.

Rose, K. (1992). Speech acts and questionnaires: The effect of hearer response. *Journal of Pragmatics 17,* 49—62.

Rose, K. (2005). On the effects of instruction in second language pragmatics. *System, 33,* 385–399.

Rose, K., & Kasper, G. (Eds.). (2001). *Pragmatics in language teaching.* Cambridge: Cambridge University Press.

Rose, K., & Ng, K. (2001). Inductive and deductive teaching of compliments and compliment responses. In K. Rose, & G. Kasper (Eds.), *Pragmatics in language teaching* (pp. 145–170). Cambridge: Cambridge University Press.

Safont, M. P. (2003). Instructional effects on the use of request acts modification devices by EFL learners. In A. Martínez Flor, E. Usó Juan, & A. Fernández Guerra (Eds.), *Pragmatic competence and foreign language teaching* (pp. 211–232). Castelló: Servei de Publicacions de la Universitat Jaume I.

Salazar, P. C. (2003). Pragmatic instruction in the EFL context. In A. Martínez Flor, E. Usó Juan, & A. Fernández Guerra (Eds.), *Pragmatic competence and foreign language teaching* (pp. 233–246). Castelló: Servei de Publicacions de la Universitat Jaume I.

Sasaki, M. (1997). Investigating EFL students' production of speech acts: A comparison of production questionnaires and role plays. *Journal of Pragmatics, 30*, 457–484.

Schmidt, R. (1993). Consciousness, learning, and interlanguage pragmatics. In G. Kasper, & S. Blum-Kulka (Eds.), *Interlanguage pragmatics* (pp. 21–42). New York: Oxford University Press.

Schmidt, R. (1995). Consciousness and foreign language learning: A tutorial on the role of attention and awareness in learning. In R. Schmidt (Ed.), *Attention and awareness in foreign language learning* (pp. 1–63). Honolulu: University of Hawai'i, Second Language Teaching and Curriculum Center.

Swain, M. (1995). Three functions of output in second language learning. In G. Cook, & B. Seidlhofer (Eds.), *Principles and practice in the study of language: Studies in honour of H. G. Widdowson* (pp. 125–144). Oxford: Oxford University Press.

Swain, M. (2005). Verbal protocols: What does it mean for research to use speaking as a data collection tool? In M. Chalhoub-Deville, C. Chapelle, & P. Duff (Eds.), *Inference and generalizability in applied linguistics: Multiple perspectives* (pp. 97–113). Amsterdam: John Benjamins.

Takahashi, S. (2001). The role of input enhancement in developing pragmatic competence. In K. Rose, & G. Kasper (Eds.), *Pragmatics in language teaching* (pp. 171–199). Cambridge: Cambridge University Press.

Takahashi, S. (2005). Noticing in task performance and learning outcomes: A qualitative analysis of instructional effects in interlanguage pragmatics. *System, 3*, 437–461.

Thomas, J. (1983). Cross-cultural pragmatic failure. *Applied Linguistics, 4*, 91–112.

Tracy, K., & Eisenberg, E. (1990). Giving criticisms: A multiple goals case study. *Research on Language and Social Interaction, 24*, 37–70.

Tracy, K., Van Dusen, D., & Robinson, S. (1987). Good and bad criticism: A descriptive analysis. *Journal of Communication, 37*, 46–59.

Wajnryb, R. (1993). Strategies for the management and delivery of criticisms. *English Australia Journal 11* , 74–84.

Wajnryb, R. (1995). The perception of criticism: One trainee's experience. *English Australia Journal 13*, 54–68.

Wolfson, N. (1989). The social dynamics of native and non-native variation in complimenting behavior. In M. Eisenstein (Ed.), *The dynamic interlanguage: Empirical studies in second language variation* (pp. 219–236). New York: Plenum Press.

Yoshimi, D. R. (2001). Explicit instruction and JFL learner's use of interactional discourse markers. In K. Rose, & G. Kasper (Eds.), *Pragmatics in language teaching* (pp. 223–244). Cambridge: Cambridge University Press.

Yuan, Y. (2001). An inquiry into empirical pragmatics data-gathering methods: Written DCTs, field notes, and natural conversations. *Journal of Pragmatics 33*, 271–192.

Appendix 1: Target forms included in the study

target forms	examples
Statement of problems: stating the problem or errors found with R's choice, work, or products	I thought you had two conclusions. I didn't see your conclusion.
Giving advice: proposing a potential solution to the problem or errors identified	You might want to delete the comma. Perhaps you could pay more attention to grammar.

modifiers	examples
1. External: additional comments, separate from the problem identification and advice giving	
Compliment: saying something good about the thing you are going to criticize	It was an interesting paper. That was a great presentation.
Disarmer: showing awareness of the potential offence that your comment may cause R	You had a few spelling mistakes here and there *but I think that's because you're writing pretty quick, nothing too major.*
Grounder: giving reasons to justify your comment	I think "is" would be better than "are" there *because traffic is single.*
2. Internal: linguistic softeners	
Question: using questions rather than bald statements or imperatives to identify a problem or propose a potential solution	Did you summarize the main idea? Could this work?
Past tense: creating a sense of distance between the speaker and the comment	I *thought* it *would* make more sense that way. Maybe you *could've explained* it a little bit more.
Modal verbs (e.g., may, might [want to], could, would)	I'm not sure but maybe you *could* cut out the second section.
Modal adverbs	maybe, perhaps, probably *Perhaps* you *might* want to check that again.
Uncertainty phrases: showing hesitation or uncertainty about the criticism	*I wasn't sure* that was the best phrase you could've used. *I don't know* that I agree with the point you made.
Hedges (e.g., kind of, sort of, seem)	This sentence was *sort of* unclear.
Downgraders (e.g., a bit, a little [bit], quite, rather)	Your introduction seemed *a little* too long.

(adapted from Nguyen, 2005)

Pragma-linguistic conventions for realizing constructive criticism
(adapted from Nguyen, 2005)
1. Statement of problem:
    - NP was ADJ
    - You V (past tense)
    - You had (a/an) (ADJ) NP
2. Giving suggestion:
    - You can
    - You could + V
    - You could have + V (past participle)
    - You may + V
    - You might + V
    - You might want to + V
    - (If I were you) I would
    - It would be better if you + V
    - It would be better + V (infinitive)
    - If you + V, it may
    - NP may be + V (past participle)
    - Why don't you?

note: Structures to be avoided because they might produce a negative effect on the hearer:
- Imperatives: "Give more examples"
- Strong modal structures: *should, must, have to, ought to*
- Negative words: "wrong," "weak," etc.

Appendix 2: Data collection instruments

Oral Peer Feedback Task

Instruction: You have written a 250 word essay. Now show it to your friend and work in pairs. Take as much time as you need to read your friend's essay. *Try to find something you are **unsatisfied** with about the essay and comment on it. Does your friend think the same? Discuss with him or her some of the things you think are **wrong** with the essay.* Your friend will also give comments on your essay. Do you agree with his or her ideas?

Do not try to discuss two essays at the same time. Work on one at a time only. You may discuss between yourselves whose essay to work on first.

Note
1. It is important that you understand the task completely, so before you start you are encouraged to ask questions if you find any detail you are not sure of.
2. Although the task requires you to comment specifically on the points you are unsatisfied with in your friend's essay, *you can also comment on the good points (if any) in his or her essay.*

You may want to ask yourself the following questions when giving feedback on your friend's essay:

Organization
1. Does the essay directly discuss the topic?
2. Is there a clear organizational structure, i.e., does it have three parts: an introduction, a body, and a conclusion?
3. Is the introduction brief and to the point? Does it indicate the main ideas that the writer will discuss in the body?
4. Are there several paragraphs in the body, each making a different specific point?
5. Is there a brief conclusion that summarizes the main points in the argument?
6. Are the ideas properly linked?

Ideas
7. Is the writer's opinion clear or do you think the writer is not quite sure what he or she thinks?
8. Are the ideas relevant and well supported by evidence and examples?
9. Are the ideas presented logically?

10. Are the ideas developed from one paragraph to another or does the writer just repeat himself or herself?

Grammar/vocabulary
11. Is there a variety of sentence structure and vocabulary or is there a lot of repetition?
12. Are the linking words (i.e., words used to link ideas) helpful or do they confuse you?
13. Are the sentences grammatically accurate?
(adapted from Nguyen, 2005)

Discourse Completion Task

Please read the instruction and the given situations carefully and write your answers in English in the space provided under each situation. It is important that you understand the requirements completely, so before you start, you are encouraged to ask questions if you find something you do not understand.
Thank you for your assistance.

Instruction: In reference to an essay that your friend has just written, what would you say in the following hypothetical situations?

Example

Situation 0: What would you say to your friend if you thought her essay exceeded the limit of 250 words?
You: "I think ...."

Situation 1: What would you say to your friend if you thought his or her essay was not very well organized, so it was rather difficult to follow his or her ideas?
You:

Situation 2: What would you say to your friend if you thought in some instances he or she didn't support his or her arguments with relevant examples and evidence, so these arguments were hard to convince readers?
You:

Situation 3: What would you say to your friend if you thought his or her essay lacked a focus, and so it was difficult to follow his or her arguments?
You:

Situation 4: What would you say to your friend if you thought he or she didn't often make use of linking words, so the essay seemed to lack cohesion?
You:
(adapted from Nguyen, 2005)

Reflection Essay

At home write a one-page reflection on the experience you gained in giving critical peer feedback, using the following guiding questions to help you. Submit this reflection to your instructor in the next class meeting.

Guiding questions
1. Name AT LEAST one important thing about giving critical peer feedback that you have learned in the last sessions.
2. How has your idea about giving critical feedback changed as a result of this gained experience?
3. How helpful is this experience to you?
4. How are you going to make use of this experience in your other classes?

Appendix 3: Grading criteria

Scoring for pragmatic appropriateness level

Appropriateness: knowing what to say to a particular interlocutor in a particular context of situation; determined by the right choice of realization strategies, that is, giving suggestion rather than demanding changes because of the equal power status between the interlocutors.

grammatical level	score	examples
inappropriate Head Act (HA)	0	You *must* pay attention to grammar.
appropriate HA (without modifiers or with inappropriate modifiers)	4	You can rewrite your introduction (without modifiers). You can rewrite your introduction *because it's too bad* (with inappropriate modifier).
appropriate HA + appropriate modifiers	5	*Perhaps* you *could* pay more attention to grammar.

Scoring for linguistic accuracy

Accuracy: knowing the expressions for conveying intentions; determined by the correct usage of relevant linguistic structures, e.g., saying "*if I were you, I would*" but not "*If I were you, I will.*"

grammatical level	score	examples
incorrect pragma-linguistic form	0	Your ideas *would* be linked more properly (the correct form is "Your ideas *could* be linked more properly")..
correct pragma-linguistic form + incorrect connecting part/inaccurate modifiers	4	It would be better if you could *revising* it (the correct form is "if you could revise it).
correct pragma-linguistic form + correct connecting part/accurate modifiers	5	You *may want to* explain this *a little bit* more.

Note

- Scores to be assigned for the target forms only (see Appendix 1)
- Scores to be assigned for both linguistic realization strategies (i.e., identifying problem and giving advice) and modifiers (i.e., softeners).

- Scores to be assigned for both pragmatic appropriateness and linguistic accuracy but linguistic accuracy is to be scored only when pragmatic appropriateness has been achieved. In other words, pragmatic appropriateness is a necessary condition for linguistic accuracy.
- Modifiers to be awarded scores only when appropriate head act has been used. E.g., if a candidate says "Your writing is good but you must pay attention to grammar," the compliment "Your writing is good" is not to be awarded a score because the head act "You must" is not appropriate.
- A candidate's final score will be calculated following this procedure: (1) calculate the total number of criticisms he or she has made; (2) then generate the score for each criticism by adding its score for appropriateness and score for accuracy; (3) calculate the sum for all criticisms made; (4) finally divide this sum by the number of criticisms made.

(adapted from Martínez-Flor & Fukuya, 2005)

Pragmatic Awareness of Japanese EFL Learners in Relation to Individual Differences: A Cluster Analytic Approach

Kazuhito Yamato
Kobe University, Japan

Kenji Tagashira
Hiroshima University, Japan

Takamichi Isoda
Ritsumeikan University, Japan

This study investigated the relationships between pragmatic awareness and learner types drawn from profiles of learners' motivation and proficiency, thus providing insight into the interplay of learner factors in contrast to previous studies describing the relationships between single variables. In addition to a modified replication of Bardovi-Harlig and Dörnyei's (1998) study in the Japanese EFL context, this study incorporated measures of motivation based on Self-Determination Theory and learners' proficiency. Cluster analysis sorted 69 Japanese EFL learners into three distinct subgroups based on their configuration of motivation and proficiency; in particular, they differed on their levels of intrinsic motivation and proficiency. Their pragmatic awareness was later compared by use of one-way ANOVA. The results illustrated that two groups with more self-determined motivation showed sharper perception of pragmatic inappropriateness than the group with lower intrinsic motivation, even though its proficiency was higher. Based on the "noticing hypothesis" (Schmidt, 1995), we propose that intrinsically motivated learners are likely to process L2 pragmatic input at the level of 'understanding,' whereas those with lower motivational profiles only 'notice the form' but do not process it at the 'understanding' level. Proficiency is not in itself a sufficient condition for enabling 'understanding.'

Introduction

In the field of Interlanguage Pragmatics (ILP), the relationship between learners' pragmatic and grammatical awareness has been an ongoing discussion since Bardovi-Harlig and Dörnyei's (1998) seminal study, which compared learners' pragmatic and grammatical awareness from the perspective of the learning environment (e.g., EFL or ESL) and the learners' overall L2 proficiency. Successors to this type of research have dealt with the same variables (e.g., Niezgoda & Röver, 2001) as well as other variables such as the length of residence (LOR) in the ESL environment (Ran, 2007; Schauer, 2006; Xu, Case, & Wang, 2009). However, to date only a few researchers have taken into account learners' individual differences. Takahashi (2001, 2005) examined how motivational factors influence one aspect of pragmatic awareness—learners' attention in processing the target pragmalinguistic features—during instruction. Tagashira, Yamato and Isoda (2011) investigated the relationships between overall pragmatic awareness and one type of individual difference, learners' motivation. The current study, therefore, attempts to examine further the relationship between pragmatic awareness and the interplay between two individual difference factors: the motivational profiles of Japanese EFL learners and their proficiency.

Variables influencing pragmatic awareness

It is widely acknowledged that pragmatic awareness plays an important role in developing pragmatic competence. Kasper (1996) raised three conditions for the acquisition of pragmatic knowledge: "There must be pertinent input, *the input has to be noticed* [emphasis added], and learners need ample opportunities to develop a high level of control" (Kasper, 1996, p. 148). In other words, to develop pragmatic competence, learners have to notice the pragmatic information in the input and understand its function in the surrounding context, i.e., they have to be pragmatically aware. Bardovi-Harlig and Dörnyei (1998) were the first to investigate pragmatic awareness by analyzing learners' recognition of pragmatic errors and how severely they rate such errors, and the variables that play a key role in developing pragmatic awareness have become an issue since then. The major variables are: learning environment, length of residence, motivation, and proficiency.

Effect of learning environment and length of residence on pragmatic awareness

Bardovi-Harlig and Dörnyei (1998) compared US-based ESL learners' recognition and judgment of the severity of grammatical errors and pragmatic infelicities with those of high school EFL learners and teachers of English in Hungary. In that study, the participants first watched a video comprising 20 scenarios, some of which contained either grammatical or pragmatic errors, and were asked via a questionnaire to evaluate the severity of the perceived linguistic/pragmatic problems for each error when the scene played a second time. As a result, Bardovi-Harlig and Dörnyei found that the ESL learners recognized a considerably higher number of pragmatic errors than grammatical ones, whereas the EFL groups were more aware of grammatical violations than of pragmatic ones. The severity ratings for the two error types also indicated a difference in the participants' perceptions across the two learning environments: ESL learners considered the pragmatic infelicities to be more serious, whereas EFL learners perceived the grammatical errors to be more salient.

Niezgoda and Röver (2001) replicated Bardovi-Harlig and Dörnyei's (1998) study with ESL learners in Hawai'i and EFL learners in the Czech Republic and obtained contrasting results: the EFL learners recognized a higher number of pragmatic infelicities than the ESL learners. The EFL learners also assigned higher severity ratings to both the pragmatic and grammatical violations than did the ESL learners. Thus, Niezgoda and Röver's data showed that the EFL learners in their study were more aware of pragmatic infelicities than the ESL learners and also perceived them to be more serious than the ESL learners did. One agreement with the original study was that ESL learners considered pragmatic errors to be more salient than grammatical violations.

Previous studies on length of residence (LOR) (Ran, 2007; Schauer, 2006; Yamanaka, 2003; Xu et al., 2009) agree that learners' awareness of pragmatics increases as LOR in the ESL environment increases. For example, Schauer (2006) used Bardovi-Harlig and Dörnyei's video-and-questionnaire instrument accompanied by post hoc interviews, and reported that ESL learners increased their pragmatic awareness significantly during their stay in the ESL environment. Yamanaka (2003) found a significant positive relationship between L2 learners' interpretation of accuracy and their degree of proficiency and LOR. Xu et al., (2009) found both LOR and overall L2 proficiency influenced L2 pragmatics significantly, with overall L2 proficiency demonstrating a stronger influence in the ESL environment.

Overall, these previous findings have shown that ESL learners recognize more pragmatic errors and rate them more severely than grammatical errors (Bardovi-Harlig & Dörnyei, 1998; Niezgoda & Röver, 2001), and that this tendency becomes more obvious as the learners' LOR in the ESL environment increases (Schauer, 2006). More complex results, however, have been obtained for EFL learners. Bardovi-Harlig and Dörnyei (1998) found that EFL learners recognize more grammatical errors and rate them more severely, which led them to point out that language environment is the most important factor accounting for pragmatic and grammatical awareness. Niezgoda and Röver (2001), on the other hand, found no significant differences between grammatical and pragmatic error severity ratings among their EFL learners and argued that the "explanation lies in an interaction between exposure to pragmatic and grammatical input and individual learner characteristics, specifically the degree to which learners attend to input" (Niezgoda & Röver, 2001, p. 77). In Niezgoda and Röver's study, the Czech-speaking EFL learners were advanced learners enrolled in a teacher education program and were highly motivated to seek pragmatic input in their daily lives, leading the researchers to argue that this motivation toward English language learning might have influenced their sensitivity to pragmatic errors as well as grammatical errors.

Effect of motivation on pragmatic awareness

The importance of motivation in ILP is found in one of twelve basic questions proposed by Kasper and Schmidt (1996) as "Do motivation and attitude make a difference in level of acquisition?" (p. 162) Their answer is as follows:

> [It] is possible that *intrinsic motivation* (enjoyment of learning for its own sake) might be more relevant for ILP than *extrinsic motivation* (learning motivated by external reward), but then again intrinsic motivation might not be especially relevant because it is cognitive involvement and enjoyment rather than social involvement that is highlighted by the construct. (Kasper & Schmidt, 1996, pp. 161–162; emphasis in the original)

In other words, motivational factors may play a role in pragmatic development. However, only a few previous studies have dealt with motivation and pragmatic awareness to explicitly support their proposal.

Takahashi (2000, as cited in Kasper & Rose, 2002) was the first to examine the effects of motivation on L2 pragmatics, and she followed these efforts up in a successive study (Takahashi, 2005). These studies investigated the possible constraints that individual difference variables—in particular, learners' motivation—have on the processing of L2 pragmatic input in pragmatic instruction. The motivation measure used in Takahashi (2005) was the questionnaire adapted from Schmidt, Boraie, and Kassabgy (1996). This questionnaire contains 47 items, which are categorized into seven subscales of motivation, such as intrinsic motivation, extrinsic motivation, personal goals, anxiety, and so on. The findings showed that the learners' awareness of the target pragmalinguistic features in the input correlated with their motivation—in particular, intrinsic motivation—but not with their proficiency. One drawback of Takahashi's approach toward motivation (and possibly also that of Schmidt et al.), however, is that motivational factors were derived a-theoretically through an exploratory factor analysis, which was necessary to reorganize the extensive subscales of motivation set out in the questionnaire (e.g., Takahashi, 2005). Takahashi (2005) obtained nine factors, which was a different configuration from that in Schmidt et al. (1996). Although Takahashi noted "a complex interplay between learners' motivational dispositions and their attentional targets at the pragmatic level" (p. 111), she further argued that "[o]ne can assume that learners with this motivational orientation [intrinsic motivation] perceive these pragmalinguistic forms as ones that allow them to achieve their language learning goals successfully, resulting in greater attention to these features" (p. 112) and concluded that pragmatic awareness "is associated with the learners' motivation, in particular, their intrinsic motivation" (p. 113). This could result in simple dichotomous categories of motivation (intrinsic vs. extrinsic) and suggests that motivation needs to be understood through a more systematic motivational model.

Motivation as a developmental continuum— Self-Determination Theory

In order to overcome the problems inherent in using a motivation construct based on factor analysis, we prefer a theory-based psychological approach so that the notion of motivation can be captured more systematically and viewed as a developmental continuum. This study draws on Self-Determination Theory (SDT) (Deci & Ryan, 1985), which we find preferable to other motivational theories such as integrative motivation (Gardner, 1985) and the L2 motivational self system (Dörnyei, 2009). One advantage is that, rather than relying on a simple intrinsic/extrinsic dichotomy, SDT provides a detailed classification of motivation which differentiates motivation by the degree to which a person controls his or her behavior. The least autonomous, or self-determined stage of motivation is *amotivation*: a person has little or no intention to attempt the behavior. In contrast, the most self-determined stage of motivation is *intrinsic motivation*: a person is performing a behavior out of interest or enjoyment and is in a state of autonomy. Falling between them are types of *externally-regulated*, or extrinsic, motivation. Three different categories are postulated, each involving a differing degree of self-determination.[1] *External regulation* refers to the least self-determined form of extrinsic motivation, including the classic instance of being controlled by external sources such as rewards or threats. A partially internalized type of extrinsic motivation, *introjected regulation*, exists within the person but is not considered part of the integrated self (e.g., learning English in order not to feel guilty). *Identified regulation*, which is the most developmentally advanced form of extrinsic motivation, involves appreciation of valued outcomes of the behavior, such as learning English in order to pursue one's hobbies (Dörnyei, 1998; Hiromori, 2004).

These five categories can also be viewed as a developmental sequence. A person goes through the three stages of externally-regulated motivation, i.e., external regulation, introjected regulation, and identified regulation, and by gradually internalizing control of behavior eventually reaches the stage of fully-autonomous, intrinsic motivation.

Although the importance of motivation in L2 learning has been frequently addressed, few studies have dealt with the relationship between motivation and L2 pragmatic awareness, and the impact of learners' level of self-determination (i.e., autonomous self-regulation) on pragmatic awareness or pragmatic development remains unclear. Tagashira et al. (2011) is the first study to investigate the relationship between motivation and pragmatic awareness based on SDT. Through cluster analysis, the data were analyzed from the perspective of learners' motivational profiles in order to see how the profiles affected pragmatic awareness. The results revealed that learners' motivational profiles influenced not only their perception of pragmatic error identification, but also their severity ratings of errors, suggesting that motivation plays an important role in learners' pragmatic development.

Effect of proficiency on pragmatic awareness

In studies on the effects of proficiency on pragmatic awareness, it has generally been shown that learners with high proficiency are more aware of pragmatic information than those with low proficiency. This view is supported by studies such as Bardovi-Harlig and Dörnyei (1998), Niezgoda and Röver (2001), Yamanaka (2003) and Xu et al. (2009). Bialystok (1993) suggested that this is the case because learners with high proficiency have well-developed processing systems, thus allowing them to allocate selective attention to relevant aspects of input more efficiently (more accurately and faster) than those with low proficiency who struggle with processing basic semantic/syntactic features (House, 1996).

In contrast, Takahashi (2005), who studied the effects of proficiency and motivation on pragmatic awareness, found that there was no significant correlation between proficiency and pragmatic awareness. She suggested that the effects of proficiency could be overridden by motivation. This view was supported by her finding that pragmatic awareness correlated with motivation, but not with proficiency. However, the finding was not conclusive, not least because Takahashi's study dealt with proficiency and motivation separately through correlational analyses. Therefore, the question is still open as to what the relative effect of the two individual difference factors on pragmatic awareness might be.

Research questions of the present study

As seen above, previous studies have tackled the relationship between pragmatic awareness and individual differences, and have obtained mixed results. One of the reasons behind these conflicting findings is that those previous studies tended to take variables as discrete, rather than complex or integrated, concepts. For example, Bardovi-Harlig and Dörnyei (1998) considered learning environment (ESL/EFL) as a robust factor in pragmatic awareness, and Niezgoda and Röver (2001) found that overall L2 proficiency has a stronger effect on L2 pragmatics than LOR. Takahashi (2005) compared the effects of motivation and proficiency on pragmatic awareness, showing that motivation has a greater effect than proficiency, but treated them as separate variables. These studies have not dealt with the interaction or interplay between these variables. The issue here should be framed as follows: How does the interaction of proficiency and motivation relate to pragmatic awareness? Do more intrinsically motivated learners with lower proficiency levels recognize more pragmatic errors and rate them more severely than learners with less motivation and higher proficiency, and vice versa?

The objective of this study is, therefore, to clarify whether there is any difference in the pragmatic awareness of Japanese EFL learners due to their individual differences, more specifically, motivational profiles based on SDT and their proficiency (i.e., the TOEIC® score). Specifically, the research question is:

To what extent does Japanese EFL learners' complex of individual differences (i.e., motivation and proficiency) influence their pragmatic awareness?

Method

Participants

The participants were 153 Japanese university intermediate EFL learners who had studied English for at least six years as a compulsory subject at school in Japan. Their learning environment was an EFL setting and all participants were native speakers of Japanese. Data from 62 participants were excluded from the analysis, because they had been in some sort of ESL environment for more than one day at some point prior to the present study. Data from a further 22 participants were also removed due to incomplete or missing information. Therefore, the analysis reported hereafter is based on data from 69 participants (10 men and 59 women) who had never been in an ESL environment (i.e., LOR=0).

Table 1 presents the participants' background information including their proficiency levels measured by a standardized test, the TOEIC® (Test of English for International Communication), and self-evaluations of their English proficiency. The TOEIC test consists of separately timed listening and reading sections of 100 questions, each in a paper-and-pencil multiple-choice format, and reports an overall score in the range of 10 to 990. Information on the learners' self-evaluated English proficiency was also obtained through a questionnaire administered at the time of the study, using a rating scale of 1 to 10 to self-assess the four skills (1=minimal, 10=near-native).

Table 1. Participants' English language proficiency (N=69)

	min.	max.	M	SD
TOEIC® score	240	760	431.67	106.20
self-assessment (10-point scale)				
speaking	1	8	2.94	1.43
listening	1	7	3.30	1.50
reading	1	7	3.77	1.42
writing	1	7	4.17	1.43

Materials and procedure

Two questionnaires were used for the present study: one was for measuring English learning motivation, developed by Hiromori (2004, 2006) for Japanese EFL learners, and the other was for pragmatic awareness, originally devised by Bardovi-Harlig and Dörnyei (1998). The TOEIC® score was used as a proficiency measure. These instruments will be discussed in more detail below.

Language learning motivation scale

The first instrument was an English learning motivation scale, adapted from Hiromori (2004, 2006), based on SDT. The questionnaire contained a total of 18 items which asked whether various proposed reasons applied to the participants. The participants were asked to rate their agreement on a five-point scale ranging from 1 (strongly disagree) to 5 (strongly agree) (see Appendix and Hiromori, 2006, for details). On average, it took the participants approximately 20 minutes to respond to the questionnaire. All instructions were in their L1, i.e., Japanese.

Questionnaire for pragmatic awareness

The second instrument was a questionnaire on pragmatic awareness, adapted from Bardovi-Harlig and Dörnyei (1998). The original survey was made up of twenty scenes, consisting of three categories: (a) eight sentences which were grammatical but pragmatically inappropriate in the final line of the dialogues (i.e., pragmatically incorrect items), (b) eight sentences which were pragmatically appropriate, but contained grammatical errors (i.e., ungrammatical items), and (c) four sentences containing both grammatically correct and pragmatically appropriate sentences (see Bardovi-Harlig & Dörnyei, 1998, for detailed items). Following Bardovi-Harlig and Dörnyei, fourteen out of the twenty items were included for the present analysis, treating the first five items on the questionnaire as a practice block and eliminating one invalid item (see Bardovi-Harlig & Dörnyei, 1998, for a detailed explanation of the item selection).

Example of a pragmatically incorrect item (5 items)
The teacher asks Peter to help with the plans for the class trip.
T: OK, so we'll go by bus. Who lives near the bus station? Peter, could you check the bus time for us on the way home tonight?

P: No, I can't tonight. Sorry. (from Bardovi-Harlig & Dörnyei 1998, p. 260)

Example of an ungrammatical item (6 items)
Peter and George meet before class. They want to do something before class starts.
G: Hey, we've got 15 minutes before the next class. What shall we do?
P: Let's to go to the snack bar.
(from Bardovi-Harlig & Dörnyei 1998, p. 261)

For administrative and practical reasons, instead of the video-taped format used in the original study, the test items were administered through a written questionnaire (as also in Xu et al., 2009). In addition, we made an alteration in the answer sheet from the original in order to overcome its shortcomings for analyzing the data. Figure 1 is an example of the original answer sheet used in Bardovi-Harlig and Dörnyei (1998).

The teacher asks Peter to help with the plans for the class trip.

T: OK, so we'll go by bus. Who lives near the bus station? Peter, could you check the bus time for us on the way home tonight?

P: No, I can't tonight. Sorry.

Was the last part appropriate/correct?   Yes ☐   No ☐
If there was a problem, how bad do you think it was?
   Not bad at all ____ : ____ : ____ : ____ : ____ Very bad

Figure 1. Representation of the original answer sheet (Bardovi-Harlig & Dörnyei, 1998, p. 260).

In the original format, it is logically possible for the participants to check 'Yes' for a pragmatically inappropriate scenario when in fact they think it contains a grammatical error and vice versa. As Schauer (2006) rightly pointed out, in this format, "the researchers had to assume that when the participants indicated that there was an infelicity in a scenario, they had in fact detected the one planted by the researchers rather than identifying a 'false error'" (p. 272). Niezgoda and Röver (2001) attempted to overcome this vagueness by administering an extra questionnaire of grammatical judgment after completing the original format. Putting the original and Niezgoda and Röver (2001)'s format together, we devised a separate item for pragmatic and grammatical appropriateness, as shown in Figure 2.

> The teacher asks Peter to help with the plans for the class trip.
>
> T: OK, so we'll go by bus. Who lives near the bus station? Peter, could you check the bus time for us on the way home tonight?
>
> P: <u>No, I can't tonight. Sorry.</u>
>
> Was the last part ...
>
>   (a) grammatically correct?   Yes ☐   No ☐
>   If your answer is no, how serious do you think it was?
>   Not bad at all ___ : ___ : ___ : ___ : ___ : ___Very bad
>   (b) appropriate in this situation?   Yes ☐   No ☐
>   If no, how serious do you think it was?
>   Not bad at all ___ : ___ : ___ : ___ : ___ : ___Very bad

Figure 2. Representation of the modified answer sheet based on Bardovi-Harlig & Dörnyei (1998).

In the present study, therefore, the participants were (a) asked to judge whether the last sentence in each scenario was pragmatically and grammatically correct, and, if they judged the item to be 'pragmatically inappropriate' or 'grammatically incorrect,' they were (b) subsequently instructed to rate the severity of the error on a six-point scale from 1 (not bad at all) to 6 (very bad). Note here that our focus in the present study is on the pragmatic awareness measured by the learners' response to pragmatic appropriateness items (such as item (b) in Figure 2).

Data analysis

Following Bardovi-Harlig and Dörnyei (1998) and other successive studies, correct error identifications were scored as 1, and incorrect identifications were scored as 0. For error severity ratings, learners' judgments on the six-point scales were recorded as a value from 1 to 6, and participants who had not detected an error in a scenario were assigned 0 for the severity rating. For all statistical analysis, the alpha level was set at 0.05.

To examine the configurations of motivation toward English language learning and proficiency, a group of multivariate statistical methods for classification was used to profile the learners based on their scores from the motivational questionnaire and the TOEIC® test. In previous studies, the relationship between learners' pragmatic awareness and their individual differences was often analyzed by correlation: the focus of analysis was on the relationship between individual variables. The current study takes a different approach to analysis, which caters for the architecture of motivation postulated by SDT, and proficiency. SDT's motivational continuum suggests that learners show different degrees of intensity on the five motivational subtypes. This theoretical underpinning makes it necessary to analyze the relationship between pragmatic awareness and patterns of motivational factors with proficiency, i.e., learner profiles, rather than the correlational relationships among singles variables, such as pragmatic awareness, individual motivational factors, and proficiency.

In view of this requirement, the current study employed cluster analysis, a technique that has rarely been used in L2 research (Yamamori, Isoda, Hiromori, & Oxford, 2003). Based on similarities/dissimilarities of data, it sorts subjects and items into subgroups that share homogeneous characteristics (for further details, see Csizér, & Dörnyei, 2005 and Dörnyei, 2007). Of the many clustering algorithms, Ward's method was used because it is generally regarded as efficient for retrieving homogeneous subgroups (Everitt, Landau, & Leese, 2001; StatSoft, Inc., 2010). Ward's method is an agglomerative algorithm: The analysis starts with individual subjects as distinctive clusters, and larger clusters are formed by combining clusters with the closest characteristic subject until all the subjects are combined under one large cluster. This process is represented in a tree-like diagram called a dendrogram. To classify the participants, researchers need to decide a cut-point so that subgroups are formed below the cut-point. This decision is rather exploratory: researchers need to take into consideration changes in distances (dissimilarities) between clusters, characteristics of the resulting clusters, and the theoretical significance of the characteristics. The dissimilarity measure employed in this study was squared Euclidean distance as recommended for analysis using Ward's method (Hair & Black, 2000).

Results

Learner profiles (motivation and proficiency)

The number of meaningful clusters was decided by considering large changes in clustering distances and the characteristics of the resulting clusters. With the aid of the dendrogram obtained from the English learning motivation scale and proficiency measure, participants were categorized into three groups (see Figure 3). To confirm the validity of the grouping, separate ANOVAs were conducted and results indicated significant overall differences in the combination of the score on the English learning motivation scale and TOEIC scores between the clusters ($p<.01$ for all).

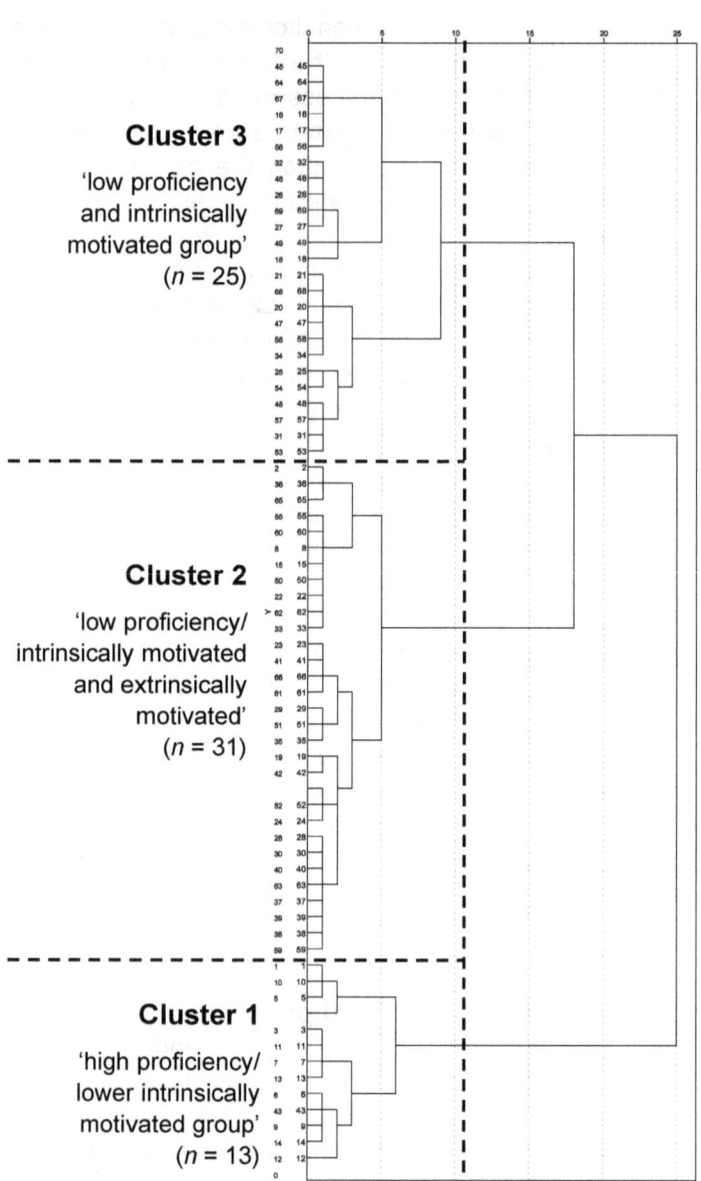

Figure 3. Dendrogram showing the classification of the participants according to the English learning motivation scale and proficiency.

As Figures 3 and 4 illustrate, the groups were named after their characteristics: cluster 1 'high proficiency/lower intrinsically motivated group' (n=13, TOEIC® scores, M=573.08, SD=86.95), cluster 2 'low proficiency/intrinsically motivated and extrinsically motivated group' (n=31, TOEIC® scores, M=396.61, SD=86.01), and cluster 3 'low proficiency and intrinsically motivated group' (*n*=25, TOEIC® scores, *M*=401.60, *SD*=74.59).'

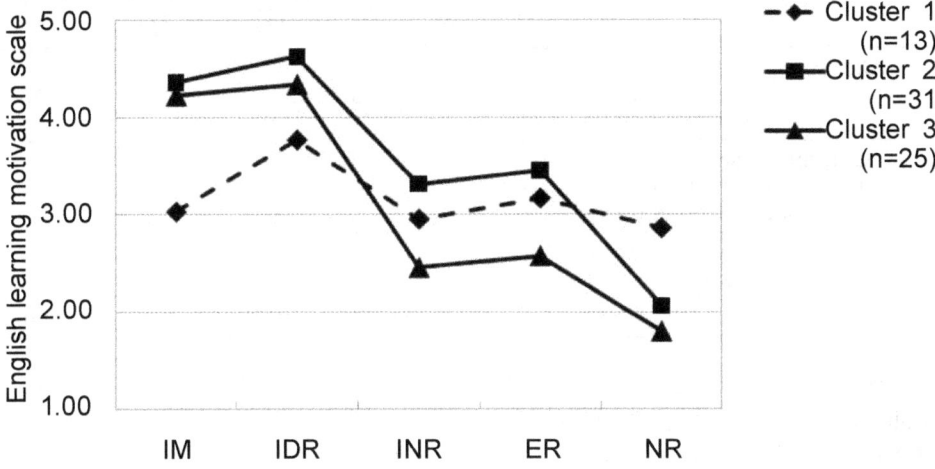

Figure 4. Motivational profiles of the groups of participants. Motivations are abbreviated as follows: IM=Intrinsic motivation, IDR=Identified regulation, INR=Introjected regulation, ER=External regulation, and NR=Non-regulation

Pragmatic awareness

Table 2 illustrates the results of error identification and severity rating of pragmatic errors by each motivational group. Cluster 1, the 'high proficiency/ lower intrinsically motivated group,' noticed errors in scenarios the most (49.20%) but perceived them as not-so-serious problems (1.99). On the other hand, cluster 3, the 'low proficiency/intrinsically motivated group,' noticed nearly as many errors (45.60%) but considered them to be serious problems (3.88). Cluster 2, the 'low proficiency/intrinsically motivated and extrinsically motivated group' found fewer errors than the other groups but rated them the most severe (35.50% and 3.90, respectively).

Separate ANOVAs were conducted to identify any differences between the score groups. A small but significant difference between the groups was found in the severity rating scores, $F(2, 66)=11.87$, $p=.01$ $\eta 2=.08$, but not in error identification, $F(2, 66)=2.59$, $p=.08$, $\eta 2=.01$. Tukey's post hoc HSD test revealed that in severity rating scores, cluster 1 (the 'high proficiency/lower intrinsically motivated group') differed significantly from cluster 2 (the 'low proficiency/ intrinsically motivated and extrinsically motivated group') and cluster 3 (the 'low proficiency/intrinsically motivated group') ($p<.01$, for all).[2]

Table 2. Error identification (%) and severity rating of pragmatic errors (N=69)

		error identification (%)		severity rating	
		M	SD	M	SD
Cluster 1: high proficiency/ lower intrinsically motivated group	(n=13)	49.20	27.83	1.99	1.18
Cluster 2: low proficiency/ intrinsically motivated and extrinsically motivated group	(n=31)	35.50	17.67	3.90	1.30
Cluster 3: low proficiency/ intrinsically motivated group	(n=25)	45.60	21.23	3.88	1.27
total	(N=69)	41.70	21.62	3.53	1.46

These results suggest that, according to the configuration of learner motivation toward English language learning and their proficiency, the groups show similar recognition of pragmatic errors in given contexts, but differ in their ratings of the severity of these errors.

Discussion

The present study sought to explore the relationship between pragmatic awareness and learner profiles of Japanese EFL learners, including motivation and proficiency. The results suggest that (a) there is no significant difference among the three distinct learner groups in terms of their ability to identify pragmatic errors, but (b) learners with self-determined motivation or a greater tendency toward intrinsic motivation (i.e., more self-regulated) show keener perception of pragmatic inappropriateness than those with less self-determined motivation but higher proficiency.

These findings are in accordance with Schmidt's (1993) claim that "those who are concerned with establishing relationships with target language speakers are more likely to pay close attention to the pragmatic aspects of input and to struggle to understand than those who are not so motivated" (Schmidt, 1993, p. 36). The notions of 'noticing' and 'understanding' may help explain the impact of motivation on the learning of pragmatics. Schmidt (1995) describes the relationship between pragmatics and 'noticing' and 'understanding' as follows:

> In pragmatics, awareness that on a particular occasion someone says to their interlocutor something like, "I'm terribly sorry to bother you, but if you have time could you look at this problem?" is a matter of noticing. Relating the various forms used to their strategic deployment in the service of politeness and recognizing their co-occurrence with elements of context such as social distance, power, level of imposition and so on, are all matters of understanding." (Schmidt, 1995, p. 30)

Noticing is a process whereby learners detect and represent a select aspect of information as input in the short-term memory so that it will be utilized for subsequent cognitive processing (Gass, 1997; Gass & Selinker, 2008; Robinson, 1996). Gass and Selinker (2008) depict noticing (or, in their terminology, apperception) as "a priming device that prepares input for further analysis" (p. 482). Noticing takes place when a learner mentally represents the utterance. The subsequent stage of processing is understanding, where the noticed input is elaborated upon for comprehension in various aspects. There are differing degrees of understanding, spanning from a simple, semantic understanding to a more elaborate, structural understanding (Gass, 1997; Gass & Selinker, 2008; Skehan, 1998). This processing is exemplified in the quote from Schmidt (1995) above as a speaker grasping the contextual meaning of the utterance by relating the noticed language (the utterance) to the social context in which it is uttered.

Previous studies such as Takahashi (2005) have pointed out the possibility that motivation affects noticing and, consequently, pragmatic awareness. However, no theoretical explanation is provided in the ILP literature about how the three are interrelated. The interplay between pragmatic awareness, the cognitive processes of noticing and understanding, and motivation need to be understood with reference to the function of attention, bridging the concept discussed in the cognitive domain of research and the concept that is treated as an effect. Motivation affects learners' control of attention, which is a crucial process for the noticing and subsequent analysis of the noticed items, or understanding. To be functional users of the target language, learners need to learn various aspects of the language, including word-level features (e.g., pronunciation, orthography, meanings of a word), sentence-level features (e.g., word order and grammar), and discourse/social-level features (e.g., organization of a text and appropriate use of language in a context). Input contains relevant information for the development of the language system in all these aspects. However, as humans' attentional capacity is limited, learners cannot process all the information in the input at one time, and they have to prioritize only what they think is important for subsequent processing by registering it in the short-term memory and discarding the rest of the information (Robinson, 1996; Skehan, 1998; VanPatten, 1990). This trade-off is an important issue because learners can notice and understand only a select range of linguistic information. This process is to some extent under the learner's active control, and this is where motivation exerts its effects: motivation affects learners' selective attention, i.e., choosing which aspects of incoming stimuli to attend to (Crookes & Schmidt, 1991; Schmidt, 1995; Manolopoulou-Sergi, 2004). Therefore, motivation, or in this study, learners' individual idiosyncratic motivational patterns, may predispose learners to pay attention to different aspects of input. Learners who are motivated to attain a good command of the target language, such as those in clusters 2 and 3, will value pragmatic aspects of language use, and they will be inclined to detect stimuli containing pragmatic information and utilize this information for more elaborate analysis. In contrast, learners who are not willing to expend effort on learning the language, such as those in cluster 1, will avoid deep analysis and engage in superficial processing. They will disregard the same information that motivated learners will process extensively, although they might at least process the input at the semantic level, without relating the detected language to social/contextual features.

Proficiency, on the other hand, does not necessarily presuppose deeper analysis of input. In addition to input processing, the characteristics of less intrinsically motivated learners with high proficiency scores (cluster 1) highlight the effects of different types of motivation on noticing and understanding. It is possible that these learners are only motivated to value those aspects that are relevant to their reasons for learning, which, considering the environment around EFL learners in Japan, are likely to be external academic and social pressures. Many people in Japan are required to learn English for academic and vocational purposes regardless of their interest in the language, and they are often required to show their ability in English through test scores. Learners in Japan are keen to perform well on school tests, as required by the school curriculum, or socially-recognized tests such as TOEFL® and TOEIC®, high scores on which are often required for job applications. Learners with these types of motivation are likely to value the learning of phonology, vocabulary, and grammar because they seem highly relevant to success in these tests, while ignoring the social aspect of language use because it is not directly tested.

By applying this concept of noticing and understanding to groups of learners classified according to their motivational profiles and proficiency in the present study, we see that learners with intrinsic motivation or more autonomous levels of extrinsic motivation have attained a pragmatic level of understanding, whereas those with less autonomous motivational profiles (even with higher proficiency) only engage in a superficial level of processing. Corresponding to the self-determination continuum of motivation, the present results could posit that, regardless of their proficiency levels, the more self-determined learners are, the more deeply they can interpret the utterance in the specific situation.

Concluding remarks

The present study confirmed that the pragmatic awareness of Japanese EFL learners is clearly associated with their individual differences (motivational profiles and proficiency), which lends support to the conclusions of previous studies such as Niezgoda and Röver (2001) and Takahashi (2005). It also adds to our understanding of the relationship between learners' pragmatic awareness and their motivational profiles and proficiency levels by indicating the possibility that learners' motivational profiles exert more influence on their severity ratings of errors than their error recognition. In other words, as learners become more self-determined, they perceive pragmatic errors as more severe in addition to identifying them, irrespective of the learners' proficiency. In order to interpret this phenomenon, the notion of 'noticing' and 'understanding' proposed by Schmidt (1995) was applied, which leads to the conclusion that the more self-determined learners reach the realm of 'understanding' over 'noticing.' This result is substantially different from the results obtained from the usual conception of a proportional relationship between pragmatic competence and overall learners' proficiency. The analysis revealed the intriguing phenomenon that the most proficient group (cluster 1) did not perceive pragmatic inappropriateness as well as the less proficient but more intrinsically motivated groups (clusters 2 and 3) did. That is, high proficiency does not necessarily facilitate deeper pragmatic awareness within an EFL context. To confirm that high proficiency does not in fact hinder high pragmatic awareness, it would be necessary to include a group of highly proficient and intrinsically motivated learners, which could not be obtained for this study, but should be included in future research in this area.[3]

While we were only able to investigate outcomes of pragmatic development applying Schmidt's notions of 'noticing' and 'understanding,' it would be interesting for future research to trace the detailed process from noticing to understanding through a longitudinal qualitative/quantitative examination of pragmatic development. In order to track learners' development pathways, the pragmatic awareness of Japanese EFL learners should be observed and described longitudinally. Qualitative approaches are also more capable of focusing on the mechanisms of change, and explain how learners move from one stage to another.

Finally, another issue for further research is the area of pedagogical intervention for facilitating pragmatic awareness. Since the current study found that the relationship between pragmatic awareness and proficiency is not simply proportional, how can language teachers help the development of pragmatic awareness? In other words, how can they change learners' 'noticing' to 'understanding'? Our findings suggest that pedagogical interventions are most beneficial if they also take learners' motivational profiles into account.

Notes

1. Deci and Ryan (1985) posit a fourth subtype of extrinsic motivation, i.e., *integrated regulation*. However, this is not dealt with in studies drawing on the SDT, such as Noels (2001) and Hiromori (2004, 2006), because it is difficult to differentiate this fourth category from identified regulation. The current study employed the measure of motivation developed by Hiromori (2004, 2006), which includes only the first three subtypes of extrinsic motivation.
2. In terms of grammatical awareness, a significant difference between the groups was found in grammatical severity rating scores, $F(2, 66)=7.27$, $p=.01$ $\eta2=.04$, but not in grammatical error identification, $F(2, 66)=0.30$, $p=.73$, $\eta2=.01$. Similar to

pragmatic awareness, Tukey's post hoc HSD test revealed that cluster 1, the 'high proficiency/lower intrinsically motivated group,' differed significantly from cluster 2, the 'low proficiency/intrinsically motivated and extrinsically motivated group' and cluster 3, the 'low proficiency/intrinsically motivated group') in their severity ratings of grammatical errors ($p<.01$, for all).

3   Such a group, for example, would be Niezgoda and Röver's (2001) EFL learners, who were exceptionally high proficiency students at the top 5% of the English students in their cohort as well as highly motivated. Their results could complement those of the present study and imply the developmental stages of pragmatic awareness.

Acknowledgments

This study was supported by a Grant-in-Aid for Scientific Research (C) (No. 22520565) from the Japan Society for the Promotion of Science (JSPS) to the first author. The authors wish to thank Tim Greer and Shusaku Kida for their insightful feedback on earlier drafts of this manuscript. We are also grateful to the two anonymous reviewers for their constructive and detailed comments that helped improve the manuscript.

References

Bardovi-Harlig, K., & Dörnyei, Z. (1998). Do language learners recognize pragmatic violations? Pragmatic versus grammatical awareness in instructed L2 learning. *TESOL Quarterly, 32*, 233–262.

Bialystok, E. (1993). Symbolic representation and attentional control in pragmatic competence. In G. Kasper & S. Blum-Kulka (Eds.), *Interlanguage pragmatics* (pp. 43–57). New York: Oxford University Press.

Crookes, G., & Schmidt, R. W. (1991). Motivation: Reopening the research agenda. *Language Learning, 41*, 469–512.

Csizér, K., & Dörnyei, Z. (2005). Language learners' motivational profiles and their motivated learning behaviour. *Language Learning, 55*, 613–659.

Deci, E. L., & Ryan, R. M. (1985). *Intrinsic motivation and self-determination in human behavior.* New York: Plenum Publishing.

Dörnyei, Z. (1998). Motivation in second and foreign language learning. *Language Teaching, 31*, 117–135.

Dörnyei, Z. (2007). *Research methods in applied linguistics.* Oxford: Oxford University Press.

Dörnyei, Z. (2009). The L2 motivational self system. In Z. Dörnyei & E. Ushioda (Eds.), *Motivation, language identity and the L2 self* (pp. 9–42). Bristol: Multilingual Matters.

Everitt, B. S., Landau, S., & Leese, M. (2001). *Cluster analysis* (4th ed.). London: Arnold.

Gardner, R. C. (1985). *Social psychology and second language learning: The role of attitudes and motivation.* London: Arnold.

Gass, S. M. (1997). *Input, interaction, and the second language learner.* Mahwah, NJ: Lawrence Erlbaum Associates.

Gass, S. M., & Selinker, L. (2008). *Second language acquisition: An introductory course* (3rd ed.). New York: Routledge.

Hair, J. F., & Black, W. C. (2000). Cluster analysis. In L. G. Grimm, & P. R. Yarnold (Eds.), *Reading and understanding more multivariate statistics* (pp. 147–205). Washington, DC: American Psychological Association.

Hiromori, T. (2004). Motivation and language learning strategies of EFL high school students: A preliminary study through the use of panel data. *JACET Bulletin, 39*, 31–41.

Hiromori, T. (2006). *Gaikokugo gakushuusha no doukizuke wo takameru riron to jissen* [Theories and practices for enhancing foreign language learners' motivation] Tokyo: Taga Shuppan.

House, J. (1996). Developing pragmatic fluency in English as a second language. *Studies in Second Language Acquisition, 18*, 225–252.

Kasper, G. (1996). Introduction: Pragmatics in SLA. *Studies in Second Language Acquisition, 18*, 145–148.

Kasper, G., & Rose, K. R. (2002). *Pragmatic development in a second language.* Oxford: Blackwell Publishing.

Kasper, G., & Schmidt, R. (1996). Development issues in interlanguage pragmatics. *Studies in Second Language Acquisition, 18*, 149–169.

Manolopoulou-Sergi, E. (2004). Motivation within the information processing model of foreign language learning. *System, 32*, 427–441.

Niezgoda, K., & Röver, C. (2001). Pragmatic and grammatical awareness: A function of the learning environment. In K. Rose, & G. Kasper (Eds.), *Pragmatics in language teaching* (pp. 63–79). Cambridge: Cambridge University Press.

Noels, K. A. (2001). Learning Spanish as a second language: Learners' orientations and perceptions of their teachers' communicative style. *Language Learning, 51*, 107–144.

Ran, L. (2007). The relationship between linguistic proficiency and pragmatic ability. *US-China Foreign Language, 5*, 13–17.

Robinson, P. (1996). *Consciousness, rules, and instructed second language acquisition.* Frankfurt: Peter Lang.

Schauer, G. (2006). Pragmatic awareness in ESL and EFL contexts: Contrast and development. *Language Learning, 56*, 269–318.

Schmidt, R. (1993). Consciousness, learning and interlanguage pragmatics. In G. Kasper, & S. Blum-Kulka (Eds.), *Interlanguage pragmatics* (pp. 21–42). Oxford: Oxford University Press.

Schmidt, R. (1995). Consciousness and foreign language learning: A tutorial on the role of attention and awareness in learning. In R. Schmidt (Ed.), *Attention and awareness in foreign language learning* (pp. 1–63). Honolulu: University of Hawai'i, Second Language Teaching & Learning Center.

Schmidt, R., Boraie, D., & Kassabgy, O. (1996). Foreign language motivation: Internal structure and external connections. In R. Oxford (Ed.), *Language learning motivation:*

Pathways to the new century (Technical Report No. 11, pp. 9–70). Honolulu: University of Hawai'i, Second Language Teaching and Curriculum Center.

Skehan, P. (1998). *A cognitive approach to language learning.* Oxford: Oxford University Press.

StatSoft, Inc. (2010). *Electronic statistics textbook.* Tulsa, OK: StatSoft. Retrieved from http://www.statsoft.com/textbook/.

Tagashira, K., Yamato, K. & Isoda, T. (2011). Japanese EFL learners' pragmatic awareness through the looking glass of motivational profiles. *JALT Journal, 33,* 5–26.

Takahashi, S. (2000). *The effects of motivation and proficiency on the awareness of pragmatic strategies in implicit foreign language learning.* Unpublished manuscript.

Takahashi, S. (2001). The role of input enhancement in developing pragmatic competence. In K. Rose, & G. Kasper (Eds.), *Pragmatics in language teaching* (pp. 171–199). Cambridge: Cambridge University Press.

Takahashi, S. (2005). Pragmatic awareness: Is it related to motivation and proficiency? *Applied Linguistics, 26,* 90–120.

VanPatten, B. (1990). Attending to content and form in the input: An experiment in consciousness. *Studies in Second Language Acquisition, 12,* 287–301.

Yamanaka, J. (2003). Effects of proficiency and length of residence on the pragmatic comprehension of Japanese ESL learners. *Second Language Studies, 22,* 107–175.

Xu, W., Case, R. E., & Wang, Y. (2009). Pragmatic and grammatical competence, length of residence, and overall L2 proficiency. *System, 37,* 205–216.

Yamamori, K., Isoda, T., Hiromori, T., & Oxford, R. L. (2003). Using cluster analysis to uncover L2 learner differences in strategy use, will to learn, and achievement over time. *International Review of Applied Linguistics in Language Teaching, 41,* 381–409.

Appendix A: Sample items from the English learning motivation scale used in the study

Intrinsic motivation (4 items)
Because learning English is fun.

Identified regulation (4 items)
Because I want to obtain English skills that will be useful in the future.

Introjected regulation (3 items)
I want to learn English in order not to feel regret later on.

External regulation (3 items)
I want to learn English because I want to get a good grade.

Amotivation (4 items)
I don't see what I gain from English classes.

about the contributors

Kathleen Bardovi-Harlig is a professor of Second Language Studies in the College of Arts and Sciences at Indiana University. Her research investigates the acquisition of second language pragmatics, and is particularly concerned with the development of linguistic resources for pragmatic expression. She is the past editor of Language Learning and has published in Studies in Second Language Acquisition, Language Learning, Intercultural Pragmatics, Pragmatics and Language Learning, and edited volumes, handbooks, and encyclopedias.

Cao Thuy Hong is a lecturer at Faculty of English Language Teacher Education at the University of Languages and International Studies, Vietnam National University, Hanoi. She has taken part in several national and regional projects on teacher training and material development. She is interested in second language acquisition, communicative language teaching, pragmatics, and sociolinguistic issues.

Wei-Lin Melody Chang is a PhD student in the School of Languages and Linguistics at Griffith University, Brisbane, Australia. Her research interests include pragmatics, intercultural communication and Chinese linguistics. She has published work on intercultural apologies (2011, *Intercultural Pragmatics* 8(3): 411-442), face and relationships (2011, *Journal of Pragmatics* 43(12): 2948-2963), and emic concepts of face in Taiwanese business interactions (2012, in Pan and Kadar, Eds., *Chinese Discourse in Interaction*, Equinox, London).

Seiko Fujii (PhD University of California at Berkeley), is a professor in the Department of Language and Information Sciences, Graduate School of Arts and Sciences at the University of Tokyo. She teaches graduate and undergraduate courses in pragmatics, discourse and grammar, child language acquisition, second language acquisition, japanese linguistics, corpus linguistics, construction grammar, language and cognition, cross-cultural pragmatics as well as EFL and JSL. Her research, encompassing the above areas, has focused on conditionals, clause-linking constructions, modality, pragmatic markers, and reported speech in cross-linguistic and/or developmental perspectives, in addition to English-Japanese academic interaction.

Averil Grieve is a research fellow and casual lecturer at the Language Testing Research Centre in the Department of Linguistics and Applied Linguistics at the University of Melbourne, Australia. Her main research interests are pragmatics, second language acquisition, cross-cultural communication, and bilingualism. Her PhD focused on the acquisition of pragmatic markers by German adolescent exchange students to Australia. As a board member of the Deutsche Schule Melbourne, she helped establish the language model and curriculum for an early immersion bilingual primary school in Melbourne.

Michael Haugh is a senior lecturer in linguistics and English in the School of Languages and Linguistics at Griffith University, Brisbane, Australia. His research interests include pragmatics, intercultural communication, conversation analysis, and more recently corpora. He is the co-editor of *Face, Communication and Social Interaction* (2009, Equinox), and *Situated Politeness* (2011, Continuum), and has edited a number of journal special issues, including "Intention in pragmatics" for *Intercultural Pragmatics* (2008, Mouton de Gruyter), "Conceptualisations of communication" for *Australian Journal of Linguistics* (2009, Routledge), and "Face in interaction" for *Journal of Pragmatics* (2010, Elsevier).

Eric Hauser holds a PhD in Second Language Acquisition from the Department of Second Language Studies of the University of Hawai'i at Mānoa. He is currently an associate professor of the University of Electro-Communications in Tokyo and a member of the affiliate graduate faculty of the Department of Second Language Studies of the University of Hawai'i. His research focuses on, but it not limited to, Conversation Analytic work with data involving second language users of English, including the use of Conversation Analysis with longitudinal data in order to study learning. He has published in *Applied Linguistics* and *Human Studies*.

Takamichi Isoda is an associate professor in the College of Letters at Ritsumeikan University in Kyoto. He has published a book on educational data analysis, a resource book for English language teachers and articles on applied linguistics and English language teaching. He received his PhD from Waseda University in Tokyo. His current research interests include the interplay between motivation and learning contexts.

Nathan P. Krug is an assistant professor in the Center for English Education and Development at Saitama University. He has research interests spanning the fields of conversation analysis, discourse analysis, and CALL. He is currently investigating language learning and second-language conversation within computer-mediated environments.

Nguyen Thi Thuy Minh is an assistant professor at National Institute of Education, Nanyang Technological University, Singapore. Her research interests are in pragmatics and language learning, language pedagogy, and language teacher education. She has published in *Journal of Pragmatics, Intercultural Pragmatics, RELC Journal of Language Teaching and Research,* and elsewhere. Her recent professional book chapters appear in the *TESOL Classroom Practices* series.

Yusuke Okada (Ph.D, Kobe University) is a lecturer at the College of Life Sciences, Ritsumeikan University, Japan. His research focuses on second language interaction in various situational contexts, such as in classrooms, speaking tests, and academic presentations. His work has been published in *Journal of Pragmatics, JALT Journal,* and several edited volumes. He is currently focusing on a socialization process in which members of a particular group become able to discursively construct themselves as more effective members of the group.

Tomomi Otsu is a senior lecturer in the Japanese Language Center for International Students at Tokyo University of Foreign Studies. Her research interests include ordinary conversation, conversation analysis, and their implications for language teaching, and learning. She is currently interested in the study of second language conversation in Japanese.

Pham Minh Tam is a lecturer at Faculty of English Language Teacher Education at the University of Languages and International Studies, Vietnam National University, Hanoi. Her research interests include language pedagogy and language teacher education.

Kenji Tagashira is an associate professor at the Institute for Foreign Language Research and Education, Hiroshima University. He has published a university English textbook and articles on applied linguistics and English language teaching. He received his EdD from Hiroshima University. His current research interests include second language vocabulary acquisition, bilingual mental lexicon, and interlanguage pragmatics.

Jean Wong is an associate professor at The College of New Jersey. Her research uses Conversation Analysis (CA) in examining repair/correction and other interactional phenomena in first and second language settings. She has published in *Applied Linguistics, International Review of Applied Linguistics, Issues in Applied Linguistics, Research on Language and Social Interaction,* and has also contributed to edited volumes (Bowles & Seedhouse, 2007; Gardner & Wagner, 2004; Houck & Tatsuki, 2011;

Richards & Seedhouse, 2005). Her book entitled *Conversation analysis and second language pedagogy* (co-authored with Hansun Waring, Routledge, 2010) serves as an introduction to CA, particularly for language educators and other practitioners who would benefit from an in-depth understanding of language in human communication.

Kazuhito Yamato is an associate professor in the School of Languages and Communication, Kobe University. He has published articles on applied linguistics and English language teaching. He received his EdD from Hiroshima University. His research interests include L2 pronunciation instruction to Japanese learners, acquiring/learning English prosody, and interlanguage pragmatics.

NATIONAL FOREIGN LANGUAGE RESOURCE CENTER
University of Hawai'i at Mānoa

ordering information at nflrc.hawaii.edu

Pragmatics & Interaction
Gabriele Kasper, series editor

Pragmatics & Interaction ("P&I"), a refereed series sponsored by the University of Hawai'i National Foreign Language Resource Center, publishes research on topics in pragmatics and discourse as social interaction from a wide variety of theoretical and methodological perspectives. P&I welcomes particularly studies on languages spoken in the Asia-Pacific region.

PRAGMATICS OF VIETNAMESE AS NATIVE AND TARGET LANGUAGE
CARSTEN ROEVER & HANH THI NGUYEN (EDITORS), 2013

The volume offers a wealth of new information about the forms of several speech acts and their social distribution in Vietnamese as L1 and L2, complemented by a chapter on address forms and listener responses. As the first of its kind, the book makes a valuable contribution to the research literature on pragmatics, sociolinguistics, and language and social interaction in an under-researched and less commonly taught Asian language.

282pp., ISBN 978–0–9835816–2–8 $30.

L2 LEARNING AS SOCIAL PRACTICE: CONVERSATION-ANALYTIC PERSPECTIVES
GABRIELE PALLOTTI & JOHANNES WAGNER (EDITORS), 2011

This volume collects empirical studies applying Conversation Analysis to situations where second, third, and other additional languages are used. A number of different aspects are considered, including how linguistic systems develop over time through social interaction, how participants 'do' language learning and teaching in classroom and everyday settings, how they select languages and manage identities in multilingual contexts, and how the linguistic-interactional divide can be bridged with studies combining Conversation Analysis and Functional Linguistics. This variety of issues and approaches clearly shows the fruitfulness of a socio-interactional perspective on second language learning.

380pp., ISBN 978–0–9800459–7–0 $30.

TALK-IN-INTERACTION: MULTILINGUAL PERSPECTIVES
HANH THI NGUYEN & GABRIELE KASPER (EDITORS), 2009

This volume offers original studies of interaction in a range of languages and language varieties, including Chinese, English, Japanese, Korean, Spanish, Swahili, Thai, and Vietnamese; monolingual and bilingual interactions; and activities designed for second or foreign language learning. Conducted from the perspectives of conversation analysis and membership categorization analysis, the chapters examine ordinary conversation and institutional activities in face-to-face, telephone, and computer-mediated environments.

430pp., ISBN 978–0–8248–3137–0 $30.

Pragmatics & Language Learning
Gabriele Kasper, series editor

Pragmatics & Language Learning ("PLL"), a refereed series sponsored by the National Foreign Language Resource Center, publishes selected papers from the biannual International Pragmatics & Language Learning conference under the editorship of the conference hosts and the series editor. Check the NFLRC website for upcoming PLL conferences and PLL volumes.

PRAGMATICS AND LANGUAGE LEARNING VOLUME 13
TIM GREER, DONNA TATSUKI, & CARSTEN ROEVER (EDITORS), 2013

Pragmatics & Language Learning Volume 13 examines the organization of second language and multilingual speakers' talk and pragmatic knowledge across a range of naturalistic and experimental activities. Based on data collected among ESL and EFL learners from a variety of backgrounds, the contributions explore the nexus of pragmatic knowledge, interaction, and L2 learning outside and inside of educational settings.

292pp., ISBN 978–0–9835816–4–2 $30.

PRAGMATICS AND LANGUAGE LEARNING VOLUME 12
GABRIELE KASPER, HANH THI NGUYEN, DINA R. YOSHIMI, & JIM K. YOSHIOKA (EDITORS), 2010

This volume examines the organization of second language and multilingual speakers' talk and pragmatic knowledge across a range of naturalistic and experimental activities. Based on data collected on Danish, English, Hawai'i Creole, Indonesian, and Japanese as target languages, the contributions explore the nexus of pragmatic knowledge, interaction, and L2 learning outside and inside of educational settings.

364pp., ISBN 978–09800459–6–3 $30.

PRAGMATICS AND LANGUAGE LEARNING VOLUME 11
KATHLEEN BARDOVI-HARLIG, CÉSAR FÉLIX-BRASDEFER, & ALWIYA S. OMAR (EDITORS), 2006

This volume features cutting-edge theoretical and empirical research on pragmatics and language learning among a wide variety of learners in diverse learning contexts from a variety of language backgrounds and target languages (English, German, Japanese, Kiswahili, Persian, and Spanish). This collection of papers from researchers around the world includes critical appraisals on the role of formulas in interlanguage pragmatics, and speech-act research from a conversation analytic perspective. Empirical studies examine learner data using innovative methods of analysis and investigate issues in pragmatic development and the instruction of pragmatics.

430pp., ISBN 978–0–8248–3137–0 $30.

NFLRC Monographs
Richard Schmidt, series editor

Monographs of the National Foreign Language Resource Center present the findings of recent work in applied linguistics that is of relevance to language teaching and learning (with a focus on the less commonly taught languages of Asia and the Pacific) and are of particular interest to foreign language educators, applied linguists, and researchers. Prior to 2006, these monographs were published as "SLTCC Technical Reports."

NEW PERSPECTIVES ON JAPANESE LANGUAGE LEARNING, LINGUISTICS, AND CULTURE
KIMI KONDO-BROWN, YOSHIKO SAITO-ABBOTT, SHINGO SATSUTANI, MICHIO TSUTSUI, & ANN WEHMEYER (EDITORS), 2013

This volume is a collection of selected refereed papers presented at the Association of Teachers of Japanese Annual Spring Conference held at the University of Hawai'i at Mānoa in March of 2011. It not only covers several important topics on teaching and learning spoken and written Japanese and culture in and beyond classroom settings but also includes research investigating certain linguistics items from new perspectives.

208pp., ISBN 978–0–9835816–3–5 $20

DEVELOPING, USING, AND ANALYZING RUBRICS IN LANGUAGE ASSESSMENT WITH CASE STUDIES IN ASIAN AND PACIFIC LANGUAGES
JAMES DEAN BROWN (EDITOR), 2012

Rubrics are essential tools for all language teachers in this age of communicative and task-based teaching and assessment—tools that allow us to efficiently communicate to our students what we are looking for in the productive language abilities of speaking and writing and then effectively assess those abilities when the time comes for grading students, giving them feedback, placing them into new courses, and so forth. This book provides a wide array of ideas, suggestions, and examples (mostly from Māori, Hawaiian, and Japanese language assessment projects) to help language educators effectively develop, use, revise, analyze, and report on rubric-based assessments.

212pp., ISBN 978–0–9835816–1–1 $20.

RESEARCH AMONG LEARNERS OF CHINESE AS A FOREIGN LANGUAGE
MICHAEL E. EVERSON & HELEN H. SHEN (EDITORS), 2010

Cutting-edge in its approach and international in its authorship, this fourth monograph in a series sponsored by the Chinese Language Teachers Association features eight research studies that explore a variety of themes, topics, and perspectives important to a variety of stakeholders in the Chinese language learning community. Employing a wide range of research methodologies, the volume provides data from actual Chinese language learners and will be of value to both theoreticians and practitioners alike. *[in English & Chinese]*

180pp., ISBN 978–0–9800459–4–9 $20.

MANCHU: A TEXTBOOK FOR READING DOCUMENTS (SECOND EDITION)
GERTRAUDE ROTH LI, 2010

This book offers students a tool to gain a basic grounding in the Manchu language. The reading selections provided in this volume represent various types of documents, ranging from examples of the very earliest Manchu writing (17th century) to samples of contemporary Sibe (Xibo), a language that may be considered a modern version of Manchu. Since Manchu courses are only rarely taught at universities anywhere, this second edition includes audio recordings to assist students with the pronunciation of the texts.

418pp., ISBN 978–0–9800459–5–6 $36.

TOWARD USEFUL PROGRAM EVALUATION IN COLLEGE FOREIGN LANGUAGE EDUCATION
JOHN M. NORRIS, JOHN McE. DAVIS, CASTLE SINICROPE, & YUKIKO WATANABE (EDITORS), 2009

This volume reports on innovative, useful evaluation work conducted within U.S. college foreign language programs. An introductory chapter scopes out the territory, reporting key findings from research into the concerns, impetuses, and uses for evaluation that FL educators identify. Seven chapters then highlight examples of evaluations conducted in diverse language programs and institutional contexts. Each case is reported by program-internal educators, who walk readers through critical steps, from identifying evaluation uses, users, and questions, to designing methods, interpreting findings, and taking actions. A concluding chapter reflects on the emerging roles for FL program evaluation and articulates an agenda for integrating evaluation into language education practice.

240pp., ISBN 978–0–9800459–3–2 $30.

SECOND LANGUAGE TEACHING AND LEARNING IN THE NET GENERATION
RAQUEL OXFORD & JEFFREY OXFORD (EDITORS), 2009

Today's young people—the Net Generation—have grown up with technology all around them. However, teachers cannot assume that students' familiarity with technology in general transfers successfully to pedagogical settings. This volume examines various technologies and offers concrete advice on how each can be successfully implemented in the second language curriculum.

240pp., ISBN 978–0–9800459–2–5 $30.

CASE STUDIES IN FOREIGN LANGUAGE PLACEMENT: PRACTICES AND POSSIBILITIES
THOM HUDSON & MARTYN CLARK (EDITORS), 2008

Although most language programs make placement decisions on the basis of placement tests, there is surprisingly little published about different contexts and systems of placement testing. The present volume contains case studies of placement programs in foreign language programs at the tertiary level across the United States. The different programs span the spectrum from large programs servicing hundreds of students annually to small language programs with very few students. The contributions to this volume address such issues as how the size of the program, presence or absence of heritage learners, and population changes affect language placement decisions.

201pp., ISBN 0–9800459–0–8 $20.

CHINESE AS A HERITAGE LANGUAGE: FOSTERING ROOTED WORLD CITIZENRY
AGNES WEIYUN HE & YUN XIAO (EDITORS), 2008

Thirty-two scholars examine the sociocultural, cognitive-linguistic, and educational-institutional trajectories along which Chinese as a Heritage Language may be acquired, maintained, and developed. They draw upon developmental psychology, functional linguistics, linguistic and cultural anthropology, discourse analysis, orthography analysis, reading research, second language acquisition, and bilingualism. This volume aims to lay a foundation for theories, models, and master scripts to be discussed, debated, and developed, and to stimulate research and enhance teaching both within and beyond Chinese language education.

280pp., ISBN 978–0–8248–3286–5 $20.

PERSPECTIVES ON TEACHING CONNECTED SPEECH TO SECOND LANGUAGE SPEAKERS
James Dean Brown & Kimi Kondo-Brown (Editors), 2006

This book is a collection of fourteen articles on connected speech of interest to teachers, researchers, and materials developers in both ESL/EFL (ten chapters focus on connected speech in English) and Japanese (four chapters focus on Japanese connected speech). The fourteen chapters are divided up into five sections:

- What do we know so far about teaching connected speech?
- Does connected speech instruction work?
- How should connected speech be taught in English?
- How should connected speech be taught in Japanese?
- How should connected speech be tested?

290pp., ISBN 978–0–8248–3136–3 $20.

CORPUS LINGUISTICS FOR KOREAN LANGUAGE LEARNING AND TEACHING
Robert Bley-Vroman & Hyunsook Ko (Editors), 2006

Dramatic advances in personal-computer technology have given language teachers access to vast quantities of machine-readable text, which can be analyzed with a view toward improving the basis of language instruction. Corpus linguistics provides analytic techniques and practical tools for studying language in use. This volume provides both an introductory framework for the use of corpus linguistics for language teaching and examples of its application for Korean teaching and learning. The collected papers cover topics in Korean syntax, lexicon, and discourse, and second language acquisition research, always with a focus on application in the classroom. An overview of Korean corpus linguistics tools and available Korean corpora are also included.

265pp., ISBN 0–8248–3062–8 $25.

NEW TECHNOLOGIES AND LANGUAGE LEARNING: CASES IN THE LESS COMMONLY TAUGHT LANGUAGES
Carol Anne Spreen (Editor), 2002

In recent years, the National Security Education Program (NSEP) has supported an increasing number of programs for teaching languages using different technological media. This compilation of case study initiatives funded through the NSEP Institutional Grants Program presents a range of technology-based options for language programming that will help universities make more informed decisions about teaching less commonly taught languages. The eight chapters describe how different types of technologies are used to support language programs (i.e., Web, ITV, and audio- or video-based materials), discuss identifiable trends in e-language learning, and explore how technology addresses issues of equity, diversity, and opportunity. This book offers many lessons learned and decisions made as technology changes and learning needs become more complex.

188pp., ISBN 0-8248-2634-5 $25.

AN INVESTIGATION OF SECOND LANGUAGE TASK-BASED PERFORMANCE ASSESSMENTS
JAMES DEAN BROWN, THOM HUDSON, JOHN M. NORRIS, & WILLIAM BONK, 2002

This volume describes the creation of performance assessment instruments and their validation (based on work started in a previous monograph). It begins by explaining the test and rating scale development processes and the administration of the resulting three seven-task tests to 90 university-level EFL and ESL students. The results are examined in terms of (a) the effects of test revision; (b) comparisons among the task-dependent, task-independent, and self-rating scales; and (c) reliability and validity issues.

240pp., ISBN 0-8248-2633-7 $25.

MOTIVATION AND SECOND LANGUAGE ACQUISITION
ZOLTÁN DÖRNYEI & RICHARD SCHMIDT (EDITORS), 2001

This volume—the second in this series concerned with motivation and foreign language learning—includes papers presented in a state-of-the-art colloquium on L2 motivation at the American Association for Applied Linguistics (Vancouver, 2000) and a number of specially commissioned studies. The 20 chapters, written by some of the best known researchers in the field, cover a wide range of theoretical and research methodological issues, and also offer empirical results (both qualitative and quantitative) concerning the learning of many different languages (Arabic, Chinese, English, Filipino, French, German, Hindi, Italian, Japanese, Russian, and Spanish) in a broad range of learning contexts (Bahrain, Brazil, Canada, Egypt, Finland, Hungary, Ireland, Israel, Japan, Spain, and the U.S.).

520pp., ISBN 0-8248-2458-X $30.

A FOCUS ON LANGUAGE TEST DEVELOPMENT: EXPANDING THE LANGUAGE PROFICIENCY CONSTRUCT ACROSS A VARIETY OF TESTS
THOM HUDSON & JAMES DEAN BROWN (EDITORS), 2001

This volume presents eight research studies that introduce a variety of novel, nontraditional forms of second and foreign language assessment. To the extent possible, the studies also show the entire test development process, warts and all. These language testing projects not only demonstrate many of the types of problems that test developers run into in the real world but also afford the reader unique insights into the language test development process.

230pp., ISBN 0–8248–2351–6 $20.

STUDIES ON KOREAN IN COMMUNITY SCHOOLS
DONG-JAE LEE, SOOKEUN CHO, MISEON LEE, MINSUN SONG, & WILLIAM O'GRADY (EDITORS), 2000

The papers in this volume focus on language teaching and learning in Korean community schools. Drawing on innovative experimental work and research in linguistics, education, and psychology, the contributors address issues of importance to teachers, administrators, and parents. Topics covered include childhood bilingualism, Korean grammar, language acquisition, children's literature, and language teaching methodology. [in Korean]

256pp., ISBN 0–8248–2352–4 $20.

A COMMUNICATIVE FRAMEWORK FOR INTRODUCTORY JAPANESE LANGUAGE CURRICULA
WASHINGTON STATE JAPANESE LANGUAGE CURRICULUM GUIDELINES COMMITTEE, 2000

In recent years, the number of schools offering Japanese nationwide has increased dramatically. Because of the tremendous popularity of the Japanese language and the shortage of teachers, quite a few untrained, nonnative and native teachers are in the classrooms and are expected to teach several levels of Japanese. These guidelines are intended to assist individual teachers and professional associations throughout the United States in designing Japanese language curricula. They are meant to serve as a framework from which language teaching can be expanded and are intended to allow teachers to enhance and strengthen the quality of Japanese language instruction.

168pp., ISBN 0–8248–2350–8 $20.

FOREIGN LANGUAGE TEACHING AND MINORITY LANGUAGE EDUCATION
KATHRYN A. DAVIS (EDITOR), 1999

This volume seeks to examine the potential for building relationships among foreign language, bilingual, and ESL programs towards fostering bilingualism. Part I of the volume examines the sociopolitical contexts for language partnerships, including:

- obstacles to developing bilingualism;
- implications of acculturation, identity, and language issues for linguistic minorities; and
- the potential for developing partnerships across primary, secondary, and tertiary institutions.

Part II of the volume provides research findings on the Foreign Language Partnership Project, designed to capitalize on the resources of immigrant students to enhance foreign language learning.

152pp., ISBN 0–8248–2067–3 $20.

DESIGNING SECOND LANGUAGE PERFORMANCE ASSESSMENTS
John M. Norris, James Dean Brown, Thom Hudson, & Jim Yoshioka, 1998, 2000

This technical report focuses on the decision-making potential provided by second language performance assessments. The authors first situate performance assessment within a broader discussion of alternatives in language assessment and in educational assessment in general. They then discuss issues in performance assessment design, implementation, reliability, and validity. Finally, they present a prototype framework for second language performance assessment based on the integration of theoretical underpinnings and research findings from the task-based language teaching literature, the language testing literature, and the educational measurement literature. The authors outline test and item specifications, and they present numerous examples of prototypical language tasks. They also propose a research agenda focusing on the operationalization of second language performance assessments.

248pp., ISBN 0–8248–2109–2 $20.

SECOND LANGUAGE DEVELOPMENT IN WRITING: MEASURES OF FLUENCY, ACCURACY, AND COMPLEXITY
Kate Wolfe-Quintero, Shunji Inagaki, & Hae-Young Kim, 1998, 2002

In this book, the authors analyze and compare the ways that fluency, accuracy, grammatical complexity, and lexical complexity have been measured in studies of language development in second language writing. More than 100 developmental measures are examined, with detailed comparisons of the results across the studies that have used each measure. The authors discuss the theoretical foundations for each type of developmental measure, and they consider the relationship between developmental measures and various types of proficiency measures. They also examine criteria for determining which developmental measures are the most successful and suggest which measures are the most promising for continuing work on language development.

208pp., ISBN 0–8248–2069–X $20.

THE DEVELOPMENT OF A LEXICAL TONE PHONOLOGY IN AMERICAN ADULT LEARNERS OF STANDARD MANDARIN CHINESE
Sylvia Henel Sun, 1998

The study reported is based on an assessment of three decades of research on the SLA of Mandarin tone. It investigates whether differences in learners' tone perception and production are related to differences in the effects of certain linguistic, task, and learner factors. The learners of focus are American students of Mandarin in Beijing, China. Their performances on two perception and three production tasks are analyzed through a host of variables and methods of quantification.

328pp., ISBN 0–8248–2068–1 $20.

NEW TRENDS AND ISSUES IN TEACHING JAPANESE LANGUAGE AND CULTURE
Haruko M. Cook, Kyoko Hijirida, & Mildred Tahara (Editors), 1997

In recent years, Japanese has become the fourth most commonly taught foreign language at the college level in the United States. As the number of students who study Japanese has increased, the teaching of Japanese as a foreign language has been established as an important academic field of study. This technical report includes nine contributions to the advancement of this field, encompassing the following five important issues:

- Literature and literature teaching
- Technology in the language classroom
- Orthography
- Testing
- Grammatical versus pragmatic approaches to language teaching

164pp., ISBN 0–8248–2067–3 $20.

SIX MEASURES OF JSL PRAGMATICS
Sayoko Okada Yamashita, 1996

This book investigates differences among tests that can be used to measure the cross-cultural pragmatic ability of English-speaking learners of Japanese. Building on the work of Hudson, Detmer, and Brown (Technical Reports #2 and #7 in this series), the author modified six test types that she used to gather data from North American learners of Japanese. She found numerous problems with the multiple-choice discourse completion test but reported that the other five tests all proved highly reliable and reasonably valid. Practical issues involved in creating and using such language tests are discussed from a variety of perspectives.

213pp., ISBN 0–8248–1914–4 $15.

LANGUAGE LEARNING STRATEGIES AROUND THE WORLD: CROSS-CULTURAL PERSPECTIVES
Rebecca L. Oxford (Editor), 1996, 1997, 2002

Language learning strategies are the specific steps students take to improve their progress in learning a second or foreign language. Optimizing learning strategies improves language performance. This groundbreaking book presents new information about cultural influences on the use of language learning strategies. It also shows innovative ways to assess students' strategy use and remarkable techniques for helping students improve their choice of strategies, with the goal of peak language learning.

166pp., ISBN 0–8248–1910–1 $20.

TELECOLLABORATION IN FOREIGN LANGUAGE LEARNING: PROCEEDINGS OF THE HAWAI'I SYMPOSIUM
Mark Warschauer (Editor), 1996

The Symposium on Local & Global Electronic Networking in Foreign Language Learning & Research, part of the National Foreign Language Resource Center's 1995 Summer Institute on Technology & the Human Factor in Foreign Language Education, included presentations of papers and hands-on workshops conducted by Symposium participants to facilitate the sharing of resources, ideas, and information about all aspects of electronic networking for foreign language teaching and research, including electronic discussion and conferencing, international cultural exchanges, real-time communication and simulations, research and resource retrieval via the Internet, and research using networks. This collection presents a sampling of those presentations.

252pp., ISBN 0–8248–1867–9 $20.

LANGUAGE LEARNING MOTIVATION: PATHWAYS TO THE NEW CENTURY
Rebecca L. Oxford (Editor), 1996

This volume chronicles a revolution in our thinking about what makes students want to learn languages and what causes them to persist in that difficult and rewarding adventure. Topics in this book include the internal structures of and external connections with foreign language motivation; exploring adult language learning motivation, self-efficacy, and anxiety; comparing the motivations and learning strategies of students of Japanese and Spanish; and enhancing the theory of language learning motivation from many psychological and social perspectives.

218pp., ISBN 0–8248–1849–0 $20.

LINGUISTICS & LANGUAGE TEACHING: PROCEEDINGS OF THE SIXTH JOINT LSH-HATESL CONFERENCE
Cynthia Reves, Caroline Steele, & Cathy S. P. Wong (Editors), 1996

Technical Report #10 contains 18 articles revolving around the following three topics:
- Linguistic issues—These six papers discuss various linguistic issues: ideophones, syllabic nasals, linguistic areas, computation, tonal melody classification, and wh-words.
- Sociolinguistics—Sociolinguistic phenomena in Swahili, signing, Hawaiian, and Japanese are discussed in four of the papers.
- Language teaching and learning—These eight papers cover prosodic modification, note taking, planning in oral production, oral testing,

language policy, L2 essay organization, access to dative alternation rules, and child noun phrase structure development.

364pp., ISBN 0–8248–1851–2 $20.

ATTENTION & AWARENESS IN FOREIGN LANGUAGE LEARNING
RICHARD SCHMIDT (EDITOR), 1996

Issues related to the role of attention and awareness in learning lie at the heart of many theoretical and practical controversies in the foreign language field. This collection of papers presents research into the learning of Spanish, Japanese, Finnish, Hawaiian, and English as a second language (with additional comments and examples from French, German, and miniature artificial languages) that bear on these crucial questions for foreign language pedagogy.

394pp., ISBN 0–8248–1794–X $20.

VIRTUAL CONNECTIONS: ONLINE ACTIVITIES AND PROJECTS FOR NETWORKING LANGUAGE LEARNERS
MARK WARSCHAUER (EDITOR), 1995, 1996

Computer networking has created dramatic new possibilities for connecting language learners in a single classroom or across the globe. This collection of activities and projects makes use of email, the internet, computer conferencing, and other forms of computer-mediated communication for the foreign and second language classroom at any level of instruction. Teachers from around the world submitted the activities compiled in this volume—activities that they have used successfully in their own classrooms.

417pp., ISBN 0–8248–1793–1 $30.

DEVELOPING PROTOTYPIC MEASURES OF CROSS-CULTURAL PRAGMATICS
THOM HUDSON, EMILY DETMER, & J. D. BROWN, 1995

Although the study of cross-cultural pragmatics has gained importance in applied linguistics, there are no standard forms of assessment that might make research comparable across studies and languages. The present volume describes the process through which six forms of cross-cultural assessment were developed for second language learners of English. The models may be used for second language learners of other languages. The six forms of assessment involve two forms each of indirect discourse completion tests, oral language production, and self-assessment. The procedures involve the assessment of requests, apologies, and refusals.

198pp., ISBN 0–8248–1763–X $15.

THE ROLE OF PHONOLOGICAL CODING IN READING KANJI
SACHIKO MATSUNAGA, 1995

In this technical report, the author reports the results of a study that she conducted on phonological coding in reading kanji using an eye-movement monitor, and draws some pedagogical implications. In addition, she reviews current literature on the different schools of thought regarding instruction in reading kanji and its role in the teaching of nonalphabetic written languages like Japanese.

64pp., ISBN 0–8248–1734–6 $10.

PRAGMATICS OF CHINESE AS NATIVE AND TARGET LANGUAGE
GABRIELE KASPER (EDITOR), 1995

This technical report includes six contributions to the study of the pragmatics of Mandarin Chinese:

- A report of an interview study conducted with nonnative speakers of Chinese; and
- Five data-based studies on the performance of different speech acts by native speakers of Mandarin—requesting, refusing, complaining, giving bad news, disagreeing, and complimenting.

312pp., ISBN 0–8248–1733–8 $20.

A BIBLIOGRAPHY OF PEDAGOGY AND RESEARCH IN INTERPRETATION AND TRANSLATION
ETILVIA ARJONA, 1993

This technical report includes four types of bibliographic information on translation and interpretation studies:

- Research efforts across disciplinary boundaries—cognitive psychology, neurolinguistics, psycholinguistics, sociolinguistics, computational linguistics, measurement, aptitude testing, language policy, decision-making, theses, and dissertations;
- Training information covering program design, curriculum studies, instruction, and school administration;
- Instructional information detailing course syllabi, methodology, models, available textbooks; and
- Testing information about aptitude, selection, and diagnostic tests.

115pp., ISBN 0–8248–1572–6 $10.

PRAGMATICS OF JAPANESE AS NATIVE AND TARGET LANGUAGE
GABRIELE KASPER (EDITOR), 1992, 1996

This technical report includes three contributions to the study of the pragmatics of Japanese:

- A bibliography on speech-act performance, discourse management, and other pragmatic and sociolinguistic features of Japanese;
- A study on introspective methods in examining Japanese learners' performance of refusals; and

- A longitudinal investigation of the acquisition of the particle *ne* by nonnative speakers of Japanese.

125pp., ISBN 0–8248–1462–2 $10.

A FRAMEWORK FOR TESTING CROSS-CULTURAL PRAGMATICS
THOM HUDSON, EMILY DETMER, & J. D. BROWN, 1992

This technical report presents a framework for developing methods that assess cross-cultural pragmatic ability. Although the framework has been designed for Japanese and American cross-cultural contrasts, it can serve as a generic approach that can be applied to other language contrasts. The focus is on the variables of social distance, relative power, and the degree of imposition within the speech acts of requests, refusals, and apologies. Evaluation of performance is based on recognition of the speech act, amount of speech, forms or formulae used, directness, formality, and politeness.

51pp., ISBN 0–8248–1463–0 $10.

RESEARCH METHODS IN INTERLANGUAGE PRAGMATICS
GABRIELE KASPER & MERETE DAHL, 1991

This technical report reviews the methods of data collection employed in 39 studies of interlanguage pragmatics, defined narrowly as the investigation of nonnative speakers' comprehension and production of speech acts, and the acquisition of L2-related speech-act knowledge. Data collection instruments are distinguished according to the degree to which they constrain informants' responses, and whether they tap speech-act perception/comprehension or production. A main focus of discussion is the validity of different types of data, in particular their adequacy to approximate authentic performance of linguistic action.

51pp., ISBN 0–8248–1419–3 $10.

www.ingramcontent.com/pod-product-compliance
Lightning Source LLC
Chambersburg PA
CBHW050104170426
43198CB00014B/2448